Management Fundamentals
A FRAMEWORK

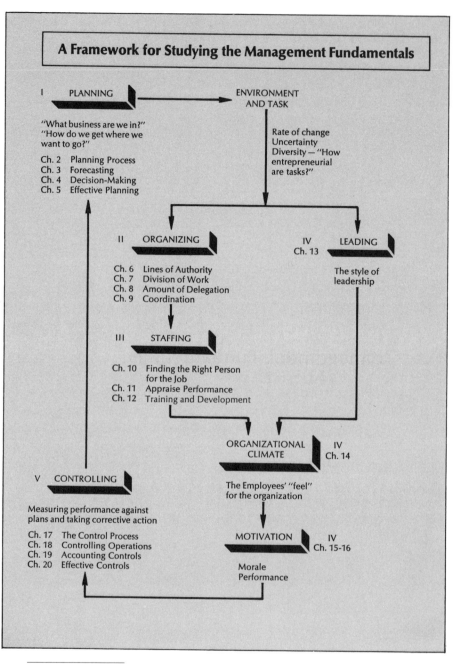

A Framework for Studying the Management Fundamentals

I PLANNING → **ENVIRONMENT AND TASK**

"What business are we in?"
"How do we get where we want to go?"

Ch. 2 Planning Process
Ch. 3 Forecasting
Ch. 4 Decision-Making
Ch. 5 Effective Planning

Rate of change
Uncertainty
Diversity — "How entrepreneurial are tasks?"

II ORGANIZING

Ch. 6 Lines of Authority
Ch. 7 Division of Work
Ch. 8 Amount of Delegation
Ch. 9 Coordination

IV LEADING
Ch. 13

The style of leadership

III STAFFING

Ch. 10 Finding the Right Person for the Job
Ch. 11 Appraise Performance
Ch. 12 Training and Development

ORGANIZATIONAL CLIMATE IV Ch. 14

The Employees' "feel" for the organization

V CONTROLLING

Measuring performance against plans and taking corrective action

Ch. 17 The Control Process
Ch. 18 Controlling Operations
Ch. 19 Accounting Controls
Ch. 20 Effective Controls

MOTIVATION IV Ch. 15-16

Morale
Performance

Source: Adapted from Gary Dessler, *Organization and Management: A Contingency Approach* (Englewood Cliffs, N.J.: Prentice-Hall, 1976), by permission.

Management Fundamentals

A FRAMEWORK

Gary Dessler

ASSOCIATE PROFESSOR AND ASSOCIATE DEAN, SCHOOL OF BUSINESS AND
ORGANIZATIONAL SCIENCES, FLORIDA INTERNATIONAL UNIVERSITY

RESTON PUBLISHING COMPANY
A PRENTICE-HALL COMPANY
RESTON, VIRGINIA

Library of Congress Cataloging in Publication Data

Dessler, Gary
  Management fundamentals.

  Includes bibliographical references and index.
  1. Management. I. Title.
HD31.D486   658.4   76–30726
ISBN 0–87909–462–1

to Claudia

TABLE OF CONTENTS

PREFACE

I wrote this book primarily for undergraduate students in introductory management courses.

When I began writing it I had three basic goals in mind, and these have governed my choice of topics and style. First, I wanted to emphasize the "nuts and bolts" of management, and the basic management functions of Planning, Organizing, Staffing, Leading, and Controlling. You'll therefore find an emphasis on practical, applicable subject matter in this book, considerable use of "hints," and other "how to"-type material, and a focus on the basic management functions.

Second, I wanted to make this a contemporary "principles" text, and to avoid the strictly "common sense" approach sometimes found in management books. I've done this by backing up conclusions (on planning, appraising performance, setting standards, and so forth) with some readable, recent behavioral science research findings. I've also used a "contingency approach" theme, showing in specific terms how the organization that's appropriate for routine, "mechanistic" tasks is different from that for entrepreneurial, "organic" tasks.

Third, I wanted this book to be readable and easy to learn from: I hope the style and learning aids help accomplish this. These aids include a "Framework for Studying the Management Fundamentals." This introduces each chapter and helps pinpoint "where we are now," and how that chapter relates to the others in the book.

Two supplementary teaching aids are available. There is a very complete Instructor's Manual. There is also a student's Study Guide. It contains case incidents for each chapter, "key concept" quizzes that can be handed in, suggested projects, chapter overviews, and "self tests" with answers.

Finally, in order to avoid constantly referring to "he or she," or "the manager" I usually just refer to "he," and I sincerely hope this doesn't insult any female readers.

*   *   *

Acknowledgments: I want to thank several people and organizations for their assistance. At Florida International University, Marian Blessing was an invaluable help during all stages of the project. Enzo Valenzi provided important input and comments on the "Staffing" chapters. George B. Simmons provided encouragement and the flexibility in my schedule that facilitated completing the book. Colleagues including Steven Altman, Wayne Cascio, Richard Hodgetts, Karl Magnusen, Myung Park, Leonardo Rodriguez, and George Sutija were always supportive.

At Reston Publishing Company, Fred Easter had a major influence in developing the basic theme of the book and Patrice LaLiberté, editor, designed it and managed its production.

At Hillsborough Community College, Robert D. Miller served as special editorial consultant. He was always a source of valuable advice and encouragement.

The following publishers (in addition to those mentioned in the text) allowed us to reproduce exhibits or other material by permission: American Management Association, "Job Description Hints," in Chapter 10, and exhibit 12-1; Harvard University Press, the "Introduction" to Chapter 15; Houghton Mifflin, exhibit 11-12; Harvard Business Review (copyright by the President and Fellows of Harvard College) exhibits 2-7, 15-1, 13-5, and material by Henry Mintzberg in Chapter 1; St. Clair Press and the *Journal of Applied Psychology*, case incident introduction in Chapter 12; Stanford University Press, the copyrighted "Strong-Campbell Interest Inventory" (exhibit 11-13); Prentice-Hall, the "Framework." Exhibits 1-1, 3-1, and 13-4 are based on *Managing: A Contemporary Introduction* by Joseph Massie and John Douglas (Prentice-Hall, 1973). The case incident introduction to Chapter 7 is from Richard Farmer, Barry Richman, and William Ryan, *Incidents in Applying Management Theory* (Belmont: Wadsworth, 1966); the case incident introduction to Chapter 21 is from John Champion and John James, *Critical Incidents in Management* (Homewood: Irwin, 1975).

Last (but not least) I want to thank my wife, Claudia, and my son, Derek, for their patience and encouragement throughout this project.

GARY DESSLER

Management Fundamentals

When you have finished studying

1

Introduction to Managing: A Contingency Approach

You should be able to:

1. *Describe what managers do.*

2. *Explain some of the differences between managers and non-managers.*

3. *List the manager's work roles.*

4. *Discuss three approaches to management.*

5. *Compare and contrast "mechanistic" and "organic" management.*

6. *Present and explain the rationale for our Framework.*

INTRODUCTION

Someone once said that people can be divided into three classes: the few who make things happen; the many who watch things happen; and the vast majority who have no idea what happened.[1]

Managers are paid to make things happen. And all you have to do is scan today's headlines to see that managers are indeed always in the center of the action:

NIXON TO BE IMPEACHED? SAYS SUBORDINATES MISLED HIM

FBI CHIEF DENIES HE PLANS TO QUIT, SAYS HE WASN'T AWARE OF ILLEGAL FBI BREAK-INS

EASTERN AIRLINES' FRANK BORMAN: TURNING THE COMPANY AROUND

THE CORPORATE WOMAN: UP THE LADDER, FINALLY

GRANT'S DECLARES BANKRUPTCY: MANAGERS EXPLAIN WHAT WENT WRONG WITH THE GAME PLAN

REBUILDING GIMBELS: RECRUITING AND DEVELOPING NEW MANAGERS

CHAMPION INTERNATIONAL: PRESIDENT ANNOUNCES REORGANIZATION

What do these headlines tell you about the manager's job?

For one thing, you can see that managers are people who get things done through others. *As a manager, you can no longer depend solely on your own efforts for getting the job done.*

Now, new skills are necessary—the skills of a manager. You have to plan the work each of your people will be doing, and set the standards they can shoot for. You have to organize them—assign each a task, and then see that you coordinate them.

You get involved in hiring, interviewing, appraising, disciplining, rewarding, and training. You have to be a leader, and to motivate others to do their best. You continually have to compare actual to expected performance, and correct any deficiencies. And all the while there is the constant pressure to produce more and better products and meet deadlines.[2]

Is the managing world for you? Do you have what it takes to be a manager? Can you get things done through others? Can you be an effective leader? Can you assume the pressure that comes from being responsible for the work, livelihood, and future of others? Just what does it take to be an effective manager? These are some of the questions you should be able to answer by the end of this book.

DO ALL MANAGERS DO THE SAME THINGS?

As you can see in Exhibit 1–1 there are three basic ways to classify managers.[3]

By Title: First, we can distinguish between executives, managers, and supervisors.

By Position: Or, we can distinguish between top management, middle management, and first-line management.

By Level: Finally, we can also distinguish between the first, second, and third (or higher) levels of management.

Exhibit 1.1   Three Ways to Classify Managers

By Title		By Position		By Level
Executives	•••	Top Management	•••	Third-Level Management
Managers	•••	Middle Management	•••	Second-Level Management
Supervisors	•••	First-Line Management	•••	First-Level Management

Different levels of managers have a lot in common. They all get work done through subordinates. They all get involved in planning for others, organizing the work of others, recruiting, and so forth. And they usually spend about two-thirds of their time with people—talking, listening, attending meetings, and so forth.[4]

But there are some differences. First of all, executives and middle managers both have managers for subordinates—they are in charge of other managers. Supervisors, on the other hand, have workers—nonmanagers—as subordinates.

Their activities are also different. Higher level managers spend more time planning and setting objectives. Middle managers then translate these objectives into specific projects for their subordinates.[5] First-level supervisors spend most of their time actually directing and controlling the work on these projects.[6] This is summarized in Exhibit 1–2.

Exhibit 1.2   The Manager's Level in the Organization and How He Spends His Time

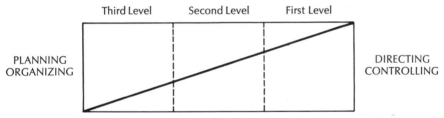

Note: Managers at different levels in the organization spend their time differently. Managers at the Third, or top, level spend more time planning and organizing. Managers at the First, or low, level spend more time supervising — actually directing and controlling the work being done.

Source: Prepared by Professor Robert Miller.

Thus the first-line supervisor is the man on the firing line. His job is getting the work out on time. He has standards to meet, and he has to press his people to keep quality up and costs down. (In fact, about one-third of his time is devoted to this.[7]) This requires skills in managing, in dealing with people, and solid knowledge of the methods of work being done.[8]

A CLOSER LOOK AT WHAT MANAGERS DO

The Management Process

The diversity of a manager's activities can be staggering. However, most writers agree that there are certain basic functions all managers perform. These are Planning, Organizing, Staffing, Leading, and Controlling. In total, they represent what is often called the "Management Process."

Here are some of the specific activities involved in each function:

Planning: Establishing goals and standards; developing rules and procedures; developing plans (both for yourself and for those who work for you); forecasting—predicting or projecting some future occurrence.

Organizing: Giving each subordinate a separate task; establishing departments; delegating authority to subordinates; establishing channels of authority and communication; coordinating the work of your subordinates.

Staffing: Determining what type of people should be hired; recruiting prospective employees; selecting employees; setting performance standards; evaluating performance; training and developing employees.

Leading: Getting others to get the job done; maintaining morale; motivating subordinates; establishing the right psychological climate.

Controlling: Setting standards—such as sales quotas, quality standards, or production levels; checking to see how actual performance compares with these standards; taking corrective action as needed.

Exhibit 1.3 The Five Main Functions of Management

THE PROCESS OF MANAGEMENT

Plan	Organize	Staff	Lead	Control

Some Characteristics of the Manager's Job

We also know that managers' jobs have certain characteristics in common.[9] These include the following.[10]

Characteristic 1: Managers work under constant pressure, at an unrelenting pace and on a wide variety of tasks.

Some writers like to characterize managers as reflective, systematic planners; but the evidence suggests just the opposite. Managers are strongly oriented to rapid-fire action and dislike reflective activities.

In a study of top managers, for example, half the activities engaged in lasted less than nine minutes and only 10 percent exceeded one hour.[11] In a study of 56 foremen, Robert Guest found that they averaged 583 activities per an eight-hour shift—an average of one activity every 48 seconds![12] Even the managers' coffee breaks and lunches were inevitably work related.

The same has been found to be true of British managers. One study of 160 British middle and top managers found that they worked for a full half hour or more without interruption only about once every two days.

As one writer points out: "[Managers] . . . seem to jump from issue to issue continually responding to the needs of the moment. . . ."

Characteristic 2: Managers strongly prefer oral means of communication.

We also know that managers don't rely as much as we once thought on summary reports or computerized management information systems for their information. Instead they strongly favor oral communictions such as meetings and telephone calls.

In two British studies, for example, managers spent an average of 66 percent and 80 percent of their time on oral communication. Henry Mintzberg found that the figure for American top executives was 78 percent. And he also found that managers depend heavily on gossip and hearsay because of its timeliness.

Ironically, this reliance on oral communications can also add to a manager's work load. Since most of his information is "in his head" rather than on paper, it's not as easy for him to assign or delegate jobs to his subordinates. He can't just hand a report to a subordinate. Instead, he has to carefully explain all he knows about the subject. This often takes so long that the manager simply ends up doing the job himself—which, of course, adds to his own work load.

Characteristic 3: Management still seems to be more of an art than a science or a profession.

In the last 25 years there has been a marked change in the way managers are educated. There is greater and greater emphasis on teaching managers how to use "management science" techniques, such as statistical inventory control, for better decisions. And there is a similar emphasis on techniques from the behavioral sciences—new techniques for motivating employees, and so forth.

These new concepts and techniques certainly have an important place in a manager's tool kit. Yet managers still rely mostly on a "seat of the pants" decision-making based on judgment and intuition. Henry Mintzberg says:

> I was struck during my study by the fact that the executives I was observing—all very competent by any standard—are fundamentally indistinguishable from their counterparts of 100 years ago (or 1,000 years ago, for that matter). The information they need differs, but they seek it in the same way—by word of mouth. Their decisions concern modern technology, but the procedures they use to make them are the same as the procedures of the 19th century manager. Even the computer, so important for the specialized work of the organization, has apparently had no influence on the work procedures of general managers. . . .

Summary: Characteristics of Managers' Jobs. Do you begin to get a feeling for the manager's job? He works at an unrelenting pace under great pressure, always pushing to meet new deadlines and new quotas. He prefers

6   rapid-fire action, jumping from activity to activity responding to the needs of the moment. He spends most of his time talking and communicating with other people. And he relies as much (or more) on judgment and intuition as on "management-science" tools for making decisions.

The Manager's Work Roles

We can get another perspective on what managers do by looking at some of the "roles" they play on a typical day.[13] Here are a few of them.

The Manager's Figurehead Role: Managers head organization units such as departments or bureaus. Because of his position as "head man," he routinely has to perform certain ceremonial duties. For example, the foreman might have to attend the wedding of a lathe operator, or the sales manager takes important customers to lunch.

The Manager's Leadership Role: A manager also must be a leader. He has to induce others to get the work out by motivating them, reconciling their differences, and so forth.

The Manager's Liaison Role: Manager's don't associate only with their superiors and subordinates. In fact, the results of several studies show that managers (both American and British) spend about 50 percent of their time with peers—people at their own level—and much of their time with those outside their organizations.[14]

This liaison role provides the manager with important information. It is his "external information system." It gets him the lowdown on the important happenings "out there" that might affect his own unit, and job.

The Manager's Monitor Role: The manager is constantly monitoring his environment. Through his liaison contacts, his superiors, and his subordinates he is constantly collecting information—via hearsay, gossip, and so on.

The Manager's Disseminator Role: The manager also has to disseminate much of the information he obtains from monitoring his environment. In his disseminator role, the manager passes on some of this privileged information to subordinates and superiors.

The Manager's Spokesman Role: The manager also has to be a spokesman for his unit. In his role as spokesman he sends information to people outside his unit—a foreman suggests a product modification to or fights for a bigger "piece of the pie" for his people, for example.

The Manager's Entrepreneur Role: The manager has to be constantly on the alert for ways to improve his organization and adapt it to changing conditions. In his monitor role he is constantly on the lookout for new ideas. When he finds one, he switches to his entrepreneur role. He initiates studies and projects aimed at allowing his unit to take advantage of the new ideas.

The Manager's Disturbance-Handler Role: Managers spend a lot of time in a "disturbance-handler" role, reacting to day-to-day crises. And the manager's day is full of such crises, from suppliers reneging on contracts, to strikes, and plant inspections by health officials.

The Manager's Resource Allocator Role: The manager is in charge of "who gets what" in his organization. One important resource he allocates is his own time. In addition, he allocates money for new equipment, raises, promotions, and so forth.

The Manager's Negotiator Role: Finally managers spend much of their time in negotiating. The foremen might have to argue a grievance problem to its conclusion with the union representative, for example; or the sales manager might be called in to negotiate a contract with an esteemed customer.

In summary, then, here are some of the roles most managers have to play:

Figurehead	Spokesman
Leader	Entrepreneur
Liaison	Disturbance Handler
Monitor	Resource Allocator
Disseminator	Negotiator

WHAT SOME FAMOUS WRITERS HAVE TO SAY ABOUT MANAGEMENT

Let's round out our picture of managing by briefly discussing what some famous writers have said about what managers do (or should do). We will focus on three approaches to management: "classical"; "behavioral"; and "contingency."

The Classical Approach to Management

Until the late 1800s managers emphasized making their companies as big as possible. They focused on rapidly accumulating men, machinery, and capital in what amounted to a race to make their companies larger than those of their competitors.

But in the late 1800s the managers' focus began to shift from growth to efficiency. They began to seek new ways to better utilize the resources they had accumulated.

Increasingly they sought new concepts and new techniques that would

8 enable them to cut costs and increase efficiency. It was out of this industrial environment that the classical school of management emerged.

Frederick Winslow Taylor and Scientific Management: Frederick Taylor was one of the first of these classical management writers.[15] His basic theme was that managers should study work scientifically in order to identify "one best way" to get the job done. He codified his ideas in terms of principles such as these:

> *Principle 1.* All jobs can be observed and analyzed in order to determine the one best way of accomplishing them.
> *Principle 2.* The best man for the job can be scientifically selected and trained.
> *Principle 3.* You can insure that the one best way is followed by paying the man on an incentive basis—tying his salary to how much he produces.
> *Principle 4.* Put a manager in charge of planning, preparing, and inspecting work. The worker simply carries out the manager's directions.

Henri Fayol and the Principles of Management: Henri Fayol had been a manager for 30 years before writing his book, *General and Industrial Management*. In it he said that managers perform five basic functions which he called planning, organizing, commanding, coordinating, and controlling.

In his book he also outlined a list of "principles" of management. He had found these useful during his years as a manager, and felt that other managers should use them in carrying out their functions of planning, organizing, and so on. Here are some of his principles:

> The principle of *division of work*. He said that each employee should be given a separate, specialized activity to perform.

> The principle of *authority and responsibility*. He said that the responsibility an employee had should be commensurate with the authority he was given.

> The principle of *unity of command*. He said that an employee should receive orders from one superior only.

> The *scalar chain* principle. He said that there should be a clear, unbroken chain of authority and communication ranging from the highest to the lowest positions in the organization.

The Behavioral Approach to Management

A series of changes swept across America and the world in the 1920s and 1930s. Increasing numbers of people moved from farms to cities and thus became more dependent on one another. Factories became more mechanized, and workers' jobs became increasingly specialized. Between 1929 and

1933 the country fell into an economic depression that saw unemployment rise from 3.2 percent to 30 percent.

Slowly the idea of individualism—that "each man is out for himself"—gave way to a feeling that "we have to help each other." This was the industrial environment out of which the behavioral writers emerged.

Elton Mayo and the Hawthorne Studies: Elton Mayo, and a research team from Harvard University, carried out an important series of studies at the Chicago Hawthorne plant of the Western Electric Company from 1927 to 1933. Their findings gave a whole new slant to the manager's job.

As their work progressed, Mayo began to feel that workers were being degraded by the highly specialized tasks they were forced to perform. He said that the production techniques of earlier times—such as when the worker would produce an entire garment by himself—provided man with an "identity." He felt that this was lacking in the mechanized, assembly line jobs.

One of his most important conclusions was that workers were not simply "cogs in the machinery." Instead the morale of workers—both individually and in groups—could have profound effects on productivity. And, he said, managers should therefore take a more "people-oriented" approach to managing.

Chris Argyris and the Mature Individual: According to Chris Argyris rigid organizations, such as those prescribed by the classical writers, hinder workers from utilizing their full potential. He says that as people mature into adults they normally move:

From a position of	*To* a position of
Dependence	Independence
Narrow interests	Broad interests
Less activity	Increased activity
Subordinate position	Superordinate position
Simple behaviors	Variety of behaviors

Argyris says that forcing people to "stick to the rules" and simply take orders inhibits these normal maturation changes. It does this by encouraging employees to be passive, dependent, and subordinate. Managers, he says, should encourage employees to take on additional responsibilities and provide them with the flexibility to grow and mature.

The Contingency Approach to Management

The classical and behavioral approaches to mangement each had different prescriptions for how managers should manage. The classicists laid down a series of principles. These held that managers should concentrate on the "things" aspects of organizations and on raising efficiency. The behaviorialists focused on the "people" aspects of organizations and on keeping the company flexible.

Today we believe that both approaches make sense, but for very different situations. Let's see why.

Burns and Stalker—Mechanistic and Organic Management: Two British researchers, Tom Burns and G. M. Stalker, studied several industrial firms in England. Their findings had a profound effect on what we know about the manager's job. Their main conclusion was that whether what they called a "mechanistic" [16] or "organic" [17] approach to management was appropriate depended on the kind of environment the organization was operating in.

A mechanistic approach to management is appropriate where the environment is unchanging. Here, for example, there is not a constant flow of new products and production processes from competitors. This approach is characterized by an emphasis on *efficiency*, very specialized, routine jobs, many elaborate rules and procedures, and an insistence that everyone "play it by the rules."

Organic Management, on the other hand, is appropriate where *innovation* and creativity is the rule. Here workers don't have very specialized jobs, and their jobs may change almost daily. There is not a rigid system of procedures, and workers are not encouraged to simply play it by the rules. These ideas are summarized in Exhibit 1–4.

Exhibit 1.4 Summary of the Burns and Stalker "Contingency" Findings

	Mechanistic	Organic
Type of Management	Mechanistic	Organic
Type of Environments	Unchanging	Rapidly Changing
Main Emphasis	Efficiency	Flexibility
How Company is Managed	Emphasis on routine jobs, many rules and procedures	Emphasis on less specialized jobs, fewer rules and procedures
Management Approach That This is Similar to	Classical	Behavioral

Alfred Chandler—Strategy and Structure: Alfred Chandler studied almost 100 of America's largest companies. He obtained information from sources like annual reports, company records, and interviews with senior executives.[18]

He found that a company's *strategy*—its basic long-term goals and plans—determined how the firm was *structured* and managed. For example, he found that firms which emphasized efficiency (such as those in the steel industry) were managed mechanistically. Here most important decisions were made by top managers, employees had to "stick to the rules," and so forth.

But companies that emphasized creativity, research, and development (such as those in the electronics industry) were managed organically. Most important decisions were made by low-level managers, employees didn't "stick to the rules," and jobs were less specialized. This is summarized in Exhibit 1–5.

Exhibit 1.5   Summary of Alfred Chandler's "Structure Follows Strategy" Approach to Management

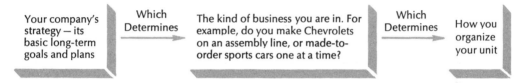

Summary: In summary, we now believe that both the classicists and behavioralists were right. But we now know that their prescriptions are appropriate for different kinds of situations. The classical or mechanistic approach fits better for very routine, unchanging tasks. The behavioral or organic approach is more appropriate for changing, entrepreneurial tasks.

THE PLAN OF THIS BOOK

The Contingency Approach: Mechanistic and Organic Management

One theme of this book is that different types of organizations are appropriate for different tasks.[19] At one extreme are organizations for tasks such as assembling autos. Here efficiency is emphasized and successful organizations tend to be bureaucratic or "mechanistic." Employees' jobs are very specialized and routine. Leadership is directive and authoritarian. The emphasis is on sticking to rules, procedures, and the chain of command.

At the opposite extreme, organizations such as new product development departments have unpredictable tasks. Here, entrepreneurial, creative activities are emphasized. To encourage such activities these organizations are "organic." They don't urge employees to "play it by the rules" or closely abide to the formal chain of command. Leadership tends to be more participative, and jobs are apt to be less specialized. Some of the most important differences between mechanistic and organic organizations are summarized in Exhibit 1–6.

Exhibit 1.6 Differences Between Mechanistic and Organic Organizations

How the Management Fundamentals Have to Fit the Task.

		MECHANISTIC	ORGANIC
		Closed (Classical Orientation)	Open (Behavioral Orientation)
P L A N	Goals-How specific?	Specific	General
	Standards	Rigid	Flexible
	Rules and Procedures	Many; specific	Few; broad
	Plan-How Detailed?	Detailed, inflexible	Broad; flexible
	Forecasts	Use historical trend	Qualitative; future projection
	Decision-making	Management science techniques	Creativity—intuition
O R G A N I Z E	Who Reports to Who	Clear—no deviations	Broad—permit deviations
	Line and Staff	Clear distinction	Little distinction
	Departmentation	By function or process	By purpose
	Specialization	Very specialized units	Broader, more "enlarged" units
	Delegation	Little	Much
	Span of Control	Narrow	Wide
	Coordination	Use chain of command	Special coordinators
S T A F F	Job Descriptions	Clear—limited scope	Broad—"open-ended"
	Job Specification	Background, skills	Background, potential
	Selection Methods	Specific performance tests—reference checks	General aptitude and interest tests
	Performance Criteria	Specific; output oriented	General; development oriented
	Performance Evaluation	Graphic rating scale	Critical incidents
	Training & Development	Skills training	Organizational development
L E A D	Leadership Style	More autocratic	More democratic
	Leadership Structure	Structured	Unstructured
	Source of Motivation	Extrinsic (money, promotion)	Intrinsic (the job itself)
	Psychological Climate	Structured, performance-oriented	Supportive, development-oriented
C O N T R O L	Standards	Specific, efficiency-oriented	General; "milestones"
	Control Measures	Imposed	Self control
	Checks on Performance	Frequent	Infrequent
	Emphasis	How work performed	The final product

Our Framework for Studying the Management Fundamentals

Throughout this book we will use the framework in Exhibit 1–7 to tie together the different topics we discuss. The framework will introduce each chapter as well as the sections on planning, organizing, staffing, leading, and controlling. Let's briefly review the rationale for the framework.

Planning: We begin with planning, and with identifying the central concept of the enterprise.[20] This determines "what business we are in." It also determines the sort of environment with which your enterprise has to deal— whether it is rapidly changing; whether many quick, entrepreneurial decisions are called for; whether efficiency or flexibility is paramount; and so on. We will discuss *planning* in Chapters 2–5.

Organizing: Next, notice that the organization and its management have to fit the demands of this environment. In Chapters 6–9, we will see that various attributes of the *organization*—whether you stick to the chain of command; how specialized jobs are, and so on—will depend on how unpredictable the environment is, and on how flexible you have to be.

Staffing: Next, the types of jobs you have determine the kinds of people you need to *staff* the organization. Also, your plans and job descriptions are standards against which performance can be *appraised* and *training* programs developed. We will discuss this in Chapters 10–12.

Leading: In Chapter 13 we will see that as a *leader* you'll have an important impact on the morale and productivity of your employees. And we will also see (as summarized in our framework) that your leadership style has to "fit" the task. For example, creative, entrepreneurial tasks call for a more participative or "hands off" leader.

In Chapters 14–16 we will see that *organizational climate*—the "feel" your employee has for the organization—is largely determined by tangible aspects of the *organization* (job descriptions, division of work, and the like) *and* by his *leaders' behavior*. In turn, the climate that *emerges* largely determines how satisfied are your employees, and how well they perform. Climate thus acts as a "bridge."

Controlling: Finally, your employees performance needs to be compared in some way with the planned standards. As you see in our framework, the *control* function serves this purpose. Performance standards are set, actual performance is measured, and corrective action is taken. We will discuss this in Chapters 17–20.

Tying It All Together: Use the framework to remind you of how the material in each chapter relates to the rest of the book. And remember that

1. Introduction to Managing

14   **Exhibit 1.7**   A Framework for Studying the Management Fundamentals

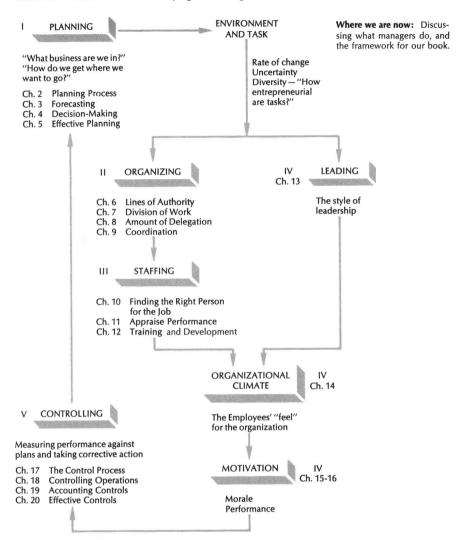

changing *any* aspect of the organization—your leadership style, how much you delegate, and so forth—clearly has implications for *everything* else in the organization. For example, change your plant layout, and you also change the pattern of communications between your employees, and thus possibly their morale as well.

Or take another example. A lot of managers are surprised when they can't "motivate" their subordinates, even after applying the sorts of motivation techniques we discuss in our "Leadership" chapters (numbers 13–16). The reason, of course, is that *everything* you do as a manager—planning, organizing, staffing, controlling, *and* leading affects motivation. Thus motivation really begins with your staffing decisions—with finding the right person for the right job. And it is further effected by the way you *organize* the job, the types of *controls* you impose, your *plans* and procedures and so forth. It is this *interrelatedness* between the management functions that our Framework helps to emphasize.

Some Important Things to Remember from This Chapter:

1. Managers are people who get things done through others. As a manager, you can no longer depend solely on your own ability for getting the job done.

2. Managers at different levels in the organization spend their time differently. Managers at the third, or top level, spend more time planning and organizing. Managers at the first, or low level, spend more time supervising—actually directing and controlling the work being done.

3. Most writers agree that there are five basic functions all managers perform: planning, organizing, staffing, leading, and controlling. In total, they represent what is often called the "management process."

4. Management is a high pressure, people-oriented job. You will always be pushing to meet new deadlines and new quotas, and in so doing communicating with other people.

5. As a manager, you will be expected to play many different roles including those of: figurehead; leader; liaison; monitor; disseminator; spokesman; entrepreneur; disturbance handler; resource allocator, and negotiator.

6. Classical-management writers said that managers should somewhat mechanically apply certain "principles of good management." Taylor, for example, said that there was "one best way" for accomplishing every task. Fayol proposed principles such as unity of command and scalar chain. These writers focused on the "things" or production aspects of organizations.

7. Behavioral writers, like Mayo and Argyris, focus on the "people" aspects of organizations. They say that managers should encourage employees to take on additional responsibilities, and also provide them with the flexibility to grow and mature.

8. According to the contingency writers, both the classical and behavioral approaches make sense—but for very different situations. For example, Burns and Stalker found that the classical, mechanistic approach is appropriate where the environment is unchanging. Behavioral, organic management is appropriate where innovation and creativity is the rule.

9. We will use our framework to tie together the material in each of our chapters. The management functions of planning, organizing, staffing, leading, and controlling are all interrelated. For example, you can't talk about motivating someone as if motivation takes place in a vacuum. Instead all of the other functions—your plans, organization, staffing, and control systems—will also influence how motivated is your subordinate.

STUDY ASSIGNMENTS

1. Describe in your own words what managers do.
2. Explain how you think your job would change if you were promoted from salesman to sales manager.
3. "Flexibility is an important management trait, since managers have to play a variety of roles." Discuss whether you agree or disagree with this statement, and why.
4. "Classical-management writers basically viewed the organization as if it was a piece of well-oiled machinery." Discuss whether you agree or disagree with this statement, and why.
5. Discuss what you think is the basic theme of the behavioral approach to management.
6. Compare and contrast the basic underlying assumptions of the classical and behavioral approaches to management.
7. How do you think the organization and management of a mechanistic firm differs from that of an organic one. Write an essay comparing and contrasting the two.
8. Think of one organic organization and one mechanistic organization to which you have belonged. What were some of the differences and similarities between the two? Can you explain what it was about the job these organizations had to perform that resulted in one being organic and the other mechanistic?
9. Draw from memory our framework for studying management.
10. In your own words, explain the rationale for our framework. Why is it important to remember that all management functions are interrelated? Give at least two examples.

NOTES FOR THE CHAPTER

1. Nicholas Murray Butler. Quoted in George Odiorne, *How Managers Make Things Happen* (Englewood Cliffs: Prentice-Hall, 1968) p. 3.
2. See William Berliner and William McLarney, *Management Practice and Training* (Homewood, Irwin, 1974).
3. See Joseph Massie and John Douglas, *Managing: A Contemporary Introduction* (Englewood Cliffs, N.J., Prentice-Hall, 1973).
4. See, for example, John Campbell, Marvin Dunnette, Edward Lawler, III, and Carl Weick, Jr., *Managerial Behavior, Performance, and Effectiveness* (New York: McGraw-Hill, 1970), p. 75; Robert Guest, "Of Time and the Foreman," *Personnel*, Vol. 32 (May 1956).

5. Berliner and McLarney, *Management Practice and Training*, p. 11.

6. T. A. Mahoney, T. H. Jerdee, and S. J. Carroll, "The Job(s) of Management," Industrial Relations, Vol. 4, No. 2 (1965) pp. 97–110.

7. See, for example, Robert H. Guest, "Of Time and Foreman," *Personnel*, Vol. 32 (May 1956) p. 481; and Lester Bittel, *What Every Supervisor Should Know* (New York: McGraw-Hill, 1974) Ch. 1.

8. Berliner and McLarney, *Management Practice and Training*, p. 12.

9. See, for example, John P. Campbell, Marvin D. Dunnette, Edward E. Lawler, III, and Carl Weick, Jr., *Managerial Behavior, Performance, and Effectiveness*, p. 75; Robert Guest, "Of Time and the Foreman," p. 482.

10. This section based on Henry Mintzberg, "The Manager's Job: Folklore and Fact," *Harvard Business Review* (July-August 1975) pp. 489–561.

11. Mintzberg, "The Manager's Job . . . ," p. 50.

12. Robert Guest, "Of Time and the Foreman," *Personnel* (May 1956) p. 478.

13. This section is based on Henry Mintzberg, "The Manager's Job," *Harvard Business Review*, July-August, 1975.

14. Mintzberg, "The Manager's Job . . . ," p. 55.

15. See Daniel A. Wren, *The Evolution of Management Thought* (New York: The Ronald Press, 1972).

16. Or "Classical."

17. Or "Behavioral."

18. Alfred Chandler, Jr., *Strategy and Structure* (Cambridge, Mass.: The M.I.T. Press, 1962). Tom Burns and G. M. Stalker, *The Management of Innovation* (London; Tavistock, 1961).

19. Based on Gary Dessler, *Organization and Management: A Contingency Approach*, p. 11–13.

20. Based on Gary Dessler, *Organization and Management* (Englewood Cliffs, N.J.: Prentice-Hall, 1976) Chapter 1.

A Framework for Studying the Management Fundamentals

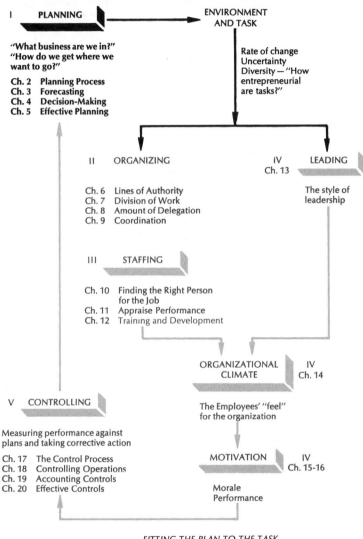

I PLANNING

ENVIRONMENT AND TASK

"What business are we in?"
"How do we get where we want to go?"

Ch. 2 Planning Process
Ch. 3 Forecasting
Ch. 4 Decision-Making
Ch. 5 Effective Planning

Rate of change
Uncertainty
Diversity — "How entrepreneurial are tasks?"

II ORGANIZING

Ch. 6 Lines of Authority
Ch. 7 Division of Work
Ch. 8 Amount of Delegation
Ch. 9 Coordination

IV LEADING
Ch. 13

The style of leadership

III STAFFING

Ch. 10 Finding the Right Person for the Job
Ch. 11 Appraise Performance
Ch. 12 Training and Development

ORGANIZATIONAL CLIMATE   IV Ch. 14

The Employees' "feel" for the organization

V CONTROLLING

Measuring performance against plans and taking corrective action

Ch. 17 The Control Process
Ch. 18 Controlling Operations
Ch. 19 Accounting Controls
Ch. 20 Effective Controls

MOTIVATION   IV Ch. 15-16

Morale
Performance

What we'll be discussing in this section:

Chap. 2
The Planning Process: Planning defined. Why planning is important. The steps in the planning process.

Chap. 3
Forecasting: Developing Planning Premises: Planning vs. forecasting. Implicit vs. explicit forecasting. Forecasting techniques.

Chap. 4
Managerial Decision-Making: The decision-making process. Identifying the central problem. Creativity in decision making. Management science decision-making techniques. Capital budgeting. How to make a decision.

Chap. 5
Effective Planning: Is planning always effective? Barriers to effective decision-making. Hints for making effective decisions.

FITTING THE PLAN TO THE TASK

Planning Characteristics	Mechanistic: Closed; classical orientation	Organic: Open; behavioral orientation
Goals — How Specific?	Specific	General
Standards	Rigid	Flexible
Rules & Procedures	Many; specific	Few; broad
The Plan — How Detailed?	Detailed; inflexible	Broad; flexible
Forecasts	Historical trend	Qualitative; future projection
Decision-Making	Management science techniques	Creativity; intuition

A Framework for Studying the Management Fundamentals

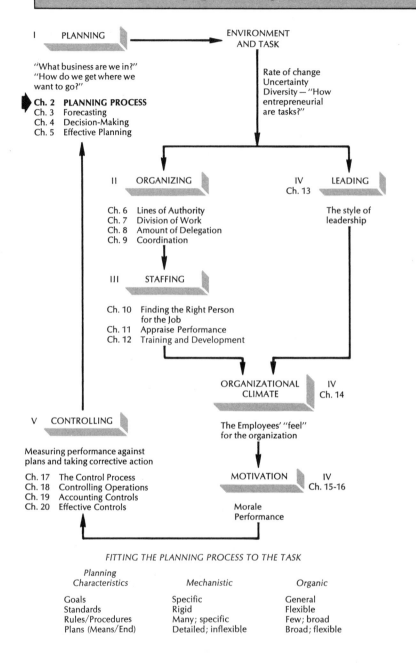

I   PLANNING

"What business are we in?"
"How do we get where we
want to go?"

Ch. 2   PLANNING PROCESS
Ch. 3   Forecasting
Ch. 4   Decision-Making
Ch. 5   Effective Planning

ENVIRONMENT
AND TASK

Rate of change
Uncertainty
Diversity — "How
entrepreneurial
are tasks?"

Where we are now:
Discussing the steps in the
planning process, which include formulating the firm's
"central concept."

II   ORGANIZING

Ch. 6   Lines of Authority
Ch. 7   Division of Work
Ch. 8   Amount of Delegation
Ch. 9   Coordination

IV   LEADING
Ch. 13

The style of
leadership

III   STAFFING

Ch. 10   Finding the Right Person
            for the Job
Ch. 11   Appraise Performance
Ch. 12   Training and Development

ORGANIZATIONAL
CLIMATE

IV
Ch. 14

V   CONTROLLING

Measuring performance against
plans and taking corrective action

Ch. 17   The Control Process
Ch. 18   Controlling Operations
Ch. 19   Accounting Controls
Ch. 20   Effective Controls

The Employees' "feel"
for the organization

MOTIVATION

IV
Ch. 15-16

Morale
Performance

FITTING THE PLANNING PROCESS TO THE TASK

Planning Characteristics	Mechanistic	Organic
Goals	Specific	General
Standards	Rigid	Flexible
Rules/Procedures	Many; specific	Few; broad
Plans (Means/End)	Detailed; inflexible	Broad; flexible

When you have finished studying

2 The Planning Process

You should be able to:

1. *Cite four dimensions of plans.*

2. *Distinguish between: goals, plans, strategies, and tactics.*

3. *List four reasons which explain why planning is important.*

4. *Give examples showing the importance of a "central concept" for the activities of a business firm.*

5. *Demonstrate how a hierarchy of plans fits together.*

6. *Give examples of goals with different "degrees of specificity."*

7. *Develop a business plan.*

INTRODUCTION

Planning is something that most people say is worthwhile, but that most people also do very little of. For example, suppose someone asked you where you wanted to be five years from now. (That's a favorite question of company recruiters.) If you want to, try answering it by filling in the chart on page 22.[1]

In filling out the chart, you had to deal with several important aspects of planning. Let's briefly review them.

First, your choice of goals probably reflected your basic concept of who you are, what you deserve, and what you are capable of. Every person (and, as we'll see, every enterprise) has his own unique "central concept." This is why one brother might become a millionaire, and another a vagabond; or why some people become teachers, while others become plumbers, sailors, or lawyers.

Next, with your self-concept to guide you, you set five-year goals. Then, for each goal (or target) you probably began developing some tentative plans (or "strategies") for getting from where you are now to where you'd like to be. For example, suppose you are now a college student, and in five years would like to be a production plant manager. Your plans would

IN TERMS OF:	WHERE I AM NOW	WHERE I'D LIKE TO BE IN FIVE YEARS
Career— my job; occupation.		
Personal Relationships— with friends; parents; family; etc.		
Learning and Education— skills; college degree; etc.		
Status and Respect— What groups you belong to; status and respect you have.		
Leisure time— The way you spend your leisure time (hobbies, sports, etc.).		

probably have to include such things as what you'd major in in school; when you have to graduate; and what sort of first job you'd look for after graduation. Also you would probably want to lay out a rough quarter-by-quarter plan as to what courses you would take, and when.

Some people might even want to go so far as to plan in advance for such details as what instructors they would take; others might decide these "tactics" on a daily basis.

Without a plan to guide you, you are clearly at a disadvantage. For example, without a goal, how can you tell you're majoring in the right subject? And without a major, how can you tell you're taking the right courses? For the same reason (and more) planning is essential for managers; thus we'll discuss management planning in the next four chapters. Remember, though, that planning is only one of the fundamentals of management. Plans also must be implemented—through organizing, staffing, leading, and controlling.

SOME BASIC DEFINITIONS

Plans

Plans are detailed methods, formulated beforehand, for doing or making something. They often come in narrative form (see Exhibit 2–1) and simply list goals (or targets) and the means for achieving them. Or they

Exhibit 2.1 Outline of Plan for Apex Bicycle Company

"CENTRAL CONCEPT" OF COMPANY

"To become the country's highest volume producer of low-cost bicycles."

↓

SUMMARY OF "STRATEGIC PLAN"

"During the next 5 years our company will become the country's highest volume producer of low-cost bicycles. We will do this by focusing our resources on increasing our efficiency in all areas of our operations, and by establishing a new retail-dealer network to market our low-cost bicycles."

↓

GOALS FOR THE:

Production Department	*Marketing Department*	*Personnel Department*
Department will lower production cost per bicycle by $12 per unit; raise production capacity by 10,000 units per year.	Obtain a minimum 500 new retail outlets for the low-cost bicycles. Initiate advertising campaigns aimed at publicising low cost of our bikes.	Cut costs by 10%

↓

TACTICS FOR THE:

Production Department	*Marketing Department*	*Personnel Department*
Buy 8 new bicycle framebuilding machines. Set up two new bicycle assembly lines. Institute new computerized inventory control system.	Eliminate current local sales force. Centralize all sales personnel in home office. Use them to obtain Woolworth's, Penney's, and 3 other large lower-cost type retail outlets as retailers for our bicycles.	Cut costs by eliminating 5 internal interviewers and relying more on outside employment agencies for advertising and recruiting clerical staff.

Note: This exhibit illustrates how *goals* become the targets which lower level managers develop *plans* to attain.

sometimes take the form of budgets, charts, or networks (see Exhibit 2–2) which show in financial or graphical terms what a unit's plans are.

Exhibit 2.2   A Plan for Building a House, Laid Out in the Form of a "Network"

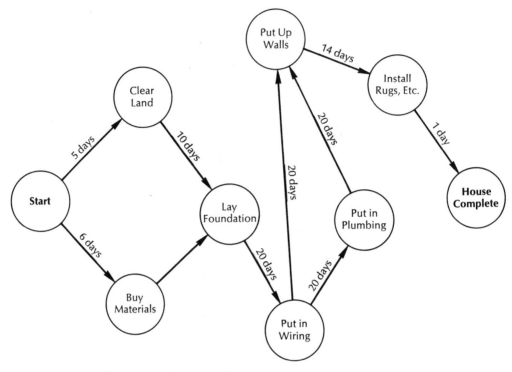

Note: A network is one of the many forms that a plan can take.

Strategies

A *strategy* is one type of plan. It specifies the central concept or purpose of your organization in terms of the service it will render to society. And it specifies the means by which it intends to create and distribute these services. It describes the basic mission of the enterprise, the goals it seeks to achieve, and the ways in which the resources of the enterprise will be used in order to achieve its goals.

Policies, Procedures, and Rules

Policies, procedures, and rules differ from each other in degree of specificity. All are sometimes referred to as "*standing plans*" because they automatically come into play when a certain event occurs.

Policies usually set broad guidelines for the enterprise. For example, it might be the policy of a department store that "if for any reason a customer is dissatisfied, her money will be cheerfully refunded."

Procedures, as the name implies, specify how to proceed in some situations. For example, "before refunding the customer's purchase price, the
salesperson should carefully inspect the garment and then obtain approval
from the floor manager for the refund."

A *rule* is an even more specific guide to action. For example: "Under
no conditions will the purchase price be refunded after 30 days."

PLANNING DIMENSIONS

Time Frame

As you can see in Exhibit 2–3, there are several ways to classify plans.
First of all, plans differ in terms of the *time dimension* they cover. Some
companies (such as those in the wood products industries) have long-range
plans that cover a hundred years or more. For most companies, though, long-
range plans cover about five years. Short-range plans typically cover one year
or less.

Exhibit 2.3 Planning Dimensions: Several Ways to Classify Plans

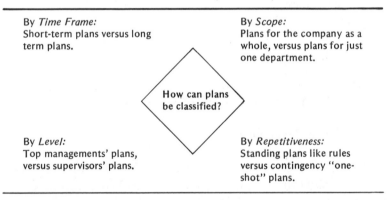

By *Time Frame:*
Short-term plans versus long
term plans.

By *Scope:*
Plans for the company as a
whole, versus plans for just
one department.

How can plans
be classified?

By *Level:*
Top managements' plans,
versus supervisors' plans.

By *Repetitiveness:*
Standing plans like rules
versus contingency "one-
shot" plans.

Source: Based partly on an idea developed by George Steiner in *Top Management Planning*
(New York, Macmillan, 1969) p. 12

Scope

Plans also differ in terms of their *scope.* Some plans are very comprehensive and lay out the overall plan for the company as a whole. Other plans
are much narrower in scope, and simply specify the plans for one department
(such as marketing). *Strategies* are typically broad in scope, and describe in
broad terms where the company is heading and how it intends to get there.
Tactics are narrower in scope and describe in more detail how, on a day-to-
day basis, the company's strategy is to be carried out. (See Exhibit 2–1.)

Level

You can also distinguish between plans on the basis of organizational level. For example, some plans—such as the firm's strategy—are typically developed by top-level management (presidents and vice presidents). Other plans, such as tactics, or those covering day-to-day production quotas, are developed and implemented by lower-level managers and foremen.

Repetitiveness

Some plans such as "standing plans" are developed for routine, repetitive application. Others, such as "contingency plans," are developed for "one-shot" projects—such as what your company will do if your employees suddenly go out on strike.

Summary

In summary, plans can be classified according to their:

1. Time Frame
2. Scope
3. Level
4. Repetitiveness

WHY IS PLANNING IMPORTANT?

It Provides Direction

Perhaps you remember the conversation that takes place between Alice and the Cheshire Cat in Lewis Carroll's *Alice in Wonderland*:

"Would you tell me, please, which way I ought to go from here?"
"That depends a good deal on where you want to go," said the cat.
"I don't much care where," said Alice.
"Then it doesn't matter which way you go," said the cat.

Their exchange helps point out what is perhaps the most important reason for planning: It provides direction and a sense of purpose for your enterprise. Thus your company's "five-year plan" typically shows what the company intends to accomplish in the five-year period as well as how it intends to accomplish it.

Planning Provides a Unifying Framework

Planning also provides a unifying framework for decision-making throughout the organization. In some situations, of course (such as Alice's), "no plan" and "no direction" go hand in hand. The problem, though, is that for a business firm the lack of a plan does not automatically entail a lack of direction.

Every company consists of various departments, such as production, sales, research and development, and personnel.[2] Usually managers in each of of these units have their own values, goals, ambitions, and ways of looking at the world. Each of these units, therefore, usually develops its own "functional strategy" or departmental direction.[3] For example, the manufacturing department may want to produce only one or two products in order to minimize production and inventory costs. The marketing department may want to offer as wide a range of products as possible in order to increase sales. The research and development unit may want to explore the frontiers of knowledge.

Imagine the chaos that could result without a unifying plan! Without a plan which tells everyone what your company hopes to accomplish, and what the contribution of each department must be, the company will be tugged in many different and competing directions. But with a clear, effective plan each department knows what it must do to contribute to the goals of the company. All the departments can then work in unison to help accomplish these goals.

Planning Helps to Reveal Future Opportunities and Threats

In a famous article entitled "Management Myopia," Theodore Levitt tells an anecdote about a famous Boston millionaire who 50 years ago unintentionally sentenced his heirs to poverty. He did this, according to Professor Levitt, by stipulating that his entire estate be forever invested exclusively in electric streetcar securities. The millionaire did this on the assumption that "there will always be a big demand for efficient urban transportation."

The problem, of course, is that the streetcar was soon replaced by automobiles and buses. The moral is that if this somewhat "nearsighted" millionaire had done some planning, he may have predicted the emergence of these alternate means of urban transportation.

Peter Drucker has pointed out that planning cannot completely eliminate the risks of such long-term decisions. Planning, however, can help identify potential opportunities and threats and at least minimize risks.[4]

28   *Planning Provides Performance Standards*

A useful plan specifies what is to be accomplished. For example, your company's five-year plan may specify that profits will double within five years. This goal can then be one of the standards against which the president's performance is measured and *controlled*. We will discuss control in Chapters 17–20.

Summary: Why is Planning Important?

In summary, as you can see in Exhibit 2–4, planning is important because:

1. It provides direction.
2. It provides a unifying framework.
3. It helps to reveal future opportunities and threats.
4. It provides performance standards.

Exhibit 2.4   Four Reasons Why Plans are Important

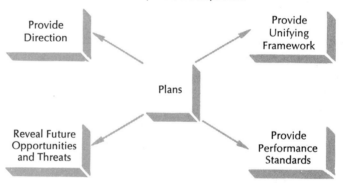

STEPS IN THE PLANNING PROCESS

Step 1—Define the Central Concept of Your Enterprise

Have you ever wondered why a company like General Motors has been so successful, while another in the same industry, such as Packard, has gone out of business? Or why a department store chain like Penney's is healthy and growing, while Grant's stores were thrown into bankruptcy?

Of course there are a great many reasons which help to explain why some enterprises are successful while others are not. But one reason seems to stand out as a common denominator for virtually all of the success stories: Companies such as Xerox, Kodak, and IBM were all built around a clearly

defined, viable, guiding concept of what their business is. As William Newman, Charles Summer, and E. Kirby Warren point out:

> Every enterprise needs a central purpose expressed in terms of the serv-
> ice it will render to society. In addition, it needs a basic concept of how
> it will create these services. Because it will be competing with other
> enterprises for resources, it must have some distinctive relevance—in
> its service or in its method of creating them.

The success of the IBM Corporation is a good example of a company built
on a well conceived central concept.[5] It has consistently viewed itself as an
information processing-system business even when most manufacturers were
still developing and selling individual pieces of equipment. Thus, while these
latter firms were fighting among themselves for a share of the separate computer or typewriter markets, IBM was growing by selling a coordinated
computer system. This included typewriter, consoles, computers, output devices, and computer programs.

The success of the Honeywell company is another example. Some
years ago, when air conditioning began growing in popularity, management
was faced with the question of whether they should begin manufacturing
and selling air conditioners. After analyzing the market and their own capabilities, they decided instead to concentrate on developing, manufacturing
and marketing the electronic switching devices and thermostats which control the air conditioners. The air conditioning market itself became highly
competitive, and many companies failed. But Honeywell thrived as the leading developer and manufacturer of control devices.

Defining your company's central concept is the first step in the planning process. *Your firm's central, guiding concept answers the question "What
business are we in?" It clearly defines the product or service your company
will render to society, as well as your company's competitive advantage—such
as high quality, low cost, rapid delivery, or extensive customer service.* These
ideas are summarized in Exhibit 2–5.

Step 2—Establish Goals

The next step in planning is to establish the goals your enterprise will
pursue. A goal is a target that you try to attain. It is also a standard against
which actual performance is measured and compared.

Step 3—Develop Forecasts

The next step in planning is to develop a forecast, which is an estimate
or prediction of what the future holds in store for the enterprise. In order to
effectively plan, you (as a manager) will need to obtain forecasts of such

Exhibit 2.5 Why Your Firm's Central Guiding Concept is so Important

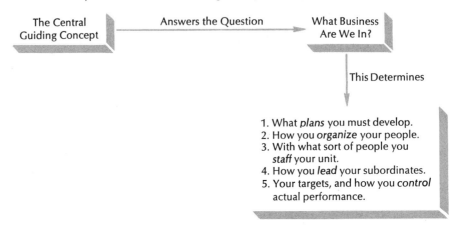

The Central Guiding Concept ——— Answers the Question ———→ What Business Are We In?

This Determines

1. What *plans* you must develop.
2. How you *organize* your people.
3. With what sort of people you *staff* your unit.
4. How you *lead* your subordinates.
5. Your targets, and how you *control* actual performance.

things as economic conditions, consumer tastes, new product developments, and political changes. Your plans are then built on these premises. We will discuss forecasting in Chapter 3.

Step 4—Evaluate Your Organization's Resources

It probably would not make much sense for a firm that produces and sells gasoline-powered lawn mowers to go into the automobile manufacturing business. Obviously its management knows something about internal combustion engines. But the men, machinery, and financial resources required for entrance into the auto industry are staggering and probably beyond the capabilities of the company. It is important, therefore, that you, as a manager, carefully assess your firm's financial, managerial, and operating resources in order to determine what is feasible and what is not.

Step 5—Develop Alternatives

After making your forecasts and auditing the resources of your company, you'll usually find that there are several alternatives—individual courses of action—that will allow you to accomplish your goals. Whether it's Ford or Jaguar, Hertz or Econo Car, Prentice-Hall or Dell, different firms within the same industry are often quite successful even with very different strategies. We will discuss developing alternatives in Chapter 4.

Step 6—Test for Consistency

In this step you compare your various alternatives with the resources, goals, and central concept of your enterprise. Obviously it is very important that your company choose an alternative which is not only consistent with its goals and concept, but also one that can be accomplished given its resources.

Step 7—Decide on a Plan

Here, you make a choice from among the available alternatives. We will discuss this step in Chapter 4.

Step 8—Implement the Plan

You are going to find that effective planning is no guarantee of success. Success also depends on effectively implementing the plan. This calls for all the skills you can muster in organizing, staffing, leading, and controlling. In fact, that's what this book is all about.

Step 9—Evaluate the Plan

If managers did business in an environment that never changed, they would probably not have to periodically reevaluate their plans. But, of course, this is not the case. We live in a world in which new products are constantly being introduced, consumers' tastes change rapidly, economic activity fluctuates, and government administrators come and go; therefore, your plans must be constantly open to evaluation and modification.

Summary: Steps in the Planning Process

In summary, the steps in the planning process are:

1. Define the central concept of your enterprise
2. Establish goals
3. Develop forecasts
4. Evaluate your organization's resources
5. Develop alternatives
6. Test for consistency
7. Decide on a plan
8. Implement the plan
9. Evaluate the plan

THE HIERARCHY OF PLANS

Many writers describe the planning process as a "means-end" chain. This chain consists of a hierarchy of ends (goals) and means (plans). This is summarized in Exhibit 2–6.

Exhibit 2.6   The "Means/End," Hierarchical Aspect of Plans

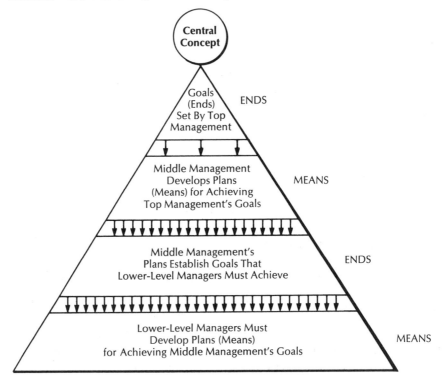

Richard Vancil and Peter Lorange have studied this planning process and in Exhibit 2–7 they have tried to summarize this hierarchical aspect of planning.[6] In their example there are three organizational levels represented: the chief executive (or highest) level; the division manager (or second) level; and the department manager (or third level).

Read Exhibit 2–7 carefully. Notice how the broad, company-wide plans and goals set by the chief executive become the targets which the division manager must establish plans for accomplishing. Similarly the plans made by the division manager result in goals which the department manager must plan to accomplish. Thus there is a hierarchy of ends (goals) and means (plans) linking the chief executive level, division manager level, and department manager level.

Exhibit 2.7 The Hierarchy of Planning

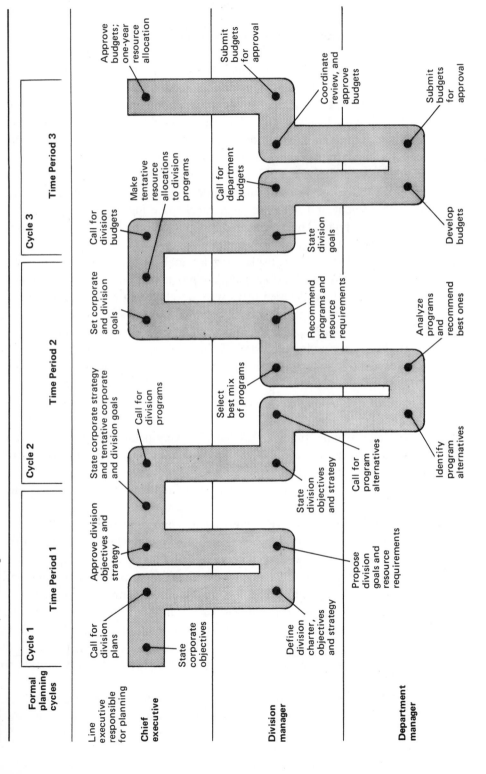

Formal planning cycles	Cycle 1		Cycle 2		Cycle 3	
	Time Period 1		Time Period 2		Time Period 3	

Line executive responsible for planning

Chief executive

- State corporate objectives
- Call for division plans
- Approve division objectives and strategy
- State corporate strategy and tentative corporate and division goals
- Call for division programs
- Set corporate and division goals
- Call for division budgets
- Make tentative resource allocations to division programs
- Approve budgets; one-year resource allocation

Division manager

- Define division charter, objectives and strategy
- Propose division goals and resource requirements
- State division objectives and strategy
- Call for program alternatives
- Select best mix of programs
- Recommend programs and resource requirements
- State division goals
- Call for department budgets
- Coordinate review, and approve budgets
- Submit budgets for approval

Department manager

- Identify program alternatives
- Analyze programs and recommend best ones
- Develop budgets
- Submit budgets for approval

Source: Richard Vancil and Peter Lorange, "Strategic Planning in Diversified Companies" *Harvard Business Review,* (January/February 1975)

34   *The Hierarchy of Plans: An Example*

The program of the National Aeronautics and Space Administration (NASA) to put a man on the moon is a good example of the hierarchy of plans.[7] In May 1961, President Kennedy formulated the broad national goal by stating: "I believe that this nation should commit itself to achieving the goal, before this decade is out, of landing a man on the moon and returning him safely to earth." With this broad goal as a target, the Office of Manned Space Flight was established within NASA, with prime responsibility for the manned lunar landing. This goal was pursued through the establishment of a sequence of manned space flight programs—Mercury, Gemini, and Apollo. This constituted a step-by-step procedure for developing America's capacity for man's exploration of space.

Given the broad goal, planning for each of these three projects was initiated and coordinated into a complete program. Operating on the premise of this broad strategy, detailed plans were developed to meet specific requirements. For example, for each launch of an orbiting manned vehicle, detailed plans had to be developed for launching, tracking, communications, and recovery. Furthermore, for each step of the process, contingency plans had to be developed for guiding activities in the event of emergencies.

Fitting Planning to the Task

Don't assume, though, that having a very detailed hierarchy of plans is always a virtue. Where you can forecast accurately and situations don't change unexpectedly then clear, precise plans are useful. They give you specific targets to shoot for, and they lay out the detailed means for attaining them.

But relying on a rigid *"means/end"* hierarchy of plans also places limits on how flexible you can be. There's always a tendency to "stick to the rules" and "go by the book" even when the rules may no longer apply. Where situations change unexpectedly or where it's hard to specify in advance how some job should be done, then a less rigid kind of planning is called for.

Some people call this *"directional"* planning.[8] Here you still have a loose hierarchy of plans. But there's more of an emphasis on the broad *direction* in which you are heading than on detailing how you will get there. This leaves you and your subordinates plenty of opportunity to react quickly to unexpected crises.

Therefore, for mechanistic situations there is more of an emphasis on standing plans—such as rules—specific goals, and detailed plans. For organic situations there is less emphasis on "sticking to the rules," goals are broader and less specific, and plans are more general. These ideas are summarized in Exhibit 2–8.

Exhibit 2.8 Fitting Planning to the Task

	How Some Important Aspects of Planning Have to Fit the Task:	
	MECHANISTIC	*ORGANIC*
Goals/Standards	Very specific	Broad
Use of standing plans such as rules and procedures:	Emphasis on many elaborate rules and procedures and "sticking to the rules"	Not as much use of pre-planned rules and procedures; employees not advised to always "stick to the rules."
How detailed plans are:	Very detailed, specific "means end" chain.	More emphasis on broad "direction" than on specifying means.

GOALS

Earlier in this chapter we defined a goal as a target or end that you strive to obtain. Once your enterprise has defined its central guiding concept and answered the question "What business are we in?" its goals become the standards against which performance is compared.

Goals Differ in How Specific They Are

Some goals are more specific (and more measurable) than others. For example, a goal such as "cut production costs by 8 percent in three years" is obviously much more specific (and measurable) than one such as "minimize costs."

You'll usually find that the goals which top managers have are less specific than those of lower-level managers. The former set broad goals (or targets) such as "minimize costs." Then it's up to the middle and first-line managers to set (with their bosses' approval) specific plans and goals for actually "minimizing costs." These might include "cut spoilage costs by 6 percent" for example.

36   *Organizations Don't Pursue Just One Goal*

What do you think is the goal of business? Probably most people would quickly answer that the goal of business is to "maximize profits." But although it is more convenient for many people—including many economists—to assume that the goal of business is to maximize profits, Professor Herbert Simon has suggested that businessmen actually pursue a number of different goals.[9]

George England carried out a study which confirmed the fact that businessmen do, in fact, pursue a variety of goals.[10] He asked over 1,000 managers to indicate which goals were "very important." Some of his findings are presented in Exhibit 2–9.

Exhibit 2.9 Managers Pursue Many Goals

Here Are the Goals England Found That Managers Felt Were Important to Them:
• Organizational Efficiency
• High Productivity
• Profit Maximization
• Organizational Growth
• Industrial Leadership
• Organizational Stability
• Employee Welfare
• Social Welfare

Source: George England, "Organizational Goals and Expected Behavior of American Managers," *Academy of Management Journal*, Vol. X, No. 2, (1967) pp. 107-17; reprinted in Stephen Carroll Jr., Frank Paine, and John B. Miner, *The Management Process* (New York: Macmillan, 1973 pp. 3-13

It seems apparent that these managers don't feel that "profit maximizing" or "efficiency" is all-important. Instead they consider *many* goals—such as growth, and employee welfare—when they make decisions.

Remember, though, that goals—whether "maximize profits," "maintain employee welfare," or some other—are only useful as targets once the central guiding concept of the enterprise has been crystalized. Your company has to have a clear answer to the question "What business are we in?" before goals such as "maximize profits" can become useful targets for management.

SOME EXAMPLES OF BUSINESS PLANS

As earlier mentioned, plans come in a variety of formats. An overall financial plan for a company is presented in Exhibit 2–10. A budget (such as shown in Exhibit 2–11) which projects revenues and expenditures, is an-

Exhibit 2.10 Outline of a Plan Presented in Financial Terms (optional)

I. NET SALES—1977-78

A. Data Supporting Sales Plan

1. The following major products will produce $ _____ in

	First Year	Second Year

Product A
Product B, etc.
Other Product
  Product in Total

2. Share of market will be improved by ___% in these products resulting in $_____ in sales.

	First Year		Second Year		Etc.
	Share of Market	$	Share of Market	$	Share of Market

Product A
Product B, etc.
  Total
Evaluate Competition

3. The following new products will produce dollar sales:

	First Year	Second Year

Product A
Product B, etc.
  Total

a. Summary of new product programs by year and effect on share market.

4. The following improvements will be made in distribution. (Sum of distribution improvements by year and effect on share of market
Examples:
  Dealer changes in weak areas
  Improvement in delivery and parts service
  Price structure revisions through lower-cost production

5. Acquisitions (if any) are anticipated as follows:
a. Summarize effect on sales and profit and dollar cost.

6. Capital Expenditures
a. Present plant capacity by major product line is as follows (expressed in terms of units):

	First Year	Second Year	Etc.

Product A
Product B, etc.

b. Percentage plant capacity utilization by major product line follows:

	First Year	Second Year	Etc.

Product A
Product B, etc.

c. Anticipated capital expenditures are as follows:

	First Year	Second Year	Etc.

Product A
Product B, etc.

d. These expenditures will result in a unit capacity increase by major product line as follows:

	First Year	Second Year	Etc.

Product A
Product B, etc.

e. After completion of plant expansion program, percentage plant utilization will be as follows:

	First Year	Second Year	Etc.

Product A
Product B, etc.   (Continued)

Exhibit 2.10 (continued)

7. Evaluation of market
   a. Size of total market (by product line, if possible).
   b. Evaluation of competition and relation to total market.
   c. Price structure effect on sales and profit.

II. PROFIT
   A. Cost reduction programs are as follows:
      Plant Overhead
      Sales Overhead
      Product Cost
      1. Summarize above programs and outline by year estimated percentage cost reductions.
   B. Product lines or products that are unprofitable are as follows:
      Product A
      Product B, etc.
      1. Summarize reasons for unprofitability. Examples:
         a. Competitive pricing
         b. High production costs, etc.
      2. Summarize steps being taken to improve profitability or to eliminate product.
   C. The following financial information by year will be included in the Long Range Plan:
      1. Profit and Loss statement
         a. Net Sales
         b. Cost of Sales
         c. Selling Expense
         d. Administrative Expense
         e. Other Deductions Net
         f. Net Profit Before Taxes
      2. Balance Sheet
         a. Assets
            1. Cash in Banks
            2. Total Net Receivables
            3. Inventories
            4. Total Prepaid Items
            5. Net Plant and Equipment
         b. Liabilities and Capital
            1. Accounts Payable and Accrued Expenses
            2. Accrued Taxes
            3. Division Capital Account
            4. Profit for Period
      3. Statement of Funds
         a. Cash on Hand—Beginning
         b. Profit
         c. Source (or Application) of Funds
            1. Notes and Accounts Receivable
            2. Inventories
            3. Net Plant and Equipment
            4. Prepaid and Deferred Items
            5. Payables and Accrued Expenses
            6. Accrued Taxes
         d. Funds Transferred
         e. Non-Cash Charges
            1. Redistributed from Head Office
            2. Sales and Franchise Taxes
            3. Unemployment and F.I.C.A.
            4. Other
         f. Cash on Hand—End

Source: Jerome B. Cohen, and Sidney Robbins, *The Financial Manager* (New York: Harper and Row, 1966) pp. 655-7

Exhibit 2.11 Example of a Budget: A Plan in Financial Terms

Darwin Books, Inc.
TENTATIVE PROFIT PLAN
For the Year Ending June 30, 19x2

	College Division	Schools Division	Total
Net sales	$4,050,000	$2,650,000	$6,700,000
Divisional expenses:			
Printing and binding	$2,400,000	$1,700,000	$4,200,000
Copy editing	100,000	80,000	180,000
Advertising and selling	650,000	470,000	1,120,000
Authors' royalties	500,000	250,000	750,000
Administration	70,000	65,000	135,000
Total divisional expenses	$3,720,000	$2,565,000	$6,285,000
Divisional profit	$ 330,000	$ 85,000	$ 415,000
General administrative expenses			300,000
Income before income taxes			$ 115,000
Income taxes			50,000
Net Income			$ 65,000

Source: Myron Gordon, and Gordon Shillinglaw, *Accounting: A Management Approach,* (Homewood; Irwin 1973) p. 510

other type of plan again in financial terms. A network (as in Exhibit 2–2) is a plan in chart form.

Plans also come in narrative form, and describe the goals of a company, and the company's planned means for accomplishing them. The outline of such a plan was presented in Exhibit 2–1.

Some Important Things to Remember from This Chapter:

1. Plans are methods, formulated beforehand for doing or making something.

2. A strategy is one important type of plan. It specifies the central concept or purpose of the enterprise as well as the means by which it intends to carry out that purpose.

3. A firm's central guiding concept answers the question "What business are we in?" It clearly defines the product or service the company will render to society as well as the company's competitive advantage.

4. Planning is important because: it provides direction; it provides a unifying framework; it helps to reveal future opportunities and threats; it provides performance standards.

5. Planning involves: defining the central concept of the enterprise; setting goals; developing forecasts; evaluating your organization's resources; developing alternatives; testing for consistency; deciding on your plan; implementing your plan; and evaluating your results.

6. It might be helpful for you to envision the planning process as a "means/ends" chain. This chain consists of a hierarchy of ends (goals) and means (plans).

40   The goals set at each level in the organization become the targets which succeedingly lower-level managers establish plans to accomplish.

7. Maximizing profits is certainly an important—perhaps *the* most important—business goal. But we also know that managers pursue other goals including growth, stability, and employee welfare. *But remember that goals are only useful as targets once the central guiding concept of the enterprise has been crystalized.*

STUDY ASSIGNMENTS

1. Define and distinguish between: goals, plans, strategies, and tactics.
2. Discuss four reasons which explain why planning is important.
3. Give two examples which show the importance of a "central concept" for the activities of a business firm.
4. Pick out three business firms with which you are familiar. Present, in two sentences or less, the central concept of each of these firms.
5. If you have not already done so, fill in the chart that we presented in the introduction to this chapter. What were some of the important aspects of planning you had to deal with in filling out this chart?
6. Briefly discuss each of the nine steps in planning.
7. Develop a hierarchy of plans for some activity (you might want to use your career plan from question 5). Make sure to specify how each of your goals are going to be attained, as well as how the "means" for each higher level becomes the "goals" for the next lower level in the hierarchy.
8. Give at least four examples of goals with different degrees of specificity.
9. Would you want to use the same approach to planning in a bookkeeping department that you would in a new product development department? Explain why you would (or would not).
10. Pick out a small business which you think you might be interested in starting. Based on whatever information may be available to you, develop a business plan in narrative form to guide you in starting up your business and taking it through its first year of operations. With what other types of plans might you want to supplement this narrative plan?

NOTES FOR THE CHAPTER

1. Adapted from David Kolb, Irwin Rubin, and James McIntyre, *Organizational Psychology* (Englewood Cliffs: Prentice-Hall, 1971) pp. 277–281.

2. This idea was developed by Hugo E. R. Uyterhoven, Robert W. Ackerman, and John W. Rosenblum, *Strategy and Organization* (Homewood: Irwin, 1973) pp. 7–9.

3. For a discussion of this point, see Paul R. Lawrence and J. W. Lorsch, "Differentiation and Integration in Complex Organizations," *Administrative Science Quarterly,* Vol. 12, No. 1 (January 1967) pp. 1–37; and D. C. Dearborne, and H. A. Simon, "Selective Perception: A Note on the Departmental Identifications of Executives," *Sociometry,* Vol. 21 (1958) pp. 140–144.

4. See Peter F. Drucker, "Long-Range Planning," *Management Science*, Vol. 5   41
(April 1959) pp. 238–249.

5. See Seymour Tilles, "How to Evaluate Corporate Strategy," *Harvard Business Review*, Vol. 41, No. 4 (July-August 1963) pp. 111–121. Reprinted in John Bonge and Bruce Coleman, *Concepts For Corporate Strategy* (New York: Macmillan, 1972) pp. 148–163.

6. Richard Vancil and Peter Lorange "Strategic Planning in Diversified Companies," *Harvard Business Review*, January/February 1975.

7. Fremont E. Kast and James E. Rosenzweig, *Organization and Management: A Systems Approach* (New York: McGraw-Hill 1974), quoted in Gary Dessler, *Organization and Management* (Englewood Cliffs: Prentice-Hall, 1976) pp. 335–336.

8. Michael McCaskey, "A Contingency Approach to Planning: Planning With Goals and Planning Without Goals," *Academy of Management Journal* (June 1974) pp. 281–291.

9. Herbert A. Simon, "On the Concept of Organizational Goal," *Administrative Science Quarterly* (1964) p. 142.

10. George England, "Organizational Goals and Expected Behavior of American Managers," *Academy of Management Journal*, Vol. 10, No. 2 (1967) pp. 107–117; reprinted in Stephen Carroll, Jr., Frank Paine, and John Miner, The Management Process: *Cases and Readings* (New York: Macmillan, 1973) pp. 3–13.

A Framework for Studying the Management Fundamentals

Where we are now: Discussing forecasting, which includes making predictions on which you build your plans.

I   PLANNING   →   ENVIRONMENT AND TASK

"What business are we in?"
"How do we get where we want to go?"

Ch. 2   Planning Process
Ch. 3   FORECASTING
Ch. 4   Decision-Making
Ch. 5   Effective Planning

Rate of change
Uncertainty
Diversity — "How entrepreneurial are tasks?"

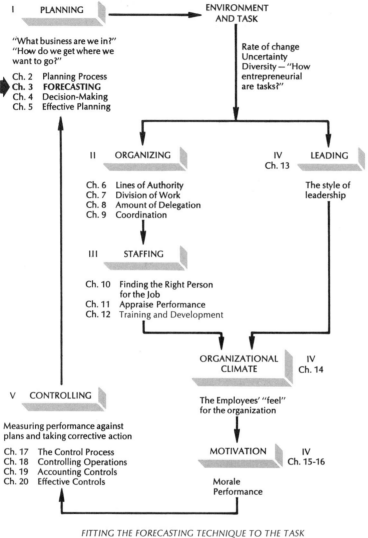

II   ORGANIZING

Ch. 6   Lines of Authority
Ch. 7   Division of Work
Ch. 8   Amount of Delegation
Ch. 9   Coordination

IV   LEADING
Ch. 13

The style of leadership

III   STAFFING

Ch. 10   Finding the Right Person for the Job
Ch. 11   Appraise Performance
Ch. 12   Training and Development

ORGANIZATIONAL CLIMATE   IV   Ch. 14

The Employees' "feel" for the organization

V   CONTROLLING

Measuring performance against plans and taking corrective action

Ch. 17   The Control Process
Ch. 18   Controlling Operations
Ch. 19   Accounting Controls
Ch. 20   Effective Controls

MOTIVATION   IV   Ch. 15-16

Morale
Performance

FITTING THE FORECASTING TECHNIQUE TO THE TASK

	Mechanistic	*Organic*
Forecasting Technique	Quantitative: Statistical forecasting, etc.	Qualitative: market research, etc.

When you have finished studying

3   Forecasting: Developing Planning Premises

You should be able to:

1. *Give examples showing the distinction between "implicit forecasting" and "explicit forecasting."*

2. *Discuss three methods for developing forecasts.*

3. *Cite at least six sources of published economic forecasts.*

4. *Describe the mechanics of "time series forecasting."*

5. *Show how "causal forecasting" techniques work.*

6. *Present an example of how you would use a forecast in planning.*

7. *Explain the DELPHI technique.*

8. *Cite the advantages and limitations of "time series," "causal," and "qualitative" forecasting techniques.*

INTRODUCTION

You don't have to look further than your own career plans to see how important forecasting can be. For example, let's suppose that you want to plan a career for yourself or for someone close to you. How could forecasts help you? For one thing, you'd probably want to check to see what the demand for different occupations is expected to be five or so years in the future. Other things equal, you'd be best off choosing a career that is expected to be in high demand, and forecasts like that in Exhibit 3–1 would therefore provide you with necessary planning assumptions or "premises." You could then begin building your career plans on these forecasts, and on your knowledge of your aptitudes and abilities. You can see that without these forecasts you'd just be "shooting in the dark." Managers also need forecasts, and so we'll discuss some specific forecasting techniques in this chapter.

Exhibit 3.1 Where the Jobs Are — and Will Be (continued)

And Where They'll Be State By State:

■ Jobs with greatest number of openings expected in the next five years.

O Worker shortage now.

✱ Openings both now and in the next five years.

Job categories (columns, left to right):
Secretaries · Bookkeepers · Typists · Salesclerks · Receptionists · Cashiers · Bank tellers · Child-care workers · Registered nurses · Licensed practical nurses · Physicians · Dentists · Health administrators · School teachers · Accountants · Managers in business, government, banking · Engineers · Farmers and farm managers · Real estate agents, brokers · Wholesale sales representatives · Insurance sales agents · Draftsmen, drafting technicians · Computer specialists · Carpenters · Truck drivers · Cosmetologists and hairdressers · Welders and flame cutters · Sewers and stitchers · Auto & truck mechanics & body workers · Plumbers and pipefitters · Electricians · Heavy-equipment mechanics, operators · Machinists · Cooks · TV & home appliance repairers · Other workers needed now; job locations; comments

State	Other workers needed now; job locations; comments
ALA.	
ALAS.	Most future openings expected in Anchorage and Fairbanks.
ARIZ.	Precision tool workers (such as grinders on close tolerance work on aerospace contracts). Most jobs are in Maricopa County, some in Pima County.
ARK.	
CAL.	Despite general surplus of workers, continuing demand for some kinds, such as nurses for night shifts and convalescent hospitals.
COLO.	
CONN.	
DEL.	Technicians to assist engineers; chemists (New Castle County).
D.C.	
FLA.	Technical writers.
GA.	
H.I.	Need for nurses is in Honolulu and Maui counties, auto mechanics in Honolulu.
IND.	Millwrights.
IOWA	Dietitians; personnel, labor relations specialists; air-conditioning mechanics; power-line repairers; telephone installers, repairers; compositors; typesetters; photographic process workers. Sales, clerical, real estate and insurance jobs mostly in Des Moines.
KAN.	Nurses needed particularly in urban areas of Topeka, Wichita, Kansas City; physicians in rural areas.
KY.	Most future openings expected in Lexington, Louisville and bordering Cincinnati areas.
LA.	
ME.	Wood harvesters.

State	Possible shortage of nurses (both LPN and RN) on Maryland's eastern shore.	Data processing machine repairers.	Legal secretaries; machine & electric motor repairers; automatic screw, special gear, jig boring, centerless grinder, bridgeport, heavy forge press operators; offset pressmen; millwrights; diesel mechanics; air-conditioning & heating designers.	Optometrists.	Auto mechanic jobs will be in southeast Nebraska.	Physician and nurse shortage is in rural areas. Other jobs mainly in Las Vegas and Reno areas.	Skilled machinists in certain specialties; medical technicians in some areas. Generally; jobs are in southern part of state.	Legal and medical secretaries; uranium miners; diesel mechanics. Nurse shortage in small towns and rural areas.	Physical and occupational therapists; job and die setter and other kinds of experienced machinists; electrical, nuclear and biomedical engineers.	Shortage of health professionals is in rural areas.	Carpenters and LPN's needed in Portland.	Textile jobs will be in the six northwest counties.	Need for physicians, nurses and other health workers is in rural areas.	Diesel mechanics; keypunch operators. Types of engineers needed are civil, mechanical. Jobs will be mostly in Dallas-Fort Worth and Houston areas.	Commission sales workers.	Jobs open now and in years ahead in crude petroleum, natural gas and coal mining; petroleum refining; construction of related facilities, including power generating plants.
MD.	○	○							○							
MASS.			■ ■		■	■		■		■ ■	■		■	✱	■ ■	✱
MICH.				○			■			■			○		■	
MINN.			■				■			■						
MO.			○			■				■			○			
MONT.			○					○		■			○			
NEB.	○			■		■		○		■			○	■	○	■
NEV.		■				■			■	■			✱		○	■
N.H.			■		■	■				■					■	
N.J.			■		■	■				■					■	
N.M.			■		■	■	■			✱ ■ ■ ■			■ ■		■ ✱	
N.Y.					○					■					○	
N.C.										■						■
N.D.										■	○		○			
OHIO						■		■		■					■ ■	
OKLA.	■			■				■		■			○		■	■
ORE.				■		✱		■		■			■	✱	■ ■	
PA.						■				■						
S.C.	○	○		○						○	○					
S.D.	○	○		○						○	○	○				
TENN.					○					✱	■	○	○			
TEX.	■	○	■		■	■ ■	○	■		■ ■	■	○	■	✱	■ ■	
UTAH	✱	■	■ ✱ ■	✱	■	✱	■	✱	■	■ ■ ✱	○	✱ ✱	■	✱	■ ■ ■	■
VT.			■							■					■	
VA.		■	■ ■	■	■	■		■		■ ■		■ ✱	■		■ ■ ■	■
WASH.		■	■ ■			■		■		■		✱				
W. VA.	■	■	■ ■ ■		■	■	■	■	■	■ ■	○	■	■ ■		■ ■ ■	■
WIS.	■	■	■ ■	■	■	■	■	■	■	■ ■	■	■	■	■	■ ■	
WYO.	■	■	■ ■	■	■	✱	■	■	■	■ ■	✱	✱	■ ■	○	■ ■	■

Note: Idaho, Illinois, Mississippi and Rhode Island did not respond.

Source: *Changing Times, The Kiplinger Magazine,* May 1976, pp. 24-25.

Exhibit 3.1   Where the Jobs are — and Will be

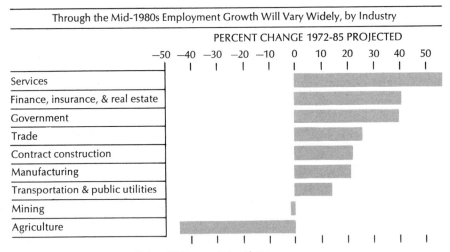

In the country as a whole:

Through the Mid-1980s Employment Growth Will Vary Widely Among Occupations

PERCENT CHANGE, EMPLOYMENT 1972-85

	−50	−40	−30	−20	−10	0	10	20	30	40	50
Professional & technical workers											
Clerical workers											
Managers, officials, & proprietors											
Service workers											
Sales workers											
Craftsmen											
Operatives											
Nonfarm laborers											
Farm workers											

Through the Mid-1980s Employment Growth Will Vary Widely, by Industry

PERCENT CHANGE 1972-85 PROJECTED

	−50	−40	−30	−20	−10	0	10	20	30	40	50
Services											
Finance, insurance, & real estate											
Government											
Trade											
Contract construction											
Manufacturing											
Transportation & public utilities											
Mining											
Agriculture											

Source: 1974-75 U.S. Department of Labor; 1974 Bureau of Labor Statistics

WHY FORECAST?

Forecasting is aimed at calculating or predicting some future event or condition.[1] It is "a service whose purpose is to offer the best available basis for management expectations of the future, and to help management understand the implications for alternative courses of action."[2]

Implicit vs. Explicit Forecasts

At one time forecasts were notoriously inaccurate, and even today you hear some managers insist that "they don't believe in forecasting." But if you spend some time watching these same managers you will see that they do, in fact, engage in forecasting. Thus, take the manager who makes a snap decision not to replace a piece of worn out machinery. He is *implicitly* forecasting that his profits will be higher than if he bought a new machine.[3]

Although this kind of intuitive approach to managing can be successful, as often as not unforeseen consequences occur and create problems for the manager. This is why—the shortcomings of forecasting notwithstanding—it is generally more useful to consciously forecast and develop *explicit* planning premises or assumptions, as Exhibit 3–2 illustrates.[4]

Exhibit 3.2 The Problems with Relying on Implicit Forecasting

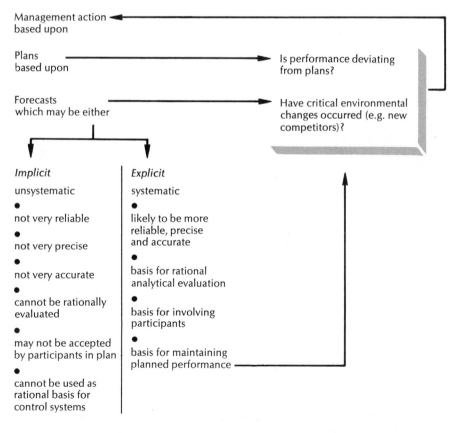

Source: Thomas E. Milne: *Business Forecasting: A Managerial Approach* (London, Longman, 1975) p. 6.

48   *THE ECONOMIC FORECAST*

What is Economic Forecasting?

It is virtually impossible to pick up a newspaper or watch a television news program and not find some reference to economic forecasting. We are told, for example, that "industrial production will rise," "gross national product is bottoming out," and that "unemployment will fall."

As its name implies, an economic forecast is a projection of the level of economic activity for a particular time period. The broadest measure of the level of economic activity is the Gross National Product (GNP). This represents the total value of the goods and services produced in this nation during a specified period, such as a year. Some economic forecasts for 1976 are summarized in Exhibit 3–3. It might be interesting for you to check how accurate they were.

Exhibit 3.3   Economic Forecasts for 1976

	1976 GNP (billions of dollars)	Real growth in GNP	Percent	
			Price increase	1976 average unemployment
ECONOMISTS				
Robert Dennis (National Planning Assn.)	1,681	6.7	6.7	6.9
Albert T. Sommers (The Conference Board)	1,677	6.9	6.1	8.0
Kerwin B. Stallings (Morgan Guaranty)	1,677	7.1	5.9	7.8
Robert Ortner (Bank of N.Y.)	1,672	6.7	6.0	7.6
Daniel A. Hodes (GT&E)	1,676	5.9	7.3	7.7
Daniel S. Ahearn (Wellington Fund)	1,669	6.6	6.5	7.8
Raymond Jallow (United California Bank)	1,666	6.0	6.7	7.6
Paul J. Markowski (Argus Research)	1,662	7.1	5.1	7.8
Robert G. Dederick (Northern Trust)	1,660	6.0	6.0	7.6
Francis H. Schott (Equitable Life Assurance)	1,660	6.0	6.2	7.8
J. Robert Ferrari (Prudential Insurance)	1,658	5.5	6.5	7.8
Bert A. Gottfried (Research Inst. of Amer.)	1,657	5.9	6.0	7.7
Peter L. Bernstein (Peter L. Bernstein Inc.)	1,656	6.4	5.5	7.5
A Gilbert Heebner (Phila. Natl. Bank)	1,650	5.6	5.8	7.8
Herbert E. Neil Jr. (Harris Trust & Savings)	1,650	6.0	5.5	8.0
Albert G. Matamoros (Armstrong Cork)	1,648	5.4	5.9	7.7
Morris Cohen (Schroder Naess & Thomas)	1,647	5.9	5.4	7.8
Don R. Conlon (Capital Strategic Services)	1,640	5.4	5.6	7.9
William C. Freund (N.Y. Stock Exchange)	1,640	5.0	5.5	7.6
Robert Eggert (RCA)	1,636	5.4	5.3	8.0
Robert H. Parks (Advest)	1,635	4.9	7.7	7.8
Gordon W. McKinley (McGraw-Hill)	1,630	5.7	4.8	8.1
James J. O'Leary (U.S. Trust)	1,627	5.1	4.9	8.4
A. Gary Shilling (White Weld)	1,607	4.9	4.1	7.5
Average	1,653	5.9	5.9	7.8

Question: How accurate were these economic forecasts for 1976?

Source: *Business Week:* December 29, 1975

Why the Economic Forecast is Important

Economic forecasting is important because the sales of virtually every product or service from ball bearings to Broadway shows is in some way related to the level of economic activity. In the case of ball bearings, the relationship may be *direct*. Thus a reduced level of economic activity implies a reduction in machine-tool orders, and therefore in orders for the ball bearings used to keep these machines running. Or the relationship may be *inverse*— as might be the case for entertainment services such as Broadway shows. These often become more attractive to consumers when economic activity is in the doldrums.

Therefore the economic forecast is important because, in one way or another, the sales of your own enterprise is tied to the general level of economic activity. As William Freund says:

> Business must plan ahead. Every business decision is predicated on some assumption about the future, whether right or wrong, whether explicit or implicit. Capital expenditure budgets, for example, must be drawn on the basis of sales estimates, which in turn depend, either directly or indirectly, on the outlook for the national economy. And with the lead time between research and marketing becoming ever longer, the need for economic projection is becoming a more vital ingredient of business decisions.[5]

Economic Forecasting

How do managers make economic forecasts? Probably there are enough books on economic forecasting to fill a small library, so we obviously can't do more here than touch on some of its most basic characteristics. In essence, there are three main approaches to economic forecasting: 1) The leading indicators approach; 2) the Gross National Product approach; and 3) the econometric approach.[6]

Indicators: The *leading indicator* approach involves closely monitoring the level of such economic "indicators" as: 1) Average hours worked per week in manufacturing; 2) new orders for durable goods; and 3) number of business failures. Some of these leading indicators are presented in Exhibit 3–4. They are called leading indicators because they tend to rise several months prior to upswings in the general level of economic activity, and fall prior to downswings. Therefore, watching these leading indicators can help you forecast what the level of economic activity will be six months or a year in advance.

Exhibit 3.4   A List of Some Important Leading Indicators

Average hours of work per week, manufacturing.	Net change in number of operating businesses; number of new incorporations.
Gross accession rate, manufacturing.	
Layoff rate, manufacturing (inverted).	Liabilities of business failures, all commercial (inverted).
Manufacturers' new orders, durable goods industry.	Corporate profits after taxes.
New private nonfarm dwelling units started; residential building contracts.	Index of all common stock prices.
	Change in business inventories.
Contracts, total commercial and industrial buildings, floor space.	Index of process of raw industrial commodities.

GNP: Economic forecasting using the GNP approach requires making estimates of the four major components of the Gross National Product. These are: Consumer spending; spending by business firms (on things such as capital equipment); spending by local, state, and federal governments; and net foreign spending (which reflects the balance between exports and imports). Based on information such as surveys of consumer-buying attitudes, a forecaster estimates the level of each of these four components. He then combines them into an estimated total GNP.

Models: Finally, the _econometric-model_ approach involves developing elaborate mathematical equations. These tie together the relationships between economic "causal" variables, (such as "new housing starts" or "equipment purchases by businesses,") and "output" variables (such as GNP). The most elaborate models may use hundreds of these variables. An econometric model is built on the assumption that you know the relationship between the economic variables in the equations, and the future level of economic activity in the country—say one year hence. Then all you need do is "plug in" the current values of these economic variables and your economic forecast will drop out. Thus, these models are supposed to work somewhat like sophisticated vending machines. Some of them, such as the model developed at the Wharton School of Business, have been fairly successful in developing forecasts. Some "instructions" for building an econometric model are presented in Exhibit 3–5.

Where to Find Economic Forecasts

There is a wealth of published economic forecasts for those managers who prefer not to develop their own.[7] In December of each year, _Business Week_ magazine presents its economic forecast for the following year; and each week it presents a snapshot of the economy on its "Outlook" page. (See Exhibit 3–6.) _Fortune_ magazine has a monthly forecast of the business outlook

Exhibit 3.5 Building Econometric Models

The Junior Econometrician's Work Kit.

Predict the U.S. Economy for 1956.
Build Your Own Forecasting Model.

DIRECTIONS:

1. Make up a theory. You might theorize, for instance, that (1) next year's consumption will depend on next year's national income; (2) next year's investment will depend on this year's profits; (3) tax receipts will depend on future Gross National Product. (4) GNP is the sum of consumption, investment, and government expenditures. (5) National income equals GNP minus taxes.

2. Use symbols for words. Call consumption, C; national income, Y; investment, I; preceding year's profits, P_{-1}; tax receipts, T; Gross National Product, G; government expenditures, E.

3. Translate your theories into mathematical equations:

(1) $C = aY + b$ (4) $G = C + I + E$

(2) $I = cP_{-1} + d$ (5) $Y = G - T$

(3) $T = eG$

This is your forecasting model. The small letters, a, b, c, d, e, are the constants that make things come out even. For instance, if horses (H) have four legs (L), then $L = aH$; or $L = 4H$. This can be important in the blacksmith business.

4. Calculate the constants. Look up past years' statistics on consumption, income, and so on. From these find values for a, b, c, d, and e that make your equation come out fairly correct.

5. Now you're ready to forecast. Start by forecasting investment from this year's profits. Look up the current rate of corporate profits — it's around $42-billion. The model won't tell what federal, state, and local governments will spend next year — that's politics. But we can estimate it from present budget information — it looks like around $75-billion.

6. Put all available figures into your model. (We've put in the constants for you.)

(1) $C = .7Y + 40$ (4) $G = C + I + 75$

(2) $I = .9 \times 42 + 20$ (5) $Y = G - T$

(3) $T = .2G$

7. Solve the equations. You want values of C, I, T, G, Y. Hints: Do them in this order — (2), (1), (4), (3), (5). In solving (1), remember that I and E are both part of G, $Y = G - T$, and $T = .2G$.

8. Results. (See if yours are the same.) For 1956, consumption will be $260.0-billion; investment, $57.8-billion; GNP, $392.8-billion; tax receipts, $78.6-billion; national income, $314.2-billion. These results are guaranteed — provided that the theories on which they're based are valid.

Source: Reprinted from the September 24, 1955 issue of *Business Week* by special permission. Copyright 1955 © by McGraw-Hill, Inc. Reproduced in Jerome Cohen and Sidney Robbins, *The Financial Manager*, (New York: Harper and Row, 1966) p. 648

that is usually buttressed in its January issue with a forecast for the coming year. Many banks, such as the *First National City Bank* (New York), *Manufacturer's Hanover Trust*, and *Chase Manhattan*, publish periodic analyses and forecasts of the economy. Each December the *Prudential Insurance Company* publishes an economic forecast for the coming year.

52   **Exhibit 3.6** Business Outlook

William B. Franklin, Chief Outlook Editor / April 19, 1976

The advance has speed and plenty of fuel

The economic advance is moving along on a fast track, propelled by continuing solid gains in employment.

Gross national product in the first quarter probably did not show any significant advance in the rate of growth compared with the preceding quarter; the size of the gain was evidently held down by a sharp decline in the net export balance and only a small advance in inventory accumulation.

The current quarter, however, is benefiting from a whole range of factors.

Business optimism is rising, and large employment gains are producing substantial increases in income.

Growth in exports and inventories is apt to give added spin to the business advance, while inflation is likely to remain subdued through the spring.

Following a sharp upsurge at the beginning of the year, Dun & Bradstreet's sales optimism index posted a further modest advance for the second quarter.

The index rose three points, to 68, the highest level since the third quarter of 1974.

Manufacturers of softgoods had the highest expectations for spring, with more businessmen in this area expecting sales increases than at any time in the past three years.

They also foresaw continued gains in new orders, with 71% of executives in hardgoods and 81% of the softgoods manufacturers expecting second-quarter gains.

The improved tone in orders is also showing up in the capital goods sector. Orders for nonelectrical machinery took a big jump in February, according to the Economics Dept. of the McGraw-Hill Publications Co.

The combined index of eight major machinery groups leaped 7% in the month, after seasonal adjustment.

This was the ninth monthly advance in the past year and brings the index one-third higher than a year earlier—and only 5% below the peak set in August, 1974.

Bright expectations in stocks and sales

The Commerce Dept.'s quarterly survey of manufacturers' inventory and sales expectations affirms the brighter hopes emerging.

According to Commerce's data, manufacturers expect a 2.2% increase in sales, seasonally adjusted, in the second quarter. (On an unadjusted basis they are anticipating a 6½% advance.)

But businessmen have been consistently underestimating the degree of improvement in sales since the recovery began last spring. Chances are sales will again outpace expectations.

Source: Part of the "Business Outlook," a weekly forecast of the economy in *Business Week* magazine (April 19, 1976, pp. 31-32)

Several agencies of the federal government also make available a wide variety of economic activity information. The *U.S. Council of Economic Advisors* prepares "Economic Indicators" every month which show the trend to date of a variety of economic indicators. The *Federal Reserve Bank of St. Louis* also publishes monthly summaries of various economic indicators.

THE SALES FORECAST

Relating Sales to the Economic Forecast

Once the economic forecast has been made, the sales forecast for your company can be developed. There are many ways to develop the sales forecast, some of which we will describe in the following sections. One of the simplest methods is to carefully study the historical relationship between the sales of your company and some economic indicator such as "machinery orders by business." For example, the manufacturer of ball bearings we mentioned earlier might be able to forecast a decline in his sales if he sees that the orders for machinery are diminishing.

Why is Sales Forecasting Necessary?

Why do managers need sales forecasts? The fundamental reason is that in the long run your company's existence depends on a continued, healthy demand for its product. Thus even the most efficiently managed streetcar company probably could not have survived after most people had transferred their business to autos and busses. On the other hand, as computer sales mushroomed, a data-system company (such as IBM) might have been successful even in the face of a number of day-to-day mistakes.

Sales forecasting also serves a second purpose: it is the foundation on which all your other forecasts are predicated. For example, you can use the sales forecasts to develop projections of production requirements (in number of units). Then, based on these projections, you can forecast what materials need to be purchased, how many employees will have to be recruited, and what your expenses (such as those for advertising, and running the plant) should amount to.

TIME SERIES FORECASTING TECHNIQUES

Time Series Forecasting Defined

A *time series* is a set of observations taken at specific times, usually at equal intervals. Examples of time series are the total Gross National Product of the United States over a number of years; the total monthly sales receipts of a department store; the daily closing price of a share on the stock exchange; and the hourly temperatures announced by the weather bureau of a city.[8] Managers who use time series forecasting are banking on past trends continuing unchanged into the future.

How to Use Time Series Forecasting

A graph of a time series—in this case the monthly sales of Bob's Air Conditioning Company [9]—is presented in Exhibit 3-7. Look at this graph for a moment; what does it tell you about their sales?

Exhibit 3.7   Monthly Sales 1965-1976 for Bob's Air Conditioning Company

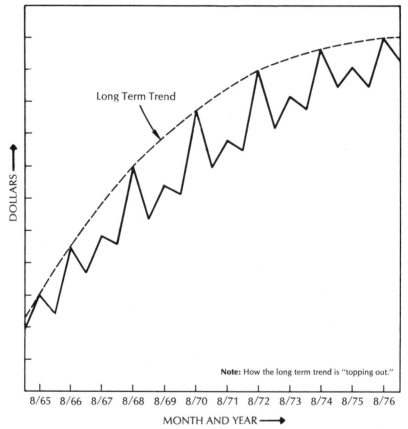

Perhaps the first thing you noticed is the regularity in the curve that is due to "seasonality." Thus Bob's sales usually begin picking up in April and May as the weather begins to turn warmer, and then peaks in August— during the hottest month of the summer season.

There is also an upward trend in Bob's sales. Notice how it has risen consistently from year to year over the past ten years. From the graph, it also seems that the *rate of growth* of this increase is slowing down—notice how the dotted line is beginning to taper off.

If you look closely you may also find that the curve seems to have a cyclical pattern which appears to repeat itself every two years. For some reason, Bob's sales tend to be a bit higher in the even-numbered years than in the odd-numbered ones.

As in the Bob's Air Conditioning example, the first thing that time series forecasting provides is a picture of *what* has happened in the past. But time series forecasting can also help you draw some tentative conclusions about *why* your sales (or earnings, etc.) have been as they have. For example, it seems obvious that the seasonal variation in Bob's sales is due to the higher summer temperatures. Management could extrapolate—project into the future—this relationship in projecting higher summer sales.

But the reasons for the cyclical patterns that repeat every two years, or for the slowing rate of growth, are not so apparent from the curve. In order for you to find out *why* these things have occurred, other and more sophisticated "causal" forecasting techniques are required.

CAUSAL FORECASTING TECHNIQUES

What are Causal Forecasting Techniques?

Causal forecasting techniques help show a manager *why* his sales are tapering off, or why they are higher every two years. They are used when enough analysis has been performed so that clear relationships between the company factor (such as sales) and other factors (such as Gross National Product) can be ascertained.

How to Use Causal Forecasting

Bob's sales curve is again presented in Exhibit 3–8, but this time you will also find some other information presented. This includes: Bob's monthly advertising expenditures; the total monthly sales of the air-conditioning industry; and the cost of electricity per kilowatt hour.

Basically causal forecasting involves estimating the company factor (such as sales) from the other factors (such as cost of electricity, or advertising expenditures). Usually "correlation analysis" (How closely are the variables related?) and "regression analysis" (How can we predict one factor if we know the values of related factors?) are used in order to develop the necessary relationships.

What does Exhibit 3–8 tell you about Bob's sales? As you can see from just "eye-balling" it, both the sales, and advertising expenditure curves seem to peak every two years. Therefore it seems likely that advertising has an important influence on Bob's sales. But why is it that while sales are increasing,

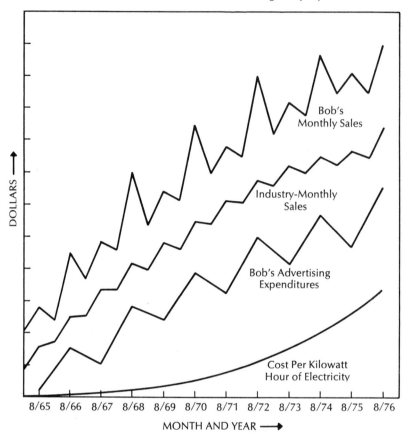

the long-term trend (the dotted line in Exhibit 3–7) seems to be "topping out"?

To help find an answer, look at the air-conditioning industry's total sales, which are presented alongside Bob's sales. Notice that Bob's share of the total market seems to be holding fairly steady. The two curves are not diverging (as they would if Bob's share of the market was falling off); or converging (as they would if his share of the market was increasing). In fact it looks as though whatever is happening to Bob's, is also happening to the rest of the industry since the entire industry's sales growth is slowing down.

What could be causing fewer people to buy air conditioners? Of course there might be any number of reasons. But for at least a partial explanation, look at how the tapering off of air-conditioner sales seems to be related to the rise in costs of electricity.

What may be happening is this. As fuel oils become more expensive, the cost of generating electricity increases. And as electricity becomes more expensive, consumers probably buy fewer and smaller air conditioners and also use their units less—which in turn slows the demand for air-conditioner parts. Thus the higher electricity costs may be "causing" air-conditioner sales to taper off. So now you know a good deal about the "causes" of Bob's sales. And with the knowledge that electricity costs are still rising you could develop a sales forecast which would show a continued slowing of sales growth, assuming some drastic steps are not taken soon.

Using the Forecast for Planning

Now suppose that you were the president of Bob's Air Conditioning. How would you use this information in developing your five-year plan?

As one alternative, you might decide to develop a new central concept for your firm and to focus on becoming "the industry leader in efficient, low-energy consuming air conditioners." Bob's could then effectively take advantage of the consumers' concern for cutting down their electric bills, and also use its advertising (which has been effective in the past) in order to help establish this "efficiency" image with the public.

Then, given this new concept, each of your divisions would develop their own plans for how they will contribute to making Bob's the "industry leader in efficient, low-energy consuming air conditioners." For example, the research and development division would lay plans for developing more efficient air-conditioning units. The manufacturing division would develop plans for implementing the more rigorous quality control needed to produce the new products. The marketing division would develop advertising plans for publicizing the new, efficient units; and a new sales distribution network might have to be developed. The personnel department would develop manpower plans for recruiting the necessary research and development engineers, and quality control engineers.

QUALITATIVE FORECASTING TECHNIQUES

Why Use "Qualitative Techniques?"

Although time series forecasting, and causal forecasting can be very useful, they clearly have some limitations. First, they are virtually useless when data are scarce—such as for an entirely new product which has no sales history. Second, they assume that historical trends will continue into the

58 future. But trends have a habit of changing, often suddenly; as a British economist once pointed out: "A trend is a trend is a trend. The question is when will it bend? Will it climb higher and higher, or eventually expire, and come to an untimely end?" [10]

A third limitation is that both of these forecasting techniques tend to disregard unforeseeable, unexpected occurrences. And yet it is these unexpected occurrences (such as the fuel shortage) that often have the most profound effects on companies.

Qualitative forecasting techniques are useful when historical data is scarce, and then you are especially interested in identifying unexpected future opportunities or threats. These techniques emphasize human judgment. They gather, in as logical, unbiased, and systematic a way as possible, all the information and judgment that can be brought to bear on the factors being forecasted. Two such techniques are Marketing Research and the DELPHI method. [11]

Marketing Research

Marketing research is "the systematic gathering, recording, and analyzing of data about problems related to the marketing of goods and services." [12] Suppose, as an example, that the Bob's Air Conditioning Company finds that their high efficiency air conditioners will have to sell at a much higher price than competing brands. Therefore, they need more market information before proceeding with their plans. For example, they need information such as "Will such an air conditioner appeal to a particular type of consumer (such as those with higher incomes)?" "Will it be a bigger seller in a particular part of the country (such as the south)?" and, "Will the high price be an insurmountable disadvantage?"

Market research is aimed at obtaining answers to questions such as these. You use it to obtain information concerning consumer buying preferences, effectiveness of advertising, and so forth. Typically data are collected through questionnaires, direct observation, and analysis of "secondary" sources of data such as census reports.

Technological Forecasting—the DELPHI Technique

In his book, *Future Shock*, Alvin Toffler says that today:

. . . . We have not merely extended the scope and scale of change, we have radically altered its pace. We have in our time released a totally new social force—a stream of change so accelerated that it influences our sense of time, [and] revolutionizes the tempo of our daily life. . .

He says that this type of rapid change is particularly evident in the many new products in use today. Although these products are widely used today, they existed only in the realm of science fiction just a few years ago. These range from nuclear generating plants and supersonic passenger planes, to electronic digital clocks and transistorized desk calculators.

How do you go about coping with such rapid change? How do you "forecast" the emergence of the sorts of opportunities and threats represented by radically new products—such as transistors and digital clocks—opportunities and threats which sometimes occur almost overnight?

William Zarecore [13] says that many managers simply depend on intuition and inspiration when it comes to such forecasting. And the fact is that many companies like Polaroid and Xerox *were* built on the inspired ideas of single individuals.

Yet the graveyard of bankrupt companies contains more than its share of firms—for example, the railroads—which simply failed to see the fundamental changes that were operating to cast their products into obsolescence.

In order to try to improve their batting averages in predicting such "unforeseeable"—or at least unexpected—changes, today many companies are engaging in what is often called "technological forecasting." According to Thomas Milne, "the role of technological forecasting is to provide information about the kinds of future developments which are possible." [14]

DELPHI: The *Delphi technique* is often used in order to make such technological forecasts. This technique involves obtaining the opinions of people who are "experts" on the future technological and economic trends which might affect your company's markets. But instead of putting all these experts together in one room (where one or two strong personalities might overwhelm the group) their opinions are solicited anonymously and individually through questionnaires. Then these opinions are analyzed, distilled, and resubmitted to the experts for a second round of opinions. This process may continue for five, six, or more rounds.

In its initial survey, for example, your company might ask its panel of experts to list the breakthroughs, important to the company, they expect to see in the next 40 years. You could then analyze these first results, and choose the ten breakthroughs most frequently mentioned.

This list of ten breakthroughs could be resubmitted to the panel for an estimate as to the *probability* that each of the ten breakthroughs would in fact occur. Then the five most probable breakthroughs could be listed and resubmitted to the experts, who would be asked to predict the *decade* in which the breakthroughs would most likely occur. You would thus have developed a "best guess" estimate of what these experts feel are the most important breakthroughs facing your company in the years ahead.

HOW TO FIT THE FORECASTING
TECHNIQUE TO THE TASK

Most products—cars, cereals, phonograph records, etc.—go through a "product life cycle." Sales climb steadily as the new product is introduced, and then more rapidly as it "catches on." Then some years in the future it reaches the maturity stage. Here competition is fierce, the product may be outdated, and sales begin to decline.[15]

The development and introduction stages are very uncertain and unstable ones for a manufacturer. Your product has no track record, and you must be ready to react quickly to unforeseen crises. Here qualitative forecasting tools like DELPHI and market research are especially useful, since they don't depend on historical data.

But in the growth and mature stages the situation is much different. Here a main concern is carefully planning production to keep efficiency high.

You have historical sales data by now, and you can make good use of times series forecasting tools and causal models. These ideas are summarized in Exhibit 3–9.

Exhibit 3.9 Fitting the Forecasting Technique to the Situation

	Product Development Stage	Marketing Testing And Early Introduction Stage	Rapid Growth Stage	Mature State Stage
Forecasting techniques	Delphi method; Historical analysis of comparable products	Consumer surveys; Market tests	Statistical techniques for identifying turning points; Market surveys; Intention-to-buy surveys	Time-series analysis and projection; Causal and econometric models

Note: During the early product development stages little historical data is available on the product so "qualitative" techniques like Delphi are appropriate. During the later stages you have more and more historical data to go on so quantitative techniques like time series analysis are appropriate.

Some Important Things to Remember from This Chapter:

1. Forecasting may not be foolproof, but without it you're just "shooting in the dark."

2. An economic forecast is a projection of the level of economic activity for a particular time period. The broadest measure of such activity is the GNP. This represents the total value of the goods and services produced in this nation during a specified period.

3. The leading indicator approach to economic forecasting involves closely   61
monitoring the level of such "indicators" as average hours worked per week in
manufacturing, and new orders for durable goods. They tend to rise several months
prior to upswings in the economy, and to fall prior to downswings.

4. Economic forecasting using the Gross National Product (GNP) approach requires making estimates of the four major components of the GNP. These
are: Consumer spending; spending by business firms; spending by governments;
and net foreign spending.

5. The econometric model approach to economic forecasting involves developing elaborate mathematical equations which tie together "causal" and economic variables.

6. Most managers probably depend on published economic forecasts. These
are available from: *Business Week* magazine; *Fortune* magazine; First National
City Bank (New York); Manufacturers' Hanover Trust Bank; Chase Manhattan
Bank; Prudential Insurance Company; the United States Council of Economic
Advisors; and the Federal Reserve Bank of St. Louis.

7. Once you have your economic forecast you can proceed to develop your
sales forecast. To do this, you can use one of the forecasting techniques (time
series, causal, or qualitative) discussed in this chapter. Your sales forecast is then
the foundation on which all your other forecasts are predicated.

8. A time series is a set of observations taken at specific times—such as the
total monthly sales receipts of a department store. By analyzing graphs of such time
series, you can identify "seasonality" and draw some tentative conclusions as to
what is causing sales to behave as they do.

9. Causal forecasting involves estimating the company factor (such as
sales) from some other factors (such as cost of electricity). Here you usually use
correlation analysis (How closely are the variables related?), and regression analysis
(How can we predict one factor if we know the values of related factors?).

10. Qualitative forecasting techniques are useful when data are scarce—
such as for entirely new products which have no sales history. These include Marketing Research, and DELPHI.

11. Qualitative techniques like DELPHI are more appropriate in the development and introduction stages of your product's "life cycle." In the rapid
growth and mature stages, historical sales data is available and here quantitative
techniques such as causal models are useful.

STUDY ASSIGNMENTS

1. Give some examples which depict the difference between *implicit* and
   explicit forecasting.
2. Discuss the pros and cons of three methods for developing forecasts.
3. Cite at least six sources of published economic forecasts. Based on this
   information, write a short essay presenting your own economic forecast for one year from today.
4. Develop a time series for some activity with which your are familiar
   (i.e., the monthly sales of a local retail store, your monthly electric bill,
   etc.).

5. Do you notice any regular variation or trend in the time series you presented in Question 4? How would you explain this variation or trend? Are there any other indicators you could use to try to explain them?

6. Your boss has asked you to make a presentation on the topic: "How our company can use causal forecasting to improve our planning." Write an essay describing what you would say.

7. Discuss the differences and similarities between qualitative, and quantitative forecasting techniques.

8. Explain the DELPHI technique. Do you think that DELPHI is only an appropriate technique for giant corporations like IBM and Xerox? Why?

9. Discuss the advantages and limitations of time-series, causal, and qualitative forecasting techniques.

10. Choose a career that is particularly attractive to you. Then, based on published data and data from your local employment service, develop one-year and five-year forecasts for the demand in your local area for people in that occupation.

NOTES FOR THE CHAPTER

1. *Webster's Seventh New Collegiate Dictionary* (Springfield, Mass.: G. & C. Merriam, 1973).

2. Thomas E. Milne, *Business Forecasting: A Managerial Approach* (London: Longman, 1975) p. 2.

3. George Steiner, *Top Management Planning* (New York: Macmillan) p. 203.

4. Thomas E. Milne, *Business Forecasting*, p. 6.

5. William C. Freund, "Long-Term Economic Projections—Some Problems, Methods, and Results," paper presented at the annual forecasting conference of the American Statistical Association, New York, May 5, 1961. Reprinted in Jerome B. Cohen and Sidney M. Robbins, *The Financial Manager* (New York: Harper & Row, 1966) p. 628.

6. See Cohen and Robbins, *The Financial Manager*, pp. 628–654.

7. Cohen and Robbins, *The Financial Manager*, Ch. 19.

8. Murray R. Spiegel, *Statistics* (New York: Schaum, 1961) p. 283.

9. A fictitious name.

10. A. Chairncross; Quoted in Thomas E. Milne, *Business Forecasting: A Managerial Approach* (London: Longman, 1975) p. 42.

11. John Chambers, Satinder Mullick, and Donald Smith, "How To Choose The Right Forecasting Technique," *Harvard Business Review* (July-August 1971) pp. 45–74.

12. Harper W. Boyd and Ralph Westfall, *Marketing Research* (Homewood: Richard D. Irwin, Inc., 1972) p. 4.

13. William D. Zarecore, "High Technology Product Planning," *Harvard Business Review* (January-February 1975) pp. 108–115.

14. Thomas E. Milne, *Business Forecasting: A Managerial Approach*, p. 129.

15. Chambers, Mullick, and Smith, "How To Choose The Right Forecasting Technique."

A Framework·for Studying the Management Fundamentals

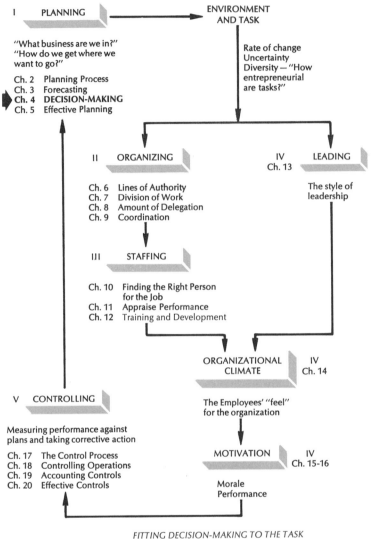

I PLANNING   →   ENVIRONMENT AND TASK

"What business are we in?"
"How do we get where we want to go?"

Ch. 2 Planning Process
Ch. 3 Forecasting
Ch. 4 DECISION-MAKING
Ch. 5 Effective Planning

Rate of change
Uncertainty
Diversity — "How entrepreneurial are tasks?"

Where we are now: Discussing the decision-making process:
1. Identifying the central problem
2. Developing alternatives
3. Evaluating the alternatives
4. Making the decision.

II ORGANIZING

Ch. 6 Lines of Authority
Ch. 7 Division of Work
Ch. 8 Amount of Delegation
Ch. 9 Coordination

IV LEADING
Ch. 13

The style of leadership

III STAFFING

Ch. 10 Finding the Right Person for the Job
Ch. 11 Appraise Performance
Ch. 12 Training and Development

ORGANIZATIONAL CLIMATE   IV Ch. 14

V CONTROLLING

Measuring performance against plans and taking corrective action

Ch. 17 The Control Process
Ch. 18 Controlling Operations
Ch. 19 Accounting Controls
Ch. 20 Effective Controls

The Employees' "feel" for the organization

MOTIVATION   IV Ch. 15-16

Morale
Performance

FITTING DECISION-MAKING TO THE TASK

	Mechanistic	*Organic*
Decision-Making Technique	Emphasis on management science, capital budgeting etc.	Emphasis on creativity, intuition, judgment

When you have finished studying

4 Managerial Decision-Making

You should be able to:

1. *Distinguish between symptoms and "the central problem" of a situation.*

2. *Use a group to develop alternative solutions to problems.*

3. *List "assets" and "liabilities" of group decision-making.*

4. *Compare, contrast, and cite some specific applications of: Linear programming techniques; waiting line techniques; and statistical decision theory techniques.*

5. *Explain how to solve Capital Budgeting problems.*

6. *Solve a "Break-even" problem.*

7. *Discuss seven hints for making a better decision.*

INTRODUCTION

Imagine that you are a management consultant. The owners of a large office building call you to tell you they have a problem. They say their elevators are moving too slowly; because of this tenants are complaining and are threatening to move out. You are asked to solve the problem.

What is the problem?

What are the symptoms?

What are some alternative solutions?

What is the best solution?

You'll find the answers in this chapter, as well as a discussion of the decision-making process: (1) identifying the central problem; (2) developing alternatives; (3) analyzing the alternatives; and (4) making the final decision.

THE DECISION-MAKING PROCESS

Decision-making is the essence of a manager's job. While Planning, Organizing, Staffing, Leading, and Controlling are the basic "functions" of management, each of these clearly involves decisions—decisions as to which plan to implement, what goals to use, and so forth.

Nowhere is the need for effective decision-making more important than in the area of planning. As we saw in Chapter 2, a company can survive many day-to-day blunders so long as its basic direction—in terms of the market it serves and the product it provides—is sound. But where a poor decision is made and a wrong road chosen, none but the luckiest survive.

It is therefore particularly appropriate that we talk about decision-making in the context of its contribution to planning. But, remember that decision-making is actually an activity which underlies all five functions of management.

Exhibit 4.1 Decision-Making Underlies All Five Functions of Management

| Planning | Organizing | Staffing | Leading | Controlling |

Decision-Making

Steps in Decision-Making

In this book, we are going to assume that making a decision involves four steps: 1) Identifying the central problem; 2) developing alternatives; 3) analyzing the alternatives; and 4) making the final decision. Let's examine each of these steps in turn.

IDENTIFYING THE CENTRAL PROBLEM

Managerial decision-making is usually sparked by the identification of a problem. Perhaps the fuel shortage is causing sales to drop, or you are faced with the problem of increased advertising by competitors. These, and a multitude like them, are the sorts of problems you are going to face daily. They require quick and effective action lest you find your enterprise at a disadvantage.

At first glance it might seem that identifying the problem is a fairly straightforward matter. But this is not the case. One common fallacy in defining problems is to emphasize the obvious or to be mislead by symptoms.

For example, take the case of a consulting team that was retained by the owners of a large office building. The office workers in the building were disturbed because they had to wait so long for an elevator to pick them up, and many tenants were threatening to move out. The owners called in the consulting team, and told them that the "problem" was that the elevators were running too slowly.

How would you have attacked the problem if you were one of the consultants? If you assume, as did the owners, that the problem could be defined as "slow-moving elevators," then the alternative solutions are fairly obvious. The elevators were running about as fast as they could, given the number of people that had to use them; so one solution might be to request that the tenants stagger their work hours. But that could cause more animosity than the slow-moving elevators. Another solution might be to add one or two more elevators, but this would be tremendously expensive.

The point of this example is that the alternatives you develop and the decision you make are tied to the way you define the basic central problem. What the consultants actually did in this case was to disregard "slow-moving elevators" as the problem, and instead define it as "the tenants are upset because they have to wait for an elevator." Then, the solution the consultants hit on was to have full-length mirrors installed by each bank of elevators so the tenants could admire themselves while waiting! The solution was both inexpensive and satisfactory, and the complaints all but disappeared.

The point is this: As a decision-maker, you have to be very careful about how you define the problem. Peel away the obvious "problems" until you hit on the heart of the matter. Then you will be ready to begin developing useful alternatives.

DEVELOPING ALTERNATIVES

To really do a good job of decision-making you have to have several alternatives to choose from. Whether you are choosing between alternative plans, job candidates, cars, or equipment, the existence of some *choice* is a prerequisite to effective decision-making. In fact, when you don't have a choice, you really don't have any decision to make—except perhaps to "take it or leave it."

You will find that sometimes developing many good alternatives is no problem. For example, you might advertise for a grounds keeper for your factory and be deluged with applications. But as often as not, developing good

Exhibit 4.2   Identifying the Central Problem

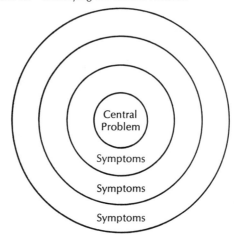

Note: Peel away the obvious "problems" or symptoms until you hit on the
heart of the matter.

alternatives is no easy matter; it takes a lot of creativity, thought, and discussion. In this section we'll discuss two very important factors in developing
alternatives: creativity, and the effective use of groups.

Creativity and Decision-Making Alternatives

Whether your organization is creative or not depends to a large extent
on the people you hire. Anyone who has ever seen a painting by a great artist,
or heard a concert by a great composer, will agree that some individuals
are clearly more creative than others.

But as you might imagine, just hiring creative people does not insure
that creativity will emerge. For example, you've probably found that creative
people you know—artists, musicians, engineers, and so on—can't be very creative when they feel closed in or under a lot of pressure. Therefore one of
your most important management jobs is to provide an atmosphere or climate
that facilitates creativity. This is one where there is: 1) Open communication
between employees; 2) an enjoyment in experimenting with new ideas; 3) an
enjoyment of work; 4) an acceptance of the need for change; 5) an emphasis
on the value of creativity; and 6) a deemphasis on control reports and "sticking to the rules." [1]

Using Groups and Committees For Developing Alternatives

Anyone who has ever sat in on an unproductive committee meeting
could quickly reel off some of the drawbacks of using groups to solve problems.
They often waste time in rambling discussions. And there is the ever-present

danger that the group will be dominated by one overpowering individual. People are often afraid to speak their minds for fear of criticism. And, once a decision is made, it is virtually impossible to identify the person who is responsible for it.

Because of problems like these many people feel that group decision-making should be outlawed. But, the drawbacks notwithstanding, we also know that under the right conditions a group *can* be very useful for developing alternatives.

Norman Maier [2] is an expert in group decision-making, and his findings help shed some light on the assets and liabilities of group decision-making. He says that the decision-making *assets* of the group are:

1. *The greater sum total of knowledge and information.* There is more information in a group than in any one of its members. Thus problems that require the utilization of knowledge should give groups an advantage over individuals.
2. *A greater number of approaches to a problem.* Since group members do not have identical approaches (to solving a problem) each can contribute by knocking others out of ruts in thinking.
3. *Participation in problem-solving increases acceptance.* Insofar as group problem-solving permits participation, it helps to make the resulting solutions more acceptable to the participants.
4. *Better comprehension of the decision.* The chances for communication failures are greatly reduced when the individuals who must work together in executing the decision have participated in making it.

The decision-making *liabilities* to watch out for include:

1. *Social pressure.* The desire to be a good group member and to be accepted tends to silence disagreement and favor consensus.
2. *"Valence" of solutions.* Each solution (or alternative) receives both critical and supportive comments. . . . When a solution receives about 15 more positive than negative comments ("valence") it tends to be accepted *regardless* of its quality. This is because a turning point between the *idea getting* and *decision-making* steps occurs here.
3. *Individual domination.* In many groups a dominant individual emerges and captures more than his share of influence on the outcomes.
4. *Conflicting secondary goal: winning the argument.* When groups are confronted with a problem the initial goal is to obtain a solution. However, the appearance of several alternatives causes individuals to have preferences, and once these emerge the desire to support a position is created . . . more and more the goal becomes that of winning the argument.

Maier says that "openmindedness"—a willingness to look for a best solution rather than to sell a particular alternative—is an important precondition to effective group problem-solving. And it's also very important that the group leader insure that all facts and alternatives are out on the table *before* the group starts criticizing alternatives or zeroing in on a solution.[3]

Some Hints. In summary, here are some hints for getting the most out of group decision-making: 1) Use people who represent different points of view; 2) carefully identify the central problem; 3) *encourage* group members to get *all* possible alternatives out on the table—don't let one or two people overwhelm everyone else (and don't just try to "sell" your own ideas!); 4) discuss the pros and cons of *all* alternatives; and 5) choose the best alternatives (perhaps combine several of them).

SOME TECHNIQUES FOR ANALYZING ALTERNATIVES

Once you have several alternatives, you have to evaluate them. Should you rent the house, or buy it? Should you open your store on the north side of the street, or on the south? Should you produce more of product "A," or of product "B?" Evaluating the pros and cons of such alternatives is the point of the *Analyzing Alternatives* step in decision-making. We'll discuss three types of analysis techniques: Operations Research; Capital Budgeting; and Break-Even Analysis.

How to Use Operations Research

During your management career you will hear a lot about something called "Operations Research" (or "Management Science"). These terms usually refer to a set of mathematical techniques through which a variety of organizational problems can be analyzed and solved. We'll briefly describe some of these techniques on the next few pages.

But operations research ("O.R.") is something more than just a bundle of tools. It is a particular approach to solving problems—a *scientific* approach. As Harvey Wagner says: ". . . you can simply define Operations Research as a scientific approach to problem-solving for executive management. . . ."[4]

In applying this approach to analyzing management problems, the management scientist typically goes through six steps:[5]

1. Formulating the problem.
2. Constructing a mathematical model to represent the system under study.
3. Deriving a solution from the model.

4. Testing the model and the solution derived from it.
5. Establishing controls over the solution.
6. Putting the solution to work: implementation.

Let's look at some specific O.R. applications.

Linear Programming: This is a mathematical method which you can use to solve resource allocation problems. These arise "whenever there are a number of activities to be performed, but limitations on either the amount of resources or the way they can be spent . . ." [6] For example, you can use it to determine how to best:

a) *Distribute* merchandise from a number of warehouses to a number of customers.
b) *Assign* personnel to various jobs.
c) Design shipping *schedules.*
d) Develop optimum *product mixes,* and
e) *Route* production.

Here are examples of two typical applications:

> *Distribution.* Company X has six manufacturing plants and 15 warehouses scattered across the country. Each plant is manufacturing the same product and operating at full capacity. Since plant capacity and location do not permit the closest plant to fully support each warehouse, company X would like to determine the factory which should supply each warehouse in order to minimize total shipping costs. Applying linear programming techniques to this problem will provide an optimum shipping schedule for the company.[7]

> *Product mix.* A poultry farmer raises chickens, ducks, and turkeys and has room for 500 birds on his farm. While he is willing to have a total of 500 birds, he does not want more than 300 ducks on his farm at any one time. Suppose that a chicken costs $1.50, a duck $1.00, and a turkey $4.00 to raise to maturity. Assume that the farmer can sell chickens for $3.00, ducks for $2.00, and turkeys for $6.00 each. How many of each should he raise in order to maximize his profits? [8]

Waiting Line (Queuing) Techniques: Waiting line problems are very commonplace. For example, supermarket managers need to know how many checkout counters they should have. If they have too many, they are wasting money on salaries; if they have too few, they may end up with many disgruntled customers. Similar problems arise when determining the optimum number of airline reservations clerks, warehouse loading docks, highway toll booths, bank tellers, and so forth.

Waiting line, or "queuing," [9] techniques can be used to analyze alternatives and arrive at optimal solutions to many of these problems. You have to know how often customers arrive; how long it takes to service them; and the order in which arriving customers are serviced. With this data, the waiting-line problem can be solved with queuing techniques. Here's an example of a typical waiting-line problem which might help to clarify its use.

> An insurance company has three claims adjusters in its branch office. People with claims against the company arrive in a predictable fashion, at an average rate of 20 per 8-hour day. The amount of time that an adjuster spends with a claimant is known, and takes 40 minutes on the average. (Claimants are processed in the order of their appearance.) (a) How many hours a week can an adjuster expect to spend with claimants? (b) How much time, on the average, does a claimant spend in the branch office? [10]

Statistical Decision Theory Techniques: When making decisions, most people intuitively assign "probabilities" to their different alternatives.[11] Thus, suppose you decide to fix your old car rather than buy a new one. Here you're probably betting that there is not much chance that something else will soon go wrong with your car. Statistical decision theory is used for formalizing this intuitive process. You assign probabilities to the outcomes of each of your alternatives, usually on a "decision tree" as shown in Exhibit 4–3. Then you calculate the "expected value" of each alternative by multiplying (1) the *probability* of the outcome by (2) the benefit (or cost) of that outcome. Let's look at an example.

Exhibit 4.3 Example of a Decision Tree

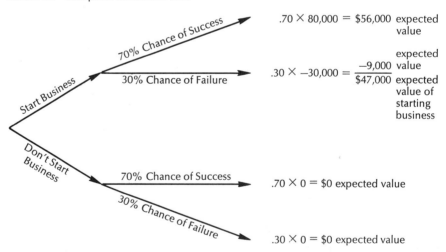

You are thinking of starting a business, and are now faced with two alternatives—to start, or not to start. As you can see in Exhibit 4–3 you think there is about a 30 percent chance that the business will completely fail, and a 70 percent chance it will be a success. If it's successful, you'll be able to turn right around and sell it for an $80,000 profit. If it's not, you'll lose your $30,000 investment. Should you start it, or not?

As in Exhibit 4–3, the "expected value" (the probability, times the profit or loss) is $56,000 (profit) for starting the business and succeeding, and $9,000 (loss) for starting it and failing. So altogether the expected value of starting the business is $56,000 — $9,000, or $47,000. The expected value of *not* starting the business is $0—there is no possible gain or loss. So in total, your best alternative seems to be to go ahead and take your chances starting the business.

How to Use Capital Budgeting

The corner druggist is thinking about buying a new cash register that will simplify his bookkeeping procedures. A manufacturer of iron gates considers buying a new welding machine in order to increase his capacity. John and Mary Smith are wondering whether to buy a new home, or stay in their rented apartment.

Capital expenditures like these involve some of the most important decisions you ever make. *They all involve an outlay of cash in return for an expected flow of future benefits.* Business decisions to invest in buildings, equipment, new products, land, or new distribution systems are all examples of capital expenditure decisions.

Capital expenditure decision-making (sometimes called "capital budgeting") involves four basic steps:

1. Generating alternative projects to invest in.
2. Evaluating the pros and cons of each of these alternatives.
3. Selecting an alternative.
4. Implementing your decision.

There are many techniques for evaluating alternatives, and we will focus on a few of them in this section. But keep in mind that regardless of which you use, there are two basic principles to follow: 1) The "bigger the better" principle. *Other things equal, bigger benefits are better than smaller ones;* 2) The "bird in the hand" principle. *Other things equal, early benefits are preferable to later benefits;* in other words, a dollar received next year is worth more than a dollar received in five years.[12]

The Payback Approach to Evaluating Alternatives: The "payback period" of an investment tells you the number of years required to recover your initial cash investment.[13] It is probably the most widely used technique for evaluating capital alternatives.

The basic approach involves ranking projects according to how long they take to pay back their initial cost. The projects having the quicker paybacks are preferred to those which take longer to pay back their initial costs.

Let's work through an example to see how you can use payback in practice. Let's assume that there are three machines you could buy to manufacture your product. As you can see in Exhibit 4–4 the initial cost of each machine is different; however, the revenue you will receive over the next few years also differs. Project C appears to be your best alternative since it pays back its initial cost in 2½ years. It would take you longer to recoup your investments in Project A or B.

Exhibit 4.4 Calculating the Payback Period for Three Machines

		Machine A	B	C
Initial Cost		5,000	7,000	10,000
Revenues:	Year 1	1,500	2,000	4,000
	Year 2	1,500	2,000	4,000
	Year 3	1,500	2,000	4,000
	Year 4	1,500	2,000	4,000
Payback Period:		$\frac{5,000}{1,500} = 3.33$ years	$\frac{7,000}{2,000} = 3.5$ years	$\frac{10,000}{4,000} = 2.5$ years

Note: Divide the Initial Cost of the Machine by the Yearly Revenues.

The payback approach is simple to use. And in an uncertain world there is a lot to be said about choosing the project that pays back its investment as quickly as possible. Notice, though, that it ignores the "bigger the better" principle: as you can see in Exhibit 4–5 it disregards any revenue that may be forthcoming after the investment has been recovered.

Exhibit 4.5 The Problem with the Payback Method

		Machine A	B	C
Initial Cost		5,000	7,000	10,000
Revenues:	Year 1	1,500	2,000	4,000
	Year 2	1,500	2,000	**4,000**
	Year 3	**1,500**	**2,000**	4,000
	Year 4	1,000	2,000	4,000
	Year 5	1,000	6,000	3,000
	Year 6	1,000	10,000	3,000

Note: Notice how the payback method disregards any revenues that may be forthcoming after the investment has been recovered. If we were to include *all* revenue for the first 6 years of the projects, machine *B* whose revenues are climbing, might be a better investment than machine *C*.

The Average Rate of Return Approach: The average rate of return represents the ratio of the average profits divided by the initial cost of the project.

In the example depicted in Exhibit 4–6 the average rate of return is 20 percent. We arrived at this by computing the project's average annual profits for a five-year period ($2,000) and dividing this by the initial cost of the project ($10,000).

Exhibit 4.6   Computing the Average Rate of Return of a Project

	Year 1	Year 2	Year 3	Year 4	Year 5	Average
Initial Cost $10,000						
Annual Yearly Profits	1,500	1,750	2,000	2,250	2,500	2,000
$\dfrac{\text{Average Yearly Profits}}{\text{Initial Cost}} = \dfrac{2,000}{10,000} = 20\%$						

This technique is simple to use. And once you compute the rate of return for your project, it is easy to compare it to your desired rate of return. You can then decide if the project should be accepted or rejected.

This approach makes sense according to our "bigger the better" principle, since the project that earns the most money would come out on top. Its main drawback is that it disregards the "bird in hand" principle. This is because it assumes that the profits from the first year are worth the same as those from the fifth year.

There are many other techniques used to evaluate capital expenditure alternatives. Most of these methods take into account the "time value" of money (remember our "bird in hand" principle). They do this through a procedure called "discounting." They include the "internal rate of return" method, and the "benefit-cost ratio" method. The latter, as the name implies, is the ratio between the sum of the benefits (or profits) from a project, divided by the costs of the project.[14]

How To Use Break-Even Analysis

Break-even analysis can help you determine whether a particular volume of sales will result in losses or profits.[15] The break-even point itself is that volume of sales at which revenues just equal expenses. Here you have neither a profit or a loss.

Break-even analysis makes use of four basic concepts: *fixed costs, variable costs, revenues,* and *profits. Fixed costs* (such as for machinery) do not change (within a fairly wide range) with changes in volume. In other words, you might use the same machine to produce ten units, 50 units, or 200 units of a product. *Variable costs* (such as for raw material) *do* rise in proportion to volume. *Revenue* is the total income you receive from sales of your product. For example, if you sell 50 widgets at $8 each, then your revenue is $8 × 50, or $400. *Profits* are what you have left after subtracting fixed and variable costs from revenues.

Break-Even Charts: A break-even chart, like that in Exhibit 4–7, can show you at a glance whether a particular volume of output will result in profits or losses. The fixed cost line is horizontal, since fixed costs remain the same regardless of your level of output. Variable costs, though, increase in proportion to output, and are shown as an upward sloping line. The total

Exhibit 4.7   Example of a Break-Even Chart

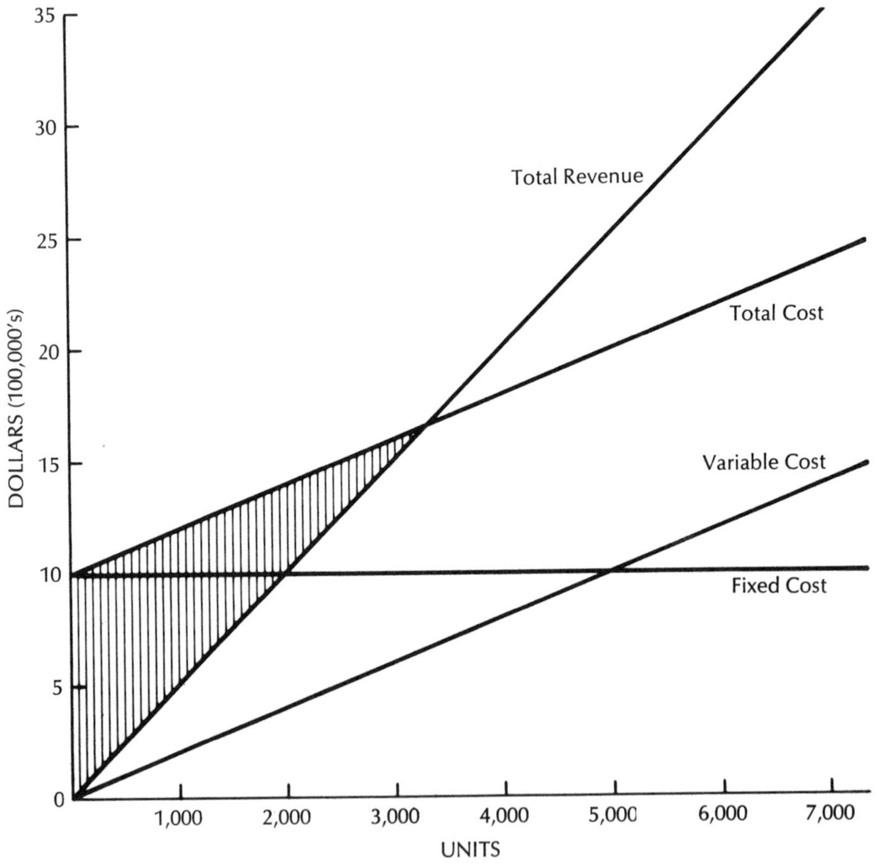

Note: To draw a break-even chart:
1. Draw in horizontal fixed cost line.
2. Draw in variable cost line (this equals # units × variable cost per unit).
3. Draw in total cost line (for each level of output, just add variable cost and fixed cost).
4. Draw in total revenue line (this equals # units × revenue per unit).

Source: James C. VanHorne, *Fundamentals of Financial Management*, (Englewood Cliffs: Prentice-Hall, 1971) p. 74.

cost line is simply equal to variable costs plus fixed costs at each level of output.

The point where the total revenue line crosses the total cost line is your break-even point. Above this point (in the shaded area) total revenue exceeds total costs. So in this particular example an output of about 3,100 units is the break-even point; above this, you would expect to earn a profit. But if your output was less than 3,100 units, you would incur losses.

The Break-Even Formula: The break-even chart gives you a quick picture of the relationship between sales volume and profits. But you do not have to use it to determine break-even points. Instead, you can use the break-even formula, which is:

$$P(X) = F + V(X),$$

where

> F = fixed costs
> V = variable costs per unit
> X = volume of output (in units)
> P = price per unit

Rearranging this formula the break-even *point* is:

$$X = F/(P - V):$$

In other words, the break-even point is that volume of output where total costs just equal total revenues. If, for example, you have a product in which:

> F = fixed costs = $1,000
> V = variable costs per unit = $.75
> P = price per unit = $1.00 per unit

then the break-even point is:

> $1,000/(1.00 - .75) = 4,000$ units.

MAKING THE DECISION

Once you've compared the pros and cons of your alternatives it's time to make the actual decision. This is where all your fact-finding, alternatives-creating, and analysis pays off. Let's see how to "fit decision-making to the task," and then discuss some hints for "making the right decision."

Fitting Decision-Making to the Task

Are different decision-making techniques appropriate for different tasks? Professor Herbert Simon would say that they are. He says that it is important to distinguish between two types of decisions: programmed and nonprogrammed. A *programmed* decision is one that can be laid out in advance, step by step. For example, deciding how many Buicks will be produced on an assembly line on a specific day is a programmed decision. A decision is *unprogrammed* to the extent that you can't adequately plan for it in advance. Sudden illness, a competitor starting a new advertising campaign, or someone opening a competing store across from yours require unprogrammed decisions.

Professor Simon says that you have to fit the decision-making technique to the situation. As you can see in Exhibit 4–8, techniques such as management science and capital budgeting are more appropriate for programmed decision-making. Here the future is more predictable, and therefore it is easier to make "rational" decisions. But for nonprogrammed decisions you have to depend more on judgment, intuition, and creativity.

Exhibit 4.8 Fitting Decision-Making to the Situation

	Mechanistic	*Organic*
Situation:	"programmed," routine decisions	"unprogrammed," nonroutine decisions
Techniques Emphasized:	Management science; capital budgeting	Judgment; intuition, creativity

Many (if not all) of the most important decisions you have to make—whether it is choosing a marriage partner, defining a central concept for your firm, or locating a new store—tend to be of the nonprogrammed variety. Therefore you can see why judgment, intuition, and creativity are still perhaps the most important tools in the manager's tool kit.

Some Hints for Making the Decision

Robert Heilbroner says that "there is nothing in the world so common and ordinary and yet so agonizingly difficult as a tough decision." [16] Here are some of his hints for making the task easier.

Marshall the Facts: Effective decision-making is based on facts—facts concerning what the real problem is; what your alternatives are; and what are the pros and cons of each. Most good managers quickly learn that when a sticky problem can't be solved, it's usually for lack of facts and they therefore send it back for more data. So the first hint is: make sure you've got all the facts.

But, don't misuse the idea of fact-collecting. Don't go on getting advice and facts so long that you never get around to making the decision!

Consult Your Feelings: Here is what Sigmund Freud had to say about making important decisions:

When making a decision of minor importance I have always found it advantageous to consider all the pros and cons. In vital matters, however, such as the choice of a mate or a profession, the decision should come from the unconscious, from somewhere within ourselves. In the important decisions of our personal life, we should be governed, I think, by the deep inner needs of our nature.

Robert Heilbroner says that usually you can tell when a decision accords with your inner nature, for it brings an enormous sense of relief. Good decisions, he says, are the best tranquilizers ever invented; bad ones often increase your anxiety. So, hint two is: consult your inner feelings.

Make Sure the Timing Is Right: Most people's behavior is affected by their passing moods. Researchers at Columbia University have found that when subjects felt "down," their actions tended to be aggressive and destructive. Yet when they felt good, their behavior swung toward tolerance and balance. People tend to be lenient when they're in good spirits, and "tough" when they're grouchy. The third hint, then, is to take account of your "emotional temperature" before making an important decision. If the "temperature" is not right, make the decision some other time.

Don't Overstress the "Finality" of Your Decision: Remember that very few decisions are "forever"; there is much more "give" in most decisions than we realize. Therefore hint four is: don't become preoccupied with the "finality" of your decision.

Talk It Over: It usually helps to talk big decisions over with others. Part of the reason is that another's opinion may point up aspects of the problem of which you weren't aware. But talking things over will also help you sort out and clarify your own thoughts and feelings. So hint five is: talk it over.

In summary, then, Heilbroner suggests:

1. Marshall the facts.
2. Consult your feelings.
3. Make sure the timing is right.
4. Don't overstress the "Finality" of your decision.
5. Talk it over.

And, finally, here are two last hints:

Analyze the Problem With an Open Mind. Herbert Simon says that people make decisions based on their own *perceptions* of the real world. Thus each of us is always looking at the world through a window tinted by our own personal values, personality, and abilities. So it's important you always remember that as a manager your own values and personality influence the way you "see" the world. And you have to be constantly on guard against seeing only those things that you *want* to see. So the next hint is: keep an open mind.

80   *Know Yourself.* The most effective managers are those who have a clear understanding of who they are.[17] Their actions are stable, consistent, and predictable. When making decisions they don't have to struggle with first deciding "who they are" that day. So the final hint is: "know yourself."

Some Important Things to Remember from This Chapter:

1. We assumed that there are four basic steps involved in making a decision: 1) Identifying the central problem; 2) developing alternatives; 3) analyzing the alternatives; 4) and making the final decision.

2. It is especially important to carefully identify the central problem. Always peel away the obvious "problems" or symptoms until you hit on the heart of the matter.

3. To really do a good job of decision-making, you should have a choice of several alternatives. Encouraging creativity—through open communication between employees; enjoyment of work, and so on—can increase the chances that your people will develop creative alternatives. Groups can be an important source of creative alternatives. This is especially so when you take advantage of their assets (such as a greater number of approaches to a problem) and try to minimize their liabilities (such as social pressure).

4. When you are leading a group discussion, try to: 1) use people who represent different points of view; 2) carefully identify the central problem; 3) encourage group members to get all possible alternatives out on the table—don't let one or two people overwhelm everyone else; 4) discuss the pros and cons of *all* alternatives; and 5) then—and only then—choose the best alternatives.

5. Operations Research (O.R.) is both a scientific approach to problem analysis and a set of mathematical techniques. These techniques include linear programming, for solving resource allocation problems; queuing, for solving waiting line problems; and statistical decision theory, for determining the "expected value" of each alternative.

6. Capital budgeting is used to analyze capital expenditure alternatives— those which involve an outlay of cash in return for an expected flow of future benefits. Remember that whether you use Payback, Average rate of return, or some other, there are two basic principles to keep in mind: The "bigger the better" principle, and the "bird in hand" principle.

7. Break-even analysis can help you determine whether a particular volume of sales will result in losses or profits. The break-even point itself is that volume of sales at which total revenues just cover total expenses.

8. Once you've compared the pros and cons of your alternatives you have to make the actual decision. One thing to remember here is the need to fit decision-making to the task—you often have to rely more on creativity and intuition than on scientific decision-making. And remember our seven hints for making better decisions: 1) Marshall the facts; 2) consult your feelings; 3) make sure the timing is right; 4) don't overstress the finality of your decision; 5) talk it over; 6) analyze the problem with an open mind; and 7) know yourself.

STUDY ASSIGNMENTS

1. Write two short incidents which illustrate the need to distinguish between symptoms and the central problem of a situation.
2. Explain how you would use a group to develop alternative solutions to problems.
3. Discuss the assets and liabilities of group decision-making.
4. Cite some specific applications of linear programming; waiting-line techniques; and statistical-decision theory.
5. What are the two basic principles to follow when analyzing any capital budgeting problem? Discuss them.
6. Discuss two techniques for solving Capital Budgeting problems.
7. The ABC Widget Factory has fixed costs of $2,000. Its variable costs per widget are $.35 and the price per widget is $.85. First find the break-even point using our break-even formula. Then draw a break-even chart illustrating the relationships involved.
8. You mention to a friend of yours that you have $5,000 to invest, and he asks you to buy a small four-family house with him. He explains that even though it is in a somewhat shoddy neighborhood, it is still a great investment since each of you would be able to take about $1,500 a year out of the building. He says that is about a 30 percent (1,500/5,000) return on your investment every year. You are not so sure just how great an investment that is. Discuss some of the capital budgeting and operations research tools you could use in evaluating this investment. What other information would you need?
9. Discuss the difference between programmed and nonprogrammed business decisions, listing at least three specific examples of each.
10. Briefly discuss each of our seven hints for making a better decision.

NOTES FOR THE CHAPTER

1. Carl E. Gregory, *The Management of Intelligence* (New York: McGraw-Hill Book Co., 1967) pp. 188–190; Larry Cummings, Bernard Hinton, Bruce Gobdel, "Creative Behavior as a Function of Task Environment: Impact of Objectives, Procedures, and Rules," *Academy of Management Journal*, Vol. 18, No. 3 (September 1975); Robert Fulmer, *The New Management* (New York: Macmillan, 1975).

2. Norman Maier, "Assets and Liabilities in Group Decision-Making: The Need for an Integrative Function," *Psychological Bulletin*, Vol. 74, No. 4 (1969) pp. 239–249; reprinted in John Turner, Alan Filley, and Robert House, *Studies in Managerial Process and Organizational Behavior* (Glenview: Scott Foresman, 1972) pp. 322–329.

3. See, for example, Norman R. F. Maier, *Psychology in Industrial Organizations* (Boston: Houghton Mifflin, 1973) Chapter 22.

4. Harvey Wagner, *Principles of Operations Research, With Applications to Management Decisions* (Englewood Cliffs, N.J.: Prentice-Hall, 1969).

5. C. West Churchman, Russel Ackoff, and E. Leonard Arnoff, *Introduction to Operations Research* (New York: Wiley, 1957) p. 13.

6. Maurice Sasieni, Arthur Yaspan, and Lawrence Friedman, *Operations Research* (New York: Wiley, 1959) p. 183.

7. From *Prentice-Hall Encyclopedic Dictionary of Systems and Procedures*, p. 364.

8. John Kemeny, Arthur Schleifer, Jr., J. Laurie Snell, Gerald Thompson, *Finite Mathematics* (Englewood Cliffs, N.J.: Prentice-Hall, 1962) p. 383.

9. A "queue" is a waiting line.

10. Sasieni, Yaspan, and Friedman, *Operations Research*, pp. 138–139.

11. Carol Gray, "Factors in Students' Decisions to Attempt Academic Tasks," *Organizational Behavior and Human Performance*, Vol. 13, No. 2 (April 1975).

12. G. David Quirin, *The Capital Expenditure Decision* (Homewood: Richard D. Irwin, 1967) p. 28.

13. James C. VanHorne, *Fundamentals of Financial Management* (Englewood Cliffs, N.J.: Prentice-Hall, 1971) p. 161.

14. For good explanations of these techniques see James C. VanHorne, *Fundamentals of Financial Management*, pp. 155–193; and G. David Quirin, *The Capital Expenditure Decision*, pp. 15–58.

15. For a good discussion of this, see VanHorne, *Fundamentals of Financial Management*.

16. Adapted from Robert L. Heilbroner, "How to Make an Intelligent Decision," *Think* (December 1960) pp. 2–4. Reproduced in Harold Lazarus, E. Kirby Warren, and Jerome E. Schnee, *The Progress of Management* (Englewood Cliffs, N.J.: Prentice-Hall, 1972) pp. 197–201.

17. John Hicks and Joics Stone, "The Identification of Traits Related to Managerial Success," *Journal of Applied Psychology*, Vol. 46, December 1962, pp. 428–432; Wendell French, *The Personnel Management Process* (Boston: Houghton Mifflin, 1974), p. 319.

A Framework for Studying the Management Fundamentals

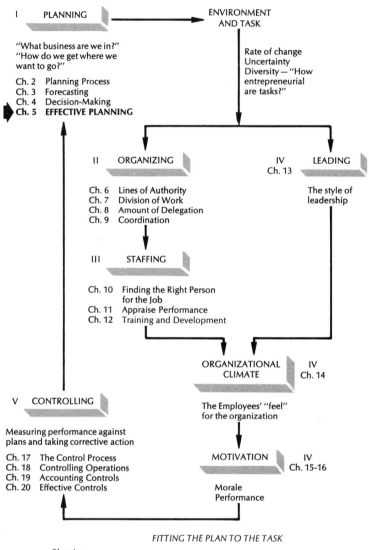

I   PLANNING

"What business are we in?"
"How do we get where we
want to go?"

Ch. 2   Planning Process
Ch. 3   Forecasting
Ch. 4   Decision-Making
Ch. 5   **EFFECTIVE PLANNING**

ENVIRONMENT
AND TASK

Rate of change
Uncertainty
Diversity — "How
entrepreneurial
are tasks?"

Where we are now: Discussing some barriers to effective planning, and some hints for making planning more effective.

II   ORGANIZING

Ch. 6   Lines of Authority
Ch. 7   Division of Work
Ch. 8   Amount of Delegation
Ch. 9   Coordination

IV   LEADING
Ch. 13

The style of
leadership

III   STAFFING

Ch. 10   Finding the Right Person
         for the Job
Ch. 11   Appraise Performance
Ch. 12   Training and Development

ORGANIZATIONAL
CLIMATE

IV
Ch. 14

V   CONTROLLING

Measuring performance against
plans and taking corrective action

Ch. 17   The Control Process
Ch. 18   Controlling Operations
Ch. 19   Accounting Controls
Ch. 20   Effective Controls

The Employees' "feel"
for the organization

MOTIVATION

IV
Ch. 15-16

Morale
Performance

FITTING THE PLAN TO THE TASK

Planning Characteristics	Mechanistic	Organic
How detailed?	Much detail	Very little detail
How specific should goals be?	Very specific	Broad
Emphasis on "milestones" vs how work should be carried out	More emphasis on how work should be carried out	Emphasis on broad milestones
Use of Standing Plans	Much use	Less use
Forecasting Techniques	Time series	Qualitative techniques
Decision-Making Techniques	Management science	Creativity, judgment, intuition

When you have finished studying

5 Effective Planning

You should be able to:

1. *Explain why planning is no guarantee of success.*

2. *List the seven barriers to effective planning.*

3. *Explain what is meant by "fitting the plan to the task."*

4. *Develop a plan for 1) a brand new product, and 2) a plan for a product which has "matured."*

5. *Give examples of "detailed, means/end" planning, and "directional" planning.*

6. *Cite eleven hints for making planning effective.*

INTRODUCTION

Planning is a necessary and useful function of management. It results in targets to shoot for, and helps you identify future opportunities and threats. And it helps to insure that all your subordinates are working toward the same goals.

But it's also important to see that planning has some major limitations. Your plan is no better than the forecast it's built on, for example, and even a brilliant plan is worthless unless effectively implemented. Therefore, in this chapter let's review some of the barriers to effective planning, with an eye toward learning how to avoid them.

Planners vs. Nonplanners

Most people probably tend to assume that planning is worthwhile. That's why phrases such as "plan ahead," "look before you leap," and "a stitch in time saves nine," are firmly embedded in our language. But (this predisposition toward planning notwithstanding), some researchers have come up with some very disconcerting findings concerning just how useful planning really is.

For example, Leslie Rue and Robert Fulmer compared "nonplan-

86 ners" and "planners" among 386 firms in three industrial groups.[1] These included nondurables (food, paper, etc.); services (transportation, finance, etc.); and durables (steel, automobiles, etc.). Their findings are summarized in Exhibit 5–1.

Exhibit 5.1   Average Performance of Planners Versus Nonplanners in Selected Industries

Financial Performance Measures	Nondurables Industry (e.g. paper)		Service Industry (e.g. financial)		Durable Industry (e.g. cars)	
	No Plan	Plan	No Plan	Plan	No Plan	Plan
Sales Growth		X	X			X
Earnings Growth	X		X			X
Earnings/Sales	X		X			X
Rate of Return	X		X			X

Note: An "X" means that on that particular financial performance measure, the no plan (or plan) companies performed the best.

Source: Adapted from Rue and Fulmer, "Is Long Range Planning Profitable?"

Notice that they found no across-the-board relationship between planning and company performance. In fact the "*non*planner" companies, in both the service and nondurables industries, seemed to outperform the "planner" companies in these industries. On the other hand, the "planners" outperformed the "nonplanners" in the durables industry.[2]

FAILURE DESPITE PLANNING

George Steiner says that "the fact that a company plans is not an open door to success." [3] Many things can happen to upset even the best-laid plans. Perhaps the clearest, most recent example of this was the demise of the Edsel automobile in the late 1950s. Let's look more closely at the Edsel situation to see what we can learn from it.

According to William Reynolds, the production of the Edsel car was one of the most carefully planned moves in business history.[4] Yet the Edsel was also one of the most stunning new-product failures in business history. How did this happen?

The Forecasts

The story begins in the early 1950s. Based on their market research and forecasts, Ford executives developed these planning premises:

a) Sales of medium-priced cars would increase.
b) Even the lower-priced cars would be sold "loaded."
c) The number of people in the income groups who bought Ford's generally low-priced cars would decrease.
d) Young people who bought Fords would usually trade them in for more luxurious Buicks, Oldsmobiles, and Pontiacs when they become more affluent.
e) People in the medium-priced car market wanted more luxurious cars.

The New Strategy

Also at about this time Ford had a solid following in the low-priced car field, a strong group of dealers, and a group of managers built around the "whiz kids." These were former Air Force officers who had worked together applying Management Science techniques to the solution of Air Force problems. These factors, combined with Ford's market research forecasts, led the executives to develop a new strategy for Ford. They decided to begin building a full line of cars, starting with a car-for-car "attack" on the wide General Motors lines. The principal focus was to be in the middle of the price range where Buick, Oldsmobile, and Pontiac were dominant.

Implementing the Plan

In contrast to the more sedate Buicks, Olds, and Pontiacs, Ford designers set about developing a "sporty, stylish, high-performing" competitor—the Edsel. It was out of this styling effort that the now famous

Exhibit 5.2   The Edsel Car Discussed in the Text

88   vertical grill emerged. The more affluent Ford executives felt that this grill was reminiscent of those found on exotic foreign sports cars (cars with which 99 percent of potential Edsel buyers were probably not familiar).

The Edsel was introduced with much fanfare; but within two months it was apparent that it was probably doomed to failure. After two agonizing years, the car was finally discontinued. How could a well-thought-out plan, based on careful research and forecasting, have resulted in such a failure?

The Problems

William Reynolds says that several factors contributed to the failure. For one thing, Ford executives apparently underestimated the impact which the job of introducing the Edsel would have on their company resources. Introducing the Edsel required the creation of an Edsel car division within Ford, and a drastic restructuring of the rest of the Ford organization. Five divisions were established in place of the former two, and overhead expenses soared. There now were five duplicate divisional controllers instead of two; five marketing managers instead of two; and so on. To make matters worse, Ford did not have enough qualified management personnel to adequately staff all these divisions.

There were other problems. A major economic recession occurred in 1958, so this turned out to be a bad year for introducing the new automobile. At about this time, Ford also signed an industrywide agreement against racing and the advertising of power and performance. This in turn undermined the publicizing of Edsel's major selling point.

Reynolds also questions whether the Ford executives completely respected the strength of the Buick, Oldsmobile, and Pontiac competition. These cars had massive, rigid shares of the market; and these shares could not be eroded by a product that was not very distinctive. Finally Ford's top management, according to Reynolds, may have been too influenced by their own values and preferences on the assumption that ". . . their own preferences [were] identical to those of the public." The executives' preference for the "sporty" vertical grill may have been one small symptom of this.

Summary

In summary it seems apparent that three factors combined to create the Edsel failure. These were: 1) *the forecast* the plan was built on; 2) *the plan itself*—to introduce a new full line to compete with General Motors; and 3) the implementation of the plan—the new organization structure and dealer network.

Remember, though, that most people have 20-20 hindsight; it is always easy to point out errors that have occurred in the past. Perhaps if there had not been a recession in 1958 we would today be lauding the planners at Ford who had the foresight and wisdom to introduce the Edsel. The moral may be that in business, as in most other human endeavors, luck still plays a big role. Perhaps the most you can expect from planning is to increase—but not insure—your chances for success.

BARRIERS TO EFFECTIVE PLANNING

Let's briefly review, then, some of the barriers to effective planning.[5]

The Accuracy of Your Forecasts

As we saw in the Edsel example, your plan can't be any better than the forecasts and planning premises on which it is built. Yet we saw that forecasting is not an exact science. Many unexpected events—recessions, actions of competitors, labor strikes, and so forth—can arise to drastically alter the premises upon which the plans are built.

Planning is Susceptible to Human Error

Planning decisions are made by people. But as discussed in Chapter 4, people look at the world through a window tinted by their own personal values, personality, and abilities. Because of this, decisions are usually not based on a completely objective evaluation of the available information. Instead, it's based on the decision-makers' *subjective* evaluation of that information. This is why we often find that two or three people can look at a single problem and come to entirely different conclusions as to what the sources and solutions of the problems are.[6]

Plans Must Be Implemented

Even the best plans, based on the best of forecasts, can fail if they are not effectively implemented. Perhaps, as in Ford's case, the plan turns out to be inconsistent with the human, financial, or capital resources available to the company. Or perhaps the company's advertising effort is inadequate; or the right employees are not recruited; or the organization structure proves inadequate. Clearly there are thousands of things that can go wrong and undermine the implementation of your plan.

Plans Are Not Always Accepted

In order to be effectively implemented, plans must be *acceptable* to the employees responsible for the implementation. But time after time you will find that management fails to win employee acceptance of their plan. The usual result is that employees do little more than pay lip service to it.

Fear of Change

Individuals tend to resist changes which they feel are not in their own best interests. This is important because the changes accompanying planning may, according to George Steiner, be countered by this human inclination. In many organizations, old ways of doing things, old methods and old procedures often become so entrenched that they simply crowd out top management's new plans.

Planning is Expensive

Planning can also be very expensive. Many companies develop elaborate planning departments and planning committees to oversee and coordinate the development of organizationwide plans. Obviously these departments can become very expensive to staff and manage. But with or without a separate planning staff, planning, to be effective, necessarily absorbs much of a manager's time and effort.[7]

Summary: Barriers to Effective Planning

As summarized in Exhibit 5–3, the following factors can limit the effectiveness of planning:

1. Inaccurate forecasts.
2. Human error.
3. Faulty implementation.
4. Lack of acceptance.
5. Fear of change.
6. The fact that planning is expensive.

FIT THE PLAN TO THE SITUATION

Why "Fitting The Plan" is Important

We know that many companies seem to be quite successful even though they appear to do no (or virtually no) planning. Until the mid-1940s Ford Motor Company, for example, was remarkably successful although Henry

Exhibit 5.3 Barriers to Effective Planning

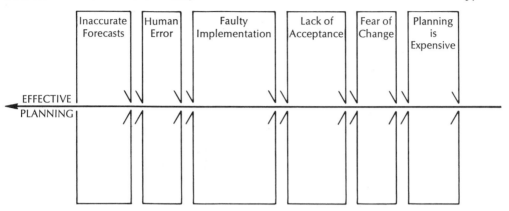

Ford scorned planning and seemingly worked in a wasteful way.[8] Recall, also, that Rue and Fulmer found that many of the "nonplanner" companies they had studied did as well, or better, than the "planners" in the same industries.

Why is it that sometimes planning is effective, and sometimes ineffective? Why is it that some companies do very little planning and are successful, and others are unsuccessful although they *do* engage in planning?

We have touched on some of the answers in the preceding sections. For one thing, some planners are simply more effective than others. For example, they develop better forecasts and choose better alternatives. Furthermore, some companies engage heavily in planning only to drop the ball when it comes to implementing their plans.

For other companies, success derives not from planning but from their good fortune at being in the right industry at the right time with the right product. The success of still other companies, such as Ford in the early 1900s, has to be credited to a few brilliant strategic decisions—such as to mass produce identical low-cost automobiles.

But there is at least one factor that influences the effectiveness of planning on which we have only briefly touched in the last few chapters: *The need to fit the plan to the "situation."*

Two Factors You Should Fit Your Plan To

There are two aspects of the situation on which we will concentrate. One is the rate at which the company's *environment* is changing; changing, for example, in terms of the introduction of new products by competitors; changes in consumers' tastes; and so forth. We will see that the more rapidly things change, the less you can rely on detailed plans, statistical forecasting, and a hierarchy of specific goals.

The second important aspect is the company's position in its *"Product life cycle."* We will see that the planning done when the market for a product is new, is very different from that done when the market has been saturated with the product. Let's look more closely at these ideas.

Planning and the Environment

How effective your plan is will depend a lot on the accuracy of your forecasts. And some firms' environments—sources of raw materials, consumer preferences, actions of competitors, and so forth—are much more predictable than others'. That is why some writers like Michael McCaskey [9] say that you should distinguish between two different types of planning: "Planning with goals," and "Directional planning."

Planning with goals is appropriate where the environment is *predictable*, and where forecasts are more reliable. Here plans can be very detailed, and goals can be established in great detail. The forecasting techniques used here can safely rely on projections of historical data. There is an emphasis on standing plans, such as policies, rules, and procedures. These specify in detail what each employee's job is and how that job is to be carried out.

Directional planning is appropriate where the environment is *unpredictable*. Here you simply identify a broad domain or area in which the organization will work, and a *general direction* in which it will move. You focus more on "what business are we in." You focus less on planning precisely how each employee is supposed to do his job. There is less emphasis on standing plans and more use of qualitative forecasting techniques, such as the DELPHI method. There is less emphasis on specifying *how* each individual is to do his job, and more emphasis on a cooperative effort to carry out the broad goals of the company. This is summarized in Exhibit 5–4.

Exhibit 5.4   How the Type of Planning Has to Fit the Situation

Type of Planning	Planning with goals; detailed, means/end planning	"Directional" planning
Appropriate Where:	Environment is stable and predictable; stress here is on efficiency.	Environment is unstable and unpredictable; stress here is on creativity, and flexibility

Planning and the Product Life Cycle

A manager who has to introduce a new product is faced with a very different task from that of a manager whose product has been sold for several years. The former's is a very uncertain world. He has no historical sales information on which to base decisions. Yet at the same time, he needs to make many difficult decisions. These include whether or not to market his new product, what the design and style of the product should be, and how to distribute his product.

On the other hand, a manager whose product has "matured" or begun to decline in popularity faces a very different situation. By this time most of the uncertainties concerning the salability of the product, or the best design for the product have disappeared. This manager no longer has to be pre-occupied with reacting quickly to the need for a drastic styling change, or revamped distribution system. There is no longer a procession of new competi-tors entering the market. His decisions and plans now focus more and more on maintaining the profitability of his product in its slowly eroding market.

A typical "product life cycle" is illustrated in Exhibit 5–5. Notice how rapidly sales and profits grow during the earliest stages of the cycle, only to begin tapering off as competitors enter the market. Finally the product enters its decline stage as the demand for the product begins dropping.

Exhibit 5.5   A Product Life Cycle

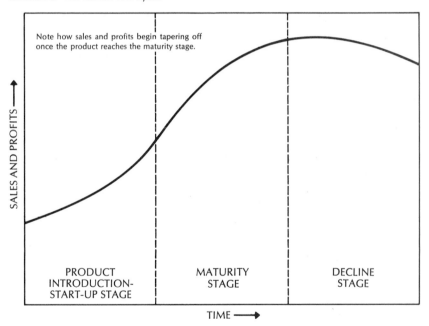

Note how sales and profits begin tapering off once the product reaches the maturity stage.

SALES AND PROFITS →

PRODUCT INTRODUCTION- START-UP STAGE

MATURITY STAGE

DECLINE STAGE

TIME →

Implications: How do you think these different stages influence the sort of planning in which each manager must engage? The manager working to develop and introduce his new product cannot afford to encumber himself with a network of ponderous plans, goals, rules, and procedures. He has little or no historical data to go on. He has to depend more on intuition and creativity and less on statistical forecasting. Because his market is growing rapidly he

94   can afford to make more day-to-day mistakes and be less efficient; the important thing is that he establish the market for his new product. Like Henry Ford in the early 1900s, his product may be successful even though planning appears to be minimal. *Directional planning* and qualitative forecasting are appropriate here.

The manager with a product in the maturity or declining stages has to develop much more specific plans. He cannot aim just for the goal of introducing his product. Instead he has to focus on profitability and on very specific goals such as "cut inventory costs by 10 percent." He cannot concern himself only with vague milestones; instead he has to plan precisely *how* each department will carry out its tasks. And, of course, this sort of *detailed means/end planning* is much easier for him because he has historical data on which to develop causal forecasts and solid planning premises.

An Example

An example might help to illustrate how you have to fit planning to the situation. Let's suppose that the Apex Bicycle Company has a very stable, predictable environment. There are few new innovations, consumer preferences don't change unexpectedly, and obtaining raw materials is not a big problem. The company knows clearly and ahead of time what kind of product it needs to sell. And it knows very quickly whether it is being successful or not.

This company could establish a very detailed "means/end chain" of plans. It could set specific goals for each department (such as cut production costs by 10 percent). And it could specify ahead of time, in detail, how each department is to accomplish those goals, (such as by installing a new assembly line, and so on).

At the other extreme, let's suppose that your company is in the business of developing and selling high quality prototypes of electronic instruments to customer specifications. Here the environment is very unpredictable. Consumer preferences are unpredictable. The company doesn't know from day to day just what kind of product it may be producing next week or next year. It always has to be ready to "jump at a moment's notice."

Your company's managers would have to rely on "directional" planning. They would have to insure that all their employees understood "what business we're in" (high quality prototypes). Beyond that, they would just set broad goals for their departments, such as "maintain high quality and a reasonable profitability on each project." They would let the departments decide on a day-to-day basis *how* they would achieve those goals. The departments could choose their own products, hire their own engineers, establish or not establish assembly lines, and so forth, as they saw fit. Thus this company stresses its

broad *direction* in its planning. The bicycle company stresses a narrower
direction *and* a specification of *how*, in detail, the company is to move in that
direction.

Summary: Fitting the Plan to the Situation

Some of the specific ways in which the plan needs to fit the situation
are summarized in Exhibit 5–6.[10]

Exhibit 5.6　Planning Under Predictable and Unpredictable Conditions

	Mechanistic	*Organic*
PLANNING CHARACTERISTICS	PREDICTABLE SITU-ATIONS/PRODUCT MATURITY-DECLINE STAGE; EMPHASIS ON EFFICIENCY.	UNPREDICTABLE SITU-ATIONS/PRODUCT DE-VELOPMENT-INTRODUC-TION STAGE; EMPHASIS ON CREATIVITY AND FLEXIBILITY.
How detailed and elaborate are plans?	A great deal of detail	Very little detail
How specific should goals be?	Very specific goals ("decrease inventory costs by 10%")	Broad goals ("maintain quality")
Emphasis on "mile-stones" vs. emphasis on how work should be carried out.	Greater emphasis on specifying how work should be carried out.	Emphasis on board, guiding milestones.
Use of standing plans	Greater use of standing plans.	Less emphasis on standing plans such as policies, rules, and proceedures
Forecasting techniques Used	Use of time series and econo-metric techniques which rely on historical data	Use of qualitative techniques like market research
Decision-making techniques	Management Science	Creativity, intuition, judgment

Source: Based on Michael McCaskey, "A Contingency Approach to Planning"; William Newman, "Strategy and Management Structure," *Journal of Business Policy*, Vol. 2, (Winter 1971/72); Fremont Kast and James Rosenszweig, *Contingency Views of Management* (Chicago, Science Research Associates, 1973); Charles Hofer, "Toward a Contingency Theory of Business Strategy," *Academy of Management Journal*, (18) 12/74.

SOME HINTS FOR MAKING YOUR PLANS WORK

Define the Central Concept of Your Enterprise

No amount of careful planning is going to overcome an ill-conceived
central concept. You have to be able to answer the question "What business
are we in?" And you have to insure that *The Business* is one that will
prosper and grow.

Forecast

Do not shrug off forecasting as a useless endeavor, or fall into the trap of implicit forecasting. Choose the appropriate forecasting technique and try to relate your sales data to other variables, such as industry sales, and Gross National Product. Then you can build your plan on as solid a set of planning premises as possible.

Define Your Problem Carefully

Do not emphasize the obvious; instead, peel away the obvious "problems" until you come to the heart of the matter.

Develop Alternatives

Remember that you must have a choice in order to make a decision. And remember that developing alternatives is a creative process which requires both creative individuals *and* a creative "climate." You can make good use of group decision-making techniques, such as brainstorming to elicit as many good alternatives as possible.

Evaluate Your Organization's Resources

Check each alternative against your organization's resources in a test of consistency. Ask questions such as: Do I have adequate financial resources to carry out the plan? Have I enough managerial talent to carry out the plan? Do my factories have the productive capacity to carry out their share of the plan?

Carefully Analyze Your Alternatives

Management Science techniques like linear programming and statistical decision-making can be useful here. But remember not to emphasize them at the expense of intuition and creativity.

Be Careful Making the Final Decision

Remember that people always look at the world through a window tinted by their own values, personalities, and abilities. Be on guard against viewing forecasts, market research information, and your various alternatives as *you* want to see them instead of as they *really are*. And remember our seven hints: Marshall the facts; consult your feelings; make sure the timing is right; don't overstress "finality"; talk it over; stay open-minded; and know yourself.

Remember: Plans Must Be Implemented

Your subordinates will also tend to view the plan from their own point of view. Remember that people tend to resist accepting plans and the changes they imply, particularly when those changes are viewed as detrimental to their own best interests.

Fit the Plan to the Situation

Remember that unpredictable, new product development-type situations call for directional planning. Predictable, market maturity situations call for more detailed, means-end planning.

Remember: Planning is Not Enough

Keep in mind that "nonplanners" sometimes do better than "planners" —and that some "planners" are dramatically unsuccessful. After all, your plan can't be any better than the *forecast* on which it's built; and some occurrences, such as economic recessions, are simply very difficult to forecast. Also, it is not enough to plan; *the plan that emerges* must be an effective one—remember that the Edsel was very carefully planned. Finally, remember that a plan is only as good as its implementation. For example, new managers must be recruited; new organizations designed; new dealers recruited; new plants constructed; and so forth. Planning is only the first function of management. Managers also Organize, Staff, Lead, and Control, and all these are ingredients of a successfully implemented plan.

Summary: Hints for Making the Plan Work

Here is a summary of the hints for making your plan work:

1. Define the central concept of your enterprise.
2. Forecast carefully.
3. Define your problem carefully.
4. Develop alternatives.
5. Evaluate your organization's resources.
6. Carefully analyze your alternatives.
7. Be careful making the final decision.
8. Fit the plan to the situation.
9. Remember: Plans must be implemented to be effective.
10. Remember: Planning is not enough.

98   **Some Important Things to Remember from This Chapter:**

1. Planning is a necessary and useful function of management; but it is also important to see that planning has some major limitations. A plan is no better than the forecast on which it is built, for example, and even a brilliant plan is worthless unless effectively implemented.

2. Some of the major barriers to effective planning include inaccurate forecasts; human errors; implementing the plan effectively; getting others to accept your plan; the fear that many have of the changes plans result in; and the fact that planning is both difficult and expensive.

3. Planning with goals, or detailed means/end planning, is appropriate where the environment is predictable and forecasts are more reliable. Here very detailed plans and goals can be set. These specify what is to be accomplished, and how it is to be accomplished.

4. Directional planning, on the other hand, is appropriate where the environment is unpredictable. Here the emphasis is on setting broad directions. There is much less emphasis on how, specifically, employees should carry out their jobs.

5. The position of your product in its life cycle also has to be considered. Directional planning is more appropriate in the start-up stage where situations change rapidly; planning with goals is more appropriate in the maturity and decline stages.

6. Some hints for making your plan more effective include: Carefully define the central concept of your enterprise; develop careful forecasts; define your problem carefully; develop alternatives; evaluate your organization's resources; carefully analyze your alternatives; be careful making the final decision; fit the plan to the situation; and remember that plans must be implemented.

STUDY ASSIGNMENTS

1. "Setting clear, measurable goals is always a virtue." Discuss why you agree or disagree with this statement.
2. Compare and contrast Planning With Goals with Directional Planning.
3. Explain why planning is no guarantee of success.
4. Discuss the seven barriers to effective planning.
5. How would you explain the fact that the "nonplanners" seem to outperform the "planners" in Rue and Fulmers service and nondurable companies?
6. Discuss some of the specific differences you would expect to find in a narrative plan for (1) a brand-new product, and (2) a product that has "matured."
7. Give some specific examples of "detailed, means/end" planning and "directional" planning.
8. What is a "product life cycle." What effect does it have on how you plan?
9. Briefly show in the form of a table some of the specific ways in which a plan needs to fit the situation.
10. Briefly discuss at least seven hints for making planning effective.

NOTES FOR THE CHAPTER

1. Leslie W. Rue and Robert M. Fulmer, "Is Long-Range Planning Profitable?" in *Proceedings* of the 1973 national meeting, Academy of Management, Boston, Massachusetts; Thad B. Green, Dennis F. Gray, Editors.

2. See also S. S. Thune and R. J. House, "Where Long-Range Planning Pays Off," *Business Horizons*, Vol. 13, No. 4 (1970) pp. 81–87; and David M. Herold, "Long-Range Planning and Organizational Performance: A Cross Validation Study," *Academy of Management Journal* (March 1972) pp. 92–102.

3. George A. Steiner, *Top Management Planning* (New York: Macmillan, 1969) p. 77.

4. Based on William H. Reynolds, "The Edsel: Faulty Execution of a Sound Marketing Plan," *Business Horizons* (Fall 1967) pp. 39–46; reprinted in Ernest Dale, *Readings in Management* (New York: McGraw-Hill, 1975) pp. 235–239.

5. Much of this discussion is based on George A. Steiner, *Top Management Planning* (New York: Macmillan, 1969) Chapter 3.

6. D. C. Dearborn and Herbert Simon, "Selective Perception: a note on the departmental identifications of executives," *Sociometry*, Vol. 21 (1958) pp. 140–144.

7. T. A. Mahoney, T. H. Jerdee, S. J. Carroll, "The Job(s) of Management," *Industrial Relations*, Vol. 4, No. 2 (1965) pp. 97–110.

8. George Steiner, *Top Management Planning* (New York: Macmillan, 1969) p. 77.

9. Michael B. McCaskey, "A Contingency Approach to Planning: Planning with Goals and Planning without Goals," *Academy of Management Journal* (June 1974).

10. See, for example, Charles W. Hofer, "Toward a Contingency Theory of Business Strategy," *Academy of Management Journal*, Vol. 18, No. 4 (December 1975) pp. 784–810; William H. Newman, "Strategy and Management Structure," *Journal of Business Policy*, Vol. 2 (Winter 1971/72); Freemont E. Kast and James E. Rosenzweig, "Contingency Views of Management" (Chicago: Science Research Associates, 1973).

A Framework for Studying the Management Fundamentals

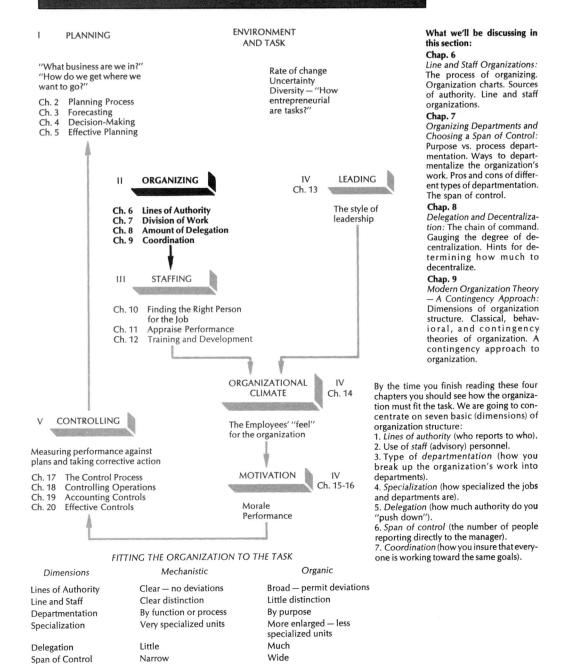

I   PLANNING

"What business are we in?"
"How do we get where we want to go?"

Ch. 2   Planning Process
Ch. 3   Forecasting
Ch. 4   Decision-Making
Ch. 5   Effective Planning

ENVIRONMENT
AND TASK

Rate of change
Uncertainty
Diversity — "How entrepreneurial are tasks?"

II   **ORGANIZING**

Ch. 6   **Lines of Authority**
Ch. 7   **Division of Work**
Ch. 8   **Amount of Delegation**
Ch. 9   **Coordination**

III   STAFFING

Ch. 10   Finding the Right Person
for the Job
Ch. 11   Appraise Performance
Ch. 12   Training and Development

IV   LEADING
Ch. 13

The style of leadership

ORGANIZATIONAL
CLIMATE

IV
Ch. 14

V   CONTROLLING

Measuring performance against plans and taking corrective action

Ch. 17   The Control Process
Ch. 18   Controlling Operations
Ch. 19   Accounting Controls
Ch. 20   Effective Controls

The Employees' "feel" for the organization

MOTIVATION

IV
Ch. 15-16

Morale
Performance

What we'll be discussing in this section:
Chap. 6
Line and Staff Organizations:
The process of organizing. Organization charts. Sources of authority. Line and staff organizations.
Chap. 7
Organizing Departments and Choosing a Span of Control: Purpose vs. process departmentation. Ways to departmentalize the organization's work. Pros and cons of different types of departmentation. The span of control.
Chap. 8
Delegation and Decentralization: The chain of command. Gauging the degree of decentralization. Hints for determining how much to decentralize.
Chap. 9
Modern Organization Theory — A Contingency Approach: Dimensions of organization structure. Classical, behavioral, and contingency theories of organization. A contingency approach to organization.

By the time you finish reading these four chapters you should see how the organization must fit the task. We are going to concentrate on seven basic (dimensions) of organization structure:
1. *Lines of authority* (who reports to who).
2. Use of *staff* (advisory) personnel.
3. Type of *departmentation* (how you break up the organization's work into departments).
4. *Specialization* (how specialized the jobs and departments are).
5. *Delegation* (how much authority do you "push down").
6. *Span of control* (the number of people reporting directly to the manager).
7. *Coordination* (how you insure that everyone is working toward the same goals).

FITTING THE ORGANIZATION TO THE TASK

Dimensions	Mechanistic	Organic
Lines of Authority	Clear — no deviations	Broad — permit deviations
Line and Staff	Clear distinction	Little distinction
Departmentation	By function or process	By purpose
Specialization	Very specialized units	More enlarged — less specialized units
Delegation	Little	Much
Span of Control	Narrow	Wide
Coordination	Use chain of command	Committees

A Framework for Studying the Management Fundamentals

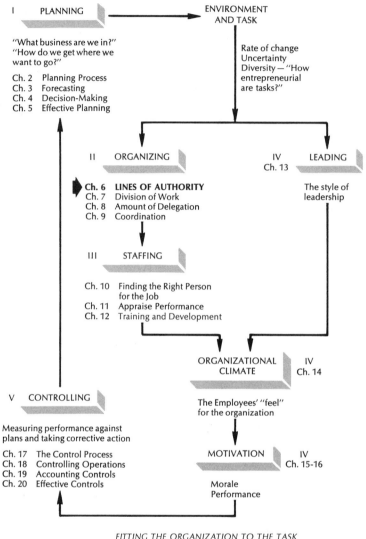

I   PLANNING   →   ENVIRONMENT AND TASK

"What business are we in?"
"How do we get where we want to go?"

Ch. 2   Planning Process
Ch. 3   Forecasting
Ch. 4   Decision-Making
Ch. 5   Effective Planning

Rate of change
Uncertainty
Diversity — "How entrepreneurial are tasks?"

II   ORGANIZING

▶ Ch. 6   LINES OF AUTHORITY
Ch. 7   Division of Work
Ch. 8   Amount of Delegation
Ch. 9   Coordination

III   STAFFING

Ch. 10   Finding the Right Person for the Job
Ch. 11   Appraise Performance
Ch. 12   Training and Development

IV   LEADING
Ch. 13

The style of leadership

ORGANIZATIONAL CLIMATE   IV   Ch. 14

The Employees' "feel" for the organization

V   CONTROLLING

Measuring performance against plans and taking corrective action

Ch. 17   The Control Process
Ch. 18   Controlling Operations
Ch. 19   Accounting Controls
Ch. 20   Effective Controls

MOTIVATION   IV   Ch. 15-16

Morale
Performance

Where we are now: Discussing some of the fundamentals of organizing, including authority in organizations, organization charts, and the use of staff.

FITTING THE ORGANIZATION TO THE TASK

Dimensions	Mechanistic	Organic
Lines of Authority (Who reports to who)	Clear — no deviations	Broad — permit deviations
Use of Staff	Much use; clear distinction between line and staff	Less use of staff; no clear distinction between line and staff

When you have finished studying

6 Line and Staff Organizations

You should be able to:

1. *Explain the purpose of organization structures.*

2. *Develop an organization chart.*

3. *Trace the sources of "authority" in organizations.*

4. *Distinguish between "line" and "staff" authority.*

5. *Show the distinction between "line" organizations and "line-staff" organizations.*

6. *Develop at least three different "line-staff" organization charts.*

7. *Explain why problems arise in "line-staff" relationships.*

8. *Identify the factors which dictate the use of "line," "staff," and "line-staff" organizations.*

INTRODUCTION

Bob Ellis started his own electronics firm two years ago. Today he has 30 employees, customers all over the country, and sales which he believes will double each year for the next five years. He manufactures three products: portable radios, dictation equipment, and calculators. He knows that you've been taking a course in management, and, over lunch one day, asks you for advice on how to reorganize his company. (Up to now he's been running it as a "one-man show," with everyone taking his orders directly from him.) Here are the specific questions he puts to you:

1. *"Should I hire an assistant to the president to handle some of the problems that normally come directly to me?"*
2. *"Should I appoint a manager to oversee the manufacturing and sales of each of our three products? Or should I put one person in charge of manufacturing all three products, and another in charge of selling all three products?"*
3. *"How can I insure that we don't start getting 'bureaucratic' and unresponsive?"*
4. *"How many people should I have reporting directly to me?"*

You may already have some ideas on how he should reorganize his firm, but delay forming detailed answers to his questions until after you've studied the next four chapters. You should then be in a much better position to answer them.

ORGANIZATION DEFINED

The purpose of organization is to give each person a separate, distinct task, and to insure that these tasks are coordinated in such a way that the organization accomplishes its goals. Except on the very rarest of occasions, organizations are never ends in themselves, but are means to an end—that "end" being the accomplishment of the organization's goals.[1] Thus:

> An organization consists of people who carry out differentiated tasks which are coordinated to contribute to the organization's goals.

THE PROCESS OF ORGANIZING

The process of organizing consists of breaking down the work necessary to achieve the goal into individual departments and jobs, and then providing the necessary coordination to insure that these departments and jobs fit together.

For very small jobs, the process of organizing is not very complicated. You'll need to ask "what tasks in my department am I responsible for accomplishing?" Then you divide up these tasks, assigning each to a subordinate.

But for larger jobs, such as running a hospital, the process of organizing can become quite complex. It involves dividing the work of the organization; combining it logically into departments; delegating authority; and establishing coordination and control systems to insure that everyone is working in unison to fulfill the organization's goals. We will spend most of the remainder of this chapter and the next three chapters discussing the process of organizing.

Is Your Unit Really Organized?

A manager can be easily lulled into a false sense of security about how well-organized his unit is. This is because the work often gets accomplished even without a lot of formal organizing. Organization structure is only one of the sources through which subordinates find out what their duties are, and how they are supposed to get their jobs done. A second source is the various standing plans—policies, procedures, and rules—which prescribe how a person is supposed to act in a particular situation. Still another source is the manager himself, who is usually available to answer questions and "put out fires" as they arise.[2]

Finally, and perhaps most importantly, the work often gets done simply because of the habitual ways of doing things and communicating that employees always develop. So even though they are not "told" how to do something (by a clear organization structure, standing plans, or their manager) they still tend to develop informal practices, procedures, and communications channels. These enable them to get their work done—though often not as well as if they were organized correctly in the first place. This is summarized in Exhibit 6–1.

Exhibit 6.1   Sources of "Structure"

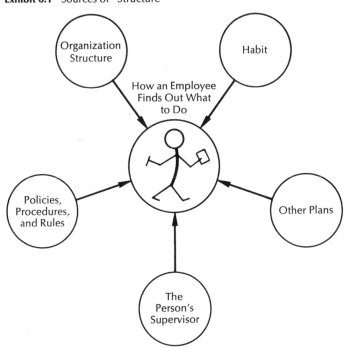

ORGANIZATION CHARTS

The usual way of depicting an organization is with an organization chart, as shown in Exhibit 6–2. These are snapshots of the organization at a particular point in time, and show the skeleton of the organization structure in chart form. They provide the title of each manager's position, and by means of connecting lines show who is accountable to whom, and who is in charge of what department.

Exhibit 6.2   An Example of an Organization Chart

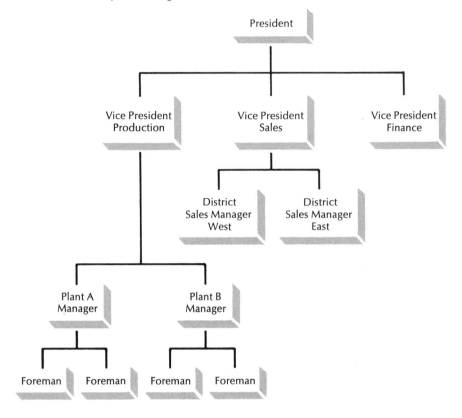

The organization chart does not tell you everything about the organization, any more than a road map tells you everything about the towns along its routes. Organization charts do not provide job descriptions (such as the one illustrated in Exhibit 6–3). These describe the specifics of each job in terms of the actual day-to-day duties and responsibilities the person is expected to perform. Nor does the organization chart show the *actual* patterns of communication in the organization. It also does not show how closely employees are controlled, or the actual level of authority and power that each position holder in the organization has. What it *does* show are the position titles and the "chain of command" from the top of the organization to the bottom.

Most organizations have, or should have, organization charts because they are helpful in informing each employee of what his job is, and how his job relates to others in the organization. On the other hand, many organizations have been quite successful without organization charts, while others have failed in spite of them.

We know, for example, that mechanistic organizations like production plants usually have very clear and complete organization charts. These show in detail who reports to whom, and what everyone's job title is. But organic organizations such as some electronics firms often make little use of organization charts. Instead, peoples' jobs and relationships change almost daily, in response to the needs of the moment.[3]

IN SUMMARY:

| Organization charts are useful because they: | **BUT** | Organization charts do *not* show you: |

Organization charts are useful because they:

1. Show titles of each manager's job.

2. Show who is accountable to whom

3. Show who is in charge of what department

4. Show what sorts of departments have been established

5. Show the "chain of command"

6. Let each employee know his job title and "place" in the organization

BUT

Organization charts do *not* show you:

1. Job descriptions of specific day-to-day duties and responsibilities

2. *Actual* patterns of communication in the organization

3. How closely employees are controlled

4. The actual level of authority and power each position holder has

AUTHORITY IN ORGANIZATIONS

Sources of Authority

Authority is the right to make decisions, the right to direct the work of others, and the right to give orders. Obviously, then, it is a very important factor in organizing. It derives from several different sources, one of which is the person's *position or rank*. The president has more authority based on rank than a vice-president, for example. And a production manager and sales manager each have authority over their own activities based on their positions in the organization.

108   **Exhibit 6.3**   Job Description for a Production Control Manager

TITLE	Production Control Manager
REPORTS TO	Assistant Plant Manager
SPECIAL REQUIREMENTS	High school graduate, college degree preferred. Background in production classes, construction, machine capacities. Ability to understand specifications. Ability to coordinate and supervise.
SUPERVISORY RESPONSIBILITY OVER:	Assistant Production Control Manager, Production Control Supervisor, Production Control Schedulers, Clerks, Hourly employees, and such other operations as designated by Plant Manager.
JOB SUMMARY	Directs the activities of: scheduling plant production; procuring raw materials; and maintaining inventory for production and shipping.
DUTIES	Receive, review, enter and promise all orders. Schedule machinery, manpower and materials in such a way that the maximum amount of efficiency is obtained from the operating departments. Prepare production schedules in accordance with customer requirements and applicable specifications. Coordinates production control with technical and production operations and maintenance. Supervises procurement of raw materials and inventory control. Responsible for all production schedules including machine operation, overtime, vacation, etc. Prepares forthcoming schedules and advises Plant Manager, Production Manager, and Department Managers of these schedules. Supervises and coordinates packing, shipping, traffic, freight consolidation operations to insure most economical freight rates and best delivery. Confers with sales offices. Follows up rush and delinquent orders. Confers with Plant Manager, Production Manager, and Plant Accountant in maintaining accurate backlogs by product class. Assist in operations report. Receives, reviews, and compiles daily production reports of plant's progress per department. Performs special projects as required. Has authority to hire, fire, promote, demote, train, discipline and supervise employees under his jurisdiction. Responsible for plant safety, housekeeping, scrap and usage where applicable to his sphere of plant influence. Implements cost reduction and efficiency improvement programs. May be responsible for execution of Union agreement.

Source: Professor Robert Miller

Other sources of authority are *personal attributes*, such as charisma, and *knowledge* and *expertise*. In other words, many people are able to command authority because of one or more personal traits they have, such as intelligence or charisma. Through their personal traits and the power of their personality they have a right to give commands and direct others well beyond the authority vested in them by their positions. Others are acknowledged *experts* in some other area, or have *knowledge* that requires others to depend on them. Through this expertise and knowledge they are able to command additional authority.

Top-Down vs. Bottom-Up Authority

Authority based on position or rank is traditionally assumed to funnel down from the top of the organization to the bottom, as illustrated in Exhibit 6–4. In a corporation, the authority stems from the owners of the company—the stockholders. They then *delegate* the authority necessary to effectively manage the firm down to the board of directors and president. As authority is delegated further and further down it becomes narrower in scope, with each succeedingly lower level of manager and worker having authority over a narrower range of activities.

Exhibit 6.4   The Delegation of Authority "Funnel"

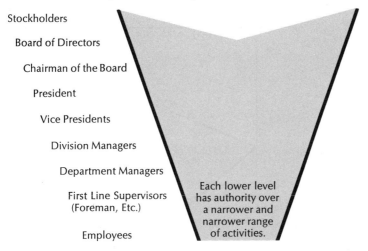

Stockholders

Board of Directors

Chairman of the Board

President

Vice Presidents

Division Managers

Department Managers

First Line Supervisors
(Foreman, Etc.)

Employees

Each lower level has authority over a narrower and narrower range of activities.

Source: Based on an idea presented in Theo. Haimann and William Scott, *Management in the Modern Organization* (Boston: Houghton Mifflin, 1970) p. 195.

Others argue against this top-down view of authority. They say that the real test of a person's authority is whether subordinates will *accept* the orders he gives them. Chester Barnard was an early proponent of this "acceptance" approach to authority. He equated giving orders with authority. He said that some orders are clearly acceptable, and others clearly unacceptable, while some lie within a "zone of indifference." Thus while your subordinate may be indifferent to some orders, for your order to be carried out—for authority to be implemented—your order, according to Barnard, must be *acceptable* to the subodinate. This is illustrated in Exhibit 6–5.

In practice, the "top-down" and "acceptance" approaches complement each other. Much of the authority in organizations (such as that based on rank or position) clearly flows from the top down. But it is also apparent that the real test of authority is whether a subordinate will accept orders based on that authority.

Exhibit 6.5   Barnard's Acceptance Theory of Authority

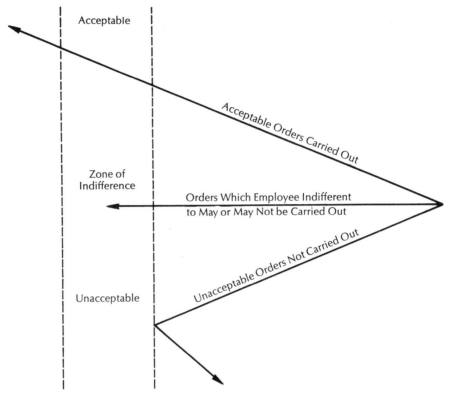

Acceptable

Acceptable Orders Carried Out

Zone of
Indifference

Orders Which Employee Indifferent
to May or May Not be Carried Out

Unacceptable Orders Not Carried Out

Unacceptable

Note: Some orders are clearly acceptable; others clearly unacceptable. Others fall within the person's "zone of indifference."

LINE AND STAFF ORGANIZATIONS

Line and Staff Authority

The two most familiar types of authority in organizations are *line* and *staff*. Line managers are authorized to *direct the work of subordinates*—they are always someone's boss. In addition, line managers have *direct responsibility for accomplishing the basic goals* of the organization.[4] Staff managers, on the other hand, are authorized to *assist and advise* line managers in accomplishing these basic goals.

You can see these ideas illustrated in Exhibit 6–6. The managers for production and marketing are line managers. They have direct responsibility for accomplishing the basic goals of the organization. They also have the authority to direct the work of various subordinates.

The "assistant to the president" is a staff position. His job is to assist and advise the president, who is himself a line manager. Notice that although the assistant to the president is a staff manager (his primary function is advisory) there is also an element of line authority associated with his job. This is because he is authorized to direct the work of his own three-man research department.

Types of Staff

You will find two types of staff in most business organizations. One is *personal staff*. This is represented by the "assistant to the president" position in Exhibit 6–6. "Personal staff" employees like this aid *one* manager in carrying out those tasks he cannot, or which he will not assign to others. This might include overall planning for his function, or policy-making, for example.[5]

Exhibit 6.6 Line and Staff Authority

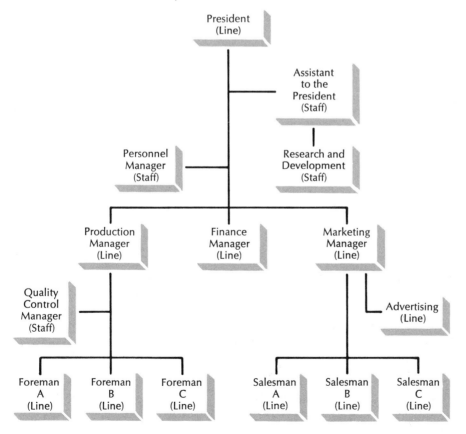

112   A second familiar type is *specialist staff*. The purpose of specialist staff is to make available to *all* line managers specialized analytical skills and advice in some specific area like collective bargaining or industrial engineering. Specialist staff is illustrated in Exhibit 6–7. Staff units are not directly in charge of the fundamental activities required to accomplish the organization's goals (as are the production manager and sales manager in Exhibit 6–7). But their assistance and advice may still be invaluable to the line managers. Many important activities, such as purchasing and personnel, normally fall into the "staff" category.

Exhibit 6.7   Examples of Specialist Staff

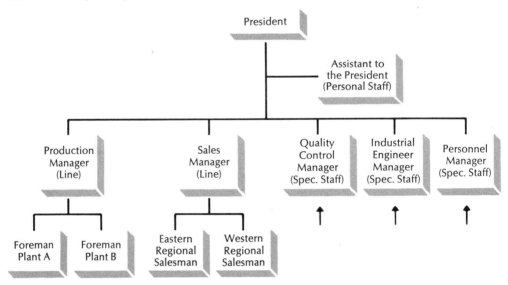

Line Organizations

Virtually all organizations are either line, or line-staff organizations. A line organization, such as that depicted in Exhibit 6–8, is the simplest and "cleanest" type of organization. Each manager is directly responsible for an activity required to accomplish the organization's goals, and there are no staff units to complicate the organization chart.

Line organizations are typical of very small organizations, as well as those that produce "made-to-order" items, such as expensive cars or wrought-iron gates.[6] Line organizations are also found in some continuous production facilities, such as oil refineries and paper mills.[7] This is because these facilities are so highly automated and complex that units which are usually considered "staff" (such as plant maintenance) become crucial and therefore take on direct-line authority.

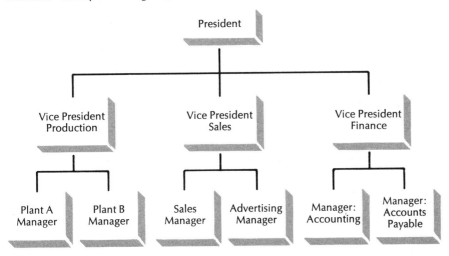

Exhibit 6.8 A Simple Line Organization

President — Vice President Production, Vice President Sales, Vice President Finance; Vice President Production — Plant A Manager, Plant B Manager; Vice President Sales — Sales Manager, Advertising Manager; Vice President Finance — Manager: Accounting, Manager: Accounts Payable

Line-Staff Organizations

The use of both line and staff units in organizations is widespread. In fact it is probably safe to say that almost every organization of any type, with more than 500 employees, utilizes staff units in one way or another.

There is no such thing as a "typical" line-staff organization because they come in a variety of configurations. In a study carried out in England, for example, the line-staff organization depicted in Exhibit 6–9 was found. In this particular company only the chief executive, general manager, and production manager were considered line managers. All the other managers, including those for sales, personnel, research and development, and finance were considered staff, and advisory to the chief executive. This company was unique in this respect. In a different company, which placed more emphasis on the sales or finance functions, these managers would probably have line authority.

Another type of line-staff organization is illustrated in Exhibit 6–10.[8] Here extensive staff specialization was carried out only within the production department, which had its own purchasing, personnel, and accounting staff units. These staff managers, however, had no responsibility outside the production department. For example, the personnel manager did not meddle in the personnel practices of the research and development or sales departments.

When to Use the Line-Staff Structure

We know that some situations are most appropriate for the use of the combined line-staff organization structure. For example, we know that the line-staff structure prevails among mass production firms such as those

114   **Exhibit 6.9**   First of Woodward's Line-Staff Organizations

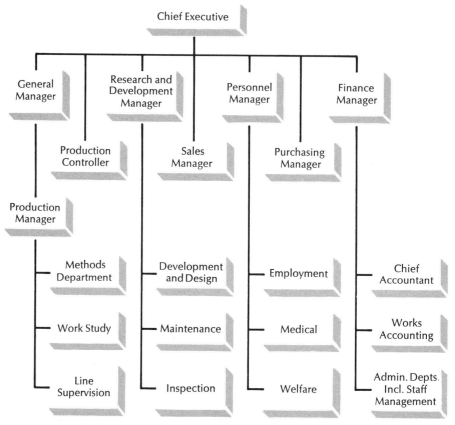

Source: Joan Woodward, *Industrial Organization: Theory and Practice,* (London: Oxford University Press, 1965) p. 105.

in the automobile industry.[9] On the other hand (to repeat) the simple-line organization prevails in smaller organizations that build products such as expensive sports cars one at a time, and in large and highly automated continuous-production facilities such as oil refineries. Thus *technology* is important.

The *size* of the organization is also an important factor. From a number of different studies in a wide range of firms we know that as the number of employees rises to about 500, the use of staff managers increases relatively quickly. After this point the ratio of staff managers to total employment remains fairly constant, with virtually all the larger firms using staff to some extent.[10]

Sources of Friction in Line-Staff Relations

Although line-staff structures are widely used, they are also the source of endless management tension and bickering. Here are some of the reasons: [11]

1. Staff personnel tend to be *younger*, more educated, of a higher social status class, and more ambitious and restless than line managers.
2. The older, often more experienced line managers tend to dislike having to take advice from younger staff managers. They fear being *"shown up."*
3. Line managers tend to view staff as *agents on trial*: as people who must constantly prove themselves. The staff person, on the other hand, views himself as an expert.
4. Line managers frequently feel that staff is *encroaching* on their duties and prerogatives.
5. Line managers also complain that staff does not give sound advice, *steals credit*, and fails to see the "whole picture."
6. Staff managers, on the other hand, feel that line managers are *"bull-headed,"* don't give staff enough authority, and resist new ideas.

With such differences in points of view, it's no wonder that the line-staff structure is often a source of tension and bickering! Let's look at a few of the things you can do to smooth out the problems.

Exhibit 6.10 Line-Staff Organization Inside Production

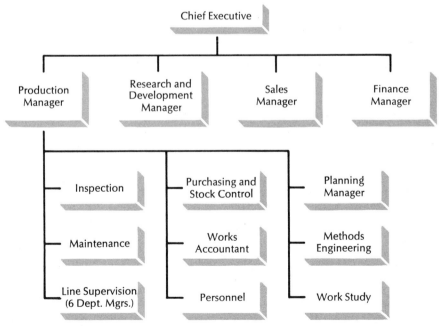

Source: Exhibit shows second kind of line-staff organization identified by Joan Woodward, *Industrial Organization; Theory and Practice*, (London: Oxford University Press, 1965) p. 106.

HINTS ON USING LINE AND STAFF STRUCTURES

Ask: Do You Really Need the Staff?

We know that line-staff structures prevail in mass production factories, and in larger organizations. This is because you usually need a fairly high volume of business to support staff personnel. After all, staff provides specialized assistance and advice but is otherwise "nonproductive"—it must be supported by the volume generated by line personnel. Therefore the first hint is to make sure that the use of staff is appropriate—that you're doing enough business to support these specialized individuals.

Make Sure Everyone Knows the Ground Rules

It's important that you avoid "power vacuums." These often occur when job assignments are not clear, and when authority is therefore "up for grabs." Remember that the staff person usually ends up doing some of the tasks formerly assigned to the line manager. And unless you make it very clear where staff's authority ends and line's begins, you're setting the stage for conflict and "power plays." So the second hint is: make sure everyone knows the ground rules; these include what (exactly) their jobs are, who does what, who reports to whom, and so forth.

Watch Out for the Staff "Gatekeeper"

Try to avoid ending up with a staff person who plays "gatekeeper" to you or to others. If it's the plant personnel manager, for example, make sure he knows that he's supposed to try working out "personnel" problems with the foremen before running to the plant manager. Or, if it's your own "assistant-to" make sure he doesn't end up as an impenetrable barrier between you and your other subordinates. So hint three is: watch out for the staff "gatekeeper."

Make Sure the Staff Person Has the Clout to Do the Job

You don't want to so completely restrict the staff person that he can't do his job. You're obviously just throwing away everyone's time and resources if staff's advice is never heeded. Therefore, you have to make it clear that the staff person does have your backing. Make it clear that he should be viewed as a valuable resource. So hint four is: make sure the staff person has the clout to do the job.

Staff people tend to be relatively ambitious. Yet often they have "nowhere to go" in the organization since they're outside the "line" hierarchy. While you don't want to give line managers the idea that the staff people might take over their jobs, you should make sure the staff person has some prospect for promotion (perhaps higher up in the parent firm). Hint five, then, is: make sure the staff person has a "ladder."

Some Important Things to Remember from This Chapter:

1. The purpose of organization is to give each person a separate distinguishable task, and to insure that these tasks are coordinated in such a way that the organization accomplishes its goals.

2. Be careful not be lulled into a false sense of security about how well organized your unit is. Standing plans, habit, and you yourself "putting out fires" all provide structure—but often not as well as if your people were organized correctly in the first place.

3. Organization charts are snapshots of the organization at a particular point in time. They show position titles and the chain of command. But they don't show you the specific day-to-day duties and responsibilities of the job incumbents. For that you need job descriptions.

4. In order for you to be an effective manager, you have to be able to give orders with authority. In other words, your subordinates must be willing to *accept* your orders and obey you. There are several sources of authority including your *position* or rank, *charisma*, or your *knowledge and expertise*.

5. Line managers direct the work of subordinates, and have direct responsibility for accomplishing the basic goals of the organization (production, sales, and so on). Staff managers are authorized to assist and advise line managers in accomplishing these basic goals. We discussed two basic types of staff: personal, and specialist.

6. A line organization is the simplest and cleanest type of organization, but most organizations—particularly those with more than 500 employees—use staff in one way or another. You want to insure that there's enough work to warrant the use of staff. This is one reason why larger organizations use more staff than do smaller ones. It is also why you often find line-staff organizations in mass production firms, which are usually geared to high-volume production.

8. Be on the alert for these sources of friction in line-staff relations: staff personnel tend to be younger and more educated; line managers tend to mistrust staff, and fear that they are trying to show them up; and they fear that staff is trying to encroach on their duties and prerogatives.

9. In setting up (or evaluating) a line and staff organization, remember our five hints: ask whether you really need the staff; make sure everyone knows the ground rules; watch out for staff "gatekeepers"; make sure the staff person has the clout to do the job; and give the staff person a "ladder."

STUDY ASSIGNMENTS

1. Answer question 1 that Bob Ellis put to you in the introduction to this chapter.
2. Explain the purpose of organization structures.
3. Without looking at its published organization chart, develop an organization chart for the business school of your local university.
4. Now look at the published organization chart of the school described in your answer to question 3. How does your chart differ from theirs? How would you explain these differences?
5. Write an essay discussing what organization charts are and are not useful for.
6. Discuss the sources of "authority" in organizations. What is the difference between line and staff authority?
7. Look at the organization chart for your local university. Distinguish between line and staff positions.
8. Develop three different line and staff organization charts.
9. Explain why problems arise in line-staff relationships.
10. Identify the factors which dictate the use of "line," "staff," and "line-staff" organizations.

NOTES FOR THE CHAPTER

1. For example, see Ernest Dale, *Organization* (New York: AMA, 1967) p. 9.
2. D. Katz and R. L. Kahn, *The Social Psychology of Organizations* (New York: Wiley, 1966) p. 334.
3. Joan Woodward, *Industrial Organization: Theory and Practice* (London: Oxford University Press, 1965).
4. Louis Allen, "The Line Staff Relationship," *Management Record*, Vol. 17, No. 9 (September 1955) pp. 346–349; 374–376. Reprinted in Max Richards and William Neilander, *Readings in Management* (Cincinnati: Southwestern, 1974) pp. 543–554.
5. Louis Allen, "The Line Staff Relationship," *Management Record*, Vol. 17, No. 9 (September 1955).
6. Joan Woodward, *Industrial Organization*, p. 101.
7. Joan Woodward, *Industrial Organization*, pp. 102–103.
8. Joan Woodward, *Industrial Organization*, p. 105.
9. Joan Woodward, *Industrial Organization*, Chapter 5.
10. See, for example, B. DeSpelder, "Ratios of Staff to Line Personnel," Research Monograph #105, Bureau of Business Research, The Ohio State University (1962); Alan C. Filly, "Decisions in Research Staff Utilizations," *The Academy of Management Journal* (September 1963) pp. 220–231; Alan Filley and Robert J. House, *Managerial Process and Organizational Behavior* (Glenview: Scott-Foresman, 1969) Chapter 11.
11. Nos. 1, 2, 3, based on Melville Dalton, "Conflicts Between Staff and Line Managerial Officers," *American Sociological Review*, Vol. 15, No. 3 (June 1950) pp. 342–350; reproduced in Ernest Dale, *Readings in Management* (New York: McGraw-Hill, 1975) pp. 170–174. Nos. 4, 5, and 6, based on Louis Allen, "The Line-Staff Relationship."

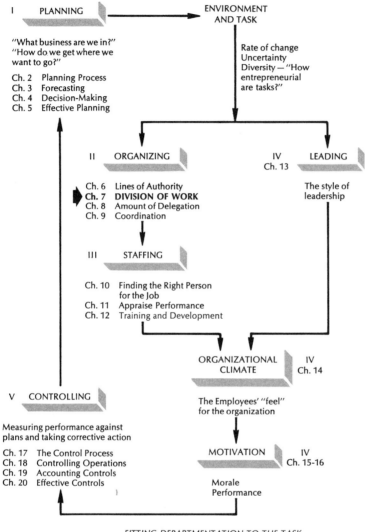

I   PLANNING   →   ENVIRONMENT
AND TASK

"What business are we in?"
"How do we get where we
want to go?"

Ch. 2   Planning Process
Ch. 3   Forecasting
Ch. 4   Decision-Making
Ch. 5   Effective Planning

Rate of change
Uncertainty
Diversity — "How
entrepreneurial
are tasks?"

Where we are now: Discussing departmentation, which involves grouping activities into "departments" and assigning them to a manager.

II   ORGANIZING   IV   LEADING
                                     Ch. 13

Ch. 6   Lines of Authority
➤ Ch. 7   **DIVISION OF WORK**
Ch. 8   Amount of Delegation
Ch. 9   Coordination

The style of
leadership

III   STAFFING

Ch. 10   Finding the Right Person
            for the Job
Ch. 11   Appraise Performance
Ch. 12   Training and Development

ORGANIZATIONAL   IV
CLIMATE   Ch. 14

V   CONTROLLING

The Employees' "feel"
for the organization

Measuring performance against
plans and taking corrective action

Ch. 17   The Control Process
Ch. 18   Controlling Operations
Ch. 19   Accounting Controls
Ch. 20   Effective Controls

MOTIVATION   IV
                      Ch. 15-16

Morale
Performance

FITTING DEPARTMENTATION TO THE TASK

Dimensions	Mechanistic	Organic
Type of Departmentation	Build departments around "processes" such as production, or sales	Build departments around "purposes" such as product lines
Degree of Specialization	Very specialized units (by process)	More *enlarged,* less specialized units (by purpose)
Span of Control	Usually narrow, but *can* be wide	Usually wide, but *can* be narrow

When you have finished studying

Organizing Departments & Choosing a Span of Control

You should be able to:

1. Compare and contrast "purpose" departmentation and "process" departmentation.

2. Explain departmentation "by product"
   "by customer"
   "by location"
   "by marketing channel"
   "by business function."

3. Cite the advantages and disadvantageous of purpose departmentation, and process departmentation.

4. Explain "matrix" departmentation.

5. Discuss the advantages and disadvantages of matrix departmentation.

6. Give an example of a "mixed" organizational design.

7. Discuss the "span of control" concept.

8. Use the Lockheed system for determining the best span of control.

INTRODUCTION

The Gross Heavy Machinery Corporation manufactures complex and expensive equipment and machinery, largely on a custom-built, job-order basis. At present the firm is functionally organized, with separate departments for sales, production, engineering (which includes design and development activities), customer service (which includes repairs and maintenance), finance, and accounting and general office functions. The company provides many of its customers with repair and maintenance service on a contractual basis.

Source: Richard N. Farmer, Barry M. Richman, and William G. Ryan, *Incidents in Applying Management Theory* (Belmont: Wadsworth Publishing Co., 1966) pp. 77–79.

Top management is presently considering a reorganization of activities along the following lines. It is felt that customer or customer-order teams could be created with a sales representative, design engineer, serviceman, cost accountant, and a secretary on each team. Each team, or possibly more than one team, could be headed by a supervisor. Through this type of setup, common interdepartmental frictions and conflicts might be substantially alleviated, or eliminated. The team members might communicate more effectively with each other than if they were in separate departments. Moreover, they might all tend to cooperate toward common objectives—including customer satisfaction, sales, cost effectiveness, and profits.

As you read this chapter, try to answer the following questions:

1. *What are the potential advantages and drawbacks of this type of organizational arrangement?*
2. *Do you think that the company should go ahead with this reorganization? Justify your position.*
3. *If the company decides to go ahead with this reorganization, what managerial functions other than "organization" should be carefully studied and why?*

WHAT IS DEPARTMENTATION?

Every organization has to carry out certain activities in order to accomplish its goals. These usually include activities such as manufacturing, selling, and accounting. *Departmentation* is the process through which these activities are grouped logically into distinct areas and assigned to managers: it is the organizationwide division of work. It results in "departments"—logical groupings of activities—which also often go by the name divisions, branches, units, groups, or sections.

Departmentation is a very important process. In fact, when most people think of "organization structure" they are usually thinking about departmentation. This is because it is departments—not "line authority," "staff authority," or "delegation"—that stand out on organization charts.

Purpose vs. Process Departmentation

Departmentation is also a very common phenomenon. The work of the federal government, for example, is divided at its highest level into the executive, judicial, and legislative branches. The executive branch itself is divided at its highest level into a number of departments, such as those for commerce, labor, and defense. Hospitals typically have such "departments" as

intensive care and radiology units. Many companies, such as General Motors,
have separate "product divisions" such as those for Buicks or Pontiacs; and
most also have separate departments for production, sales, and finance. However, though there are many ways to departmentalize organizations, most
types of departmentation can be classified as either *purpose* or *process*.[1] Let's
look at these.

PURPOSE TYPES OF DEPARTMENTATION

There are four popular "purposes" around which you can build departments: products; customers; market channels; and locations.

Departmentation by Product

Departmentation by *product* is illustrated in Exhibit 7–1, which presents part of the organization chart of the General Motors Corporation.
Notice how, at the operating divisions level, the car and truck group is
organized around product lines. The division is managed by an executive vice-
president, and there are separate divisions for Buick, Oldsmobile, Pontiac, and
so forth.

Exhibit 7.1 Product Departmentation at General Motors

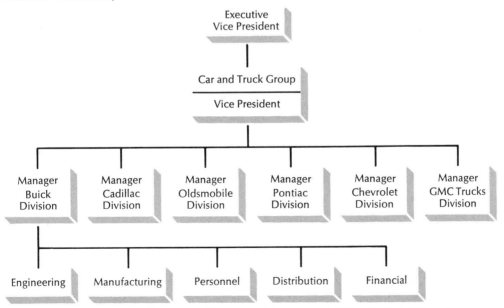

Note: The GM Car and Truck Group is departmentalized by product, and there are separate divisions for Buick, Cadillac, etc.

Departmentation by Customer

Departmentation by *customer* is illustrated in Exhibit 7–2, which shows the General Electric Company organization chart. Notice how the company is organized to serve as a supplier for many different "customers." These include aerospace, construction, consumer products, and power generation.

Departmentation by Marketing Channel

Marketing channel departmentation is illustrated in Exhibit 7–3. A marketing channel is the conduit (wholesaler, drugstore, grocery, etc.) through which a manufacturer distributes his products to his ultimate customers.

This type of departmentation is similar to customer departmentation, but there are several differences. In *customer* departmentation, each customer-oriented department is usually responsible for *both* manufacturing and selling its own products to its own customers. In *marketing channel* departmentation, the *same* product (such as a brand of facial soap) is typically marketed through two or more different channels. Thus a decision is usually made as to which department will manufacture the product for all the other marketing-channel departments.[2] This is illustrated in Exhibit 7–3.

From Exhibits 7–2 and 7–3 you may be able to see another of the differences between customer- and marketing-channel departmentation. With *customer* departmentation the *ultimate* "customers" (such as the defense department, consumers, or industrial purchasers) are the "purposes" around which departments are organized. But the manufacturer's product may actually reach some of these ultimate customers through several different marketing channels. For example, your firm might sell to consumers through *both* drugstores and grocery supermarkets. But the problems of doing business in each marketing channel may be very different. So it may make more sense to organize your departments to service the drugstore and supermarket channels rather than the ultimate customers.

Departmentation by Location

Departmentation by *location or area* is illustrated in Exhibit 7–4. Many agencies of the federal government are departmentalized by area. For example, the Federal Reserve System is divided into twelve geographical areas centered in cities such as Boston, New York, and San Francisco.

Exhibit 7.2 Customer Departmentation at General Electric

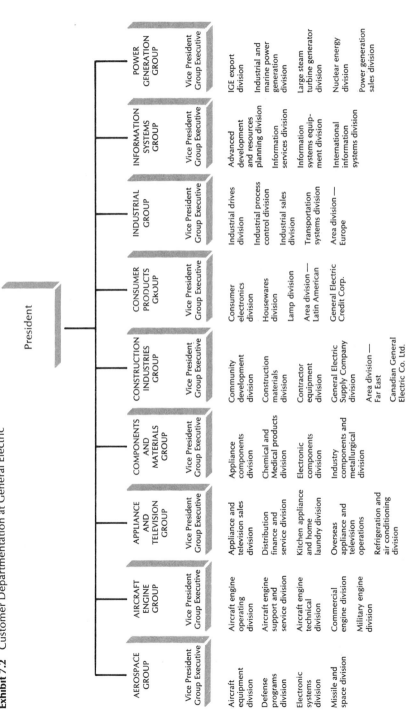

Note: Departments are built around such "customers" as aerospace, appliances and televisions, and construction.

Source: Adapted from *Corporate Organization Structures,* National Industrial Conference Board, Inc. No. 210 (1968), p. 59; Reproduced in James Gibson, John Ivancevich, and James Donnelly, Jr. *Organizations* (Dallas: Business Publications, Inc., 1973) p. 139.

Exhibit 7.3   Market Channel Departmentation at Apex Face Soap Company

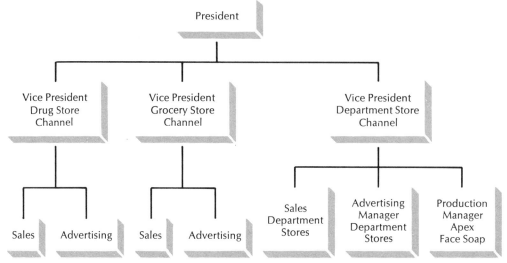

Note: 1. Only the department-store channel produces the soap, and 2. Each channel may sell to the same *ultimate* consumers.

Advantages of Purpose Departmentation

Whether you build departments around products, customers, marketing channels, or locations, purpose types of departmentation all have certain advantages in common. *They all result in units which are self-contained,*[3] *and in which a single person can give his continuous and undivided attention to the "purpose." Usually this means that each department can be more sensitive and adaptive to the needs of its product, customer, market, or location.*[4] They are therefore more appropriate in organic situations where quick, responsive decisions and flexibility (rather than efficiency) are paramount.[5]

Here each department manager is usually also less dependent on what other managers do. And as you might imagine, being put in charge of the "whole ball game"—even if it is just one product line—makes for clearer recognition of the manager's performance. This can help motivate him to better performance. Furthermore, the self-contained purpose departments can be good training grounds for your company's future executives. This is because they come in contact with a wider range of problems—production, sales, finance, and so on.

But in the final analysis, their biggest advantage is that they help lift some of the management burden from the shoulders of the company's top management. Imagine if the president of General Motors had to coordinate the tasks of designing, producing, and marketing each of G.M.'s different products. The diversity of problems he would face—from overseeing spark-plug

production to marketing Cadillacs—would clearly be enormous. Therefore virtually all large companies which have diverse products and customers have
opted for some type of purpose departmentation.[6]

Disadvantages of Purpose Types of Departmentation

Although these advantages can be very real, purpose types of departmentation also have some serious disadvantages. For one thing, you can see
from Exhibits 7–1 through 7–4 that they breed duplication of effort. The very
fact that each product, customer, marketing channel, or area department is
self-contained implies that there are *several* production plants instead of one
and *several* sales forces instead of one, and so on. This kind of duplication
is not only very expensive but can also create other problems. For example, the
company's customers may become annoyed at being visited by salesmen
representing different divisions.

Furthermore, the autonomy with which each department's manager
operates can lead to an attitude of independence. This can result in the
department drifting away from the central purpose of the organization.[7] In
fact, striking a balance between providing each department manager with
adequate authority while still maintaining control can be a ticklish business.

Finally, purpose types of departments also require more managers with
"general" managerial abilities. This is because each department is in a sense
a miniature company, often with its own production plant, sales force, personnel department, and so forth.

Exhibit 7.4   Departmentation by Area or Location

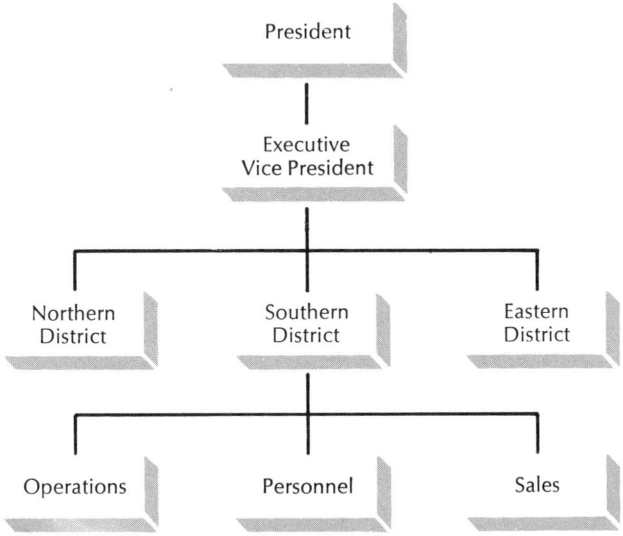

128   The advantages and disadvantages of purpose types of departmentation are summarized in Exhibit 7–5.

PROCESS TYPES OF DEPARTMENTATION

With process types of departmentation, closely related activities such as advertising, selling, and sales promotion are grouped together into a single department such as marketing.[8]

Exhibit 7.5   Advantages and Disadvantages of Purpose Types of Departmentation

Advantages	Disadvantages
You can give your continuous, undivided attention to the "purpose."	Results in duplication of effort.
Each department is relatively self-contained and self-sufficient in terms of its ability to service its purpose.	The autonomy given each department can lead to independence and drifting away from organization's central concept.
Each department tends to be relatively sensitive and adaptive to the needs of its purpose.	Requires more managers with "general" managerial ability.
Helps remove part of the management burden from the shoulders of the chief executive.	Increases the problem of top management control.
The performance of each department can be clearly identified and recognized.	
Departmental managers tend to be more motivated.	
Provides a good training ground for future corporate executives.	
Facilitates the growth of the company into new products and services.	

Some Guidelines: When To Use Purpose Types*

1. Where the company's products, customers, market channels, or areas are very diverse.

2. Where the company is so large that one man can no longer alone coordinate the functions, (production, marketing, etc.) for all products, customers, market channels, or areas.

3. Where being sensitive and adaptive to the "purpose's" changing needs is more important than being efficient.

4. Where adequate controls can be implemented by top management so as to prevent a division's "drifting away."

5. Where developing "general" managers is a major consideration.

*Note: We'll discuss these guidelines at length in Chapter 9.

This type of departmentation is typically the basis on which a new
business is organized. The head of a new company asks himself, "What basic
functions will have to be performed if the business is to meet its goals?" As
illustrated in Exhibit 7–6, in a manufacturing business these usually would
include (at least) manufacturing, sales, and finance and accounting.

Departmentation by Business Function

Thus departmentalizing a company by business function is probably the
most familiar form of division of work. It is depicted in Exhibit 7–6. Here
activities are grouped around business functions such as production, marketing, and finance.

Exhibit 7.6   Departmentation by Business Function

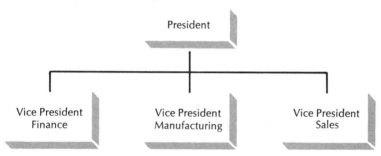

Other Types of Process Departmentation

You will also occasionally see organizations which have been departmentalized by *managerial* functions. Here, for example, you might find departments for organization, planning, or controlling. In another process type
of departmentation, activities are grouped on the basis of *technology*, with
separate departments for plating, welding, or assembling, for example.

Advantages of Process Types of Departmentation

Process types of departments (and their employees) tend to be more
specialized than purpose types. They focus on *specialized* occupational skills
such as production, planning, or welding. Because of this *they often lead to
increased proficiency and technical competence, and therefore to improved
efficiency.*[9] They are therefore more appropriate in mechanistic situations
where efficiency (rather than flexibility) is paramount.

Furthermore, since the managers' duties are also more specialized it is not as necessary to look for or train "general" managers. This can simplify both recruiting and training. Department managers are also privy to only a part of the "big picture" of the company—that which concerns their own specialized function. This makes it easier for top management to exercise tight control over the activities of department managers.

A final important advantage of this type of departmentation is that it is logical and proved. It has been widely used from the dawn of history, and has a simplicity and cleanness which has served it well.

Disadvantages of Process Types of Departmentation

Process types of departmentation also have some serious disadvantages. Responsibility for overall performance lies squarely on the shoulders of one man, usually the president. This may not be a serious problem when your firm is small, or where there is not a diversity of products. But as size and diversity of products increase, the job of coordinating the various functions may prove too great for a single individual.[10] Your company can lose its responsiveness.

Process types of departmentation also tend to result in highly specialized managers (finance experts, production experts, sales experts, and so forth). Although this may increase their proficiency, it also makes it more difficult to develop managers with the breadth of experience necessary to promote them to executive ranks.

The advantages and disadvantages of process types of departmentation are summarized in Exhibit 7–8.

Exhibit 7.7　Process Departmentation Based on Technology

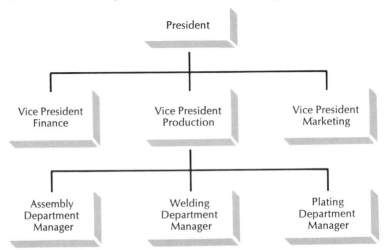

Exhibit 7.8   Advantages and Disadvantages of Process Types of Departmentation   131

Advantages	Disadvantages
Managers are functionally specialized and therefore more efficient. Less duplication of effort than in purpose types.	Responsibility for overall performance lies with chief executive only.
	Can overburden chief executive.
Training is simplified.	Reduces the attention paid to specific products, customers, markets, or areas.
Simple and proven over time.	Results in functionally specialized managers rather than "general" managers.
Facilitates tight control by chief executive level.	

Some Guidelines: When To Use Process Types*

1. Where jobs are high in volume and the "environment" (things such as sources of raw material, labor, customer demand, which are important to the organization but beyond its control) is stable and predictable.

2. Where efficiency is more important than flexibility.

3. Where products, customers, or markets are not extremely diverse.

4. Where developing "general" managers is not an acute problem.

*Note: We'll discuss these guidelines at length in Chapter 9.

MATRIX DEPARTMENTATION

What is Matrix Departmentation?

Purpose types of departmentation are very useful for insuring continuous, responsive and undivided attention to some product, customer, market, or area. *Process* types of departmentation, on the other hand, tend to be more efficient and to have less duplication of effort. *Matrix* organization structures are a newer approach to departmentation. They attempt to combine the advantages of both purpose and process types of departmentation.[11]

Many companies, such as those in the aerospace industry, often find it necessary to organize around a series of one-time projects. In the example in Exhibit 7–9, the company's aerospace products division is functionally (process) oriented (production, engineering, and so forth). Notice, though, there is also a purpose-oriented departmentation superimposed over this functional organization. There are three purpose-oriented groupings for the Venus project, Mars project, and Saturn project.

This is a typical matrix organization. A manager is put in charge of each project and given the authority and responsibility for completing the project. He is assigned a number of personnel from the various functional departments (production, engineering, etc.). He has the authority for re-

Exhibit 7.9 Matrix Departmentation

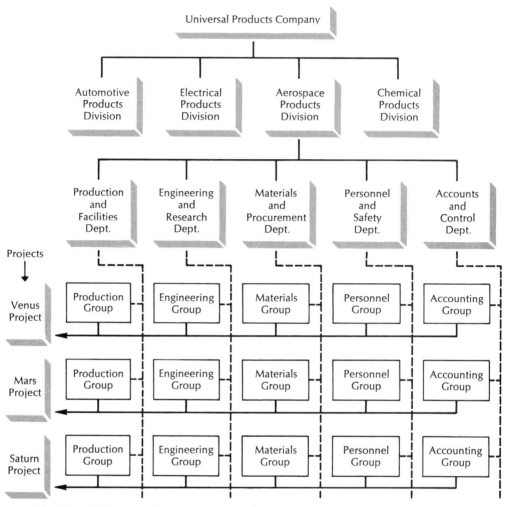

Source: Adapted from John Mee, "Matrix Organizations," *Business Horizons,* Vol. VII (1964) pp. 70-72; reprinted in David Hampton *Modern Management Issues and Ideas* (Belmont: Dickenson, 1969) pp. 92-95.

lieving his personnel from their "regular" functional group assignments and for rewarding them with promotions, salary increases, and so on. This is a temporary kind of departmentation, and on completion of the project the personnel return to their functional departments for reassignment.

Advantages and Disadvantages of Matrix Designs

Matrix departmentation has some important advantages. It insures a self-contained department which can devote its continuous and undivided attention to the needs of its own project. Yet it does not require that the entire organization be permanently organized around what are in fact temporary projects. You therefore avoid having to set up duplicate functional departments for each project.

On the other hand, matrix organizations have one important disadvantage not usually shared by purpose or process types of departmentation. Functional employees—such as those from the production department—can be caught between the conflicting demands of their functional and project managers. As you can imagine, this "role conflict" can be very demoralizing to employees and severely hamper the usefulness of the matrix organization.[12]

DEPARTMENTATION IN PRACTICE

In practice, most organizations are not simply "product"-oriented, "customer"-oriented, or "functionally"-oriented. In most organizations—particularly larger ones—the types of departmentation are mixed with several different types playing an important role.

The General Motors organization structure, presented in Exhibit 7–10, is a good example of this. There is *product* departmentation, as evidenced by the different product divisions for Buick, Cadillac, and so on. There is also departmentation by area, since separate divisions have been established for domestic markets and Canadian markets.

GM also has functional departmentation, with separate departments for marketing, design, auto assembling, and the like. But notice again, that these functional departments are themselves all self-contained within separate purpose-oriented divisions (as in Exhibit 7–11).

THE SPAN OF CONTROL

The "span of control" is the number of subordinates reporting directly to a supervisor. In Exhibit 7–12, the span of control of the president is 8, and the span of control of the production vice-president is 4.

Arguments over what the "best" span of control is have been going on for decades. Early writers recommended a very "narrow" span of only five or six subordinates. The assumption was that the boss could then keep a closer eye on each subordinate.[13] But studies of spans in actual companies clearly show that spans are often much wider. Ernest Dale, for example, found that the number of managers reporting to the chief executive in 100 companies varied from 1 to 24. Half the chief executives had spans greater than 9, and half less than 9. Only about a quarter of the companies had spans as narrow as 6.[14]

Exhibit 7.10 The Organization of General Motors

An Example of Mixed Departmentation

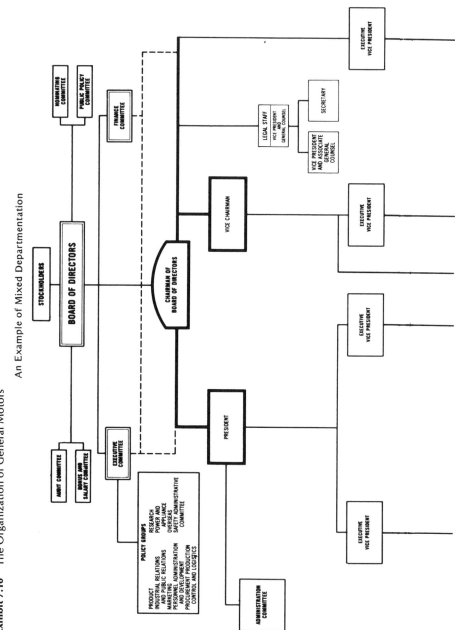

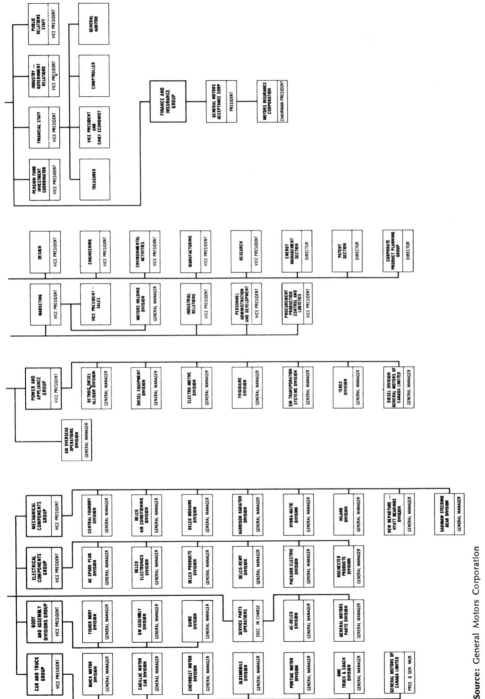

Source: General Motors Corporation

Exhibit 7.11   Functional Departmentation in G.M. Oldsmobile Division

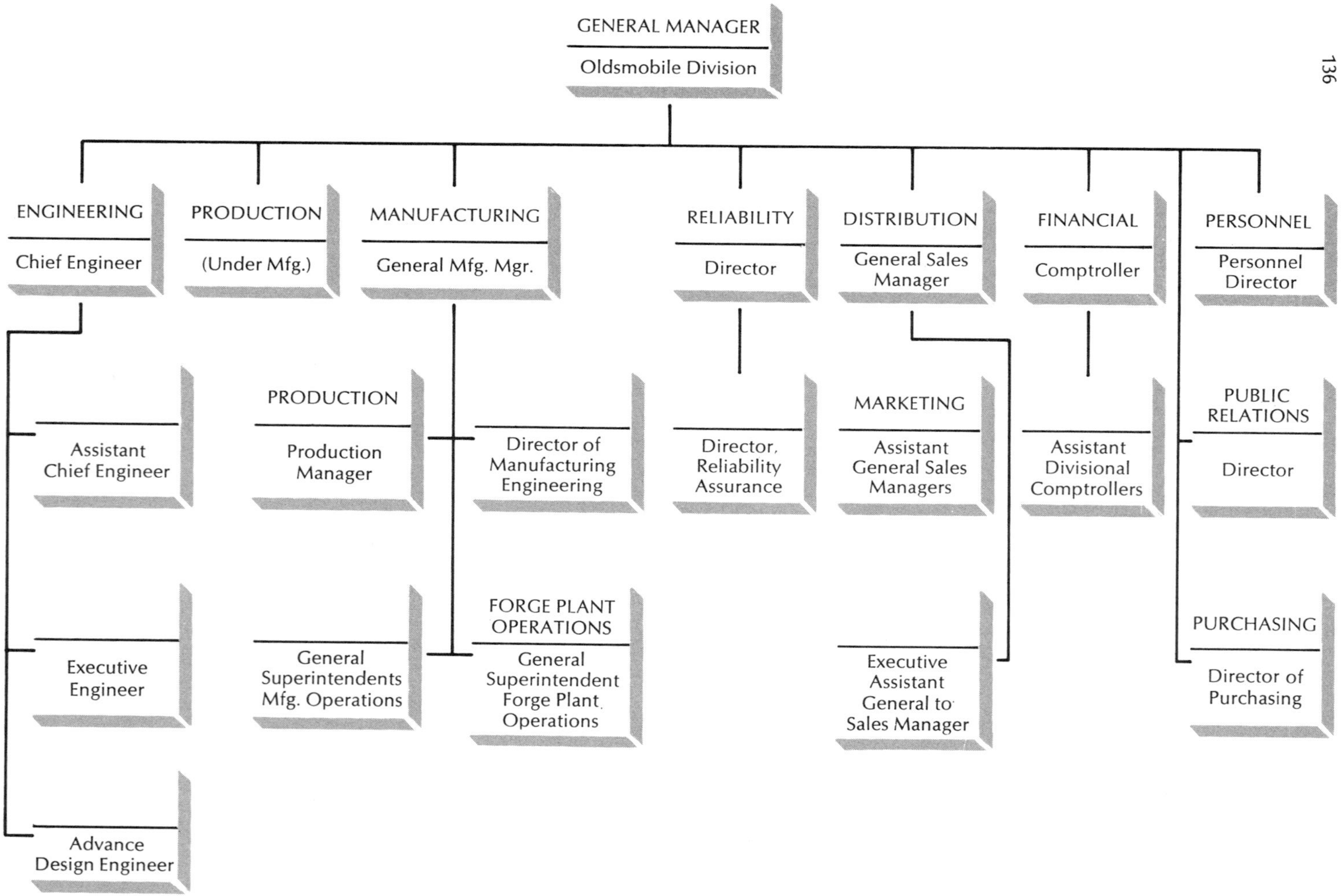

Source: From *Corporate Organization Structures*, National Industrial Conference Board, Inc., No. 210 (1968), p. 67; reproduced in Gibson, Donnelly, Ivancevich, *Organizations*, p. 146.

Exhibit 7.12   Span of Control

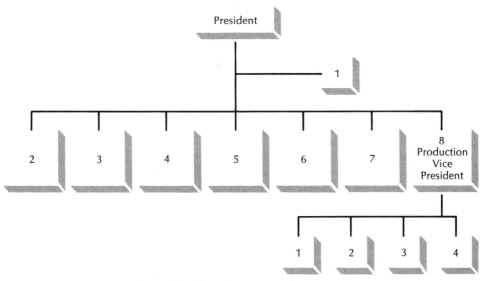

Note: The span of control of the President is 8; that of the Production Vice President is 4.

Many factors combine to determine the best span of control. We know, for example, that the spans of control of lower-level managers such as foremen are usually much wider than those of top-level executives. Furthermore, managers in mass-production, assembly-line types of companies tend to have the widest spans of control.[15] Similarly we know that jobs which are very routine, such as those in assembly lines, allow for much wider spans of control than nonroutine jobs such as managing a sales force.[16]

The Lockheed System for Determining the Best Span— A Practical Approach

But in a real situation, what is your "best" span of control? To answer this question, the Lockheed company has developed a special system which it has found to be useful.[17]

Lockheed management identified several factors which they felt should be taken into consideration when determining the best span of control for some particular situation. These included:

1. How similar are subordinates' jobs?
2. The geographic closeness of subordinates.
3. How complex are subordinates' jobs?
4. The direction and control required by subordinates.
5. The coordination required by subordinates.
6. The importance and complexity of the planning subordinates must engage in.

In the Lockheed system, points are allocated to each of these factors (similarity of jobs, geographic closeness, etc.) based on the point values in Exhibit 7–13. For example, if your subordinates' tasks are all "essentially alike" then the factor "similarity of jobs" would receive a point value of 2.

Exhibit 7.13   Lockheed Point Values

Span Factor	Point Values for Each Factor				
Similarity of functions	Identical	Essentially alike	Similar	Inherently different	Fundamentally distinct
	1	2	3	4	5
Geographic closeness	All together	All in one building	Separate building. 1 plant location	Separate locations, 1 geographic area	Dispersed geographic areas
	1	2	3	4	5
Complexity of functions	Simple, repetitive	Routine	Some complexity	Complex, varied	Highly complex, varied
	2	4	6	8	10
Direction and control	Minimum supervision and training	Limited supervision	Moderate, periodic supervision	Frequent, continuing supervision	Constant, close supervision
	3	6	9	12	15
Coordination	Minimum relationships with others	Relationships limited to defined courses	Moderate relationships, easily controlled	Considerable close relationships	Extensive mutual non-recurring relationships
	2	4	6	8	10
Planning	Minimum scope and complexity	Limited scope and complexity	Moderate scope and complexity	Considerable effort required; guided only by broad policies	Extensive effort required; areas and policies not chartered
	2	4	6	8	10

Once point values are assigned to all six factors, they are added together to provide a "supervisory index" which is then compared with the *index and suggested span of control* chart in Exhibit 7–14. This gives the supervisor his "suggested span of control." Obviously, the more routine are your subordinates tasks, the wider can be your span of control.

An Example. Let's look at an example to see how this might work in practice. Robb House, manager of employee relations at the Apex Company, is interested in determining what the best span of control would be for him. In the Lockheed point values chart, which we have repeated in Exhibit 7–15, Robb has circled the point values that seem appropriate for each of the six

Exhibit 7.14   Lockheed Index and Suggested Span of Control

Supervisory Index	Suggested Standard Span
40-42	4-5
37-39	4-6
34-36	4-7
31-33	5-8
28-30	6-9
25-27	7-10
22-24	8-11

factors. He then adds up these circled points, and finds that his "supervisory index" is 33. According to the chart in Exhibit 7–14, this 33 means that his best span is somewhere between 5 and 8 subordinates.

Notice that the Lockheed system does not tell you exactly what your best span is. Instead it gives you a narrow "optimal" range to consider, and therefore allows you some leeway in choosing exactly the best span for your situation.

Span of Control and Employee Morale

As we mentioned earlier, most early writers felt that organizations with narrow spans of control improved performance by permitting managers to closely supervise their subordinates.

One of the first studies to dispute this assumption was carried out by James Worthy in the Sears, Roebuck & Company. He found that the merchandising vice-president and store managers each had over 40 managers reporting directly to them.[18] According to some of the earlier classical-management writers this situation should have led to chaos.

Instead it was found that because of this wide span, managers could not "be running constantly to superiors for approval of their actions."[19] Therefore, this flat-type of organization structure with its wide spans of control apparently:

1. Prevented superiors from meddling too much in the business of their subordinates (since they had so many subordinates).
2. Forced the subordinates to use their own resources for getting their jobs done.
3. Resulted in improved manager development.
4. And also increased employee morale, since each subordinate had more of the feeling that he was his "own boss."

Exhibit 7.15 Lockheed System Point Values for Rob House's Span of Control

Span Factor	Point Values for Each Factor				
Similarity of functions	Identical	Essentially alike	Similar	Inherently different	Fundamentally distinct
	1	②	3	4	5
Geographic closeness	All together	All in one building	Separate building, 1 plant location	Separate locations, 1 geographic area	Dispersed geographic areas
	①	2	3	4	5
Complexity of functions	Simple, repetitive	Routine	Some complexity	Complex, varied	Highly complex, varied
	2	4	⑥	8	10
Direction and control	Minimum supervision and training	Limited supervision	Moderate, periodic supervision	Frequent, continuing supervision	Constant, close supervision
	3	6	9	⑫	15
Coordination	Minimum relationships with others	Relationships limited to defined courses	Moderate relationships, easily controlled	Considerable close relationships	Extensive mutual non-recurring relationships
	2	4	⑥	8	10
Planning	Minimum scope and complexity	Limited scope and complexity	Moderate scope and complexity	Considerable effort required; guided only by broad policies	Extensive effort required; areas and policies not chartered
	2	4	⑥	8	10

Although we don't have any hard-and-fast rules, most studies do support the idea that employees in organizations with wider spans have the higher morale.[20] Thus in one recent study of nearly 300 salesmen in three organizations, salesmen whose managers had wide spans reported that they were more satisfied; under less stress; and also performed better than salesmen whose managers had narrow spans.[21]

How Many Levels Should Your Organization Have?

For any particular organization, the wider its span of control (the number of people reporting to a supervisor) the fewer levels it will have. We know that in practice most companies have between five and eight levels of

management, including first-line supervisors at the bottom, and the company
president at the top. Here were the most frequently mentioned reasons the
companies gave as to why they preferred more (or fewer) levels: [22]

REASONS COMPANIES GAVE FOR PREFERRING MORE LEVELS (AND NARROW SPANS)	REASONS COMPANIES GAVE FOR PREFERRING FEWER LEVELS (AND WIDE SPANS)
Executives can give more time to planning and decision-making (fewer subordinates to supervise).	Better and easier communications.
It makes possible better direction and control.	Better decisions (quicker, more direct action, decisions closer to the point of action).
You necessarily develop more managers.	Fewer supervisors, so lower administrative costs.
	And, finally remember that *morale* tends to be higher.

A SUMMARY: FITTING THE ORGANIZATION TO THE TASK

Departmentation

We know that departments organized around purposes such as products, locations, and so on, are more flexible and adaptable. Here managers can focus on their "Purposes," and so quick, on-the-spot decisions are easier to make. Thus purpose departmentation is more appropriate for *organic* tasks where flexibility is paramount. On the other hand, departmentation by process is more appropriate for routine, *mechanistic* tasks where efficiency is paramount.

Span of Control

We know also that routine, assembly-line tasks do permit wider spans of control. That's what the Lockheed system is based on, for example. Yet we also know that many writers and managers recommend *narrow* spans—especially for assembly-line type tasks—since this permits "closer" supervision. So for mechanistic tasks you *can* have wider spans; but whether you do or not, depends on how closely you think you have to watch your people.

IN SUMMARY:

	Mechanistic	*Organic*
Departmentation	By Process: more specialized.	By Purpose; less specialized.
Span of Control	*Can* be wide—but depends on how much close supervision is required	*Can* be narrow—but again depends on how much close supervision is required.

Some Important Things to Remember from This Chapter:

1. Departmentation is the organizationwide division of work. It results in departments—logical groupings of activities—which also often go by the name of divisions, branches, groups, or sections.

2. Purpose types of departments are output-oriented. They include work arrangements built around specific products, geographic locations, markets, or customers. Each department is built around a specific, self-contained purpose.

3. Process types of departments are internally oriented. They involve arranging activities around such basic business functions as manufacturing, sales, and finance.

4. The advantages and disadvantages of purpose types of departmentation are summarized in Exhibit 7–5. The basic advantage is that you can give your continuous, undivided attention to the "purpose." A major disadvantage is that it results in duplication of effort. Purpose-oriented departments are more appropriate where being sensitive and adaptive to the purpose is more important than being efficient.

5. The advantages and disadvantages of process types of departmentation are summarized in Exhibit 7–6. The basic advantage is that managers are functionally specialized and more efficient. The disadvantage is that it can reduce the attention (and responsiveness) given to specific products, customers, markets, or areas. It is most appropriate where jobs are high in volume, and efficiency is paramount.

7. In a matrix organization, project managers are assigned personnel from the various functional departments. This insures a self-contained department for each project; yet the entire organization need not be permanently organized around the temporary projects.

8. The span of control is the number of subordinates reporting directly to a supervisor. In general, the more routine or similar are your subordinates' jobs, the wider can be your span of control.

STUDY ASSIGNMENTS

1. Answer the "Gross Heavy Machinery" corporation questions from the introduction to this chapter.
2. Compare and contrast purpose departmentation and process departmentation.

3. Explain departmentation by product; by customer; by location; by marketing channel; and by business function.

4. Discuss the advantages and disadvantages of purpose departmentation and process departmentation.

5. Explain matrix departmentation, and discuss its advantages and disadvantages.

6. Look at the organization chart of your university. In what way is this a "mixed" organizational design?

7. Which type of departmentation (purpose or process) do you think would be most appropriate for a bookkeeping department? For a new product development department? Why?

8. "It is up to you," your boss tells you. "You can either have the ten salesmen reporting to you, or you can hire two sales managers to report to you. They, in turn will manage five salesmen each." What are the pros and cons of a narrow vs. wide span of control? What will you tell your boss in this case?

9. What are the factors that the Lockheed span of control system takes into consideration? Explain how you would go about using the Lockheed system in practice.

10. Which department is more specialized—one departmentalized by process, or by purpose? Why is this important when you are trying to fit the organization to the task?

NOTES FOR THE CHAPTER

1. See Joseph Litterer, *The Analysis of Organizations* (New York: Wiley, 1965) pp. 174–182; Ernest Dale, *Organizations* (New York: AMA, 1967) pp. 104–130; James March and Herbert Simon, *Organizations* (New York: Wiley, 1958) pp. 24–29.

2. Harold Koontz and Cyril O'Donnell, *Management* (New York: McGraw-Hill, 1966) p. 116; M. Hanen, "Reorganize your Company Around its Markets," *Harvard Business Review*, Vol. 52, No. 6 (November-December 1974) pp. 63–74.

3. Notice how the Buick (and other) managers in Exhibit 7–1 have their own engineering, manufacturing, distribution, and personnel units.

4. James March and Herbert Simon, *Organizations*, pp. 24–25; Litterer, *The Analysis of Organizations*, p. 176; Dale, *Organizations*, pp. 109–110.

5. Tom Burns and G. M. Stalker, *The Management of Innovation* (London: Tavistock Publications, 1961).

6. Alfred Chandler, Jr., *Strategy and Structure* (Cambridge: M.I.T. Press, 1962).

7. Litterer, *Analysis of Organizations*, p. 176.

8. Ernest Dale, *Organizations*, p. 104.

9. March and Simon, *Organizations*, p. 29; Litterer, *Analysis of Organizations*, p. 181.

10. Alfred Chandler, *Strategy and Structure*, pp. 361–368; March and Simon, *Organizations*, p. 329.

11. John F. Mee, "Matrix Organization," *Business Horizons*, Vol. 7, No. 2 (Summer, 1964) p. 70–72.

12. John Rizzo, Robert J. House, and Sydney Lirtzman, "Role Conflict and Ambiguity in Complex Organizations," *Administrative Science Quarterly*, Vol. 15 (June 1970) pp. 150–163; Robert T. Keller, "Role Conflict and Ambiguity: Correlation with Job Satisfaction and Values," *Personnel Psychology*, Vol. 28, No. 1 (Spring 1975).

13. Ernest Dale, *Organizations*, p. 30.

144

14. Ernest Dale, *Organizations*, 1967, p. 95.

15. Joan Woodward, *Industrial Organization: Theory and Practice* (London: Oxford University Press, 1965) pp. 32; 69; 70.

16. Lawrence and Lorsch, *Organization and Environment* (Boston: Harvard University Press) p. 32.

17. Harold Steiglitz, "Optimizing Span of Control," *Management Record*, Vol. 24 (September 1962) p. 27; reprinted in James Gibson, John Ivancevich, and James Donnelly, *Organizations* (Dallas: BPI, 1976) pp. 246–247.

18. James Worthy, "Organization Structures and Employee Morale," *American Sociological Review*, Vol. 15 (1950) pp. 169–179; James Worthy, *Big Business and Free Men* (New York: Harey, 1959) p. 109, quoted in Rocco Carzo and John Yanouzas "Effects of Tall and Flat Organization Structures," *Administrative Science Quarterly*, Vol. 14 (June 1969) p. 178.

19. Quoted in Edwin Ghiselli and J. B. Siegal, "Leadership and Managerial Success in Tall and Flat Organization Structures," *Personnel Psychology*, Vol. 25 (September 1972) p. 623.

20. See, for example, Lyman Porter and Edward E. Lawler, III, "Properties of Organizational Structure in Relation to Job Attitudes and Job Behavior," *Psychological Bulletin*, Vol. 64, No. 1 (1965) pp. 23–51; reprinted in W. E. Scott, Jr. and L. L. Cummings, *Readings in Organizational Behavior and Human Performance* (Homewood: Richard D. Irwin, 1973) pp. 303–327.

21. John Ivancevich and James Donnelly, Jr., "Relation of Organizational Structure to Job Satisfaction, Anxiety, Stress, and Performance," *Administrative Science Quarterly* (June 1975).

22. Ernest Dale, *Organizations*, p. 146; 147–149.

A Framework for Studying the Management Fundamentals

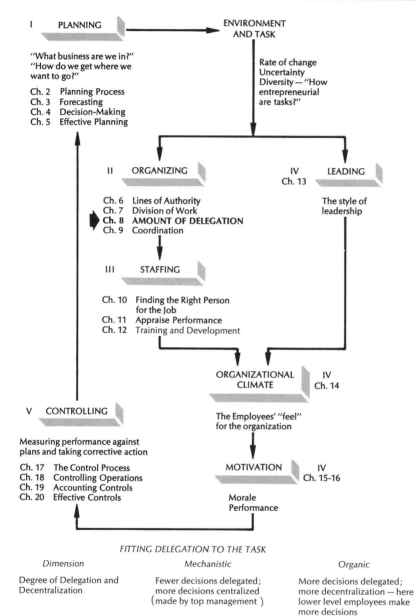

I   PLANNING → ENVIRONMENT AND TASK

Where we are now: Discussing delegation (or "pushing down") authority, and how to decentralize.

"What business are we in?"
"How do we get where we want to go?"

Ch. 2   Planning Process
Ch. 3   Forecasting
Ch. 4   Decision-Making
Ch. 5   Effective Planning

Rate of change
Uncertainty
Diversity — "How entrepreneurial are tasks?"

II   ORGANIZING

Ch. 6   Lines of Authority
Ch. 7   Division of Work
Ch. 8   AMOUNT OF DELEGATION
Ch. 9   Coordination

IV   LEADING
Ch. 13

The style of leadership

III   STAFFING

Ch. 10   Finding the Right Person for the Job
Ch. 11   Appraise Performance
Ch. 12   Training and Development

ORGANIZATIONAL CLIMATE   IV   Ch. 14

V   CONTROLLING

Measuring performance against plans and taking corrective action

Ch. 17   The Control Process
Ch. 18   Controlling Operations
Ch. 19   Accounting Controls
Ch. 20   Effective Controls

The Employees' "feel" for the organization

MOTIVATION   IV   Ch. 15-16

Morale
Performance

FITTING DELEGATION TO THE TASK

Dimension	Mechanistic	Organic
Degree of Delegation and Decentralization	Fewer decisions delegated; more decisions centralized (made by top management)	More decisions delegated; more decentralization — here lower level employees make more decisions

When you have finished studying

8 Delegation and Decentralization

You should be able to:

1. *Define delegation.*

2. *Distinguish between delegation and decentralization.*

3. *Explain how authority, responsibility, and accountability are related.*

4. *Define decentralization.*

5. *Describe the relationship between decentralization and departmentation.*

6. *List seven guidelines for determining how much decentralization exists in an organization.*

7. *Cite six factors which determine the right amount of decentralization.*

8. *Explain why you would (or would not) increase the degree of decentralization in a particular organization.*

INTRODUCTION

How often have you asked someone to do something for you—fill up the tank with gas, pick up clothes at the cleaners, write a report—only to find that the job isn't done?

This kind of day-to-day problem illustrates one of the major problems you'll face as a manager. As a manager, you will have to get the work done through others—each subordinate will be delegated his own task. But how can you be sure that the work is in fact accomplished? What can, and cannot be delegated? How do you monitor performance of tasks you have delegated? What are some of the pitfalls in delegating? These are some of the questions you should be able to answer after studying this chapter.

THE PROCESS OF DELEGATION

Organizing departments and jobs would be impossible without delegation, which we'll define as the pushing down of authority from superior to subordinate. This is because the assignment of responsibility for some depart-

148   ment or job usually goes hand in hand with the delegation of adequate
authority to get the task done. For example, it would be inappropriate for
you to assign a subordinate the responsibility for designing a new product,
and then tell him he hasn't the authority to hire designers or choose the
best design.

It should be clear, though, that while *authority* can be delegated,
responsibility cannot. You can *assign* responsibility to a subordinate. However, most managers and management writers would agree that you are still
ultimately responsible for seeing to it that the job gets done properly. Since
you retain the ultimate responsibility for the performance of the job, delegation of authority also usually entails the creation of *accountability*. Thus
your subordinate automatically becomes accountable to you for the performance of the tasks assigned to him.

FUNDAMENTALS OF DECENTRALIZATION

Decentralization Defined

Decentralization is one of those "in" words that you frequently hear
tossed about by political candidates, school board members, and business
managers. Many of them view decentralization as a panacea—a magical device
that will compensate for poor top management, encourage participation, increase efficiency, and raise morale.

Ironically, though, most people do not have a clear idea of what decentralization is. And, as often as not, when an organization is "decentralized"
it is for the wrong reasons and in the wrong way.

The way many people use the term, decentralization means about the
same thing as delegation—simply pushing authority down to subordinates.
Decentralization, according to them, is the opposite of "centralization" in
which all, or nearly all, of the authority to make decisions and take action
is retained by top management.[1]

But decentralization is and was always meant to be much more than
simply delegation. Decentralization is a philosophy of organization and management, one that implies both selective disbursal *and* concentration of
authority.[2] It involves selectively determining what authority to push down
into the organization; developing standing plans (such as policies) to guide
subordinates who have this authority delegated to them; and implementing
selective but adequate controls for monitoring performance. Thus:

> Decentralization is a philosophy of organization and management
> which involves both selective delegation of authority, as well as con-
> centration of authority through the imposition of policies and selec-
> tive but adequate controls.

Example: Let's look at a simple example in order to contrast delegation and decentralization.

Suppose that you, as plant manager, put one of your foremen in charge of getting a new production line operating. You tell him what you want him to accomplish, and then don't check with him until the end. Here you're dealing with *delegation*. But if you also give him a specific day-to-day schedule to follow, and require him to report his daily progress to you, you're dealing with *decentralization*. So the way we'll define it:

$$decentralization = delegation + control$$

Decentralization and Departmentation

Although they are related, you should clearly see that decentralization and departmentation are two very different things. The former involves delegating authority and imposing selected controls; the latter refers to dividing the work of the organization into logical groupings of activities. The two, however, are sometimes confused. This is because the term "decentralization" is also used to describe an organization which has been departmentalized in a certain way—usually around product divisions.

The reason for this—and this is extremely important—*is that the authority for making a decision can and should be delegated to the level at which the impact of the decision is local*.[3] In an organization departmentalized by business functions (such as that depicted in Exhibit 8–1) the president could delegate sales-related decisions to the sales manager, and production-related decisions to the production manager. For each of these managers, the decisions they would be making would be localized to their own departments. On the other hand, decisions having *companywide* impact—such as those concerning companywide union agreements—would have to be centralized in the president's office.[4]

Exhibit 8.1 Departmentation by Business Function

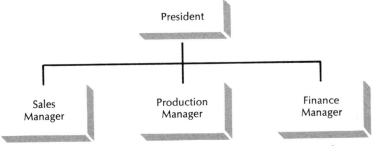

Note: Each manager could only be delegated authority to make decisions involving his own department. Decisions having company-wide impact would have to be centralized in the presidents office.

This is where product departmentation (sometimes called "divisionalization") comes in. As you can see in Exhibit 8–2, the managers of product-oriented divisions are often in charge of what amount to their own miniature companies. All or most of the decisions which have anything to do with their product (whether production, sales, design, or personnel) are "local"— concerned only with their own unit—as far as these product managers are concerned.

Exhibit 8.2 The "Self-Contained" Aspect of Product-Oriented Departments

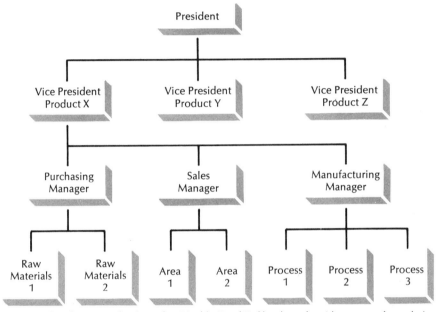

Note: Notice how the vice president for product X (and for Y, and Z, although not shown) has managers for purchasing, sales, and manufacturing reporting to him. His division is "self-contained" in that it can manufacture and sell product X with little or no help from other divisions.

Therefore, what happens when a company opts for product departmentation? It is automatically establishing a situation in which the president can delegate authority for a wider range of decisions to his product managers than he could if each was responsible for only one specific function, such as production, sales, or personnel. It is because you can delegate *more* decisions, and a *wider range* of decisions to subordinates that this type of departmentation has become so closely associated with decentralization. In summary:

1) You can and should delegate authority for a decision to the level where the impact of that decision is local.
2) With product departmentation, each manager is in charge of his own self-contained unit. Thus a wider range of decisions (for pro-

duction, sales, personnel, etc.) are therefore localized to and per-
tain to his division only.

3) Because of this, delegation and decentralization usually proceed
further in companies departmentalized by product (or perhaps
some other "purpose") than by process.

Gauging the Degree of Decentralization

Is there any way to tell just how decentralized some particular company is? There are no hard and fast rules, but the following guidelines are
useful:

1. *The greater the number of decisions* made at lower levels in the organization, the greater the decentralization.
2. *The closer the level* at which the decision is made in relation to the
point where the problem arose the greater the decentralization. Suppose a customer in California has a problem, and the western
division manager is authorized to make the necessary decisions.
Then to that extent the company is more decentralized than if the
boss in New York had to make the decisions.
3. *The more important* are the decisions that can be made at the
lower levels, the greater the decentralization. For example, a company in which division managers can make equipment purchase
decisions for up to $500,000, is more decentralized than one in
which they are authorized to make these decisions up to a limit of
$50,000.
4. *The greater the breadth of decisions* in terms of the number of functions they cover, the more the decentralization. Thus the company
in which division managers are authorized to make production, marketing, and personnel decisions is more decentralized than one in
which the managers can make only production and personnel decisions.
5. *The less a subordinate has to check* with his superior before making
decisions, the greater the degree of decentralization. Thus a company in which a manager does not have to check at all with his
supervisor (or only needs to consult with him after all results are
in), is more decentralized than one in which the manager must get
most of his decisions approved beforehand.
6. *The greater the discretion* permitted by the company's policies, procedures, and rules, the greater the decentralization. Standing plans
such as policies, procedures, and rules, tell employees how they are
to proceed in a given circumstance and therefore can limit the employee's authority.
7. *The narrower the breadth of the controls* imposed on managers,
the greater the degree of decentralization. For example, a company
in which each product-division manager simply has to report once
or twice a year on the rate of return his division earned on its in-

vestment [5] is more decentralized. One in which a variety of day-to-day production, marketing, personnel, etc., decisions are monitored is less decentralized. In the typical "decentralized" company, controls are imposed selectively, carefully giving the manager enough "breathing space" to do his job his way. But they still provide enough feedback to the manager's boss to allow for early identification of problems. [6]

Why Managers Decentralize

Why do managers decentralize? There are several reasons. [7]

Decentralization is said to result in "enlarged," more meaningful (and motivating) jobs for managers. It is also supposed to lead to more prompt attention to problems, and generally to result in more flexible and adaptable organizations. There are several reasons for this. First, the greater delegation means that managers lower in the organization have the authority to make quick, on-the-spot decisions. Also, the (usually) *purpose-oriented* units are more self-contained and their managers can more completely focus on the problems of their "purposes."

With claims like these you can begin to see why many people view decentralization as a panacea; yet decentralization often fails. To understand why, let's look at some of the factors that determine where it is and is not appropriate.

FACTORS THAT DETERMINE HOW MUCH YOU SHOULD DECENTRALIZE

Behavioral Considerations

Instituting the right amount of decentralization—whatever that amount is—assumes that superiors are willing to delegate authority, and that subordinates are willing to assume it. William Newman [8] says that some supervisors are often reluctant to delegate authority, and that many subordinates avoid the responsibility that comes with increased delegation. He cites the following reasons:

Reasons for reluctance to delegate:
1. Some managers get trapped in the "I can do it better myself" fallacy.
2. Some managers lack the ability to direct their subordinates.
3. Some lack confidence in their subordinates.
4. There may be an absence of selective controls that warn of impending difficulties.
5. Some managers have a temperamental aversion to taking a chance and delegating.

Why subordinates avoid responsibility:

1. Often the subordinate finds it easier to ask the boss than to decide for himself how to deal with a problem.
2. Many subordinates fear criticism for mistakes.
3. Some hesitate accepting new assignments when there are a lack of necessary information and resources to do a good job.
4. Some subordinates lack the necessary self-confidence.
5. Positive incentives for assuming the additional load may be inadequate.

What many of these reasons boil down to is that some supervisors and subordinates simply have an aversion to the delegation process. Therefore, the first factor influencing how much decentralization your firm should have is the human factor. You must have superiors and subordinates who are both willing and able to delegate authority and assume additional responsibilities.

Diversification: The Chandler Study

One of the most important things we have discovered about decentralization is that most often it is found in companies which market a diverse, wide range of products. Historian Alfred Chandler was one of the first to discover this.[9]

While Chandler focused on four major companies—General Motors, Standard Oil of New Jersey, Dupont Chemical, and Sears, Roebuck—he also analyzed volumes of information about almost 100 of America's largest companies. Time after time he found that the same pattern had emerged. Certain companies, such as General Electric and Westinghouse, went through three stages—*from expansion of volume* to growth through *geographical disbursion*, and finally to growth through *product diversification. And time after time these diversified companies had opted for more decentralization, and product-oriented departmentation.*

The reason was that the problems of doing business in many diverse markets were so different and varied that a single manager simply could not handle all of them. As one Westinghouse executive, recalling the days prior to decentralization, pointed out:

> All the activities of the company were divided into production, engineering, and sales, each of which was the responsibility of a vice-president. The domain of each vice-president covered the whole diversified and far-flung operations of the corporation. Such an organization of the corporation's management lacks responsiveness. There was too much delay in recognition of problems and in the solution of problems after they were recognized.[10]

In response to problems like these, companies such as Westinghouse and General Electric opted for increased decentralization. They pushed authority for a wide range of decisions down to their product divisions.

The Size of the Organization

We also know from studies of both American [11] and British [12] firms that larger organizations are usually more decentralized than smaller ones.

Occasionally, though, you will find very large organizations which have not decentralized. Here most important decisions remain centralized with top management. This is the case with the largest companies in the steel and paper industries, for example.[13] For these companies, having efficient manufacturing functions is of overriding importance. Flexibility is not a key concern. Thus they have retained the more efficient functional, centralized organization structures.

The "Environment" of the Organization

The environment of your organization—all those things, such as customers and suppliers, which are important to your organization but are largely beyond its control—also helps determine how much you should decentralize.

For example, we know that where companies are very dependent on a large single purchaser (such as a Sears, Roebuck supplier might be) it usually retains a more centralized structure. On the other hand, where the environment is less predictable then firms are usually more decentralized.[14] Here, for example, there may be many suppliers vying for positions with many purchasers. Or research and development may be constantly bringing forth a stream of new products. This is why, as summarized in Exhibit 8–3, organic firms are usually more decentralized than mechanistic ones.[15]

Exhibit 8.3   Fitting Delegation and Decentralization to the Task

	Mechanistic; Routine; mass production	Organic; Unpredictable; made-to- order production
Delegation/ Decentralization	Little	Much

Local Impact of Decisions

Remember, too, that authority can and should be delegated to the lowest level at which the impact of the decision is localized.

In a company departmentalized by business function, the production manager can be delegated authority to make production decisions (since these decisions will only impact his area). However, he could not be delegated

authority to make marketing decisions, since these would impact another
division. But in a company departmentalized around product divisions, the
product manager may have his own production, design, and marketing units.
He could therefore be delegated authority over a wider range of decisions;
this firm would then be more decentralized. These ideas are illustrated in
Exhibit 8–4.

Having Adequate Controls

Finally, remember that how much you can decentralize also depends
on how adequate, and sensitive are your available controls. Without adequate
control devices (such as accounting information feeding back from the depart-

Exhibit 8.4 Delegation and Decentralization

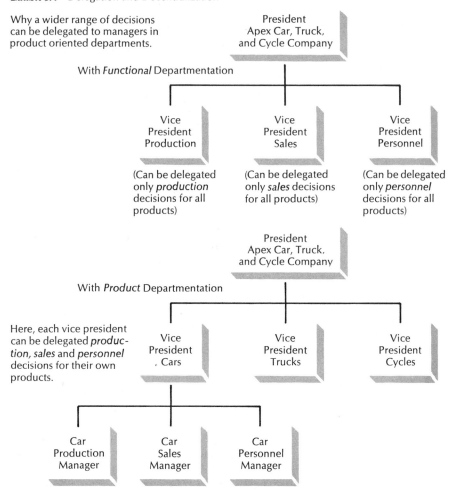

Why a wider range of decisions
can be delegated to managers in
product oriented departments.

President
Apex Car, Truck,
and Cycle Company

With *Functional* Departmentation

Vice
President
Production

Vice
President
Sales

Vice
President
Personnel

(Can be delegated
only *production*
decisions for all
products)

(Can be delegated
only *sales* decisions
for all products)

(Can be delegated
only *personnel*
decisions for all
products)

President
Apex Car, Truck,
and Cycle Company

With *Product* Departmentation

Here, each vice president
can be delegated *produc-
tion, sales* and *personnel*
decisions for their own
products.

Vice
President
. Cars

Vice
President
Trucks

Vice
President
Cycles

Car
Production
Manager

Car
Sales
Manager

Car
Personnel
Manager

156   ments, inventory control systems, etc.) decentralization would be hard to achieve. This is because it would be difficult for you to monitor performance for the decisions you have delegated to subordinates. We will discuss control systems at length in Chapters 17 through 20.

Summary: Some Hints For Determining the Right Amount of Decentralization

First, decentralization requires:
1. Managers and subordinates who are willing and able to assume the responsibilities that go with the increased decentralization.
2. That the impact of the decision a subordinate is delegated authority to make is localized to his department; decentralization, therefore, proceeds further in companies departmentalized by purpose than by process.
3. That adequate controls are available.

In addition, there are three factors which determine the appropriate amount of decentralization for an organization:

4. *The degree of diversification.* Other things equal, the more diversified a company, the more decentralized it will be.
5. *The size of the organization.* Other things equal, the larger the organization, the more decentralized it will be.
6. *The organization's environment.* Other things equal, the more unpredictable the firm's environment, the more decentralized it will be.

One final word. If you look at the factors which determine the "right" amount of decentralization—(numbers 4, 5, and 6) you will notice that they have something in common. From your point of view, *diversity*, *large size*, or an *unpredictable environment* all mean that you have to make many more quick decisions and handle much more information than you might otherwise. As a person beset by a multitude of diverse problems, you could quickly become "overloaded" and incapable of making many necessary decisions.

It is exactly this "information overload" [16] that decentralization is aimed at coping with. It allows you to delegate—push down—a big part of your work load to subordinates, while simply monitoring performance through some well placed controls.

Some Important Things to Remember from This Chapter:

1. Although authority can be delegated, responsibility cannot. You can assign responsibility to a subordinate, but ultimately you are still responsible for seeing to it that the job is done properly.
2. Decentralization is a philosophy of organization and management. It

involves both selective *delegation* of authority as well as *concentration* of authority
through the use of policies and selective but adequate controls.

3. The authority for making a decision can and should be delegated to
the level at which the impact of the decision is local. Because you can delegate
more decisions, and wider range of decisions to subordinates in a "divisionalized,"
product-oriented department, decentralization proceeds further with this type of
departmentation.

4. An organization is more decentralized:

The greater the number of decisions made at lower levels—

The closer the decision-making is to the point where the problems arose—

The more important are the decisions made at the lower level—

The greater the breadth of decisions made by employees at lower levels—

The less a subordinate has to check with his superior—

The greater the discretion permitted by the companies standing plans—

The narrower the breadth of controls imposed on managers.

5. There are six useful guidelines that you can use for determining the
optimum amount of decentralization. First, remember that decentralization requires: managers and subordinates who are willing and able to assume the added
responsibilities; that the impact of the decision which a subordinate is delegated
authority to make is localized to his department; and that adequate controls are
available. In addition, the "right amount" of decentralization depends on: the
degree of diversity your unit faces; the size of your organization; your organization's environment. Remember that diversity, large size, or an unpredictable
environment all mean that you have to make many more quick decisions and
might become "overloaded" if you don't decentralize.

STUDY ASSIGNMENTS

1. "Delegation is essential for organizing. You simply cannot have an
   organization without delegation." Discuss whether you agree or disagree with this statement, and why.
2. Define delegation and decentralization, and distinguish between the
   two.
3. Explain how authority, responsibility, and accountability are related.
4. What is the difference between decentralization and departmentation?
   How are the two related?
5. Discuss seven guidelines for determining how much decentralization
   exists in an organization.
6. Discuss six factors that determine the right amount of decentralization.
7. "Authority for making a decision can and should be delegated to the
   level at which the impact of the decision is local." Discuss the importance of this statement in decentralization and departmentation.

8. "You can talk about delegating all you wish. Some managers will still always delegate too much, and some will delegate too little—it all depends on their personalities." Discuss whether you agree, or disagree with this statement, and why.

9. How would you summarize Chandler's findings on the relationship between diversification and decentralization? How would you account for these findings?

10. Choose an organization with which you are familiar and use our seven guidelines to determine how much decentralization exists in that organization. Then explain why you would (or would not) increase the degree of decentralization in that organization.

NOTES FOR THE CHAPTER

1. Joseph Litterer, *The Analysis of Organizations* (New York: Wiley, 1965) p. 379.

2. Harold Koontz and Cyril O'Donnell, *Management* (New York: McGraw-Hill, 1976) p. 375.

3. See Harold Stieglitz, *Organizational Planning* (New York: The National Industrial Conference Board, Inc., 1962); in Harold Lazarus and E. Kirby Warren, *The Progress of Management* (Englewood Cliffs, N.J.: Prentice-Hall, Inc., 1968) p. 72.

4. Gary Dessler, *Organization and Management* (Englewood Cliffs, N.J.: Prentice-Hall, 1976) pp. 107–108.

5. Rate of Return on Investment (ROI) is usually calculated by dividing net income ("profits") by the investment in such things as plant, equipment, and inventories.

6. For discussions of points 1–7, see Arlyn Melcher, *Structure and Process of Organizations* (Englewood Cliffs: Prentice Hall, 1976). He presents a questionnaire for measuring degree of delegation on pp. 153–154: Ernest Dale, *Planning and Developing the Company Organization Structure*, Research Report No. 20 (New York: American Management Association, 1952) p. 107; and Harold Koontz and Cyril O'Donnell, *Management* (New York: McGraw-Hill, 1976) pp. 374–375, present good discussions of decentralization.

7. Based on Joseph Litterer, *The Analysis of Organizations*, p. 375.

8. See William Newman, Charles Summer, and E. Kirby Warren, *The Process of Management* (Englewood Cliffs, N.J.: Prentice-Hall, 1967) pp. 95–98.

9. Alfred Chandler, *Strategy and Structure* (Cambridge: The M.I.T. Press, 1962).

10. Chandler, *Strategy and Structure*, p. 366.

11. Ernest Dale, *Organization* (New York: American Management Association, 1967) p. 110.

12. John Child, "Predicting and Understanding Organization Structure," *Administrative Science Quarterly* (June 1973) pp. 168–185.

13. Ernest Dale, *Organization*, p. 10; Alfred Chandler, *Strategy and Structure*, p. 335.

14. Sergio Mindlin and Howard Albrich present a good review of this in "Interorganizational Dependence: A Review of the Concept and a Re-Examination of the Findings of the Aston Group," *Administrative Science Quarterly*, Vol. 20 (September 1975) pp. 382–391.

15. Tom Burns and G. M. Stalker, *The Management of Innovation* (London: Tavistock Publications, 1961).

16. Daniel Katz and Robert L. Kahn, *Social Psychology of Organizations* (New York: John Wiley & Sons, Inc., 1966) p. 233.

A Framework for Studying the Management Fundamentals

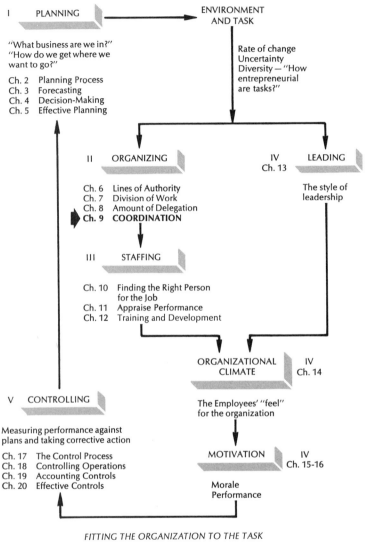

I   PLANNING   ENVIRONMENT
                                 AND TASK

"What business are we in?"
"How do we get where we
want to go?"

Rate of change
Uncertainty
Diversity — "How
entrepreneurial
are tasks?"

Ch. 2   Planning Process
Ch. 3   Forecasting
Ch. 4   Decision-Making
Ch. 5   Effective Planning

II   ORGANIZING   IV   LEADING
                            Ch. 13

Ch. 6   Lines of Authority   The style of
Ch. 7   Division of Work   leadership
Ch. 8   Amount of Delegation
Ch. 9   COORDINATION

III   STAFFING

Ch. 10   Finding the Right Person
            for the Job
Ch. 11   Appraise Performance
Ch. 12   Training and Development

ORGANIZATIONAL   IV
CLIMATE   Ch. 14

V   CONTROLLING

The Employees' "feel"
for the organization

Measuring performance against
plans and taking corrective action

Ch. 17   The Control Process
Ch. 18   Controlling Operations   MOTIVATION   IV
Ch. 19   Accounting Controls   Ch. 15-16
Ch. 20   Effective Controls

Morale
Performance

Where we are now: Discussing how to fit each of our seven dimensions of organization (lines of authority, etc.) to the task.

FITTING THE ORGANIZATION TO THE TASK

Dimensions of Organization	Mechanistic	Organic
Lines of Authority	Clear — no deviations	Broad — permit deviations
Line and Staff	Clear distinction	Little distinction
Departmentation	By process	By purpose
Specialization	Very specialized units	More enlarged, less specialized units
Delegation	Little	Much
Span of Control	Narrow	Wide
Coordination	Use "chain of command"	Use special committees

When you have finished studying

Modern Organization Theory: A Contingency Approach

You should be able to:

1. Cite the characteristics of Bureaucracy.

2. List the implications that Weber's bureaucracy and Fayol's principles have for our six dimensions of organizational structure.

3. Cite the characteristics of McGregor's "Theory Y" assumptions, and of Likert's System IV organization.

4. List the implications which the behavioral theories have for our six dimensions of organizational structure.

5. Discuss the findings of three "contingency theory" writers.

6. Present the characteristics of mechanistic and organic organization.

7. Develop sample organization structures for mechanistic and organic types of situations.

INTRODUCTION

William Levitt was the founder of the firm that had built "Levittowns"—communities of low-cost homes—throughout the country. The firm was amazingly successful until it was taken over by ITT, a large conglomerate. When asked why his firm did so poorly after the takeover, William Levitt replied:

> *"The system [which ITT] so successfully built up does not apply to Levitt and Sons. . . . In an entrepreneurial enterprise such as this the rigid system of controls necessary to a conglomerate like [ITT] just won't work. . . . It works beautifully with a routine, repetitious business. You can run hotels with it, you can rent cars with it, you can make refrigerators with it. . . . But you can't build homes with it."*

What was it about Levitt that made ITT's rigid organizational structure inappropriate? Can you think of any other situations where a more organic, "entrepreneurial" structure such as Levitt previously had would be appropriate? These are some of the questions you should be able to answer by the end of this chapter.

162   *DIMENSIONS OF ORGANIZATION STRUCTURE*

The purpose of a theory is to explain a set of facts and their relation to one another. When thousands of businessmen recently introduced "bicentennial" products they were all theorizing that Americans would be caught in a bicentennial spirit that would create a demand for these products. When a doctor diagnoses a patient, his diagnosis is actually a theory (or a tentative theory—a *hypothesis*) which *explains* how some illness may be causing the observed symptoms. Based on his diagnosis (or theory) the doctor can then *predict* the effects which alternative medications may have on the patient.

Exhibit 9.1   The Three Purposes of a Theory

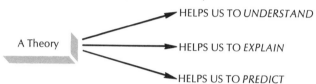

Over the past 50 years we have developed theories of organizations. These theories help us to *understand* and *explain* the structure and behavior of organizations. And they help us to *predict* how some change—such as widening the span of control—may influence the rest of the structure of the organization. Several different theories have been proposed, and we will discuss some of the most important ones in this chapter. At the end of this chapter you should be able to explain why:

1. Clear *lines of authority* and adherence to the chain of command are appropriate for some companies, but not others;
2. Some companies make *use of staff* personnel, and others do not;
3. Some companies *departmentalize* by process, and others do so by purpose;
4. Jobs in some companies are *highly specialized*, and in others they are self-contained, and "enlarged";
5. Why some companies are far more *decentralized* than others;
6. Why some companies have narrow *spans of control*, and some have wide ones.

Finally toward the end of this chapter, we will discuss a *seventh* important dimension of organization structure which up to this point we have neglected —*coordination*.

CLASSICAL ORGANIZATION THEORIES 163

Weber's Bureaucracy

Today when we hear the word "bureaucracy" it immediately brings to mind visions of a ponderous, slowly moving organization—one steeped in red tape, meaningless hurdles, and inefficiency.

Most people are therefore surprised to find out that one of the earliest proponents of bureaucracy, Max Weber, heralded it as a faster, more efficient way to get things done. As he put it:

> The fully developed bureaucratic mechanism compares with other organizations exactly as does the machine with nonmechanical modes of production . . . precision, speed, unambiguity, continuity, discretion, unity, . . . these are raised to the optimal point in a strictly bureaucratic administration.[1]

Bureaucracy, to Weber, was an ideal or "pure form" of organization, the standard against which all organizations should be measured. He said that this ideal type of organization structure had the following characteristics:

1. A *well-defined hierarchy* of authority with clear lines of authority and control and responsibility concentrated at the top of the hierarchy.
2. A *high degree of specialization.*
3. A division of work based on *functional departmentation.*
4. A *system of rules* covering the rights and duties of employees.
5. A definite *system of procedures* for dealing with the work situation and "rationally" coordinating activities.
6. A *centralized* system of *written documents* ("the files") for collecting and summarizing the activities of the organization.
7. *Impersonality* of relationships between employees.
8. *Recruitment* of managers on the basis of *ability* and technical knowledge.[2]

This bureaucracy, or "bureaucratic model," was one of the first theories of organization. It was a theory that Weber hoped would be used to understand how and why organizations were structured as they were, and the standard against which other organizations would be compared.

But like most "ideal" forms of anything it was an extreme, an exaggeration. Having *some* specialization, *adequate* procedures and rules, and *some* centralization was and is clearly better than having no organization at all. But Weber's bureaucratic model quickly became synonymous with a rigid, unbending, inflexible structure manned by "robots."

Whereas Max Weber was a philosopher, Henri Fayol was a practicing manager. He had spent 30 years as top executive of a coal and steel company. His model of organization, which was codified in a number of "principles," clearly reflected this "hands on" experience. Here are some of his more important principles of organization:

1. *Division of work.* Fayol felt that for both management and labor there should be a "specialization of functions," such that different people carry out different, *specialized* activities.

2. *Authority and responsibility.* Authority is the "right to give orders and the power to exact obedience." It was Fayol who first stated the classic case as to why authority must be commensurate with responsibility.

3. *Unity of command.* This principle held that an employee should receive orders from only one superior.

4. *Centralization.* Unlike Weber, Fayol did not prescribe that all authority should be centralized at the top of the organizational hierarchy. Instead he believed that the degree of delegation was a simple "question of proportion," something that depended on the nature of the situation and the subordinate's competence. He said that "the degree of centralization must vary according to different cases."

5. *Scaler chain.* The scaler chain was "the chain of superiors ranging from the ultimate authority to the lowest ranks." According to this principle, there should be a clear, unbroken chain of command ranging from the top to the bottom of the organization structure.[3]

In some respects Weber's bureaucracy and Fayol's principles were quite different. For one thing, bureaucracy was proposed as the "ideal" model of organization against which all organization's should be rated. On the other hand, Fayol's principles were supposed to be applied flexibly. Fayol said that centralization, degree of specialization, and so forth, had to vary from situation to situation.

But the word "principles" has a connotation of rigidity. And Fayol's emphasis on a clear chain of command, unity of command, and specialization, has over the years left most people with the impression that his model is as unbending and as extreme as Weber's.

What the Classical Theories Mean for Organization Structure

In terms of our six dimensions of organization structure, we can summarize these classical organization theories as follows:

1. *Lines of authority.* There should be clear, unbroken lines of authority stretching from the top to the bottom of the organization. Each person should have only one superior.

2. *Line and staff.* Fayol and Weber espoused specialization. So we
   could assume that they would prescribe the use of both line managers and staff specialists in the management of the organization.
3. *Departmentation.* Organizations should be functionally departmentalized, since this type of specialization is more efficient.
4. *Degree of specialization of jobs.* Employee's jobs should be highly
   specialized, with each man an expert at carrying out his duties.
5. *Delegation and decentralization.* In the bureaucratic model, delegation is minimized and as many decisions as possible are made at
   the top of the organizational hierarchy. Fayol was flexible on this
   point.
6. *Span of control.* A narrow span of control, usually less than six, was
   prescribed for most managers (see Exhibit 9–2).

BEHAVIORAL THEORIES OF ORGANIZATION

The Changing Business Environment

The classical theories of the early 1900s faced increasing criticism during the '30s and '40s. They had been developed during a simpler era, one in
which smaller, less complex organizations and the "protestant ethic" of hard
work prevailed. But as the population shifted from farms into cities, workers
increasingly were pushed into close proximity to each other and the values
in America began to change.[4]

People began to think less of individualism and the protestant ethic,
and more about their mutual dependence on their fellow man. This shift in
values was reinforced by the Great Depression, which occurred between 1929
and 1933. Unemployment rose from 3.2 percent to 30 percent. And gradually
at first, the notion of the hard-working, self-made man as a guarantee of a
successful economy was rejected. Increasingly the prevailing values played
down achievement by individuals and emphasized the importance of security
and getting along with others.

Increasingly the classical theories were brought under fire. Writers said
that they assumed that employees were little more than robots, people who
always acted rationally and in their own self-interest, and who required and
preferred detailed guidance and close supervision. As the pendulum began
to swing away from the classicists, these criticisms became exaggerated. Soon
all classicists were being accused of assuming that employees were little more
than cogs in the machinery.

New theories of organization began to emerge—theories which placed
greater emphasis on the morale of employees, and on their need to interact
within work groups. Let us look at two of these "Behavioral" theories, Mc-
Gregor's "Theory Y" and Likert's "System IV."

Exhibit 9.2   The Organization as Viewed by the Classicists

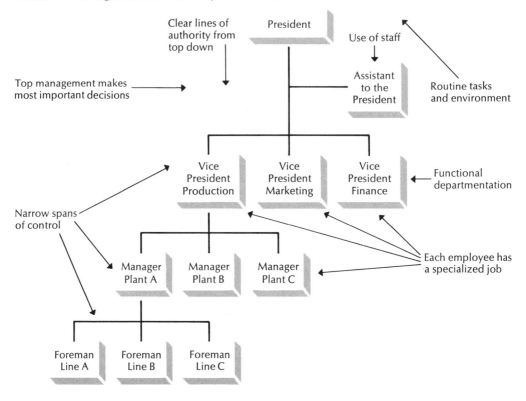

McGregor's Theory X and Theory Y

According to Douglas McGregor, the classical organization (with its centralized decision-making, highly specialized jobs, and close supervision) was a reflection of certain basic assumptions the classical writers held about human nature. These assumptions, which McGregor somewhat arbitrarily classified as Theory X, held that:

1. The average human being has an inherent dislike of work and will avoid it if he can. . . .
2. Because of this human characteristic of dislike of work, most people must be coerced, controlled, directed, and threatened with punishment to get them to put forth adequate effort. . . .
3. The average human being prefers to be directed, wishes to avoid responsibility. . . .[5]

In their place he proposed "Theory Y," a set of assumptions which he brought forth as a "modest beginning for a new theory with respect to the management of human resources." The assumptions of Theory Y were that:

1. The average human being does not inherently dislike work.
2. External control and the threat of punishment are not the only means for bringing about effort toward organizational objectives.
3. People are motivated best by satisfying their "higher order" needs for achievement, esteem, and self-actualization.
4. The average human being learns, under proper conditions, not only to accept but to seek responsibilities.
5. The capacity to exercise a relatively high degree of imagination, ingenuity, and creativity in the solution of organizational problems is widely, not narrowly distributed in the population.[6]

As you can imagine, this new set of assumptions had some very profound implications for the way organizations would be structured. Many of the prescriptions of the classical theories—for centralization of authority, close supervision, highly specialized functional divisions of work, and so forth— were overturned. In their place, as we will see, McGregor and his associates prescribed a very different organization structure. Theirs was built on delegation of authority, more general, less close supervision, and enlarged and more interesting jobs.

Likert's System IV

Like McGregor, Rensis Likert opposed the kinds of organizations which classical writers seemed to be prescribing. He referred to these classical organizations as System I. In these organizations, he said:

1. Management is seen as having no confidence or trust in subordinates.
2. The bulk of decisions and the goal-setting of the organization are made at the top.
3. Subordinates are forced to work with fear, threats, and punishment.
4. Control is highly concentrated in top management.[7]

In their place, Likert proposed System IV, an organization built on Theory Y-type assumptions. In System IV organizations:

1. Management is seen as having complete confidence and trust in subordinates.
2. Decision-making is widely disbursed and decentralized.
3. Workers are motivated by participation and involvement in decision-making.
4. There is extensive, friendly superior-subordinate interaction.
5. There is widespread responsibility for control with the lower echelon fully involved.[8]

What the Behavioral Theories Mean for Organization Structure

McGregor's Theory Y assumptions and Likert's System IV organization prescribe a very different type of organization structure than did the assumptions and principles of classical theory. In terms of the six dimensions

168   of organization structure we have been using, these behavioral theories can
be summarized as follows:

1. *Lines of authority.* Less emphasis on clear lines of authority, and
   less adherence to the chain of command.
2. *Line and staff.* Less specialized jobs in which line authority and staff
   authority can overlap.
3. *Departmentation.* Departmentation based more around enlarged,
   self-contained, purpose-types of departments.
4. *Degree of specialization of jobs.* Much less emphasis on specialization, and an emphasis on "job enlargement."
5. *Delegation and decentralization.* High degrees of delegation and
   decentralization; a minimum number of decisions centralized at the
   top of the hierarchy.
6. *Span of control.* Wide span of control, on the assumption that the
   employees can be trusted and need not be closely supervised (see
   Exhibit 9–3).

Exhibit 9.3   The Organization as Seen by Behavioralists

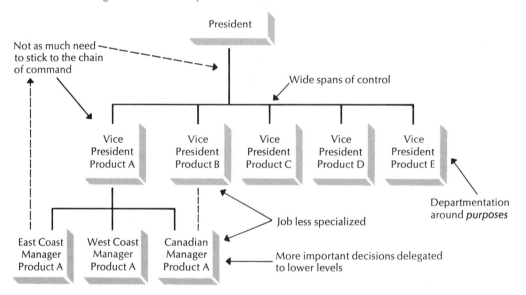

CONTINGENCY APPROACHES TO ORGANIZATION

Why a "Contingency" Approach?

The classical and behavioral theories of organization each arrived at
very different conclusions about how organizations should be structured. However, they both had one important thing in common. Both were "universal"
theories, since their proponents prescribed them as the "best" type of organi-

zation regardless of the situation. Whether you were organizing a production plant, a hospital, or a business school, *classical* theorists generally recommended centralization, high degrees of specialization, functional departmentation, and so on. *Behavioral* theorists recommended decentralization, purpose-types of departmentation, and enlarged jobs.

In the past few years a third type of organization theory has developed. This "contingency" theory holds that the "best" organization structure varies from situation to situation. The "contingency" theory does not render useless the classical, or behavioral theories; it merely helps to place them in their proper perspective.

The Woodward Studies

Almost from their outset, the studies by Joan Woodward and her associates were aimed at trying to understand why organization structure seemed to have no relation to success for the companies they studied. The research team spent months analyzing volumes of data on company history and background, size, and policies and procedures. None of these factors seemed to explain why some successful firms had classical mechanistic structures, while others had behavioral, organic ones. Finally the Woodward team decided to classify the companies according to their "production technologies," as follows:

1. *Unit and small-batch production.* These companies produced one-at-a-time prototypes and specialized units to customers' requirements.
2. *Large batch and mass production.* These companies produced large batches of products on assembly lines.
4. *Process production.* These companies produced products such as paper and petroleum products through continuously running facilities.

Now their findings began to make sense. It was clear that a *different type of organization structure was appropriate for each type of technology.* Some of Woodward's findings are summarized in Exhibit 9–4. Notice that organic structures prevailed in the unit and process productions firms; mass productions firms had mechanistic structures.

In terms of our six dimensions of organization structure, the Woodward findings can be summarized as follows:

1. *Lines of authority.* The lines of authority and adherence to the chain of command are rigid in mass production firms, but more informal and flexible in unit and process production firms.
2. *Line and staff.* Line and staff distinctions are clearest in mass production firms. There is little distinction between line and staff authority in unit and process production firms.

Exhibit 9.4   Summary of Joan Woodward's Research Findings

	Unit and Small Batch Firms (Example: Custom Built Cars)	Large Batch and Mass Production (Example: Mass-Produced Cars)	Process Production (Example: Oil Refinery)
Chain of command	Not Clear	Clear	Not Clear
Line-Staff	No distinction	Clear distinction	No distinction
Span of Control	Narrow	Wide	Narrow
Departmentation	Purpose	Process	Purpose
Overall Organization	Organic	Mechanistic	Organic

Note: Summary of data showing how production technology and organization structure are related.

3. *Departmentation.* There is a *functional* departmentation in mass production firms, and *purpose* types of departmentation in unit and process production firms.
4. *Degree of specialization of jobs.* Jobs are highly specialized in mass production firms, and less so in unit and process production firms.
5. *Delegation and decentralization.* Organizations tend to be centralized in mass production firms, and decentralized in unit and process production firms.
6. *Span of control.* Unit and process production firms have smaller supervisory level spans of control than do mass production firms.[9]

The Burns and Stalker Studies

Tom Burns and G. M. Stalker studied about 20 companies in the United Kingdom. They sought to determine what type of organization structure was best for different types of industries. The companies studied came from a variety of industries, and included a rayon mill, and several electronics firms.

Rayon Mill: The rayon mill was at one extreme. In order to be successful in this highly competitive industry, the firm had to keep costs to a minimum and be as efficient as possible. Therefore their very existence depended on keeping unexpected occurrences to a minimum and maintaining steady, high volume production runs.

The researchers found that this organization was a "pyramid of knowledge." It was highly centralized and run on the basis of elaborate policies, procedures, and rules. Job descriptions were carefully defined, and everyone from the top of the organization to the bottom had a very specialized job to do.[10]

Electronics Firms: The electronics firms were at the other extreme.
These firms' existence depended on their ability to continuously introduce new
and innovative electronic components. They also had to be constantly on the
alert to new innovations by their competitors. Flexibility and creativity (rather
than efficiency) were paramount for these companies.

Here the researchers found that there was a "deliberate attempt to
avoid specifying individual tasks." Not only did employees not have highly
specialized jobs; their jobs often changed from week to week and day to day.
These firms usually did not even have organization charts, and there was no
careful adherence to the chain of command. When a problem arose, an
employee simply took it to the person he felt was in the best position to solve
it. This often meant bypassing the "formal" chain of command. Decision-
making authority was pushed down to the lowest levels, where the employees
were in the best position to cope with problems as they arose.

Conclusions: Their analyses of these different firms led Burns and
Stalker to distinguish (as we saw in Chapter 1) between two different types of
organization which they called *Mechanistic* and *Organic*. The rayon mill was
typical of Mechanistic organizations; the electronics firms were typical of the
Organic ones.

In terms of the six dimensions of organization structure we have discussed, the Burns and Stalker findings can be summarized as follows:

1. *Lines of authority.* In mechanistic organizations the lines of authority are clear, and everyone closely adheres to the chain of command. In organic organizations, employees' jobs are always changing
   and the lines of authority are not so clear. Here there is less emphasis on sticking closely to the chain of command, and much more
   emphasis on speaking directly with the person who might have an
   answer to the problem.
2. *Line and staff.* In mechanistic organizations there is a clear distinction between line authority and staff authority. In organic organizations jobs are constantly being revised, and employees with "staff"
   authority one day may well have "line" authority the next day.
3. *Departmentation.* In mechanistic organizations, (with their emphasis
   on efficiency), process types of departmentation prevail. In organic
   organizations, (where flexibility is the rule), purpose types of departmentation prevail.
4. *Degree of specialization of jobs.* In mechanistic organizations each
   employee has a highly specialized job at which he is expected to
   become an expert. In organic organizations, "job enlargement" is the
   rule.
5. *Delegation and decentralization.* In mechanistic organizations, most
   important decisions are centralized. In organic ones, more important
   decisions are made at lower levels; they are more decentralized.

172

6. *Span of control.* The span of control is narrow in mechanistic organizations, and there is close supervision. Spans are wider in organic organizations, and supervision is more general.

The Lawrence and Lorsch Studies—Departmentation and Coordination

Two Harvard professors, Paul Lawrence and Jay Lorsch, set out to determine "what kind of organization does it take to deal with various economic and market conditions?" [11] They focused on two important aspects of organization structure: "differentiation" (the division of work of the organization into departments) and "integration" (coordination).

The researchers studied several firms in the plastics, and container industries.[12] Their findings are summarized in Exhibit 9–5.

Container Firms: In the *container* firms the tasks which the marketing, research, and production departments had to accomplish were all quite routine. There was little difficulty in determining what kind of products should be developed, manufactured, and sold. And all departments could usually get very quick feedback concerning the success of their job performance. *All* departments, therefore, had similar "classical" structures. Since all the departments were similar (and classical) coordination was a straightforward matter. Coordination was accomplished through the use of policies, procedures, rules, and through the company's chain of command. The manager of each department brought his problems to the president, who saw to it that the three departments were working in unison.

Plastics Firms: In the *plastics* firms, on the other hand, only the production and marketing departments faced such routine tasks. And they, too, had the more efficient classical-type structures.

Exhibit 9.5   Summary of Lawrence and Lorsch Findings

	Production Departments	*Marketing Departments*	*Research Departments*
Plastics Firms	Very predictable tasks	Very predictable tasks	Very *unpredictable* tasks
	"Classical" organization structures	"Classical" organization structures	"*Behavioral*" organization structures
	Much "Differentiation"; coordination achieved by special committees, departments and individuals		
Container Firms	Very predictable tasks	Very predictable tasks	Very predictable tasks
	"Classical" organization structures	"Classical" organization structures	"Classical" organization structures
	Little "Differentiation"; coordination achieved by use of the "chain of command," and standing plans		

But the research departments faced much uncertainty. The employees   could not accurately predict what would be the best type of product to develop. It took them much longer to get feedback on the success of their job performance than it did the people in the production and marketing departments. *The structures of the research departments were therefore much different from those of the other departments.* They were structured for flexibility and creativity and had "behavioral," organic-type structures.

Because of this "differentiation" between departments in the plastics firms, special coordinating committees and departments had been established. Instead of relying on standing plans and adherence to the chain of command, special full-time coordinators were appointed. They cut across the hierarchy and kept the lines of communication open between employees in the marketing, production, and research departments.

In terms of the dimensions of organization structure we have been using, we can summarize the Lawrence and Lorsch findings as follows:

1. *Line of authority.* Where tasks were routine and predictable (such as for the departments in the container firms) lines of authority were very clear. There was also strict adherence to the chain of command. Where tasks were more ambiguous and unpredictable (as in the research departments of the plastics firms) it was not so clear "who reported to who." Here there was much less adherence to the chain of command.
2. *Line and staff.* Lawrence and Lorsch did not specifically deal with this dimension.
3. *Departmentation.* Where tasks were routine and predictable, process types of departmentation prevailed. Where tasks were ambiguous and unpredictable, purpose types of departmentation prevailed.
4. *Degree of specialization of jobs.* Where tasks were routine and predictable, jobs were much more specialized. Where tasks were ambiguous and unpredictable, jobs were more enlarged.
5. *Delegation and decentralization.* Where tasks were routine and predictable, decision-making was centralized toward the top of the hierarchy. Where tasks were ambiguous and unpredictable, there was much more delegation.
6. *Span of control.* Where tasks were routine and predictable, a narrow span seemed appropriate. Where tasks were ambiguous and unpredictable, wider spans prevailed.
7. *Coordination.* In situations such as faced by the container firms, coordination is achieved through standing plans and adherence to the chain of command. In situations such as faced by the plastics firms, coordination can be achieved by special "coordinators." Their job is to cut across the organizational hierarchy and keep the lines of communication open between employees in different departments.

Exhibit 9.6   Fitting Our Seven Dimensions of Organization Structure to the Task

	Mechanistic Structures	*Organic Structures*
Type of Tasks You'll Find here	Predictable, routine tasks and environment; ability to forecast accurately; job requirements very clear; little difficulty in determining the product to be developed, manufactured, or sold; quick feedback concerning the success of job performance.	Unpredictable, nonroutine entrepreneurial tasks and environment; inability to forecast accurately; job requirements are not at all clear in most instances and may change from day to day; there is a great deal of difficulty in determining what the best type of product to be developed, manufactured, and sold is; adding to the ambiguity is the fact that it takes a long time to get feedback concerning the success of job performance.
Examples of Organizations With This Type of Structure	Assembly-line factory, and a bookkeeping department.	New product, research and development departments.
Emphasis	Here the stress is on *efficiency*.	The stress here is on *creativity* and *flexibility*.
Dimensions of Organization Structure:		
Lines of Authority.	Very clear lines of authority from superior to subordinate, and rigid adherence to the chain of command.	Lines of authority often "fuzzy" with much less emphasis on rigidity adhering to the chain of command. The unity of command principle is often violated here and an employee will often find himself taking orders from more than one superior.
Line and staff.	A very clear distinction between line and staff authority. Extensive use of staff personnel.	Here there is often little distinction between line, and staff authority. Instead, everyone turns to any employee who is considered an expert on the problem at hand, and he is given the resources and authority to get the problem solved. There is less use of formal staff personnel.
Departmentation.	Emphasis here on the more efficient process types of departmentation such as by business function.	Emphasis here on the more self-contained, adaptable, purpose types of departmentation such as by product, customer, marketing channel, or location.
Degree of Specialization of Units and jobs	Highly specialized jobs in which each person is expected to become an expert within his own very limited field.	More emphasis here on self-contained, enlarged or enriched jobs.

(Continued)

	Mechanistic Structures	Organic Structures
Delegation and Decentralization.	There are fewer, and less important decisions made at the lower levels and the subordinates have little discretion and must check constantly with their superiors before making decisions. Thus, there is a minimum of delegation and decentralization here.	Many more decisions made at the lower levels, and the decisions are more important and cover a wider range of functions. Subordinates have a great deal of discretion and need only check occasionally with their superiors before making a decision. Thus, there is a great deal of delegation and decentralization here.
Span of Control	While routine tasks should permit wider spans, these mechanistic structures are usually associated with close supervision, and therefore narrower spans.	While more unpredictable tasks *should* require *narrower* **spans**, these organic structures are usually associated with "general" supervision, and wider spans of control that help keep morale high.
Coordination	Emphasis here is on the use of policies, procedures, and rules as well as use of hierarchy for coordination.	Emphasis here is on special coordinators—individuals, departments or committees—whose job it is to cut across the hierachy and keep communications between departments open.

A CONTINGENCY MODEL OF ORGANIZATION— MECHANISTIC AND ORGANIC STRUCTURE

These "contingency" findings can help us to understand why different organization structures are appropriate for different tasks.[13] At one extreme are the organizations for performing predictable, routine tasks, such as assembling autos or bookkeeping. Here efficiency is emphasized, and successful organizations are *mechanistic*.[14] They stress adherence to rules and to the chain of command; highly specialized jobs; close supervision; and functional departmentation.

At the opposite extreme, organizations such as research labs and new product development departments have unpredictable, nonroutine tasks. Here creativity and entrepreneurial activities are emphasized. To facilitate such activities these organizations are *organic*.[15] They don't urge employees to "play it by the rules," or to closely abide to the formal chain of command. Jobs are more enlarged and self-contained, and departments are organized around purposes. In Exhibit 9–6 we have summarized the characteristics of each of our dimensions of organization structure as they would appear in mechanistic, and organic organizations.

Some Important Things to Remember from This Chapter:

1. The purpose of a theory is to explain a set of facts and their relation to each other.

2. In terms of our six dimensions of organization structure we can summarize the classical organization theories of Weber and Fayol as follows. They had: clear unbroken lines of authority; clear distinctions between line and staff; functional departmentation; highly specialized jobs; minimum delegation and decentralization; a narrow span of control.

3. The behavioral theories of organization emerged during an era in which the prevailing values played down achievement by individuals and emphasized the importance of the group. In terms of our six dimensions of organization structure, the prescriptions of behaviorists like Likert and McGregor can be summarized as follows. Organizations should have: less emphasis on clear lines of authority; less distinction between line and staff authority; purpose types of departmentation; less specialization of jobs; more delegation and decentralization; wider spans of control.

4. Remember that both the classical and behavioral theories of organization were "universal" theories. Proponents described them as the "best" types of organization regardless of the situation.

5. Contingency organization theory helps us put the classical and behavioral prescriptions into their proper place. The work of people like Joan Woodward, Burns and Stalker, and Lawrence and Lorsch clearly show that the "best" type of organization varies from situation to situation. At one extreme are mechanistic organizations; these are best for performing routine, predictable tasks such as assembling autos, or bookkeeping. Here efficiency is emphasized. At the other extreme are organic organizations; these are best for accomplishing the creative, entrepreneurial tasks carried out in units such as research labs and new product development departments.

STUDY ASSIGNMENTS

1. The introduction to this chapter described the problem that Levitt had running his building business in the rigid manner prescribed by ITT. Could ITT have gone through with the purchase of Levitt, and still avoided this problem? How?

2. What is the purpose of a theory? Give some examples of theories with which you are familiar.

3. What are the characteristics of bureaucracy?

4. Discuss the implications that Weber's Bureaucracy and Fayol's principles have for our six dimensions of organizational structure.

5. Briefly describe the assumptions of McGregor's "Theory Y" and Likert's "System IV" organization.

6. Discuss the implications which the behavioral theories have for our six dimensions of organization structure.

7. Discuss the findings of three "contingency theory" writers.
8. You have been asked to give a lecture on "the basics of mechanistic and organic organization structures." Discuss how you would compare and contrast the two.
9. Answer the four questions Bob Ellis put to you in the Introduction to Chapter 6.
10. Choose one very familiar organization that you feel is either organic or mechanistic. Look closely at the management functions in this organization. Pay particular attention to our seven dimensions of organization structure. What makes this organization particularly appropriate for dealing with the type of tasks it has? If you chose an organic organization, why do you think it would be *inappropriate* for routine tasks? If you chose a mechanistic organization, what is it about this organization that you think would make it particularly *inappropriate* for dealing with entrepreneurial, creative tasks?

NOTES FOR THE CHAPTER

1. Max Weber, "Bureaucracy." From Max Weber: *Essays in Sociology*, translated and edited by H. H. Gerth and C. Wright Mills. Copyright 1946, by Oxford University Press. Reprinted in Joseph A. Litterer, *Organizations: Structure and Behavior* (New York: John Wiley and Sons, Inc., 1969) p. 34.
2. Based on Richard D. Hall, "Intraorganizational Structural Variation," *Administrative Science Quarterly*, Vol. 7, No. 3 (December 1962) pp. 295–308, in W. Scott, Jr., and L. L. Cummings, *Readings in Organizational Behavior and Human Performance* (Homewood: Irwin, 1973); and Rolf Rogers, *Organizational Theory* (Boston: Allyn and Bacon, 1975) pp. 5–6.
3. Daniel A. Wren, *The Evolution of Management Thought* (New York: The Ronald Press, 1972) p. 220; James Gibson, John Ivancevich, James Donnelly, Jr., *Organizations* (Dallas: BPI, 1976) pp. 268–273.
4. See Daniel Wren, *The Evolution of Management Thought*.
5. Douglas McGregor, *The Human Side of Enterprise* (New York: McGraw-Hill, 1960) pp. 16–18, quoted in Daniel Wren, *The Evolution of Management Thought*, p. 449.
6. Daniel Wren, *The Evolution of Management Thought*, p. 450.
7. Based on Paul Hersey and Kenneth Blanchard, *Management of Organizational Behavior* (Englewood Cliffs, N.J.: Prentice-Hall, Inc., 1969) pp. 52–56.
8. Hersey and Blanchard, *Management of Organizational Behavior*, pp. 52–54.
9. Joan Woodward, *Industrial Organization: Theory and Practice* (London: Oxford, 1965).
10. Tom Burns and G. M. Stalker, *The Management of Innovation* (London: Tavistock Publications, 1961) p. 82.
11. Paul R. Lawrence and J. Lorsch, *Organization and Environment* (Boston: Division of Research, Graduate School of Business Administration, Harvard University, 1967) p. 1.
12. They also studied several food industry companies.
13. Quoted from Gary Dessler, *Organization and Management* (Englewood Cliffs, N.J.: Prentice-Hall, Inc., 1976) pp. 11–14.
14. Or "Classical," "Theory X," or "System I."
15. Or "Behavioral," "Theory Y," or "System IV."

A Framework for Studying the Management Fundamentals

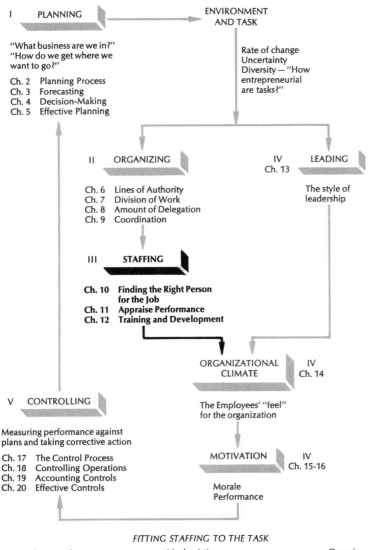

I PLANNING

"What business are we in?"
"How do we get where we want to go?"

Ch. 2   Planning Process
Ch. 3   Forecasting
Ch. 4   Decision-Making
Ch. 5   Effective Planning

ENVIRONMENT AND TASK

Rate of change
Uncertainty
Diversity — "How entrepreneurial are tasks?"

II   ORGANIZING

Ch. 6   Lines of Authority
Ch. 7   Division of Work
Ch. 8   Amount of Delegation
Ch. 9   Coordination

IV   LEADING
Ch. 13

The style of leadership

III   STAFFING

Ch. 10   Finding the Right Person for the Job
Ch. 11   Appraise Performance
Ch. 12   Training and Development

ORGANIZATIONAL CLIMATE

IV
Ch. 14

The Employees' "feel" for the organization

V   CONTROLLING

Measuring performance against plans and taking corrective action

Ch. 17   The Control Process
Ch. 18   Controlling Operations
Ch. 19   Accounting Controls
Ch. 20   Effective Controls

MOTIVATION

IV
Ch. 15-16

Morale
Performance

What we'll be discussing in this section:
Chap. 10
Staffing: Job analysis: Developing job descriptions and job specifications. Application blanks, interviews, and personnel tests. Orienting employees.
Chap. 11
Performance Appraisal and Counseling: Developing performance appraisal tools. Problems in appraising performance. Counseling.
Chap. 12
Training and Development: Developing and implementing a training program. Training and development techniques.

FITTING STAFFING TO THE TASK

Aspects of Staffing	Mechanistic	Organic
Job Descriptions	Clear; limited scope	Broad; — "open-ended"
Job Specification	Background, skills	Background, potential
Selection Methods	Specific performance tests — reference checks	General aptitude & interest tests — interview
Performance Criteria	Specific	General; more emphasis on milestones
Performance Evaluation	Graphic rating scale	Critical incidents
Training & Development	On the job training	Organizational development

A Framework for Studying the Management Fundamentals

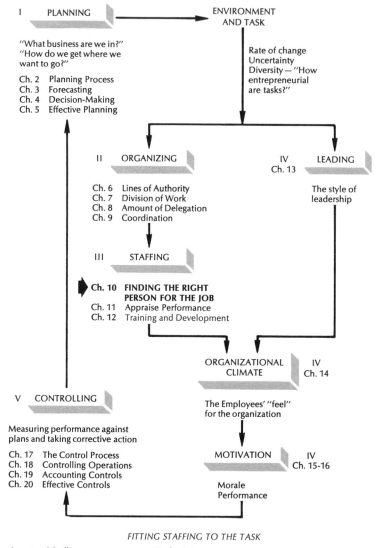

I   PLANNING   ENVIRONMENT AND TASK

"What business are we in?"
"How do we get where we want to go?"

Rate of change
Uncertainty
Diversity — "How entrepreneurial are tasks?"

Ch. 2   Planning Process
Ch. 3   Forecasting
Ch. 4   Decision-Making
Ch. 5   Effective Planning

Where we are now: Discussing staffing, which includes:
1. Determining job requirements
2. Recruiting applicants
3. Selecting the best person for the job
4. Orienting that person to his new job.

II   ORGANIZING   IV   LEADING
                           Ch. 13

Ch. 6   Lines of Authority
Ch. 7   Division of Work
Ch. 8   Amount of Delegation
Ch. 9   Coordination

The style of leadership

III   STAFFING

Ch. 10   **FINDING THE RIGHT PERSON FOR THE JOB**
Ch. 11   Appraise Performance
Ch. 12   Training and Development

ORGANIZATIONAL CLIMATE   IV   Ch. 14

V   CONTROLLING

The Employees' "feel" for the organization

Measuring performance against plans and taking corrective action

Ch. 17   The Control Process
Ch. 18   Controlling Operations
Ch. 19   Accounting Controls
Ch. 20   Effective Controls

MOTIVATION   IV   Ch. 15-16

Morale
Performance

FITTING STAFFING TO THE TASK

Aspects of Staffing	Mechanistic	Organic
Job Descriptions	Clear — limited scope	Broad — "open-ended"
Job Specification	Background, skills	Background, potential
Selection Methods	Specific performance tests — reference checks	General aptitude and interest tests — interview

When you have finished studying

10   Staffing

You should be able to:

1. *Perform a "job analysis."*

2. *Prepare job descriptions and job specifications.*

3. *Design an employment application blank.*

4. *Discuss the advantages and limitations of application blanks, interviews, references, and formal tests as selection tools.*

5. *Employ the nine steps for developing and using a personnel test.*

6. *List the important factors in an employee orientation program.*

INTRODUCTION

How well do you think you would do on the following jobs? If you're like most people, your answers will range from "very well" for some jobs, to "don't know" for others. Try to place a checkmark in the column that corresponds to your thoughts:

	Very Well	So-So	Poorly	Don't Know
ACCOUNTANT				
ARCHITECT				
ASSEMBLY-LINE WORKER				
DOCTOR				
ENGINEER				
EXECUTIVE				
FOREST RANGER				
LAWYER				
LIFE-INSURANCE SALESMAN				
LIGHTHOUSE WATCHMAN				
MECHANIC				
POLICEMAN				
SECRETARY				
TAILOR				
TEACHER				
VETERINARIAN				

182   *On what did you base your predictions? First, you already have some feel for your* aptitudes *in such areas as creativity and leadership, and for your* interests *for things like working outdoors or with other people. You also have a good idea of what your* achievements *have been in terms of what you have learned in school or on your jobs. Finally, you have an idea of what your* personality *is in terms of self-confidence, for example. Thus your predictions were probably based on a conscious (or unconscious) assessment of how your interests, aptitudes, achievements, and personality fit each job.*

This job/person matching is what staffing the organization is all about. The first step is to analyze the job. *Here you find out what the duties of the job are, and what kind of skills, interests, aptitudes, achievements, and personality a person should have to do the job well.*

Second, you have to recruit *applicants for the job in order to build up a pool of qualified candidates. Third, you* select *the best person for the job. Here you try to find the one whose achievements, interests, aptitudes, and personality are "right" for the job. Then, to make sure the person's entry into the job is smooth, you* orient *him to the job, supervision, and company. The purpose of this chapter is to discuss each of these steps in detail.*

JOB ANALYSIS—DETERMINING WHAT THE JOB REQUIRES

What is Job Analysis?

Dividing the work of the organization results in jobs which have to be staffed. Job analysis is the procedure through which you find out 1) what the job entails, and 2) what kinds of people should be hired for the job. It provides you with data on job requirements which is then used to develop *job descriptions* (what the job entails) and *job specifications* (what kinds of people should be hired for the job?).[1] This is summarized in Exhibit 10–1.[2]

But keep in mind that job analysis is not used only for making recruiting and hiring decisions. As we will see in the next two chapters, you also need data on job requirements for evaluating performance and designing training programs.

Techniques for Analyzing Jobs

There are many ways to do a job analysis, but most companies use some combination of 1) observation of the job being analyzed; 2) interviewing the person doing the job; and 3) filling out some type of job analysis

Exhibit 10.1   The Functions of Job Analysis

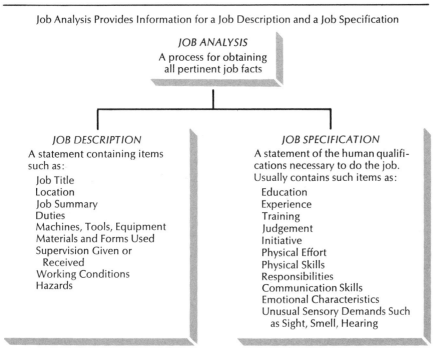

Job Analysis Provides Information for a Job Description and a Job Specification

JOB ANALYSIS
A process for obtaining
all pertinent job facts

JOB DESCRIPTION
A statement containing items
such as:
   Job Title
   Location
   Job Summary
   Duties
   Machines, Tools, Equipment
   Materials and Forms Used
   Supervision Given or
     Received
   Working Conditions
   Hazards

JOB SPECIFICATION
A statement of the human qualifi-
cations necessary to do the job.
Usually contains such items as:
   Education
   Experience
   Training
   Judgement
   Initiative
   Physical Effort
   Physical Skills
   Responsibilities
   Communication Skills
   Emotional Characteristics
   Unusual Sensory Demands Such
     as Sight, Smell, Hearing

Source: Dale S. Beach, *Personnel* (New York; Macmillan, 1970) p. 187.

questionnaire. We will focus on four specific techniques for analyzing jobs. In practice you could use any one of them, or combine the techniques that best fit your purpose.

Technique (1): U.S. Civil Service Procedure

The U.S. Civil Service Commission has published a guide entitled *Job Analysis*.[3] In it they recommend that:

1. Gathering information about work performed should be done through the most *practical* means possible.
2. The *basic purpose* of gathering the information is to determine what workers *actually* do, how they do it, and why they do it. This information in turn is used to determine what skills, knowledges, and abilities it takes to perform the duties.
3. The information gathered must be reported in a manner that is *understandable* to others.[4]

They say that there are several practical, simple methods for gathering information about a job. Perhaps the simplest involve *interviews*—with the worker, groups of workers, or the workers' supervisor. Another technique is

Exhibit 10.2   Model Worksheet for Obtaining Job Analysis Data

Step by step: the information to obtain when doing a job analysis.

IDENTIFYING INFORMATION: (such as)
   Name of incumbent
   Organization/unit
   Title and series
   Date
   Interviewer

BRIEF SUMMARY OF JOB: (This statement will include the primary duties of the job. It may be prepared in advance from class specifications, job descriptions or other sources. However, it should be checked for accuracy using the task statements resulting from the analysis.)

JOB TASKS:
   What does the worker do?   How does he do it?   Why? What output is produced?
   What tools, procedures, aids are involved?   How much time does it take to do the task?
   How often does the worker perform the task in a day, week, month, or year?

SKILLS KNOWLEDGE, AND ABILITIES REQUIRED:
What does it take to perform each task in terms of the following?
1. Knowledge required.
   a) What subject matter areas are covered by the task?
   b) What facts or principles must the worker have an aquaintance with or understand in these subject matter areas?
   c) Describe the level, degree, and breadth of knowledge required in these areas or subjects.
2. Skills required.
   a) What activities must the worker perform with ease and precision?
   b) What are the manual skills that are required to operate machines, vehicles, equipment, or to use tools?
3. Abilities required.
   a) What is the nature and level of language ability, written or oral, required of the worker on the job? Are there complex oral or written ideas involved in performing the task, or simple instructional materials.
   b) What mathematical ability must the worker have? Will he use simple arithmetic, complex algebra?
   c) What reasoning or problem solving ability must the worker have?
   d) What instructions must the worker follow? Are they simple, detailed, involved, abstract?
   e) What interpersonal abilities are required? What supervisory or managing abilities are required?
   f) What physical abilities such as strength, coordination, visual acuity must the worker have?

PHYSICAL ACTIVITIES:
   Describe the frequency and degree to which the incumbent is engaged in such activities as: pulling, pushing, throwing, carrying, kneeling, sitting, running, crawling, reaching, climbing.

ENVIRONMENTAL CONDITIONS:
   Describe the frequency and degree to which the incumbent will encounter working under such conditions as these: cramped quarters, moving objects, vibration, inadequate ventilation.

TYPICAL WORK INCIDENTS:
   a) Situations involving the interpretation of feelings, ideas, or facts in terms of personal viewpoint.
   b) Influencing people in their opinions, attitudes, or judgments about ideas or things.
   c) Working with people beyond giving and receiving instructions.
   d) Performing repetitive work, or continuously performing the same work.
   e) Performing under stress when confronted with emergency, critical, unusual, or dangerous situations; or in situations in which work speed and sustained attention are make-and-break aspects of the job.
   f) Performing a variety of duties often changing from one task to another of a different nature without loss of efficiency or composure.
   g) Working under hazardous conditions that may result in: violence, loss of bodily members, burns, bruises, cuts, impairment of senses, collapse, fractures, electric shock.

(Continued)

WORKER INTEREST AREAS:
Identify from the list below, the preferences for work activities suggested by each task.
A preference for activities:
a) dealing with things and objects;
b) concerning the communication of data;
c) involving business contact with people;
d) involving work of a scientific and technical nature;
e) involving work of a routine, concrete, organized nature;
f) involving work of an abstract and creative nature;
g) involving work for the presumed good of people;
h) relating to process, machine, and technique;
i) resulting in prestige or the esteem of others;
j) resulting in tangible, productive satisfaction.

Source: U.S. Civil Service Commission

the *"participant log."* Here you ask the worker to keep a daily log or list of the things he does during the day. *Questionnaires* of various kinds (either filled in by the worker or by you) are also popular.

In Exhibit 10–2 you'll find a work sheet you can use as a guide for collecting, compiling, and reporting the data. Notice that it includes information on things such as "What does the worker do?" "Knowledge required on the job"; and "Physical activities the worker typically has to engage in." You can use this worksheet, as a guide for writing out job descriptions, and job specifications.

Technique (2): Job Analysis Questionnaires

Many companies use job analysis *questionnaires* to obtain information on job requirements. You will find one such questionnaire presented in Exhibit 10–3. It is aimed at collecting job related information such as typical duties and tasks; tools and equipment used; and how much responsibility for machinery the job entails. It can also be used for writing out job descriptions, and job specifications.

Technique (3): The U.S. Department of Labor Procedure

The U.S. Department of Labor (DOL) has published a *Handbook for Analyzing Jobs.*[5] The heart of their procedure is a description of what your worker does in terms of *data, people,* and *things.*[6]

For example, look at Exhibit 10–4. It lists many activities (such as "analyzing") that a worker might do as part of his job. Notice that there are separate activities ("analyzing," "instructing," "operating," etc.) for each of the three basic categories—*data, people,* and *things.* If you were analyzing

186   **Exhibit 10.3**   A Job Analysis Questionnaire

Name   Department

Payroll Title   Name, Immediate Supervisor

Insrructions: Please read the entire form before making any entries. Answer each question as accurately and carefully as possible. When completed return this form to your supervisor. If you have any questions ask your supervisor.

Your Duties

What duties and tasks do you personally perform daily?

What duties do you perform only at stated intervals such as semi weekly, weekly or monthly? Indicate which period applies to each duty.

What duties do you perform only at irregular intervals?

Supervision of Others

How many employees are directly under your supervision? (List job titles and number of people assigned to each job.)

Do you have full discretionary authority to assign work; correct and discipline; recommend pay increases, transfers, promotions and discharge; and to answer grievances?

Do you only assign work, instruct, and coordinate the activities of your subordinates?

Materials, Tools, and Equipment

What are the principal materials and products that you handle?

List the names of the machines and equipment used in your work.

List the names of the principal hand tools and instruments used in your work.

What is the Source of Your Instructions? (e.g. oral, written, blue prints, specifications, etc.)

What Contacts Are You Required to Make with Persons Other Than Your Immediate Supervisor and Departmental Associates?

  a) Give the job titles and the department or organization of those with whom you deal.

  b) Describe the nature of these contacts.

Decisions

What decisions do you have to make without consulting your supervisor?

Responsibility

  a) Describe the nature of your responsibility for money, machinery, equipment, and reports.

  b) What monetary loss can occur through an honest error?

---

the job of a receptionist/clerk, for example, you might code the job 5, 6, 7 (copying data, speaking-signalling people, and handling things). On the other hand, a psychiatric aid in a hospital might be coded 2, 7, 5 in terms of data, people, and things.

Records and Reports

  a) What records and reports do you personally prepare?

  b) What is the source of the data?

Checking of Your Work

  a) How is your work inspected, checked or verified?

  b) Who does this?

Physical Requirements

  a) What percentage of the time do you spend in the following working positions?

     Standing _____ %,   Sitting_____ %,   Walking about_____ %?

  b) What weight in pounds must you personally lift and carry? _____ pounds

  c) What percentage of the working day do you actually spend lifting and carrying this weight? _____ %

  d) Are any special physical skills, eye-hand coordination, and manual dexterity skills required on your job?

Working Conditions

Describe any conditions present in the location and nature of your work, such as noise, heat, dust, fumes, etc., which you consider unfavorable or disagreeable.

Hazards

Describe the dangers or accident hazards present in your job.

THIS PORTION IS TO BE FILLED OUT BY YOUR SUPERVISOR.

Education Requirements

What is the lowest grade of grammar school, high school, or college required of a person starting in this job?

Previous Experience

  a) What kind of previous work experience is necessary for minimum satisfactory performance for a new employee on this job?

  b) Give the length of experience required.

Training

Assuming that a new employee on this job has the necessary education and experience to qualify for the work, what training is necessary after the employee is on the job to achieve an acceptable performance level? (Specify training needed and period of time to acquire it.)

| _____ | _____ |
| Date | Signature of Supervisor |

Source: Dale S. Beach, Personnel (New York: Macmillan, 1970) pp. 194-5

The data used in doing an analysis of this sort is obtained by observing and interviewing the workers. Then you have to make your own judgment about the major functions he performs, as well as write a short narrative summary of the job.

Exhibit 10.4   Basic Work Activities

		Data		People		Things
		Data		*People*		*Things*
	0	Synthesizing	0	Mentoring	0	Setting up
	1	Coordinating	1	Negotiating	1	Precision working
	2	Analyzing	2	Instructing	2	Operating-controlling
Basic	3	Compiling	3	Supervising	3	Driving-operating
Activities	4	Computing	4	Diverting	4	Manipulating
	5	Copying	5	Persuading	5	Tending
	6	Comparing	6	Speaking-signaling	6	Feeding-offbearing
			7	Serving	7	Handling
			8	Taking instructions-helping		

Note: You determine your employee's job "score" on *data, people,* and *things* by observing his job and determining, for each of the three categories, which of the basic activities illustrates his job.

Source: U.S. Department of Labor, Manpower Administration, Handbook for Analyzing Jobs (Washington, D. C., U.S. Government Printing Office, 1972) p. 73; reproduced in Schneider, *Staffing Organizations,* p. 25

In addition to identifying the data/people/things *quantitative* score for the job, you are also asked to identify the work field (like "cooking") to which the job belongs. On the form you also indicate the worker traits (aptitudes, temperaments, interests, etc.) that seem necessary for adequate job performance.

A sample of a completed DOL job analysis form for a "dough mixer" in a bakery is presented in Exhibit 10–5. It gives you a brief summary of the job, and a *quantitative score* for the job—in this case, 5, 6, 2. (You can use this to *classify* your jobs.) And, it specifies the *traits* of the people you need to staff this job.

Technique (4): The Position Analysis Questionnaire

Researchers at Purdue University [7] have developed a relatively "sure-fire" procedure for *quantitatively* describing jobs. Their "Position Analysis Questionnaire" (PAQ) [8] is a very structured job analysis questionnaire. It can be used for analyzing many different types of jobs. [9] The PAQ itself is filled in by a job analyst (perhaps yourself), a person who should already be acquainted with the particular job to be analyzed. It has 194 questions, divided into six major divisions:

1. *Information input* (where and how does the worker get the information that he uses in performing his job?)
2. *Mental processes* (what reasoning, decision-making, planning, and information processing activities are involved in performing the job?)

Sample of the End Result of Using the Department of Labor Job Analysis Technique.

U.S. Department of Labor
Manpower Administration

JOB ANALYSIS SCHEDULE

1. Established Job Title ___ DOUGH MIXER ___

2. Ind. Assign ___ (bake prod.) ___

3. SIC Code(s) and Title(s) ___ 2051 Bread and other bakery products ___

---

4. JOB SUMMARY:

Operates mixing machine to mix ingredients for straight and sponge (yeast) doughs according to established formulas, directs other workers in fermentation of dough, and curs dough into pieces with hand cutter.

5. WORK PERFORMED RATINGS: (From Exhibit 10-4)

	D	P	(T)
Worker Functions	Data	People	Things
	5	6	2

Work Field ___ Cooking, Food Preparing ___

6. WORKER TRAITS RATINGS: (To fill in, you'd need the "Handbook for Analyzing Jobs.")

Training time required

Aptitudes

Temperaments

Interests

Physical Demands

Environment Conditions

Source: Adapted from Schneider, *Staffing Organizations,* p. 27

3. *Work output* (what physical activities does the worker perform, and what tools or devices does he use?)

4. *Relationships with other persons* (what relationships with other people are required to perform the job?)

5. *Job context* (in what physical and social context is the work performed?)

6. *Other job characteristics* (what activities, conditions, or characteristics other than those described above are relevant to the job?) [10]

Exhibit 10.6 "Position Analysis Questionnaire"

INFORMATION INPUT

1 INFORMATION INPUT

1.1 Sources of Job Information

Rate each of the following items in terms of the extent to which it is used by the worker as a source of information in performing his job.

	Extent of Use (U)
NA	Does not apply
1	Nominal/very infrequent
2	Occasional
3	Moderate
4	Considerable
5	Very substantial

1.1.1 Visual Sources of Job Information

1 |U___ Written materials (books, reports, office notes, articles, job instructions, signs, etc.)

2 |U___ Quantitative materials (materials which deal with quantities or amounts, such as graphs, accounts, specifications, tables of numbers, etc.)

3 |U___ Pictorial materials (pictures or picturelike materials used as *sources* of information, for example, drawings, blueprints, diagrams, maps, tracings, photographic films, x-ray films, TV pictures, etc.)

4 |U___ Patterns/related devices (templates, stencils, patterns, etc., used as *sources* of information when *observed* during use; do *not* include here materials described in item 3 above)

5 |U___ Visual displays (dials, gauges, signal lights, radarscopes, speedometers, clocks, etc.)

6 |U___ Measuring devices (rulers, calipers, tire pressure gauges, scales, thickness gauges, pipettes, thermometers, protractors, etc., used to obtain visual information about physical measurements; do *not* include here devices described in item 5 above)

7 |U___ Mechanical devices (tools, equipment, machinery, and other mechanical devices which are *sources* of information when *observed* during use or operation)

8 |U___ Materials in process (parts, materials, objects, etc., which are *sources* of information when being modified, worked on, or otherwise processed, such as bread dough being mixed, workpiece being turned in a lathe, fabric being cut, shoe being resoled, etc.)

9 |U___ Materials *not* in process (parts, materials, objects, etc., not in the process of being changed or modified, which are *sources* of information when being inspected, handled, packaged, distributed, or selected, etc., such as items or materials in inventory, storage, or distribution channels, items being inspected, etc.)

10 |U___ Features of nature (landscapes, fields, geological samples, vegetation, cloud formations, and other features of nature which are observed or inspected to provide information)

11 |U___ Man-made features of environment (structures, buildings, dams, highways, bridges, docks, railroads, and other "man-made" or altered aspects of the indoor or outdoor environment which are *observed* or *inspected* to provide job information; do not consider equipment, machines, etc., that an individual uses in his work, as covered by item 7)

Source: One page from the Position Analysis Questionnaire, Occupational Research Center, Department of Psychological Sciences, Purdue University, West Lafayette, *Indiana,* 47097, Copyright © Purdue Research Foundation, 1969. Reprinted by permission.

You would start by familiarizing yourself with the questionnaire (a sample of which is illustrated in Exhibit 10–6), and the job. Next you would interview the worker and fill in the questionnaire. For each item on the questionnaire (such as "written materials" in Exhibit 10–6), you select the rating (1—very infrequent, 2—occasional, etc.) which you consider to be the most appropriate for his job. We know that by filling out this questionnaire for all jobs in your unit you can describe, profile, or rate all of them by using five basic dimensions:

1. Having decision-making/communication/social responsibilities.
2. Performing skilled activities.
3. Being physically active.
4. Operating vehicles/equipment.
5. Processing information.

Thus the PAQ provides you with *a quantitative profile* or score of any job based on these five dimensions. Notice that the PAQ is not a substitute for a job description (which describes in detail what the worker does), although it *can* help in *developing* one. The PAQ's real strength is in two areas.[11] First, since most jobs can be described in terms of five basic dimensions, you can use the PAQ to classify jobs into different classes (such as Secretary II, Secretary III, etc.). And, since you also arrive at a quantitative rating or value for each job (or job class) you can also use the PAQ to establish salary levels for each job, or job class.

Job Descriptions

Most job analyses result in job descriptions. These are statements, such as that in Exhibit 10–7, which describe the specific tasks, duties, and responsibilities of the job. Also included are the situational factors, such as working conditions, equipment used, and relationships involved in it.

Hints for Writing Up Job Descriptions. Here are some hints for finally writing up your job descriptions: [12]

1. *Be clear.* The job description should portray the work of the position so well that the duties are clear without reference to other job descriptions.
2. *Indicate scope.* In defining the position, be sure to indicate the scope and nature of the work by using phrases such as "for the department," or "as requested by the manager." Include all important relationships.
3. *Be specific.* Select the most specific words to show: (1) the kind of work; (2) the degree of complexity; (3) the degree of skill required; (4) the extent to which problems are standardized; (5) the

extent of the worker's responsibility for each phase of the work; and (6) the degree and type of accountability. Use "action words" such as analyze, gather, assemble, plan, devise, confer, deliver, transmit, maintain, supervise, and recommend. Generally speaking, positions at the lower levels of organization have the most detailed duties or tasks, while higher-level positions deal with broader aspects of business.

4. *Show supervisory responsibility.* Show clearly whether the responsibilities are carried out by the incumbent of the position, or through incumbents of other positions. The specialist or professional usually carries out the duties himself, or provides technical guidance when he assigns work to other persons. The manager or supervisor generally delegates the actual work to others.

Exhibit 10.7 A Job Description, and Job Specification

A Job *Description* for a Washer Assembly Stockman

JOB TITLE _____ WASHER ASSEMBLY STOCKMAN _____

DEPARTMENT Lock Washer and Nut Assembly JOB CODE NO. ___89-262___

NO. OF EMPLOYEES ON JOB___1___SEX—M ☐ F ☐ DATE ___6-10-77___

STATEMENT OF THE JOB

Under the direction of the WASHER ASSEMBLY SETUP MAN, receives and breaks down mill box loads of incoming stock, sorting according to classification of product, in preparation for distribution in department; services WASHER HAND ASSEMBLERS by lifting mill boxes of work on to assembly tables, weighs completed work on floor scale to measure production, and delivers to Department 96 on hand truck to be packed.

DUTIES OF THE JOB

1. Receives, sorts, and delivers stock; carries mill boxes of washers and bolts from stock to selected locations on floor according to size and type of plating, as directed by WASHER ASSEMBLY SETUP MAN; selects proper boxes by reading travel ticket and lifts onto work tables to be assembled by WASHER HAND ASSEMBLERS or places on hand truck, pulls loaded truck to Washer Assembly machines, and selects proper boxes to place at each machine, as directed, according to type of stock.

2. Weighs completed work in mill boxes; hauls completed work to scales on lift truck to weigh by placing boxes on scale in groups according to shift and work group as shown on production ticket; records weight on production ticket to show amount produced by shift and work group.

3. Delivers all mill boxes of completed work to Department 96 by hand truck to be packed.

4. Does errand work for the department such as hauling mill box loads of work by lift truck from the Plating Department and to the Heat Treat Department.

Exhibit 10.7   (continued)

A Job *Specification* for a Washer Assembly Stockman

JOB TITLE ___WASHER ASSEMBLY STOCKMAN_____ CODE NO.89-262

DICTIONARY TITLE _____ CODE NO. _____

DEPARTMENT   Lock Washer & Nut Assembly   TOTAL POINTS   CLASS

EXPERIENCE

Two to three months' experience required to learn which work goes to automatic assembly and which to hand assembly, and to become familiar with travel tickets to determine size and be able to recognize kinds of plating in order to properly sort material and service the WASHER HAND ASSEMBLERS.

SCHOOLING

Must be able to read travel tickets and sort material accordingly. Equivalent of eighth grade education.

RESPONSIBILITY FOR PRODUCT OR MATERIALS

Small losses might occur through misplacing product, mixing travel tickets, or incorrect pairing of washers and bolts in servicing WASHER HAND ASSEMBLERS.

RESPONSIBILITY FOR MACHINERY AND EQUIPMENT

Only equipment involved is lift truck and scales. Little responsibility for even small loss.

RESPONSIBILITY FOR WORK OF OTHERS

No supervision of others. Negligence in servicing WASHER HAND ASSEMBLERS or distribution and weighing up work would not seriously affect work of others.

RESPONSIBILITY FOR SAFETY OF OTHERS

Reasonable care in handling mill boxes and hand lift trucks around other workers in the department will prevent endangering safety of others.

RESOURCEFULNESS

Worker has a variety of duties which include lining up work for WASHER AND ASSEMBLERS, but these tasks are standard and any variation results from instructions of WASHER ASSEMBLY SETUP MAN.

MONOTONY AND COMFORT

Worker does considerable standing and walking with complete freedom to vary routine.

VISUAL EFFORT

Visual effort involved in weighing and in reading travel tickets to identify work.

PHYSICAL EFFORT

Considerable moving, handling and lifting of mill boxes.

Source: Jay Otis and Richard Leukart, *Job Evaluation* (Englewood Cliffs, N. J.; Prentice-Hall, Inc., 1961) pp. 275; 292-3

5. Be brief. Remember that brief, accurate statements will best accomplish your purpose.

6. Recheck. Finally, to check whether the description fulfills the basic requirements, ask yourself: Would a new employee understand the job if he read the position description?

Job Specifications

The *job specifications* takes the job description and then answers the question "What human traits and experience are necessary to do this job well?" It tells you what kind of person to recruit for, and for what qualities that person should be tested. See Exhibit 10–7.

There are basically two ways to develop a job specification. The more popular approach is to base them on the educated guesses of people like supervisors and personnel managers. Here you ask them (or yourself) "What do you think it takes in terms of education, intelligence, training, etc. to do this job well?" The second method is more accurate, and is based on statistical analysis. It entails testing workers and determining what traits distinguish successful from unsuccessful ones. Those human traits which are found to be related to high job performance are then included in the job specification.

Fitting Job Analysis to the Situation

You'll probably find that the job analysis approach you take for assembly-line jobs is quite different from the one you'd take if analyzing jobs in, for example, a research facility. Here are some things to keep in mind:

	in Mechanistic Organizations	*in Organic Organizations*
Job descriptions—Nature of jobs	Jobs specialized and clearly defined; clear, detailed job descriptions	Jobs more enlarged and often change day to day; job descriptions less detailed
Type of staff—Job specifications	Emphasis is on technical expertise and skills	Emphasis on creativity and ability to learn

RECRUITING JOB CANDIDATES

After you have developed a clear picture of the requirements of a job,[13] your next step is to obtain an adequate pool of applicants. As depicted in Exhibit 10–8, this is a very important step.

Exhibit 10.8 Why Obtaining a Pool of Job Applications is Important

"He has one big qualification for the job — he's the only man who answered our ad!"

Source: STRICTLY BUSINESS cartoon by Dale McFeatters reproduced through the courtesy of Publishers-Hall; in Herbert Chruden and Arthur W. Sherman, Jr., *Personnel Management* (Cincinnati: South Western, 1972)

The particular source of applicants you will use varies with different occupations and geographical areas. Some good sources include:

1. Unions.
2. Employers or trade associations.
3. Public employment services.
4. Private employment agencies.
5. Direct hiring.
6. Friends and relatives.
7. Advertising in newspapers.
8. Professional associations or journals.
9. Colleges and universities.
10. High schools, business colleges, etc.
11. In-house transfers.
12. Transfers from other firms.[14]

196   *SELECTING THE RIGHT PERSON*

After you have a pool of candidates, the next step is to select the best person for the job. The selection process usually entails the use of application blanks, interviews, tests, and reference checking.

Using Application Blanks as Selection Tools

Most companies use application blanks to obtain from the candidate biographical information, and information on prior work experience, educational background, and other personal items.

There are obviously many items that can be included on the application blank. For example, George England has found that the 86 application-blank items listed in Exhibit 10–9 had all proved useful in predicting job success for various types of jobs. Thus the Exhibit gives you a good "menu" from which to choose items for your own application blank.

An important thing to remember, though, is that for some jobs some items will be better predictors of job success than others. For example, the Ajax Life Insurance Company might find that the following characteristics are related to success for life insurance sales jobs: Participation in at least one competitive sport in college; election to at least three collegiate offices; and average college grades. Once these more important characteristics have been identified, scores or "weights" can be assigned to these items on the application blank, and each candidate's total score summed up.

Using Interviews as Selection Tools

Almost every organization of any size uses the interview as a selection device. It provides a good way for you to size up a candidate and appraise him directly rather than through application blanks, tests, or references. And the interview also gives you a good opportunity to provide the candidate with information about the available job and the company.

Interviews can be either directed or nondirected. In the directed interview, you use a form such as shown in Exhibit 10–10 to guide the conversation.

The basic idea behind the *nondirected* interview is to get the candidate to talk freely. One good way to do this is by restating or repeating his key phrases. For example, if the candidate says "I really enjoyed that job," you might say "you really enjoyed that job?" This will probably get him to elaborate on why he liked the job. It is usually more effective than asking him a direct question like "why did you like that job?"

Exhibit 10.9 Personal History Items Useful in Developing Your Application Blank

---

PERSONAL
Age
Age at hiring
Marital status
Number of years married
Dependents, number of
Children, number of
Age when first child born
Physical health
Recent illnesses, operations
Time lost from job for certain previous period
  (last 2 years, etc.)
Living conditions, general
Domicile, whether alone, rooming house, keep
  own house, etc.
Residence, location of
Size of home town
Number of times moved in recent period
Length of time at last address
Nationality*
Birth place*
Weight and height
Sex

GENERAL BACKGROUND
Occupation of father
Occupation of mother
Occupation of brothers, sisters, other relatives
Military service and rank
Military discharge record
Early family responsibility
Parental family adjustment
Professionally successful parents
Stable or transient home life
Wife does not work outside home

EDUCATION
Education
Educational level of wife
Educational level of family relatives
Education finances—extent of dependence on
  parents
Type of course studied—grammar school
Major field of study—high school
Specific courses taken in high school or college
Subjects liked, disliked in high school
Years since leaving high school
Type of school attended, private/state
College grades
Scholarship level, grammar school and high school
Graduated at early age compared with classmates

---

*Some items, such as these may violate fair employ-
ment practice legislation.

EMPLOYMENT EXPERIENCE
Educational—vocational consistency
Previous occupations (general type of work)
Held job in high school (type of job)
Number of previous jobs
Specific work experience (specific jobs)
Previous (selling) experience
Previous (life insurance sales) experience
Total length of work experience (total years,
  months)
Being in business for self
Previous employee of company now considering
  application
Seniority in present employment
Tenure on previous job
Minimum current living expenses
Salary requests, limits set for accepting job
Earnings expected (in future, 2 yrs., 5 yrs.,
  etc.)

SOCIAL
Club memberships (social, community, campus,
  high school)
Frequency of attendance at group meetings
Offices held in clubs
Experience as a group leader
Church membership

INTERESTS
Prefer outside to inside labor
Hobbies
Number of hobbies
Specific type of hobbies, leisure time activities
  preferred
Sports
Number of sports active in
Most important source of entertainment

*PERSONAL CHARACTERISTICS,
ATTITUDES EXPRESSED*
Willingness to relocate or transfer
Confidence (as expressed by applicant)
Basic personality needs (5 types) as expressed by
  applicant in reply to question on application
  blank
Drive
Stated job preferences

MISCELLANEOUS
Time taken for hiring negotiations between appli-
  cant and company
Former employer's estimate of applicant

Source: George W. England, *Development and Use of Weighted Application Blanks*, Rev. Ed., (Minneapolis: Industrial Relations Center, University of Minnesota, 1971) pp. 16-19

Exhibit 10.10   Structured or Patterned Form for Directed Interviews

PATTERNED INTERVIEW FORM — EXECUTIVE POSITION

Date_____ 19_____

SUMMARY

Rating: | 1 | 2 | 3 | 4 | Comments:_____

In making final rating, be sure to consider not only what the applicant can do but also his stability, industry, perseverance, loyalty, ability to get along with others, self-reliance, leadership, maturity, motivation, and domestic situation and health.

Interviewer:_____ Job considered for:_____

Name_____ Date of birth_____ Age_____; Phone No. _____

Present address_____City_____State_____How long there?_____
Is this a desirable neighborhood? Too high class? Too cheap?

Previous address_____City_____State_____How long there?_____
Is this a desirable neighborhood? Why did he move?

What kind of a car do you own?_____ Age_____Condition of car_____
Will he be able to use his car if necessary?

Were you in the Armed Forces of the U. S.? Yes, branch_____ Dates_____19_____to_____19_____

_____19_____to_____19_____

If not, why not?_____

Are you employed now? Yes ☐ No ☐. (If yes) How soon available?_____
What are his relationships with present employer?

Why are you applying for this position?_____
Is his underlying reason a desire for prestige, security, or earnings?

WORK EXPERIENCE. Cover all positions. This information is very important. Interviewer should record last position first. Every month since leaving school should be accounted for. Experience in Armed Forces should be covered as a job.

LAST OR PRESENT POSITION

Company_____City_____From_____19____to_____19_____
Do these dates check with his application?

How was job obtained?_____Whom did you know there?_____
Has he shown self-reliance in getting his jobs?

Nature of work at start_____Starting salary_____
Will his previous experience be helpful on this job?

In what way did the job change?_____
Has he made good work progress?

Nature of work at leaving_____ Salary at leaving_____
How much responsibility has he had?   Any indication of ambition?

Superior_____Title_____What is he like?_____
Did he get along with superior?

How closely does (or did) he supervise you?_____What authority do (or did) you have?_____

Number of people you supervised_____What did they do?_____
Is he a leader?

Responsibility for policy formulation_____
Has he had management responsibility?

To what extent could you use initiative and judgment?_____
Did he actively seek responsibility?

Form No. EP-302-R

Source: Published by the Dartnell Corporation, Chicago, by permission.

Remember, though, that whether you're using a directed or nondirected approach, the important thing is to get the *interviewee* to talk.

While interviews are widely used, there is much debate about just how useful they are. We know, for example, that several interviewers who examine the same applicant often come away with different opinions concerning his abilities.

In Exhibit 10–11 we have presented a summary of some typical interviewing problems. You will also find there some specific hints which should make you a more effective interviewer.

Using References as Selection Tools

Almost all companies carry out some sort of reference check on their candidates. The problem, though, is that most people prefer not to give bad references, and the ones you receive will probably be unrevealing (at best). The reference check is therefore not very useful for evaluating a person's strong points. But given the fact that most people don't like giving bad references, when you *do* receive some negative comments they can provide a good "red flag." Many firms now use the telephone to check references using forms such as that in Exhibit 10–12.

One of the problems with using references is that they are, as their names implies, *referred* to you by the job applicant. Therefore many managers use the applicant's suggested references as a *source* for *other* references who may know of the applicants performance. Thus you might want to ask each of your applicant's references "Could you please give me the name of a person who might be familiar with the applicant's performance?" In that way you begin getting information from references other than those referred to you by the applicant himself.

Using Formal Tests as Selection Tools

For many companies, formal tests are an important component in the selection process. There are thousands of standardized tests available, ranging from performance tests, to interest inventories. Most of these have been checked for *validity* (will it accurately measure what it is supposed to measure?) and *reliability* (will the same person be rated about the same in several different trials with the same test?). Most tests also have established *norms* or standards for different groups like college graduates, minorities, and different age brackets.

Tests are not infallible, and you should not rely solely on their results when evaluating a candidate. Not only are tests far from "perfect"—in terms of

Exhibit 10.11   Avoiding Interviewing Problems

What Two Researchers Found Out About Interviewing Problems:

First Researcher	*Second Researcher*	*And Some Hints for Avoiding These Problems*
1. Interviewers seem to develop stereotypes about a good applicant and seek to match interviewees with their stereotype.	1. Interviewers agree on which facts they say they consider in making decisions, and can agree on the goodness or badness of an interviewee's record, but they do not agree on whether they should *hire* the person.	1. Provide interviewers an *accurate picture* of the "good" employee so that all interviewers can work with the same stereotype. Put the stereotype in behavioral terms and require the interviewer to make a prediction about job behavior.
2. Unfavorable information about an interviewee is more influential on the interviewer's decision than favorable information.	2. The impact of favorability of information is a function of the characteristics of the people *already* interviewed and/or the others with whom the interviewee is presented; an average applicant after or among poor applicants is rated above average. Further, when "bodies" are needed (when the interviewer has a quota to fill) an average applicant receives a higher rating. Interviewers agree more on unfavorable applicants.	2. Require interviewers to *consider all relevant information* in making decisions.
3. Interviewer decisions are affected by whether the information is provided a little piece at a time or all at once.	3. The impact of factual information on the interviewer's judgment is a function of (1) whether the interviewer follows a structured interview schedule and (2) whether the interviewer takes notes. Those who do neither seem to make decisions based on a global impression ("halo").	3. Do not give interviewers *quotas* for bodies. 4. Require interviewers to use a standardized, highly *structured interview schedule* and to take extensive notes to be used *later* in making their decisions. The guidelines should concentrate on assessment of factual material, not on evaluations.
4. Biases for or against an interviewee are established early in the interview.	4. Only highly structured interviews generate information that enables interviewers to agree with each other; experience is not the important element *unless interviewers receive feedback on their interviews.* Then more experienced interviewers are more reliable. Experience also makes the interviewer less susceptible to external pressure such as quotas (see number 2 above).	
5. Experienced interviewers can agree on the rankings (from best to worst) to be given a group of interviewees.		5. Make sure the information to be sought *in* the interview *and* the interviewer have been validated. *Provide feedback to interviewers* on their performance so they can engage in self-correction behavior. Some people seem to be better users of information than others.

Source: Developed by Schneider, *Staffing Organizations,* p. 196

Exhibit 10.12   A Form for Checking References Over the Telephone   201

Applicant: Date:
Former Company:
Former Supervisor:
Title:
Telephone Number:
      (Please respect confidentiality of information in this file)
1.   This is _____ speaking, I'm with _____ , Inc., in _____ .
        We are considering _____ for a position in our department.
        Is this a convenient time for you to talk with me a moment?
2.   What were the dates of his (her) employment with your company?
3.   (a) What did you hire him to do?
        (b) What was his position before leaving?
        (c) What were his primary responsibilities?
        (d) How well did he meet your expectations?
4.   He states his salary as _____ . Is this correct?   Yes   No
5.   What other types of compensation did he receive?
6.   How much time did he lose from work?
7.   Did he supervise others?   Yes   No   How many?
8.   What was his approach to the supervision of others?
9.   How much direction or support did he require?
10.   (a) How has he shown creative ability?
        (b) How practical are his ideas?
        (c) How receptive is he to others' ideas?
        (d) How well does he follow through on projects?
        (e) What percentage of his work has been (research/design)?
        (f) What are his technical strong points?
11.   Can you describe briefly one of his assignments that will show his level of capability?
12.   How extensive is his knowledge of his field?
13.   How broad are his interests?
14.   How well does he organize and present his ideas?
15.   What type of situation do you think is best for him?
16.   (a) What were his outstanding strong points?
        (b) Weak points?
17.   Do you have any additional comments regarding _____ ?

Thank you for your help. May we ask you to keep our inquiry confidential?

Source: Tektronix, Inc., reproduced in Wendell French, *The Personnel Management Process* (Boston: Houghton Mifflin, 1974) p. 299

predicting who will or will not be successful on the job—but they are also viewed by some candidates as an invasion of privacy. Furthermore, recent equal employment opportunity legislation has laid down severe penalties for companies who make discriminatory use of tests. The Equal Employment Opportunity Commission (EEOC) specifies strict guidelines for proving how valid and reliable a test is and for insuring that it is properly administered.

Let's look at four basic types of tests.

Achievement and Performance Tests.   These tests measure the applicant's abilities. The simplest example is the performance test in which the applicant is asked to demonstrate his ability to do some job—secretaries are usually asked to take typing tests, for example. Classroom examinations in statistics, finance (or management!) are also examples of achievement tests.

Aptitude Tests. These measure an applicant's aptitude or potential to do some job. Some, like the General Aptitude Test Battery (used by the U.S. Department of Labor) measure a broad range of aptitudes such as verbal ability, numerical ability, and motor coordination. Others focus on specific aptitudes, such as to do creative work, or to understand the workings of machinery. Intelligence (or IQ) tests are one kind of aptitude test.

Personality Tests. These are really not tests at all but are devices for measuring different facets of an applicant's personality. They include "tests" like the Rorschach (or "ink blot") Test and the Edwards Personal Preference Schedule. These are used to measure such aspects of the applicant's personality as his self confidence; or to determine which basic motives are the most important to him. These tests are the most difficult to administer and evaluate.

Interest Tests. These "interest inventories" usually compare the applicant's interests with those of people working in various occupations who have previously taken the test. An example of the results of one of these inventories—"the Strong Vocational Interest Inventory"—is presented in Exhibit 10–13. The "Kuder Preference Record" is another widely used interest inventory.

As you might imagine, interest inventories such as these can be very useful for career counseling. But they are also useful for evaluating an applicant's potential for the job. If you can hire an applicant whose interests are about the same as those of successful incumbents in the job for which you are recruiting, you're obviously well ahead of the game.

Some Hints on Developing Ideal Test Procedures: George Strauss and Leonard Sayles say that the ideal test development procedure contains the following nine steps: [15]

1. *Analyze job.* Personnel specialist interviews current managers to find characteristics that distinguish "'good" from "bad" employees on a particular job (or use one of our four techniques).

2. *Write job specification.* Interview results are analyzed and consensus summarized in list form. These listed characteristics are sent back to managers to rank order.

3. *Prepare test items.* Psychologist prepares test items that he believes will measure highly ranked characteristics in job applicants. (The ones you identified with step 2.)

4. *Try out test items.* These items are tried out on a random sample of applicants to see which items do the best job.

5. *Construct tentative test.* On the basis of these results, a tentative test is prepared.

6. *Measure employee performance.* A decision is made as to how to distinguish between high and low performing employees (the "criterion"). This may be in terms of overall performance as subjectively rated by the supervisor, or in terms of objective measures such as aver-

Exhibit 10.13 Report on Vocational Interest Blank for Men

Name................................. Age............. Date............. Agency or school................................. Case no.................................

Group	Occupation	Raw Score	Standard Score
I	Artist		37
	Psychologist		23
	Architect		48
	Physician		22
	Psychiatrist		23
	Osteopath		20
	Dentist		15
	Veterinarian		10
II	Mathematician		16
	Physicist		11
	Chemist		18
	Engineer		21
III	Production Manager		25

Scale: C (0–35) | B− | B | B+ | A   0 5 10 15 20 25 30 35 40 45 50 55 60 65

Note: Individual report blank for the Strong Vocational Interest Blank (for men, revised) showing thirteen of the forty-eight occupations covered, the grouping of occupations into interest areas, the letter ratings, and a hypothetical pattern of interest scores.

Source: Strong-Campbell Interest Inventory, Form T-325 of the Strong Vocational Interest Blank by Edward K. Strong, Jr., and David P. Campbell.

age daily sales, percentage of production passing inspection, or absentee rates. If several criteria are used, some formula must be developed to weigh them so that a single overall dimension can be determined.

7. Give test to applicant. Test is then given to all new applicants, but not used for selection.

8. Compare "highs" and "lows." After some time (say 18 months) the scores of those tested *and hired* are compared with their performance as measured by the criterion (such as sales per day). Test items that seem to be closely related with the criterion are used in the test battery, which is now introduced into the employment procedure. (Or, you could administer the test to *current* job incumbents. Then determine who are the high and low performers, and which test items are most closely related to performance.)

9. Repeat process. Several years later, "revalidate" the test (as in steps 7 and 8) to insure that the test is still adequately predicting performance.

ORIENTING THE EMPLOYEE TO HIS NEW JOB

Why Use Orientation?

Think back for a moment about how you felt during your first day on a job. If you were like most people, you were a little tense and your anxiety level was probably higher than usual. Remember how relieved you were when some of the other people at work invited you to lunch! These kinds of "first-day jitters" are typical for new employees. Thus in one study at the Texas Instruments Company, researchers discovered the following about new employees: [16]

The first days on the job were anxious and disturbing ones.

"New employee initiation" practices by peers intensified anxiety.

Anxiety interfered with the training process.

Turnover of newly hired employees was caused primarily by anxiety.

The new workers were reluctant to discuss problems with their supervisors.

Employee orientation is aimed at minimizing such problems. Its purpose is to introduce the new employee and the organization to each other, to help them to become acquainted, and to help them to accommodate each other.

What Orientation Entails   205

Orientation programs range from brief informal introductions to lengthy, formal programs. In the latter, the new employee is usually given a handbook or printed materials as well as a tour of the facilities. (Exhibit 10–14 shows the table of contents from staff-orientation handbook used at a university.)

The information provided in orientation programs typically covers things such as employee compensation benefits; personnel policies; the employee's daily routine; company organization and operations; and safety measures and regulations. The new employee's supervisor is often given an orientation checklist similar to that in Exhibit 10–15.[17] This helps to insure that the supervisor has covered all of the necessary orientation steps.

Some companies have also found it useful to provide new employees with special "anxiety-reduction seminars." For example, when the Texas Instruments Company found out how high the anxiety level of its new employees was, they initiated special full-day seminars. These focused on information about the company and the job, and allowed many opportunities for questions and answers. The new employees were also told what to expect in terms of rumors and hazing from old employees. They were also told that it was very likely they'd succeed on their jobs. These special seminars proved to be very useful. By the end of the first month, the new employees who had participated in the seminar were performing much better than those who had not.

Some Important Things to Remember from This Chapter:

1. You use job analysis to determine what the job entails, and what kind of people should be hired for the job. Whether you use the *Civil Service* procedure, the *job analysis questionnaire*, the *Department of Labor* procedure, or the *PAQ*, job analysis basically entails: 1) Gathering information about the job through observations, interviews, or questionnaires; and 2) compiling and presenting information in job descriptions and job specifications.

2. The Civil Service procedure for job analysis is a simple, practical procedure that can be applied to almost any job. It involves filling out a worksheet (Exhibit 10–2) usually by observing the work being done and interviewing the worker. A job analysis questionnaire (Technique 2) is another simple, practical approach to job analysis.

3. The U.S. Department of Labor procedure and the Position Analysis Questionnaire both allow you to assign numerical values or scores to your workers' jobs. These techniques are not quite as useful for developing job descriptions and job specifications. But they are very useful for assigning jobs to different classes

Exhibit 10.14   Table of Contents for Employee Orientation Handbook

Source: Florida International University, University Staff Orientation Guide

Exhibit 10.15 Supervisor's Orientation Checklist

Employee's Name:	*Discussion Completed (please check each individual item)*
I. Word of welcome	_____
II. Explain overall departmental organization and its relationship to other activities of the company	
III. Explain employee's individual contribution to the objectives of the department and his starting assignment in broad terms	_____
IV. Discuss job content with employee and give him a copy of job description (if available)	_____
V. Explain departmental training program(s) and salary increase practices and procedures	_____
VI. Discuss where the employee lives and transportation facilities	_____
VII. Explain working conditions: 　*a.* Hours of work, time sheets 　*b.* Use of employee entrance and elevators 　*c.* Lunch hours 　*d.* Coffee breaks, rest periods 　*e.* Personal telephone calls and mail 　*f.* Overtime policy and requirements 　*g.* Paydays and procedure for being paid 　*h.* Lockers 　*i.* Other _____	_____
VIII. Requirements for continuance of employment—explain company standards as to: 　*a.* Performance of duties 　*b.* Attendance and punctuality 　*c.* Handling confidential information 　*d.* Behavior 　*e.* General appearance 　*f.* Wearing of uniform	_____
IX. Introduce new staff member to manager(s) and other supervisors. Special attention should be paid to the person to whom the new employee will be assigned.	_____
X. Release employee to immediate supervisor who will: 　*a.* Introduce new staff member to fellow workers 　*b.* Familiarize the employee with his work place 　*c.* Begin on-the-job training	_____

If not applicable, insert N/A in space provided.

_____	_____
Employee's Signature	Supervisor's Signature
_____	_____
Date	Division

Form examined for filing:

_____	_____
Date	Personnel Department

Source: Joan Holland and Theodore Curtis, "Orientation of New Employees," in Joseph Famulard (ed.) *Handbook of Modern Personnel Administration* (New York: McGraw-Hill, 1972) ch. 23; reproduced in William Glueck, Personnel (Dallas: B.P.I., 1974) p. 238

208   (since each job has a numerical score) and also for deciding on an appropriate salary for each job classification.

4. Remember that it is very important to build up an adequate pool of candidates for your job. The more of a choice you have, the easier it is for you to pick the best person for the job.

5. Most companies use some combination of application blanks, interviews, reference checking, and personnel tests in selecting their employees. In Exhibit 10–11 we have summarized some hints for making your interview as useful as possible. For example, we know that it helps to give all interviewers an accurate picture of the "good" employee, and to require all interviewers to use a standardized interview form.

6. Psychological tests are highly personal in nature, and there is always the possibility that you may be invading someone's privacy by requiring him to take the test. Obtain the services of a qualified industrial psychologist before developing a testing procedure or choosing the test. And make certain that the test validly predicts performance on the job for which you are testing, and that the information you obtain is held in the strictest confidence.

7. Employee-orientation is aimed at introducing new employees to the company. The aim is to help them become acquainted, and to help them accommodate to their new jobs. We know that even a short orientation can drastically reduce the "first-day jitters" and the turnover in your unit.

STUDY ASSIGNMENTS

1. Choose· two positions in an organization with which you are familiar and carry out a job analysis of them, using one of the techniques discussed in this chapter. Develop both a job description and a job specification for each job.

2. Write an essay discussing the main factors typically found in job descriptions and job specifications.

3. Develop a job description and a job sepcification for a: student; professor; accountant; salesman; and for a job that you want after graduation.

4. Design and write an employment application blank for the following jobs: bank teller; forest ranger; professor.

5. Discuss the advantages and limitations of application blanks, interviews, references,.and formal tests as selection tools.

6. Discuss the nine steps you would use to develop a test for job applicants.

7. Develop a table of contents for the manual you will distribute as part of your company's orientation program.

8. In this chapter we discussed four techniques for analyzing jobs. Compare and contrast 1) the Civil Service procedure and job analysis questionnaire with 2) the Department of Labor procedure, and position analysis questionnaire. For example, are the latter two useful for writing job descriptions? For what *are* they particularly useful? Why?

9. Summarize our six hints for writing job descriptions.

10. "Interviews can be effective selection tools if used properly." Discuss
    whether you agree or disagree with this statement, and why. Be sure to
    include some specific hints for making the interview as effective as pos-
    sible.

NOTES FOR THE CHAPTER

1. Benjamin Schneider, *Staffing Organizations* (Santa Monica: Goodyear, 1976) p. 19.

2. Dale Beach, *Personnel* (New York: Macmillan, 1970) p. 187.

3. United States Civil Service Commission, Bureau of Intergovernmental Personnel Programs, *Job Analysis*, BIPP152-35 (December 1973).

4. U.S. Civil Service Commission, *Job Analysis*, p. 1.

5. This section based on Benjamin Schneider, *Staffing Organizations*, pp. 24–29.

6. U.S. Department of Labor, Manpower Administration, *Handbook for Analyzing Jobs* (Washington: U.S. Government Printing Office, 1972).

7. Based partly on Schneider, *Staffing Organizations*, pp. 26–30.

8. Ernest J. McCormick, Paul Jeanneret, and Robert Mecham, "A Study of Job Characteristics & Job Dimensions as Based on the Position Analysis Questionnaire," *Journal of Applied Psychology*, Vol. 56, No. 4 (August 1972) pp. 347–368.

9. See *Position Analysis Questionnaire*, Occupational Research Center, Department of Psychological Sciences, Purdue University, West Lafayette, Indiana 47907.

10. *Position Analysis Questionnaire*, Occupational Research Center, p. 1.

11. Technical Manual for the Position Analysis Questionnaire, PAQ Services, Inc., 1315 Sunset Lane, West Lafayette, Indiana 47906, p. 13.

12. Based on Ernest Dale, *Organizations*, 1967 (New York: American Management Association, 1967) p. 301.

13. This section based partly on Benjamin Schneider, *Staffing Organizations*, pp. 99–105.

14. F. T. Malm, "Recruiting Patterns and the Functioning of Labor Markets," *Industrial and Labor Relations Review*, 7 (1954) pp. 507–525; quoted in Schneider, p. 103.

15. Based on George Strauss and Leonard Sayles, *Personnel* (Englewood Cliffs: Prentice-Hall, 1972) Ch. 19.

16. Earl Gomerjail and M. Scott Myers, "Breakthrough in on-the-job Training," *Harvard Business Review* (July-August 1966). Quoted in Wendel French, *The Personnel Management Process* (Boston: Houghton Mifflin, 1974) p. 333.

17. William Glueck, *Personnel: A Diagnostic Approach* (Dallas: Business Publications, Inc., 1974) p. 238.

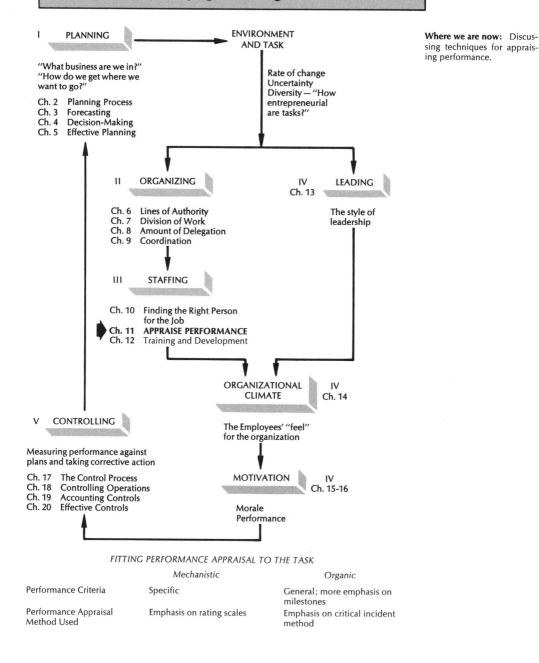

A Framework for Studying the Management Fundamentals

I PLANNING → ENVIRONMENT AND TASK

Where we are now: Discussing techniques for appraising performance.

"What business are we in?"
"How do we get where we want to go?"

Ch. 2 Planning Process
Ch. 3 Forecasting
Ch. 4 Decision-Making
Ch. 5 Effective Planning

Rate of change
Uncertainty
Diversity — "How entrepreneurial are tasks?"

II ORGANIZING

Ch. 6 Lines of Authority
Ch. 7 Division of Work
Ch. 8 Amount of Delegation
Ch. 9 Coordination

IV LEADING
Ch. 13

The style of leadership

III STAFFING

Ch. 10 Finding the Right Person for the Job
➤ Ch. 11 **APPRAISE PERFORMANCE**
Ch. 12 Training and Development

ORGANIZATIONAL CLIMATE IV Ch. 14

The Employees' "feel" for the organization

V CONTROLLING

Measuring performance against plans and taking corrective action

Ch. 17 The Control Process
Ch. 18 Controlling Operations
Ch. 19 Accounting Controls
Ch. 20 Effective Controls

MOTIVATION IV Ch. 15-16

Morale
Performance

FITTING PERFORMANCE APPRAISAL TO THE TASK

	Mechanistic	*Organic*
Performance Criteria	Specific	General; more emphasis on milestones
Performance Appraisal Method Used	Emphasis on rating scales	Emphasis on critical incident method

When you have finished studying

11 Performance Appraisal and Counseling

You should be able to:

1. *Develop, evaluate, and administer at least four effective performance appraisal tools.*

2. *List and discuss the pros and cons of: graphic rating scales; the alternation ranking method; the paired comparison method; the forced distribution method; the critical incident method; a behaviorally anchored ranking scale.*

3. *Explain the problems to be avoided in appraising performance.*

4. *Discuss the pros and cons of using different potential raters to appraise a person's performance.*

5. *Carry out an effective counseling interview.*

INTRODUCTION

As a manager, appraising your subordinates' performances will be a very important part of your job. And to be effective, you will have to know as much as possible about the "nitty gritty" of developing and administering performance appraisal tools.

Actually you've probably already had some experience with performance appraisal scales. For example, some colleges ask students to rank instructors on scales like the one in Exhibit 11–1. Do you think this is an effective scale? Do you see any ways to improve it? These are two of the important questions you should be in a better position to answer by the end of this chapter.

WHY SHOULD YOU APPRAISE PERFORMANCE?

There are actually several reasons to appraise performance.[1] First, performance appraisals provide information on which *promotion* and *salary* decisions can be made. These are the most frequent uses of performance appraisals.

Exhibit 11.1   A Scale for Appraising Instructors

INSTRUCTOR

DEPARTMENT

COURSE NUMBER OR TITLE

I. The following items reflect some of the ways teachers can be described in and out of the classroom. For the instructor named above, please circle the number which indicates the degree to which you feel each item is descriptive of him or her. In some cases, the statement may not apply to this individual. In these cases, check *Does not apply or don't know* for that item.

	Not at all Descriptive	Very Descriptive	Doesn't apply or don't know
1. Has command of the subject, presents material in an analytic way, contrasts various points of view discusses current developments, and relates topics to other areas of knowledge	1 2 3	4 5 6 7	( )
2. Makes himself clear, states objectives, summarizes major points, presents material in an organized manner, and provides emphasis.			
3. Is sensitive to the response of the class, encourages student participation, and welcomes questions and discussion.			
4. Is available to and friendly towards students, is interested in students as individuals, is himself respected as a person, and is valued for advice not directly related to the course.			
5. Enjoys teaching, is enthusiastic about his subject, makes the course exciting, and has self-confidence			

Note: (Additional items may be presented by instructor and/or department.)

Source: Richard Miller, *Developing Programs for Faculty Evaluation* (San Francisco: Jossey-Bass Publishers, 1974), p. 43.

Second, performance appraisal provides an opportunity for you and your subordinate to sit down and *review* the subordinate's work-related behavior. Most people need and want some feedback concerning their performance (especially when it is favorable!) and the appraisal provides this feedback. Finally, it also allows you and your subordinate to map out a *plan* for rectifying any performance deficiencies which might be identified.

TOOLS FOR APPRAISING PERFORMANCE

Graphic Rating Scales

Graphic rating scales are probably the most widely used performance appraisal tools. This is because they are relatively easy to develop and use. A typical rating chart is presented in Exhibit 11–2.[2] Notice that the chart lists a number of traits (job knowledge, versatility, etc.) as well as a range of performance (from Unsatisfactory to Exceptional) for each. You rate your

subordinates by circling or checking the score that best describes his level
of performance for each trait. The circled values for each trait are then added
up and totaled.

The Alternation Ranking Method

Another popular, simple method for evaluating employees is to rank
them from best to worst on some characteristic. Since you will usually find
it is easier to distinguish between your worst and best employees than to
simply rank them, an "alternation" ranking method is most popular. First,
you list all subordinates to be rated and then cross out the names of any you
don't know well enough to rank. Then, on a form such as that in Exhibit
11–3, you indicate the employee who is the highest on the characteristic being
measured and also the one who is the lowest. Then you choose the next
highest and the next lowest, *alternating* between highest and lowest until
you've ranked all the employees to be rated.

Paired Comparison Method

The paired comparison method is supposed to make the ranking
method more effective. For every trait (quantity of work, quality of work,
etc.) every subordinate is compared to every other subordinate in pairs.

Suppose, as in Exhibit 11–4, there are five employees to be rated. In
the paired comparison method you would make a chart of all possible pairs
of employees (A and B; A and C; B and D, etc.). Then for each trait you
indicate who is the better employee of the pair. Next, the number of times
an employee is rated "high" is added up. In Exhibit 11–4, employee "B" was
ranked highest for quality of work, while "A" was ranked highest for creativity.

Forced Distribution Method

The forced distribution method is similar to "grading on a curve."
With this method predetermined percentages of rates are placed in various
performance categories. For example, you may decide to distribute your employees as follows:

15% HIGH PERFORMERS

20% HIGH AVERAGE PERFORMERS

30% AVERAGE PERFORMERS

20% LOW AVERAGE PERFORMERS

15% LOW PERFORMERS

Exhibit 11.2　Example of a Graphic Rating Scale

Employee: _____　Job title: _____ Date: _____

Department: _____　Job number: _____ Rater: _____

FACTOR	SCORE - RATING				
	UNSATISFACTORY So definitely inadequate that it justifies release	FAIR Minimal; barely adequate to justify retention	GOOD Meets basic require-ment for retention	SUPERIOR Definitely above norm and basic requirements	EXCEPTIONAL Distinctly and consistently outstanding
QUALITY Accuracy, thoroughness, appearance and acceptance of output					
QUANTITY Volume of output and contribution					
REQUIRED SUPERVISION Need for advice, direction or correction					
ATTENDANCE Regularity, dependability and prompness					
CONSERVATION Prevention of waste, spoilage; protection of equipment					

Reviewed by: _____　(Reviewer comments on reverse)

Employee comment: _____

　　　Date: _____ Signature or initial: _____

Note: In this form, the supervisor checks the appropriate box.

Source: Dale Yoder, *Personnel Management and Industrial Relations* (Englewood Cliffs, N. J.: Prentice-Hall, 1970) p. 240

Exhibit 11.3   Rating-Ranking Scale Using Alternation-Ranking Technique   215

RATING-RANKING SCALE

Consider all those on your list in terms of their (quality). Cross out the names of any you cannot rate on this quality. Then select the one you would regard as having most of the quality. Put his name in Column I, below, on the first line, numbered 1. Cross out his name on your list. Consult the list again and pick out the person having least of this quality. Put his name at the bottom of Column II, on the line numbered 20. Cross out his name. Now, from the remaining names on your list, select the one having most of the quality. Put his name in the first column on line 2. Keep up this process until all names have been placed in the scale.

COLUMN I (MOST)   COLUMN II (LEAST)

1. ....   11. ....

2. ....   12. ....

3. ....   13. ....

4. ....   14. ....

5. ....   15. ....

6. ....   16. ....

7. ....   17. ....

8. ....   18. ....

9. ....   19. ....

10. ....   20. ....

Source: Dale Yoder, Personnel Management, p. 237

One practical way for doing this is to write each employee's name on a separate index card. Then, for each trait being appraised (quality of work, creativity, etc.) you simply place the employee's card in one of the appropriate categories.

Critical Incident Method

One of the problems with the appraisal tools we have discussed so far is that they are filled in only once or twice a year. Because of this, they may only reflect the employees performance over the two- or three-week period immediately preceding the appraisal. And when you sit down with your subordinate to review his appraisal, you could also find yourself with very few "hard facts" for explaining his good or poor performance.

Exhibit 11.4 Ranking Employees by the Paired Comparison Method

FOR THE TRAIT "QUALITY OF WORK"					
Men Rated:					
As Compared to:	A	B	C	D	E
A		+	+	−	−
B	−		−	−	−
C	−	+		+	−
D	+	+	−		+
E	+	+	+	−	

↑ B Ranks Highest Here

FOR THE TRAIT "CREATIVITY"					
Men Rated:					
As Compared to:	A	B	C	D	E
A		−	−	−	−
B	+		−	+	+
C	+	+		−	+
D	+	−	+		−
E	+	−	−	+	

↑ A Ranks Highest Here

Note: + means "better than"; − means "worse than." For each chart, add up the number of +'s in each column to get the highest ranked employee.

Because of these kinds of problems many more companies are using the "critical incident" appraisal technique. Here you keep, for each subordinate, a running record of uncommonly good or undesirable incidents (like those in Exhibit 11–5). Then every six months or so, you and your subordinate sit down and discuss his performance based on these specific incidents.

Exhibit 11.5 Examples of Critical Incidents for an Assistant Plant Manager

Continuing Duties	Targets	Critical Incidents
Schedule Production for Plant	Full utilization of personnel and machinery in plant; orders delivered on time	Instituted new production scheduling system; he decreased late orders by 10% last month; he increased machine utilization in plant by 20% last month
Supervise procurement of raw materials and inventory control	Minimize inventory costs while keeping adequate supplies on hand	He let inventory storage costs rise 15% last month; over-ordered parts "A" and "B" by 20%, underordered part "C" by 30%
Supervise machinery maintenance	No shutdowns due to faulty machinery	Instituted new preventive maintenance system for plant; he prevented a machine breakdown by discovering faulty part

Behaviorally Anchored Rating Scales (BARS)   217

A new appraisal technique has recently been developed; it is called a Behaviorally Anchored Rating Scale (BARS). Its proponents claim that it provides better, more equitable appraisals than do the other tools we have discussed.[3]

Developing a BARS usually requires five steps: [4]

1. *Generate critical incidents.* Persons with knowledge of the job to be appraised (job holders and/or supervisors) are asked to describe specific illustrations (critical incidents) of effective and ineffective performance behavior.

2. *Develop performance dimensions.* The people developing the BARS then cluster these incidents into a smaller set (say five or ten) of performance dimensions. Each cluster (dimension) is then defined.

3. *Reallocate incidents.* Another group of people who also know the job then reallocate the original critical incidents. They are given the clusters definitions, and critical incidents, and asked to reassign each incident to the dimension it best describes. Typically a critical incident is retained if some percentage (usually 50 to 80%) of this group assigns it to the same cluster as did the group in step 2.

4. *Scale the incidents.* This second group is generally asked to rate (seven- or nine-point scales are typical) the behavior described in the incident as to how effectively or ineffectively it represents performance on the appropriate dimension.

5. *Develop final instrument.* A subset of the incidents (usually six or seven per cluster) are used as "behavioral anchors" for the performance dimensions.

Example: Let's look at an example to see how this works in practice. Three researchers set out to develop a BARS for grocery clerks who were working in a large western grocery chain.[5] They collected a number of critical incidents, and then clustered them into eight performance criteria or dimensions:

KNOWLEDGE AND JUDGMENT.

CONSCIENTIOUSNESS.

SKILL IN HUMAN RELATIONS.

SKILL IN OPERATION OF REGISTER.

SKILL IN BAGGING.

ORGANIZATIONAL ABILITY OF CHECK-STAND WORK.

SKILL IN MONETARY TRANSACTIONS.

OBSERVATIONAL ABILITY.

218   In Exhibit 11–6 you will find the Behaviorally Anchored Rating Scales for one of these dimensions, "Knowledge and Judgment." Notice how there is a scale (ranging from one to seven) for rating performance from "extremely poor" to "extremely good." Notice also how the BARS is "behaviorally anchored" with specific critical incidents. For example, there is a specific critical incident ("by knowing the price of items, this checker would be expected to look for mismarked and unmarked items") that helps "anchor" or specify what is meant by "extremely good" performance. Similarly there are other critical incident "anchors" all along the scale.

Exhibit 11.6   A Behaviorally Anchored Rating Scale for the Trait "Knowledge and Judgment"

Extremely good performance	7	
		By knowing the price of items, this checker would be expected to look for mismarked and unmarked items.
Good performance	6	You can expect this checker to be aware of items that constantly fluctuate in price.
		You can expect this checker to know the various sizes of cans—No. 303, No. 2, No. 2½.
Slightly good performance	5	When in doubt, this checker would ask the other clerk if the item is taxable.
		This checker can be expected to verify with another checker a discrepancy between the shelf and the marked price before ringing up that item.
Neither poor nor good performance	4	
		When operating the quick check, the lights are flashing, this checker can be expected to check out a customer with 15 items.
Slightly poor performance	3	
		You could expect this checker to ask the customer the price of an item that he does not know.
		In the daily course of personal relationships, may be expected to linger in long conversations with a customer or another checker.
Poor performance	2	
		In order to take a break, this checker can be expected to block off the checkstand with people in line.
Extremely poor performance	1	

* Notice how the scale (from 1-7) is "Behaviorally anchored" by the "Critical incidents."

Source: Lawrence Fogli, Charles Hulin, Milton Blood, "Development of First Level Behavioral Job Criteria" *Journal of Applied Psychology* Vol. 55, (1971) No. 1, p. 6

Advantages: Developing a BARS can obviously be more time-consuming and expensive than developing other appraisal tools (such as graphic rating scales). But BARS are also said to have some important advantages.[6,7,8] Here are some of them:

1. *A more accurate gauge.* People who know the job and its requirements better than anyone else develop BARS. The resulting BARS should therefore be a very good gauge of performance on that job.

2. *Clearer standards.* The critical incidents along the scale help to clarify what is meant by "extremely good" performance, "average" performance, and so forth.

3. *Feedback.* The use of the critical incidents may be more useful in providing feedback to the people being appraised.

4. *Independent dimensions.* Systematically clustering the critical incidents into five or six performance dimensions (such as "knowledge and judgment") should help to make the dimensions more independent of one another. For example, a rater should be less likely to rate his employee high on *all* dimensions simply because he was rated high in "cooperativeness."

Mixing the Methods

Actually, there is no reason why you cannot combine two or more appraisal tools, and many companies do exactly that. An example of one such "mixed" method is illustrated in Exhibit 11–7. This presents a rating form used to appraise the performance of professional accountants in a large certified public accounting firm. Notice that basically it is a graphic rating scale, with descriptive phrases included to define the traits being measured. But in addition, notice that there is a "comments" section below each trait. This allows the rater to jot down several relevant critical incidents.

Fitting Performance Appraisal to the Task

In terms of fitting performance appraisal to the task, here's what you should keep in mind, based upon the research findings that we discussed in Chapter 9:

	in Mechanistic Organizations YOU WOULD EXPECT:	*in Organic Organizations* YOU WOULD EXPECT:
Performance Standards	Many, clear-cut standards	Few, broad performance standards. Emphasis on milestones
Performance Appraisal method used	Emphasis on rating scales	Emphasis on critical incident method

Exhibit 11.7   A "Mixed" Performance Appraisal Tool

Combining a Graphic Rating Scale with Critical Incident Comments

PERFORMANCE REPORT – IN-CHARGE ACCOUNTANT

Classification   Senior ☐ _____ _____ ____
Supervisor ☐ Name   Evaluated By   Date

Preliminary ☐ Final ☐   #Staff Supervised _____ Engagement _____
Special ☐
From _____ To _____   Total Engagement Hours:_____ Total Hours Assigned: _____
Dates Assigned

Engagement Partner _____
Describe Duties Assigned:_____
_____

Was the work assigned: Complex ☐ Difficult ☐ Routine ☐

	Outstanding	Above Average	Satisfactory	Needs Improvement	Unsatisfactory	Not Rated
TECHNICAL COMPETENCE:						
Knowledge and application of accounting and audit standards						
Knowledge and application of the Firm's Uniform Audit Approach						
Knowledge and application of tax principles and procedures						
Knowledge and application of SEC practices and procedures						
Identification and review of management letter comments						
Preparation and review of reports						
Preparation and review of engagement documentation						
Recommendations for improvements to the audit program						
Knowledge of client's business						

Comment _____
_____

	Outstanding	Above Average	Satisfactory	Needs Improvement	Unsatisfactory	Not Rated
BUSINESS SENSE & ADMINISTRATION OF THE ENGAGEMENT						
Planning and coordination of the engagement						
Utilization of staff and client personnel, assignment and delegation of duties						
Use of own budgeted time to perform assigned tasks						
Control of engagement time and expenses						
Promptness in responding to manager and client requests						
Promptness and accuracy in preparation of administrative reports, planning summaries, budgets, time reports						
Keeping manager advised of progress and difficulties encountered						

Comment _____
_____

	Outstanding	Above Average	Satisfactory	Needs Improvement	Unsatisfactory	Not Rated
LEADERSHIP						
Attitude, self-motivation, dedication, initiative, accepting responsibility						
Problem-solving, conceptualizing, creativity, imagination						
Judgment, common sense						
Motivation, direction, coaching, evaluation of staff						
Relationship with manager						
Relationship with staff						

Comment _____
_____
_____

Source: Courtesy of Mr. Patrick Conway, Coopers and Lybrand C.P.A. This exhibit is adapted and summarized from their form, and does not necessarily represent the firm's current practices.

SOME PROBLEMS TO WATCH OUT FOR   221
WHEN APPRAISING PERFORMANCE

Most of us are quite familiar with the types of inequities that can arise in appraisal systems. For example, you have probably noticed that some instructors are "easy" graders and tend to give higher grades on the average than others. And some students (or subordinates) become "teacher's pet" and tend to get rated high regardless of their actual performance.

Problems like these can destroy the usefulness of your performance appraisal system. They not only result in inaccurate, invalid appraisals, but in unfair ones as well. And once your subordinates find out that the appraisal system is unfair, you may find yourself in a worse predicament than if you had no appraisal system at all. It would be helpful, therefore, to discuss some of the specific problems you may run into when appraising performance.

The Clarity of Standards Problem

One problem concerns the clarity of the performance standards. For example, look at the graphic rating chart in Exhibit 11–8. While the chart seems objective enough, actually it might result in very unfair ratings. This is because the traits and degrees of merit are open to various interpretations. For example, different supervisors would probably define "good" performance, "fair" performance, and so on, differently. The same is true of traits such as "quality of work," or "creativity." Some traits, such as "integrity," may be almost impossible to rate objectively.

Exhibit 11.8   A Graphic Rating Scale — With Unclear Standards

	EXCELLENT	GOOD	FAIR	POOR
Quality of Work				
Quantity of Work				
Creativity				
Integrity				

For example, What is meant by "good"; quantity of work; and so forth.

Therefore, it's important that you obtain consensus among your supervisors regarding the meanings of the traits and degrees in the rating form. One way to do this is by including descriptive phrases which define each trait—as was the case in Exhibit 11–2. Training the raters can also help alleviate this problem.

The Halo Effect Problem

There is a "halo effect" in the appraisal when the appraiser assigns the same rating to *all* traits regardless of an employee's actual performance on these traits. The problem often occurs with employees who are especially friendly (or unfriendly) toward the supervisor. For example, the "unfriendly" employee will often be rated as unsatisfactory for all traits rather than simply for the trait "gets along well with others." A five- or ten-minute training program, showing supervisors what to avoid, can help alleviate this problem.[9]

The Central Tendency Problem

Perhaps you have noticed that most people have a "central tendency" when filling in questionnaires or rating scales. For example, if the scale ranges from one through seven, many people will tend to avoid the highs (six and seven) and lows (one and two), and put most of their checkmarks between three and five.

On a graphic rating chart, such as shown in Exhibit 11–2, this central tendency could mean that all employees are simply rated "average." Needless to say, this restriction can seriously distort the evaluations. It can make them almost useless for promotion, salary, or counseling purposes. The *ranking* tools we discussed are aimed at avoiding this central tendency problem.

The Leniency or Strictness Problem

You have probably noticed that some supervisors (or instructors) tend to rate all their subordinates consistently high (or low). For example, some instructors are notoriously high graders, and others are not. This strictness/ leniency problem is much more acute with graphic rating scales, since the supervisor can conceivably rate *all* his subordinates either high or low. When using some form of ranking system, on the other hand, the supervisor is forced to distinguish between high and low performers. Thus, strictness/ leniency is not as much of a problem with ranking systems.

The Problem of Bias

There is another problem in performance appraisal which in many ways is much more difficult to deal with than the other problems we have discussed. This is the problem of how the employee's sex or race affects the rating he or she obtains.

One reason this problem is more difficult to deal with is that the bias is sometimes for and sometimes against the person being rated. For example, we know that some people are prejudiced against blacks, or against females, or against some other minorities. They tend to rate them low, regardless of their actual performance. Yet we also know that even when objective performance measures (such as graphic rating scales) are used, *high* performing *females* are often rated significantly higher than *high* performing *males*. Similarly *low* performing *blacks* are often rated significantly higher than *low* performing *whites*.[10]

At present there is no easy way to predict just what effect this "bias" problem may have on an appraisal. About the best you can do is be on guard against being a "biased" appraiser.

Some Hints for Avoiding the Appraisal Problems

The performance appraisal problems we just discussed are very real. Yet the fact is that virtually all companies still use some type of appraisal system, since the information they provide is crucial.[11] Your main concern should be to effectively implement your system, so as to keep the problems to a minimum. There are at least two things you can do in this regard.

First, we know that *providing clear instructions, and training* can help to minimize or eliminate problems like the halo effect. In fact (to repeat) even where the training is just for five or ten minutes, managers who are trained to minimize rating errors do far better than those who are not trained.[12]

You can also minimize many of the problems by choosing *the right appraisal tool*. Each of the tools, such as the graphic rating scale, or forced choice method, has a number of advantages and disadvantages which you should consider before implementing your own system. These are summarized in Exhibit 11–9.

WHO SHOULD DO THE APPRAISING?

Look at the organization chart in Exhibit 11–10. How many different potential raters could appraise Jones? Actually there are at least four:

1. Smith, Jones' *immediate supervisor*.
2. Brown and Green, Jones' *peers*.
3. A *committee* comprised of the three vice-presidents, and president.
4. Jones himself (*self-appraisal*).

Exhibit 11.9 Important Advantages and Disadvantages of Appraisal Tools

	Advantages	Disadvantages
Graphic Rating Scales	Simple to use: provides a quantitative rating for each employee.	Standards may be unclear; halo effect, central tendency, leniency, bias can also be problems here.
Alteration Ranking	Simple to use (but not as simple as graphic rating scales). Avoids central tendency and other problems of rating scales.	Ranking may still not be precise.
Paired Comparison Method	Results in more precise rankings than does alternation ranking.	More difficult than ranking.
Forced Distribution Method	Here you end up with a predetermined number of people in each group.	But your appraisal results depend on the adequacy of your original choice of cut-off points.
Critical Incident Method	Helps specify what is "right" and "wrong" about the employee's performance; forces manager to evaluate subordinates on an ongoing basis.	Difficult to rate or rank employees relative to one another.
BARS	Participation of employees in developing the BARS should lead to a more accurate gauge; the critical incidents help "anchor" and clarify the scale.	Very difficult to develop.

Needless to say, each of these raters will see a somewhat different facet of Jones' performance, and will therefore come to different conclusions about his performance.

Appraisal by the Immediate Supervisor

Supervisors' ratings are the heart of most appraisal systems. This is because getting a supervisor's appraisal is relatively easy and also makes a great deal of sense. The supervisor should be—and usually is—in just about the best position to observe and evaluate his subordinate's performance. Therefore most appraisal systems rely heavily on the supervisor's evaluation.

Using Peer Evaluations

The evaluation of an individual by his peers has proven to be effective in predicting future management success. From a study of military officers, for example, we know that peer ratings were quite accurate in predicting which officers would be promoted-and which would not.[13] And in another study that involved over 200 industrial managers, peer ratings were similarly useful in predicting who was promoted.[14] One thing to watch out for, of course, is "logrolling," in which all the peers simply get together to rate each other high.

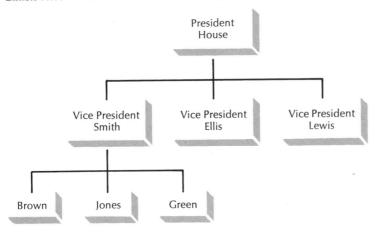

Using Rating Committees

Many companies use rating committees to evaluate employees. As in Exhibit 11–10, these committees are usually composed of the employees' immediate supervisor and three or four other supervisors. Needless to say, everyone on the committee should be able to intelligently evaluate some aspect of the employee's performance.

You will often find quite a discrepancy in the ratings made by the different supervisors, and this was formerly considered a major drawback of the committee approach to appraisals. But in the past few years we have discovered two things which suggest that committee ratings can in fact be quite useful. First, the combined use of several raters can help "cancel out" problems such as bias and halo effect on the part of the individual raters. Second, we now accept the fact that raters at different levels in the organization usually observe different facets of an employee's job performance and the appraisal ought to reflect these differences.[15]

Using Self-Appraisals

Companies have had mixed success using self-appraisals for evaluating performance. On the one hand, many companies use "Management by Objectives" programs. Here subordinates and superiors jointly establish goals and periodically evaluate the subordinate's performance with respect to these goals. Many of these programs are quite effective. And for some reason self-ratings usually do not exhibit the central tendency—or halo—problems we previously discussed.[16]

On the other hand, we also know that when a person appraises himself his rating is usually higher than it would be if he were rated by his superior.[17] Because of this fairly consistent upward bias in self-appraisals, your best bet is probably to use them for counseling and developing subordinates. They are not as useful for making salary and promotion decisions.

COUNSELING SUBORDINATES

What Counseling Should Not Involve

Once the performance appraisal is completed you'll probably want to feedback the results to your subordinate. In a majority of cases this involves getting together with him once or twice a year to review the ratings.

As often as not, these meetings turn out to be frustrating, tense, and useless affairs for all concerned. Most supervisors and subordinates are more than a little uncomfortable when having to engage in these meetings in the first place. And the problem is compounded by the fact that most managers spend all their time criticizing the subordinate, rather than trying to work out plans for constructive change.

What Counseling Should Involve

Chances are your subordinate is as aware as you are of what he has done wrong, and simply criticizing him probably won't change his behavior. In light of this, what goals should you aim to accomplish? Here are a few to keep in mind:

1. To bring about some *constructive change* in your subordinate's behavior.
2. To *locate the root cause* of the performance deficiency.
3. To *reduce frustration* by allowing a subordinate to express his attitudes and feelings about his job.
4. To *stimulate problem solving* for the purpose of finding solutions to the subordinate's performance problems.

Your approach to the counseling meetings should be governed by the above four goals. Needless to say, you're going to have to take a different approach than if your goal was simply to "let your subordinate know where he is falling down on the job."

Three Problems to Watch Out for When Counseling

Defensiveness: Psychiatrists know that if each of us had to absorb the full impact of the problems and tensions of daily living we would probably crack under the pressure.[18] Therefore we all set up defense mechanisms which help us screen out painful experiences.

Defenses are thus a very important and familiar aspect of our lives. When a person is accused of poor performance, for example, his immediate reaction will often be *denial.* By denying that he was at fault he avoids having to question or analyze his own competence. Still others react to criticism with *anger and aggression.* This helps them to let off steam and postpone confronting the immediate problem until they are better able to cope with it. Still others react to criticism by *retreating* into a shell.

In any event, understanding and dealing with defensiveness can help you avoid one of the big barriers to effective counseling. Psychologist Mortimer Feinberg suggests the following:

1. *Recognize that defensive behavior is normal.*
2. *Never attack a man's defenses.* Don't try to "explain a man to himself" by saying things like "You know the real reason you're using that excuse is because you can't bear to be blamed for anything." Instead, try to concentrate on the act itself (inadequate sales, decreasing profits, etc.) rather than on the man.
3. *Postpone action.* Sometimes the best thing to do is nothing at all. People frequently react to sudden threats by instinctively hiding behind their "masks." But, given sufficient time, a more rational reaction takes over.
4. *Recognize your own limitations.* Don't expect to be able to solve every problem that comes up—especially the human ones. More important, remember that a supervisor should not try to be a psychologist. Offering your people understanding is one thing, trying to deal with deep-seated psychological problems is another matter entirely.

Criticizing: Criticism can drastically undermine your subordinate's future performance. For example, in one study at the General Electric Company, subordinates who were criticized by their managers during counseling subsequently performed much more poorly than those who were not. And, as you might imagine, the criticism had an especially damaging effect on those subordinates who were more insecure to start with.[19] Where some constructive criticism *is* necessary, psychologist Feinberg suggests following the "Do's and Don'ts" summarized in Exhibit 11–11.

228   **Exhibit 11.11**   Some Hints for "How to Criticize"

DO	DON'T
Try to make your negative comments immediately on his completion of the act which you want to criticize. Correct him *immediately*.	Don't bother criticizing your subordinate unless you feel that he is capable of making some *improvement*.
Criticize your man in an environment where he knows you are *paying direct attention* to him. If possible, go to his work station rather than have him go to yours.	Many managers tend to give their subordinates a critical *"broadside."* Don't overcriticize your people, take one point at a time.
Know the man you are criticizing. Is he receptive? Defensive? Is he looking for ways to improve?	*Never say "always."* No one "always" does anything wrong, or everything right.
Keep it private. Open criticism can be, and frequently is, disastrous.	Don't use the *"sandwich technique"* by prefacing your remarks with praise, and then sandwiching him in with the criticism.
Criticize constructively. Be specific. Use "critical incidents." Give specific suggestions of what could be done and why.	Make a *joke* of it. What seems humorous to you, might well seem sarcastic and in bad humor to the person being criticized.
Make sure your criticism is *objective* and free of any personal feelings on your part. Direct the criticism at what can be done, rather than to the person.	Expect to win any *popularity* contests. There are going to be times when you simply have to criticize a subordinate, and criticism is bound to strike a sour note occasionally.
Make sure that you don't let your own need to give advice and be respected force you into *selling* your own ideas.	
Criticize *without comparison.*	

Source: Based on Mortimer Feinberg, *Effective Psychology for Managers* (Englewood Cliffs, N. J.: Prentice-Hall, Inc., 1967) pp. 169-177

Pursuing Multiple Goals: Some supervisors attempt to accomplish several different goals during the same counseling meeting. Yet Norman Maier says that discussing "future development" calls for a different approach than does telling an employee "where he stands." In the latter case a "tell and sell" approach is called for. Here doses of criticism and persuasion are intermixed throughout the meeting. But for development purposes, you have to encourage your subordinate to appraise himself. This calls for a give-and-take problem solving approach throughout the meeting.[20]

Hints for Effective Counseling

1. *Remember that defenses are normal.*
2. *Don't just try to sell your own ideas.* Listen carefully to what your subordinate is trying to tell you. Carefully restate and reflect his feelings so that he can more objectively analyze them. Norman Maier says that an active listener must show by his behavior that he is trying to understand, and that he accepts the person as well as what he says. "For a counselor or a listener to indicate doubt, surprise, disagreement, or criticism, places him in the role of a judge or critic; for him to

express agreement, pity, or even sympathy, places him in the role of a   229
supporter." [21]

3. *Reflect feelings.* Professor Maier also says that a counselor should serve as a "selective mirror." Incidents, justifications, details of arguments and reasons, and so forth, are relatively unimportant, he says. But how the person *feels* about any of these things *is* important. Thus, as shown in Exhibit 11–12, you should reflect these feelings back to your subordinate. In other words, try to help your subordinate get a more objective view of his feelings by restating them in different words.

Exhibit 11.12   The Counselor Serves as a Selective Mirror

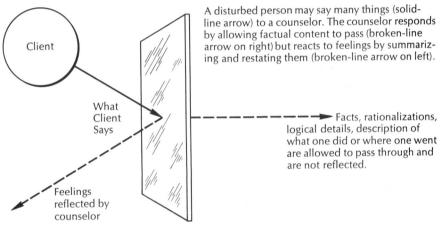

A disturbed person may say many things (solid-line arrow) to a counselor. The counselor responds by allowing factual content to pass (broken-line arrow on right) but reacts to feelings by summarizing and restating them (broken-line arrow on left).

Client

What Client Says

Facts, rationalizations, logical details, description of what one did or where one went are allowed to pass through and are not reflected.

Feelings reflected by counselor

Source: Norman R. F. Maier, *Psychology in Industrial Organizations* (Boston, Houghton Mifflin, 1973) p. 534.

4. *Don't criticize.* Try to avoid being critical, especially where you are trying to bring about some constructive change in your subordinate's behavior. Where some constructive criticism is necessary, try following psychologist Feinberg's "Do's and Don'ts."

5. *Aim for constructive change.* Remember that the purpose of counseling is to bring about a constructive change. Therefore, problem solve with your subordinate—set joint goals, and mutually review his accomplishments. Mutually discuss minimizing any roadblocks that may be in his way.[22]

6. *Counsel day to day.* You want to avoid "critical broadsides," and to give feedback immediately. You also want to avoid mixing "tell and sell" with "problem solving and development." Therefore try to counsel often, on a day-to-day basis, rather than just once or twice a year.[23]

7. *Don't try to be an expert.* Don't try to psychoanalyze your subordinate or to "explain him" to himself—leave that to a trained psychologist. Concentrate on mutually setting goals and reviewing achievements.

230   ## Some Important Things to Remember from This Chapter:

1. Appraising performance will be a very important part of your management job. It is the basis on which your subordinates' promotion and salary decisions are made. And it provides you with an opportunity to review with your subordinate his work-related behavior.

2. All the performance appraisal tools we discussed have their own advantages and disadvantages. Graphic rating scales are simple to use, but are susceptible to problems such as halo effect and central tendency. Ranking methods, such as alternation ranking or the paired comparison method, are still fairly simple to use (though not nearly as easy as the graphic rating scales). They also help you avoid many of the problems to which graphic rating scales are susceptible (such as central tendency). The critical incident method is very useful for coaching subordinates, since it focuses on specific instances of good or bad performance. But it is difficult to rate or rank employees relative to one another with this method, so it is not quite as useful for making salary decisions. BARS appear to have great potential in performance appraisal, but they are relatively difficult to develop and implement.

3. You also have to give some thought as to who actually does the appraising. You might, for example, choose between the person's immediate supervisor, his peers, an appraisal committee, or even allow the person to appraise himself. Most appraisal systems depend on either the supervisor, or on some logical committee for the appraisal.

4. Once the results of the performance appraisal are in, you should make an honest attempt to sit down with your subordinate and counsel him. Remember that the aim of this counseling session is not just to tell him what he has done wrong. Instead, you want to locate the root cause of the problem and bring about some constructive change. In doing so, try to avoid making him defensive, avoid criticizing him, and try not to mix the goals of "development" with "where you stand now."

STUDY ASSIGNMENTS

1. List and discuss the pros and cons of at least four performance appraisal tools.
2. Develop a graphic rating scale for the following jobs: secretary; engineer; professor.
3. Evaluate the rating scale in Exhibit 11–1. Discuss ways to improve the scale.
4. Explain how you would use the alternation ranking method; the paired comparison method; and the forced distribution method.
5. Over the period of a week, develop a set of critical incidents covering the classroom performance of one of your instructors.
6. Explain in your own words how you would go about developing a behaviorally anchored rating scale.
7. Explain the problems to be avoided in appraising performance.

8. Discuss the pros and cons of using different potential raters to appraise
   a person's performance.
9. Your boss has asked you to give a lecture on the topic "How to counsel
   subordinates." Explain what you would cover in your lecture.
10. The performance of one of your workers has dropped markedly over
    the past four months. His work has become sloppy and his attendance
    poor, and he has gotten into several arguments with his co-workers.
    Have one of your classmates take on the role of this worker, and have
    a counseling interview with that person.

NOTES FOR THE CHAPTER

1. William Glueck, *Personnel: A Diagnostic Approach* (Dallas: BPI, 1974) p. 286.
2. Source: Dale Yoder, *Personnel Management and Industrial Relations* (Englewood Cliffs, N.J.: Prentice-Hall, Inc., 1970).
3. See, for example, Timothy Keaveny and Anthony McGann, "The Comparison of Behavioral Expectation Scales and Graphic Rating Scales," *Journal of Applied Psychology*, Vol. 60, No. 6 (1975) pp. 695–703.
4. Based on Donald Schwab, Herbert Heneman, III, and Thomas DeCotiis, "Behaviorally Anchored Scales: A Review of the Literature," *Personnel Psychology*, Vol. 28 (1975) pp. 549–562.
5. Lawrence Fogli, Charles Hulin, and Milton Blood, "Development of First Level Behavioral Job Criteria," *Journal of Applied Psychology*, Vol. 55, No. 1 (1971) pp. 3–8.
6. Timothy Keaveny and Anthony McGann, "A Comparison of Behavioral Expectation Scales and Graphic Rating Scales."
7. Schwab, Heneman, DeCotiis, "Behaviorally Anchored Rating Scales: A Review of the Literature."
8. James Goodale and Ronald Burke, "Behaviorally Based Rating Scales Need Not Be Job Specific," *Journal of Applied Psychology*, Vol. 60, No. 3; June 1975.
9. Gary Latham, Kenneth Wexley, and Elliot Pursell, "Training Managers to Minimize Rating Errors in the Observation of Behavior," *Journal of Applied Psychology*, Vol. 60, No. 5 (October 1975).
10. William J. Bigoness, "Effect of Applicants Sex, Race, and Performance on Employer's Performance Ratings: Some Additional Findings," *Journal of Applied Psychology*, Vol. 61, No. 1 (February 1976).
11. Allen Patz, "Performance Appraisal: Useful But Still Resisted," *Harvard Business Review* (May-June, 1975).
12. Gary P. Latham, Kenneth Wexley, and Elliot Pursell, "Training Managers to Minimize Rating Errors in the Observation of Behavior," *Journal of Applied Psychology*, Vol. 60, No. 5 (October 1975); Walter Borman, "Effect of Instructions to Avoid Halo Error on Reliability and Validity on Performance Evaluation Ratings," *Journal of Applied Psychology*, Vol. 60, No. 5 (October 1975).
13. R. G. Downey, F. F. Medland, and L. G. Yates, "Evaluation of a Peer Rating System and for Predicting Subsequent Promotion of Senior Military Officers," *Journal of Applied Psychology*, Vol. 61, No. 2 (April 1976).
14. Allan Krautt, "Prediction of Managerial Success by Peer and Training Staff Ratings," *Journal of Applied Psychology*, Vol. 60, No. 1 (February 1975).
15. Walter C. Borman, "The Rating of Individuals in Organizations: An Alternate Approach," *Organizational Behavior and Human Performance*, Vol. 12 (1974) pp. 105–124.
16. Herbert G. Heneman, III, "Comparison of Self- and Superior Ratings of Managerial Performance," *Journal of Applied Psychology*, Vol. 59, No. 5 (1974) pp. 638–642; Richard J. Klimoski and Manuel London, "Role of the Rater in Performance Appraisal," *Journal of Applied Psychology*, Vol. 59, No. 4 (1974) pp. 445–451.

232   **17.** J. W. Parker et al., "Rating Scale Content: III. Relationships Between Supervisory and Self-Ratings," *Personnel Psychology*, Vol. 12, pp. 49–63, in John B. Miner, "Management Appraisal: A Review of Procedures and Practices," reprinted by W. Clay Hamner and Frank Schmidt, *Contemporary Problems in Personnel* (Chicago: St. Clair, 1974) p. 247.

18. Mortimer Feinberg, *Effective Psychology for Managers* (Englewood Cliffs, N.J.: Prentice-Hall, Inc., 1967) p. 80.

19. H. H. Meyer, E. A. Kay, and J. French, "Split-Roles in Performance Appraisal," *Harvard Business Review*, Vol. 43 (1965) pp. 123–129.

20. Norman R. F. Maier, *Psychology in Industrial Organizations* (Boston: Houghton Mifflin, 1973) pp. 558–559.

21. Norman Maier, *Psychology in Industrial Organizations*, p. 532.

22. H. H. Meyer, E. A. Kay, and J. French, "Split Roles in Performance Appraisal," *Harvard Business Review*, Vol. 43 (1965) pp. 123–129; Norman Maier, *Psychology in Industrial Organizations*, pp. 556–558.

23. Meyer, Kay, and French, "Split Roles in Performance Appraisal."

A Framework for Studying the Management Fundamentals

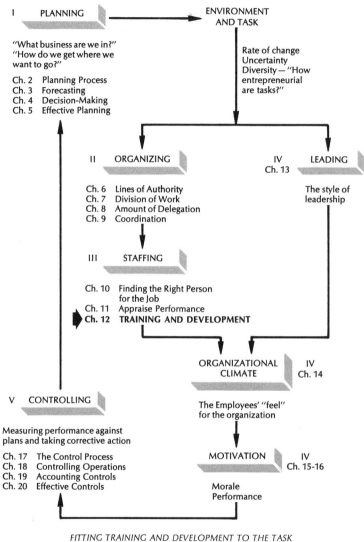

I PLANNING

"What business are we in?"
"How do we get where we
want to go?"

Ch. 2 Planning Process
Ch. 3 Forecasting
Ch. 4 Decision-Making
Ch. 5 Effective Planning

ENVIRONMENT
AND TASK

Rate of change
Uncertainty
Diversity — "How
entrepreneurial
are tasks?"

Where we are now: Discussing the process and techniques of training and development.

II ORGANIZING

Ch. 6 Lines of Authority
Ch. 7 Division of Work
Ch. 8 Amount of Delegation
Ch. 9 Coordination

III STAFFING

Ch. 10 Finding the Right Person
for the Job
Ch. 11 Appraise Performance
▶ Ch. 12 TRAINING AND DEVELOPMENT

IV LEADING
Ch. 13

The style of
leadership

ORGANIZATIONAL
CLIMATE

IV
Ch. 14

V CONTROLLING

Measuring performance against
plans and taking corrective action

Ch. 17 The Control Process
Ch. 18 Controlling Operations
Ch. 19 Accounting Controls
Ch. 20 Effective Controls

The Employees' "feel"
for the organization

MOTIVATION

IV
Ch. 15-16

Morale
Performance

FITTING TRAINING AND DEVELOPMENT TO THE TASK

	Mechanistic	*Organic*
Training and Development Technique	Emphasis here on "surface" techniques like lectures, programmed learning, and on the job training	Emphasis here on "in depth" techniques like sensitivity training

When you have finished studying

12 Training and Development

You should be able to:

1. *Develop and implement a training program.*

2. *Explain how to distinguish between "training" problems and those not amenable to training.*

3. *Cite at least eight training and development techniques.*

4. *Discuss at least five training and development techniques.*

5. *Explain the difference between "surface" and "in-depth" training and development techniques.*

INTRODUCTION

The Sanitary Company is a small company that provides building maintenance services on a contract basis. Employees work part time cleaning buildings and offices during the evening. Most employees work four hours a night. They are paid at an hourly rate.

Employees work in groups ranging in size from two to 25 persons. There are about 15 such "work groups" in the company. Each group is responsible for doing all the cleaning in one building. The actual cleaning work is similar for each group.

Employees are expected to report for work each night at the building to be cleaned. The company has managers who are responsible for supervising the cleaning crews, but they are not members of the actual work groups.

Employees tend to have low levels of education. Some of them are illiterate. About half of the employees are women. Many of the women are housewives during the day. For most of the male employees, work with the Sanitary Company is a second job. The employees range in age from 16 to over 70.

Assume that you have been hired as a consultant to the company that is described in the case.* The company president, Mr. N., has told you that

---

* *Source:* Douglas Hall, Donald Bowen, Roy Lewicki, and Francine Hall, *Experiences in Management and Organizational Behavior* (Chicago: St. Clair, 1975) pp. 178–79. Reprinted by permission.

he is concerned with the high rate of turnover and absenteeism in his company. He has asked you to diagnose his company's problem, and to recommend a plan for solving it. He specifically wants your answers to the following questions:

1. *What do you think the real problem is? Why?*
2. *What solution(s) would you propose? Why? Would you recommend training?*
3. *How would you implement your plan? What reasons would you give for doing it this way?*

What will you tell the company president? Think about these questions as you read this chapter. By the end of the chapter you should be in a much better position to answer them.

STEPS IN THE TRAINING PROGRAM

Step 1. Analyzing the Organization

Training and development programs should be aimed at preparing employees to better achieve the goals of the organization. Therefore, the first step in developing a training program is for you to analyze the organization's goals and current performance.[1] This is one reason why "organizational analysis"—reviewing the organization's goals, plans, environment, practices, and problems—is important: it helps you identify problems. For example, you might find that morale is low throughout the organization; or that communications do not flow freely from one level to the next. Problems like these are often identified by having a consultant interview a number of employees, or by administering questionnaires.

Organizational analysis is also important because many of the training programs that fail do so because they lack the backing and full commitment of top management.[2] One way to insure this commitment is to have top management participate in developing training programs which it sees as vehicles for achieving the goals it has set for the organization.

Step 2. Identify Important Performance Discrepancies

Your next step is to *determine if there is a discrepancy between your employee's actual and desired performance.* For this you'll need the person's job description and job specification. These describe his *desired* performance.

One way to identify discrepancies is through performance appraisal, which we discussed in Chapter 11. Here you determine his actual performance.

Robert Mager and Peter Pipe say that you next have to decide whether
the performance discrepancy is *important* or not.[3] They suggest completing
the sentence: "The discrepancy is important because. . . ." Ask: "What will
happen if I leave the discrepancy alone?" This will "force into the open the
reasons why someone says the discrepancy is important."

Step 3. Problem Identification

In Chapter 4 we emphasized the importance of identifying the "central problem." Identifying this problem is also very important when developing a training program. For example, let's suppose that you analyze your
organization. You discover important conflicts between members of two departments; they are always arguing with one another, they don't return each
other's calls, and so on. How would you define the problem?

Many managers would probably fall into the trap of identifying "interdepartment conflict" as the problem. They would assume that it could be
alleviated by training employees to be more sensitive and understanding
toward each other. But if they dug deeply enough they might find that the
real problem does not lend itself to a training solution at all.

For example, in one company the kind of conflict we just described
resulted because the company had very inadequate job descriptions; it was
therefore hard to pinpoint who was responsible for what. A tug-of-war
ensued, in which each department tried to obtain more responsibility and
authority for itself. Thus the central problem in this case was "inadequate job
descriptions." As soon as the consultants assigned clear, unambiguous job
descriptions to each employee the tug-of-war ceased and conflict all but disappeared.

If It's Not a "Training" Problem, What Is It? In Exhibit 12–1,
William Tracy has summarized some suggested procedures for identifying
training and development requirements. Notice that very often "training" is
not the solution. Instead reorganization, clearer policies, improved job design,
or better work methods are called for. Robert Mager and Peter Pipe suggest
trying to isolate the real problem by asking four questions:

> 1. *Is the desired performance punishing?* For example, ask: What
> is the consequence of performing as desired? Is it punishing to perform
> as expected?
> 2. *Is nonperformance rewarding?* For example, ask: What is the
> result of doing it his way instead of my way? What does he get out
> of his present performance in the way of rewards? Does he get more
> attention for misbehaving than for behaving?
> 3. *Does performing really matter?* For example, ask: Does per-
> forming as desired matter to the performer? Is there a favorable out-

Exhibit 12.1   A Checklist for Identifying Training and Development Requirements

1: Determine immediate needs.
- a. Evaluate current training and development programs to determine whether the training produces the desired behavioral changes.
  - (1) Evaluate ongoing training programs.
    - a) Review training documents for adequacy.
    - b) Observe trainers, trainees in learning environment of classroom, shop, laboratory.
    - c) Analyze in-course and end-of-course test results.
    - d) Interview trainers and trainees.
  - (2) Evaluate the *products* of the training system.
    - a) Interview line supervisors.
    - b) Interview and observe trainees at the workplace.
    - c) Review personnel records and performance ratings.
    - d) Administer questionnaires to supervisors and trainees; analyze questionnaires.
    - e) Analyze work samples.
- b. List and analyze shortfalls in process or product. Determine whether they are due to:
  - 1) Poor organization.
  - 2) Inadequate supervision.
  - 3) Unclear policies.
  - 4) Poor communications.
  - 5) Improper personnel selection policies or procedures.
  - 6) Poor job design.
  - 7) Equipment or material problems.
  - 8) Work methods.
  - 9) Inappropriate work standards.
  - 10) Inadequate operator or supervisor training.
- c. Survey all aspects of enterprise operations to determine areas where additional training is required.
  - 1) Compare job descriptions and applicant specifications with personnel records.
  - 2) Analyze performance ratings.
  - 3) Analyze all enterprise records for areas of possible deficiency.
  - 4) Identify and analyze operating problems.
  - 5) Use interviews, questionnaires, group conferences, tests, and work samples to determine training problems.
  - 6) Subject each problem to careful analysis to determine whether the problem is due to:
    - a) Poor organization.
    - b) Inadequate supervision.
    - c) Unclear or ambiguous policies.
    - d) Poor communications.
    - e) Improper personnel selection policies.
    - f) Poor job design
    - g) Equipment or material deficiencies.
    - h) Improper work methods.
    - i) Inappropriate work standards.
    - j) Training deficits.
2: Determine long-range training needs.
- a. Analyze enterprise plans, policies, and forecasts to determine their potential impact on staffing needs.
- b. Identify and analyze future systems, equipment, techniques, and procedures to determine their impact on personnel requirements.
- c. Determine whether current training systems will support future personnel requirements in terms of
  - 1) Operative personnel (workers)
  - 2) Supervisory personnel.
  - 3) Managerial personnel.
- d. Identify training system shortfalls.
3: For each training requirement, determine whether the training should be provided on or off the premises, and whether it should be formal or on-the-job. Consider:
- a. Comparative costs
- b. Availability of in-house personnel, equipment, and facilities resources.
4: Summarize training needs.
5: For off-the premises programs, develop objectives, prepare contract specifications, solicit and evaluate proposals and select a contractor.
6: For in-house programs, develop objectives and guidelines following the procedures described in the remainder of this chapter.

Source: William Tracey, *Designing Training and Development Systems*, pp. 37–40; copyright © 1971 by American Management Association. Reprinted by permission.

come for performing? Is there an undesirable outcome for not performing?

    4. *Are there obstacles to performing?* For example, ask: What
prevents him from performing? Does he know what is expected of him?
Does he know when to do what is expected of him? Are there conflicting demands on his time? Does he lack the authority, time, or
tools? Is he restricted by policies or by a "right way of doing it" that
ought to be changed?

Step 4. Choosing the Training Objectives and Techniques

    Let's suppose that after carefully analyzing the situation you come to
the conclusion that training and development are the solution. You are now
faced with the problem of crystalizing your training objectives, and of choosing the best training and development technique.

    As you can see in Exhibit 12–2, one way to distinguish between train-
ing techniques is to classify them according to whether they 1) impart knowledge; 2) develop skills; or 3) change attitudes. For example, if your objective
is simply to impart knowledge, then programmed instruction, lectures, or
conferences are called for. But if your goal is to develop the skills of your
employees, then simply "lecturing" them probably won't suffice. What you
need here is to get them "involved" through on-the-job training, case studies,
or computerized management games.

Exhibit 12.2 The Primary Uses of Training and Development Techniques

	Impart Knowledge	Develop Skills	Change Attitudes
Lectures	x		
Programmed Learning	x		
Conferences	x		
On the Job Training	x	x	
Management Games		x	
Role Playing		x	x
Sensitivity Training			x
Grid Training		x	x

    On the other hand, you will sometimes find it necessary to change the
attitudes of employees in order to solve the problem. For example, in establishing minority recruiting/affirmative action programs many companies find
it necessary to "sensitize" their managers to the needs of the new minority
recruits. In this case, a more "in-depth" training and development technique
aimed at changing employees' attitudes is called for.

TECHNIQUES FOR IMPARTING KNOWLEDGE

Lectures

Lectures are one of the most simple ways of imparting knowledge to trainees. Here the training instructor presents a series of facts, concepts, or principles, and explains relationships.[4] As most students are painfully aware, lectures are usually a means of "telling" trainees something. The students (or trainees) participate mainly as listeners. In training, the most important uses of lectures include:

1. Reducing anxiety about upcoming training programs or organizational changes by explaining their purposes.
2. Introducing a subject and presenting an overview of its scope.
3. Presenting basic material that will provide a common background for subsequent activities.
4. Illustrating the application of rules, concepts, or principles; reviewing, clarifying, or summarizing.[5]

The main *advantage* of the lecture method is that it is simple and efficient. The trainer can present more material in a given amount of time than he can by any other method.[6] And he can do so with very large groups.

But as most students know, lectures have some important *drawbacks*. They usually don't provide for student participation, and unless the material is very interesting, little learning may take place. People learn skills by doing, and therefore lectures are inadequate by themselves for teaching new skills or for changing attitudes. We also know that the necessary stress on verbal communication can prove very frustrating to some students.[7] And while a skillful lecturer can adapt his material to the specific group, usually it is almost impossible for him to adjust it for individual differences *within* a group.

Programmed Learning

Whether the programmed learning device itself is a textbook or a machine, programmed learning always consists of three functions:

1. Presenting questions, facts, or problems to the learner.
2. Allowing him to respond.
3. Providing feedback on the accuracy of his answers.

A page from a programmed textbook is presented in Exhibit 12–3. The main advantage of programmed learning is that usually it reduces training time by about one-third.[8] And since it lets people learn at their own rate, provides immediate feedback and reduces the risk of error, it should also facilitate learning.

Exhibit 12.3 A Page from a Programmed Textbook

Sec. 2	Graphs

17
    The most direct way to plot the graph of a function $y = f(x)$ is to make a table of reasonably spaced values of x and of the corresponding values of $y = f(x)$. Then each pair of values (x,y) can be represented by a point as in the previous frame. A graph of the function is obtained by connecting the points with a smooth curve. Of course, the points on the curve may be only approximate. If we want an accurate plot we just have to be very careful and use many points. (On the other hand, crude plots are pretty good for most purposes.)

Go to 18.

18
    As an example, here is a plot of the function $y = 3x^2$. A table of values of x and y is shown and these points are indicated on the graph.

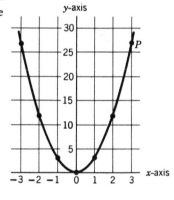

x	y
-3	27
-2	12
-1	3
0	0
1	3
2	12
3	27

    To test yourself, encircle below the pair of coordinates that corresponds to the point P indicated in the figure.

⌈(3,27) | (27,3) | none of these⌉

    Check your answer. If correct, go on to 19. If incorrect study frame 16 once again and then go to 19.

Source: Daniel Kleppner and Norman Ramsey, *Quick Calculus* (New York: John Wiley & Sons, 1965) p. 11.

N.B. The right answer to frame 18 is (3, 27).

We know, however, that trainees usually do *not* learn much more with programmed learning than they would with a conventional textbook approach.[9] Yet the costs of developing the manuals, books, and machinery for programmed learning can be quite high. Therefore you have to carefully weigh the cost of developing such programs against the accelerated (but not better) learning which should occur.

Conferences

There are three types of conferences.[10] In the *directed discussion* the trainer guides the discussion in such a way that the facts, principles, or concepts are explained. In the *training conference* the instructor's job is to get the group to pool its knowledge and past experiences and bring different points of view to bear on the problem. The purpose of the *seminar conference* is to find an answer to a question or a solution to a problem. Here the group is used to develop the best solution. The instructor's job is to define the problem, and encourage and insure full participation in the discussion.

The main advantage of conferences is that they permit your people to actively engage in discussions. This is important because, for most people, the opportunity to express one's own views can be very stimulating.

The main limitation to using conferences is probably the lack of good conference leaders.[11] A good conference leader can:

1. Clearly identify the central problem.
2. See to it that all participants are encouraged to present points of view and develop alternatives.
3. See to it that there's a clear agenda to follow.
4. Minimize debate over unimportant details.
5. Prevent domination by one or two individuals.
6. Provide clear summaries on each point.

TECHNIQUES FOR DEVELOPING SKILLS

On-the-Job Training (OJT)

Virtually every employee, from mail-room clerk to company president, gets some "on-the-job training" when he joins a firm. This is why William Tracey calls it "the most common, the most widely accepted, and the most necessary method of training employees in the skills essential for acceptable job performance."[12] In many companies, OJT is the *only* type of training available to employees.

There are a variety of OJT methods. Probably the most familiar is the *"coaching"* or *"understudy"* method. Here the employee is trained on the job by his immediate superior. At lower levels, the coaching may simply involve having the trainee observe his supervisor so as to develop the skills necessary for running a machine. But this technique is also widely used at top management levels. Here the positions of "assistant" and "assistant to" are often used for the purpose of training and developing the company's future top executives.[13] Some hints for using OJT are presented in Exhibit 12–4.

Job rotation, in which the employee (usually a management trainee) moves from job to job at planned intervals, is another OJT technique. The

Exhibit 12.4   The Four Step Method of on the Job Training: Some Hints

STEP 1:   *Preparation of the Learner*

    1. Put the learner at ease—relieve the tension.
    2. Explain why he is being taught.
    3. Create interest, encourage questions, find out what the learner already knows about his job or other jobs.
    4. Explain the why of the whole job, and relate it to some job the worker already knows.
    5. Place the learner as close to his normal working position as possible.
    6. Familiarize him with the equipment, materials, tools, and trade terms.

STEP 2:   *Presentation of the Operation*

    1. Explain quantity and quality requirements.
    2. Go through the job at the normal work pace.
    3. Go through the job at a slow pace several times, explaining each step. Between operations, explain the difficult parts, or those in which errors are likely to be made.
    4. Go through the job at a slow pace several times, explain the key points.
    5. Have the learner explain the steps as you go through the job at a slow pace.
    6. Have the learner explain the key points as you go through the job at a slow pace.

STEP 3:   *Performance Tryout*

    1. Have the learner go through the job several times, slowly, explaining to you each step. Correct his mistakes, and, if necessary, do some of the complicated steps for him the first few times.
    2. You, the trainer, run the job at the normal pace.
    3. Have the learner do the job, gradually building up skill and speed.
    4. As soon as he demonstrates that he can do the job put him on his own, but don't abandon him.

STEP 4:   *Follow Up*

    1. Designate to whom the learner should go for help if he needs it, or if he needs to ask questions.
    2. Gradually decrease supervision, checking his work from time to time against quality and quantity standards.
    3. Correct faulty work patterns that begin to creep into his work, and do it before they become a habit. Show him why the learned method is superior.
    4. Compliment good work; encourage him and keep him encouraged until he is able to meet the quality/quantity standards.

Source: William Berliner and William McLarney, *Management Practice and Training* (Homewood, Richard D. Irwin, 1974) pp. 442-443.

244   jobs usually vary in content, and you will often find the trainee being moved periodically from production, to finance, to sales, and so on.

Special assignments and *committees* are OJT techniques used to provide lower-level executives with first-hand experience in working on actual problems. Executives from various functional areas serve on "boards" and are required to analyze problems and recommend solutions to top management.[14]

Management Games

People learn best by getting actively involved in the activity itself, and management games can be very useful for gaining such involvement. In the typical game, trainees are divided into five- or six-man "companies." They are given a goal, such as "maximize sales," and are told that they can make several specific decisions. For example, they may be allowed to decide 1) how much to spend on advertising; 2) how much to produce; 3) how much inventory to maintain; 4) and how many of which product to produce. Usually the game itself compresses a two- or three-year period into hours, days, or months.

As in the real world, each company usually doesn't get to see what decisions the other companies had made, although these decisions obviously affect their own sales. For example, if a competitor decides to increase his advertising expenditures he may end up increasing his sales at the expense of yours.

There is usually a great sense of excitement and enjoyment in playing the game. And in addition to being an enjoyable way to develop problem solving skills, games also help focus attention on the need for planning rather than on "putting out fires." The companies are apt to elect their own officers and develop their own organization structures. They can therefore be useful for developing leadership skills, and for fostering cooperation and teamwork.

A major problem with games is that they can be very expensive to develop and implement, particularly when the game itself is computerized. Also, management games usually force the decision-maker to choose his alternatives from a "closed" list. In real life (as we discussed in Chapter 4) managers are more often rewarded for creating new alternatives.[15] On the whole, though, trainees almost always react favorably to a well-run game, and it is a good technique for developing problem solving and leadership skills.

Role Playing

Role playing involves the spontaneous acting out of a situation by two or more persons under the direction of a trainer.[16] A dialogue usually ensues and, before anyone realizes it, the trainees are enthusiastically playing out their roles.

To give you a feeling for what role playing is like we've reproduced the roles from a famous role-playing exercise in Exhibit 12–5. The exercise is called "The New Truck Dilemma." Each person gets to see only his own role—the general instructions given to all the role players are presented in Exhibit 12–6.[17]

Exhibit 12.5   Several Roles from the "New Truck Dilemma"

Role Sheet: Walt Marshall, Foreman

You are the foreman of a crew of repairmen, each of whom drives a small service truck to and from his various jobs. Every so often, you get a new truck to exchange for an old one and you have the problem of deciding which of your men should have the new truck. Often there are hard feelings because each man seems to feel he is entitled to the new truck, so you have a tough time being fair. As a matter of fact, it usually turns out that whatever you decide, most of the men consider it wrong. You now have to face the same issue again because a new Chevrolet truck has just been allocated to you for distribution.

In order to handle this problem, you have decided to put the question to the men themselves. You will tell them about the new truck and ask them what is the fairest way to distribute the trucks. Do not take a position yourself because you want to do what the men think is fair.

Role Sheet: Hank, Repairman

You have the worst truck in the crew. It is five years old and had been in a bad wreck before you got it. It has never been good, and you have put up with it for three years. It's about time you got a good truck to drive and it seems only fair that the next one should be yours. You have had only one accident. That was when you sprung the door of Charlie's truck as he opened it when you were backing out of the garage. You hope the new truck is a Ford, since you prefer to drive that make.

Role Sheet: John, Repairman

You have to do more driving than most of the other men because you work in the suburbs. You have a fairly old truck and you think you should have the new one because you do so much driving.

Role Sheet: Charlie, Repairman

The heater in your present truck is inadequate. Since Hank backed into the door of your truck, it has never been repaired correctly. The door lets in too much cold air and you attribute your frequent colds to this. You want to have a warm truck since you have a good deal of driving to do. As long as it has good tires and brakes and is comfortable, you don't care about its make.

Role Sheet: George, Repairman

When a new Chevrolet truck becomes available, you think you should get it because you have the most seniority and don't like your present truck. Your own car is a Chevrolet and you prefer a Chevrolet truck such as you drove before you got the Ford.

Role Sheet: Bill, Repairman

You think you deserve a new truck; it certainly is your turn. Your present truck is old, and since the more senior man has a fairly new truck, you should get the next one. You have taken excellent care of your present Dodge and have kept it looking like new. A man deserves to be rewarded if he treats a company truck like his own.

Role-playing exercises like this one can develop conference-leader skills, as well as the decision-making skills of the entire group. With "The New Truck Dilemma," participants also learn the importance of *fairness* in bringing about *acceptance* of resource allocation decisions. The role players can also

Exhibit 12.6   General Instructions for "New Truck Dilemma"

You work for the telephone company and one of you is the foreman while the others are repairmen. The job of a repairman is to fix phones that are out of order, and it requires knowledge and diagnostic skills as well as muscular skills. Repairmen must climb telephone poles, work with small tools, and meet customers. The foreman of a crew is usually an ex-repairman; this happens to be true in this case. He has an office at the garage location but spends a good deal of time making the rounds, visiting the places where the men are working. Each repairman works alone and ordinarily does several jobs in a day. The foreman gives help and instruction as needed.

The repairmen drive to various locations in the city to do repair work. Each of them drives a small truck and takes pride in its appearance. The repairmen have possessive feelings about their trucks and like to keep them in good running order. Naturally, they like to have new trucks, because new trucks give them a feeling of pride.

Here are some facts about the repairmen and their trucks.

	Years With Company	Type of Truck Used
George	17	2-year-old Ford
Bill	11	5-year-old Dodge
John	10	4-year-old Ford
Charlie	5	3-year-old Ford
Hank	3	5-year-old Chevrolet

Most of the men do all their driving in the city, but John and Charlie cover the jobs in the suburbs.

In playing your part, accept the facts as given and assume the attitude supplied in your specific role. From this point on, let your feelings develop in accordance with the events that occur during the role play. When facts or events arise that are not covered by the roles, make up things that are consistent with the way it might be in a real-life situation.

Source: Role instructions are taken from an article by N. R. F. Maier and I. F. Zerfoss, "MRP: A Technique for Training Large Groups of Supervisors and Its Potential Use in Social Research," *Human Relations.* 1952. 5, 180-181. Permission to reproduce the roles has been granted by the Plenum Publishing Company, London, England. Reproduced in N. R. F. Maier, Allen Solem, Ayesha Maier, *The Role-Play Technique* (LaJolla, University Associates, 1975) pp. 27-30.

drop their inhibitions and experiment with new ways of acting. For example, a foreman could experiment with being both considerate (people-oriented) and autocratic (production-oriented). In the real world he might not have this opportunity to experiment with different styles. However, role playing can be very time-consuming, and without competent leadership it can be a waste of time. But, on the whole, we do know that role playing is an effective technique for developing leadership skills,[18] and probably other skills as well.

ORGANIZATIONAL DEVELOPMENT— TECHNIQUES FOR CHANGING ATTITUDES

Training and development techniques like lectures, programmed learning, and on-the-job training, are not highly personal in nature. In other words, they are aimed at imparting knowledge or improving skills, and do not require

much emotional involvement on the part of the trainees. Psychologists refer
to these as "surface interventions."

In this section we are going to turn our attention to a very different
group of techniques called "organizational development" (OD). OD *does*
require high levels of emotional involvement on the part of trainees. It's stated
objective is to change the attitudes, beliefs, and values of the trainees. Psychologists therefore call it an "in-depth" intervention.

Why Use OD?

In Chapter 9 (Organization Theory) we saw that new forms of organizations are emerging—ones that are more organic and adaptable to change.
They are characterized by less adherence to the chain of command, more
enlarged jobs, and "Theory Y" values which emphasize openness, trust, and
participative leadership.

Managers sometimes find it necessary to make their own organizations
more organic. Perhaps your organization suddenly has to adapt to a competitor's new and unique product. Or perhaps you're faced with emerging conflict
between several of your department heads, conflict that is undermining your
unit's creativity and flexibility. These are the kinds of situations that lead
managers to turn to OD.[19]

Objectives of Organizational Development

While there are many different OD techniques, they are all aimed at
accomplishing the following objectives:

1. Increasing the level of support and trust among participants.
2. Increasing open confrontation of organizational problems.
3. Increasing the openness and authenticity of organizational communications.
4. Increasing personal enthusiasm and self-control.[20]

This emphasis on the "people" aspects of organizations does not mean that
OD practitioners don't try to bring about changes in organization structure,
policies, or practices; they often do. But the typical OD program is aimed
at changing the attitudes, values, and beliefs of the employees so that *the
employees themselves* can identify and implement such organizational changes.

Characteristics of OD

We might be able to get a better feel for what OD is by looking at
some of its distinguishing characteristics. Here are a few of them: [21]

1. OD is an *educational strategy* intended to bring about some planned organizational change.
2. The organizational changes sought are usually the result of some *"exigency"* or outside problem. This often results in intergroup conflict, or questions of organizational identity.
3. OD almost always relies on a technique which involves *direct experience*.
4. OD programs utilize *change agents* who are almost always outside consultants.
5. A change agent usually has a social philosophy or set of values concerning people in organization which are like those of McGregor's *Theory* Y (see Chapter 9).
6. The goals that the change agent seeks to accomplish through OD tend to reflect his *"Theory Y" orientation*. For example, he aims for better conflict resolution, increased understanding, more considerate leadership, and better conflict resolution.

No two OD programs are exactly alike but they all tend to follow a basic three-step process:

1. *Gathering data* about the organization and its operations and attitudes.
2. *Feedback* of data about the organization and its problems to the parties involved.
3. *Team Planning* of the solution to these problems.

An Actual OD Change Program: An Optional Example

Here is a brief summary of an actual OD program which was carried out recently: [22]

1. *Initial diagnosis:* The diagnosis consisted of three stages. First a series of *interviews* was held with a sample of 15 supervisory and managerial personnel (including the plant manager and his immediate staff). Second, *group meetings* were held with those interviewed to examine the results and to identify problem areas and priorities. Finally the plant manager, his immediate staff, and the external consultants met to finalize the *"change design"* (the OD training program).

2. *Team skills training:* Foremen, general foremen, assistant superintendents, and superintendents participated with their peers (in groups of approximately 25 individuals) in a series of experience-based exercises during a two-and-a-half-day workshop.

3. *Data collection:* Immediately following the team skills training, all foremen completed two questionnaires. The first concentrated on organizational "health" and effectiveness. The second asked them to describe the behavior of their immediate supervisor—general foremen or assistant superintendents.

4. *Data confrontation:* In this phase various work groups were asked to review the data described above, and determine problem

areas, establish priorities in these areas, and develop some preliminary recommendations for change.

   5. *Action planning:* Based on the data and conversation during the data confrontation, each group developed some recommendations for change, and plans for the changes to be implemented. The plans included what should be changed, who should be responsible, and when the action should be completed.

   6. *Team building:* Each natural work group in the entire system, (including the plant manager and his immediate staff of superintendents), then met for two days. The agenda consisted of identifying blocks to effectiveness for the specific group, and the development of change goals and plans to accomplish the desired changes.

   7. *Intergroup building:* This phase consisted of two-day meetings between groups that were interdependent in the plant. The groups met for the purpose of establishing mutual understanding and cooperation and to enhance collaboration on shared goals or problems.

   The sequence in which the interventions occurred is outlined in Exhibit 12–7.

Exhibit 12.7   Actual Timetable for O.D. Program Described in Text

Intervention	Initiated	Completed
Initial diagnosis	12-1-69	12-31-69
Team skills training	1-9-70	2-28-70
Data collection	1-10-70	3-1-70
Data confrontation	5-9-70	8-19-70
Action planning	9-1-70	12-31-70
Team building	1-1-71	2-1-71
Intergroup building	2-2-71	2-28-71
Data Collection	3-15-71	3-15-71

Source: Kimberly and Warren, *"Organization Development and Change in Organizational Performance"* p. 193.

Specific OD Techniques.   As you can see in Exhibit 12–8, there are many different OD techniques. In the next few sections we will concentrate on two representative ones: sensitivity training, and the managerial grid.

Sensitivity Training

Sensitivity, Laboratory, or *T-group* training (the T is for Training) is a very controversial development method. According to Chris Argyris, it is:

> A group experience designed to provide maximum possible opportunity for the individuals to expose their behavior, give and receive feedback, experiment with new behavior, and develop . . . awareness of self and of others. . . .[23]

Exhibit 12.8   Different Types of O.D. "Interventions," and their Target Groups

Target Group	*Types of Techniques or "Interventions"*
Interventions designed to improve the effectiveness of INDIVIDUALS	Life- and career-planning activities Role analysis technique Coaching and counseling T-group (sensitivity training) Education and training to increase skills, knowledge in the areas of technical task needs, relationship skills, process skills, decision making, problem solving, planning, goal setting skills Grid OD phase 1
Interventions designed to improve the effectiveness of DYADS/TRIADS	Process consultation Third-party peacemaking Grid OD phases 1, 2
Interventions designed to improve the effectiveness of TEAMS & GROUPS	Team building—Task directed —Process directed Family T-group Survey feedback Process consultation Role analysis technique "Start-up" team-building activities Education in decision making, problem solving, planning, goal setting in group settings
Interventions designed to improve the effectiveness of INTERGROUP RELATIONS	Intergroup activities —Process directed —Task Directed Organizational mirroring (three or more groups) Technostructural interventions Process consultation Third-party peacemaking at group level Grid OD phase 3 Survey feedback
Interventions designed to improve the effectiveness of the TOTAL ORGANIZATION	Technostructural activities Confrontation meetings Strategic planning activities Grid OD phases 4, 5, 6 Survey feedback

Source: Wendell French and Cecil Bell, Jr., *Organization Development* (Englewood Cliffs, N. J., Prentice-Hall, Inc., 1973) p. 107.

Here is an outline of a typical T-group program: [24]

1. A group of 10 to 15 meets away from the job without a planned agenda.
2. The discussion focuses on the "here and now." In other words, the participants are encouraged to let each other know how "they're coming across" to each other *in the group* rather than in terms of their past behavior.
3. Some trainees usually try to impose some "structure" on the discussion; for example, by developing agendas. The trainer usually heads off such attempts.
4. The feedback process is all-important. Thus the trainees have to

feel secure enough to inform each other truthfully about how their behavior is being seen, and to interpret the kind of feelings it produces.

5. The success of the T-group, therefore, depends on the level of "psychological safety" the trainees perceive. In other words the trainees have to feel safe to reveal themselves, and to expose their feelings, and drop their defenses.

Does sensitivity training work? We know that trainees usually do become more sensitive to others, and more open after going through T-group training.[25] Furthermore, researchers have found that sensitivity training can also result in increased company performance and profits.[26]

Criticisms of T-Group Training: Yet sensitivity training is still a very controversial technique. The reason for this is the depth of emotional involvement required of trainees. They literally need to bare their souls in the training session, and so the training is thus very personal in nature. Sensitivity training has therefore been widely criticized. Writers point out, for for example, that:

Sensitivity training is based on creating *stress situations* for their own sake.

The participants (and trainers) are often unaware of what the *outcome* of a session will be.

Its ultimate goals and techniques are often *inconsistent* with the business and economic world in which we live.

"*Anybody*" with a registration fee can attend.

When you suggest that a subordinate participate in a T-group program, his attendance cannot be considered strictly "*voluntary*."

T-group training has been known to result in nervous *breakdowns* of trainees.[27]

T-Group Hints.   In light of these criticisms, here are some *hints* for setting up a T-group program.

1. *T-group training is more appropriate for developing organic organizations.* When this type of openness and flexible organization structure is not appropriate—such as on an assembly line—sensitivity training is not appropriate.[28]
2. Programs should be strictly *voluntary*.
3. Careful *screening* of participants should take place.
4. The training consultant should be an *experienced* T-group professional.
5. Make sure that you give a great deal of attention to building in mechanisms for *transferring the learning* back to your organization.
6. Make sure that all trainees know *ahead of time* what sort of "training" they are getting into.[29]

Grid Training

The "managerial grid" is another OD technique. The grid itself is presented in Exhibit 12–9. It represents several possible leadership "styles." Each style represents a different combination of two basic orientations—*concern for people* and *concern for production*. For example, the 9–1 leader emphasizes production but deemphasizes the needs of his people. On the other hand, the 1–9 leader is very concerned about people and not too concerned about production.

Exhibit 12.9   The Managerial Grid ©

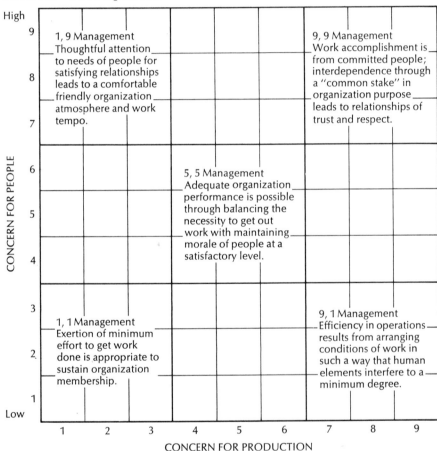

Note: The Managerial Grid Illustrates Different Combinations of People and Production Orientation.

Source: Robert Blake and Jane Morton, *Corporate Excellence Through Grid Organization Development,* "The Managerial Grid" © 1968 (Houston, Texas: Gulf, 1968).

There is an entire training and development program built around the managerial grid. It is aimed at developing open confrontation of organizational problems, and "9–9" (high people-high production) leaders.

The following is an outline of the program, which usually lasts three to five years.[30]

Phase 1. This usually involves a one-week conference. Here trainees are taught the fundamentals of grid training.

Phase 2. Here you and your subordinates discuss, analyze, and solve your unit's practices and problems: *teamwork* is stressed.

Phase 3. Here you use the techniques developed in Phase 2 to discuss, analyze, and jointly solve problems between your unit and others in the organization.

Phase 4. Next, top management meets with various groups. Here the aims are to work out companywide problems, and to set some development targets for the company as a whole.

Phase 5. In this step, specific procedures are outlined for accomplishing the company's development targets.

Phase 6. Here you evaluate your unit's and your company's accomplishments, and begin work on any remaining (or new) problems.

Some Important Things to Remember from This Chapter:

1. Training and development programs should be aimed at preparing employees to better achieve the goals of the organization; therefore, the first step in developing a training program is to analyze the organization's goals and current performance. You do this with "organizational analysis." Through interviews, questionnaires, and analysis of company records, you review the organization's goals, plans, environment, practices, and problems.

2. There are four basic steps in developing a training program. The first (to repeat) involves analyzing the organization. The next steps are: Identify important performance discrepancies; identify problems (and make sure they are indeed "training" problems!); and finally choose the training objectives and techniques.

3. Techniques such as lectures, programmed learning, and conferences are especially useful for imparting knowledge. On the other hand, if your aim is to develop your subordinate's skills then techniques such as on-the-job training or management games are more appropriate. If changing attitudes is your objective, techniques such as role playing, sensitivity training, and grid training are appropriate.

4. Sensitivity (or "t-group") training can be effective. It can result in managers who are more sensitive to their subordinates, and a climate that is more open and less hostile. But remember that it is also widely criticized. So before embarking on such a program you should be sure that your aim is to develop an open, organic organization; that the program is strictly voluntary; that participants are carefully screened; and that the consultant is an experienced professional.

STUDY ASSIGNMENTS

1. Answer the questions concerning the sanitary company from the introduction to this chapter. Prepare to give the president a three-part plan: (1) diagnosis; (2) change strategy; and (3) implementation.
2. Discuss each step in developing a training program.
3. Explain how you would distinguish between "training" problems and those not amenable to training.
4. Discuss the pros and cons of five training and development techniques.
5. You recommend to your boss that he hire someone to be in charge of training and development of your company, and he replies, "Train- and development is useless. No one's ever shown that it's effective, and you know darn well you just can't change people." How would you respond to his remarks?
6. Explain the difference between "surface" and "in-depth" training and development techniques.
7. With a group of your classmates, carry out "the New Truck Dilemma" role-playing exercise discussed in this chapter. Afterward discuss your experiences. Did everyone enjoy the role playing? Did the foreman use good group decision-making techniques?
8. Write an essay on organizational development. Make sure to discuss its objectives, characteristics, and an outline of a typical OD program.
9. What are the criticisms of t-group training? In the light of these criticisms, discuss some hints for setting up t-group training.
10. Explain the managerial grid development program.

NOTES FOR THE CHAPTER

1. Irwin Goldstein, *Training: Program Development and Evaluation* (Monterey, Brooks/Cole, 1974) p. 19.
2. Robert J. House, *Management Development* (Ann Arbor: University of Michigan) p. 45–64.
3. Robert Mager and Peter Pipe, *Analyzing Performance Problems* (Belmont, California; Fearon, 1970) p. 7–15.
4. William R. Tracey, *Designing Training and Developing Systems* (New York: American Management Association, 1971) p. 192.
5. William R. Tracey, *Designing Training and Developing Systems*, p. 192; G. H. Proctor and W. M. Thornton, *Training: A Handbook for Line Managers* (New York: American Management Assoc., 1961).
6. William R. Tracey, *Designing Training and Developing Systems*, p. 192.
7. F. Reissman, "The Culturally Deprived Child: A New View," *Mental Health and Achievement*, edited E. P. Torrence and R. D. Strom (New York: John Wiley & Sons, 1965) pp. 312–319; J. Tiffin and E. McCormick, *Industrial Psychology*, (Englewood Cliffs: Prentice-Hall, 1965).
8. G. N. Nash, J. P. Muczyk, and F. L. Vettori, "The Role and Practical Effectiveness of Programmed Instruction," *Personnel Psychology*, Vol. 24 (1971) pp. 397–418; Ernest McCormick and Joseph Tiffin, *Industrial Psychology* (Englewood Cliffs: Prentice-Hall, 1974).
9. R. Hedberg, H. Steffen, D. Baxter, "Insurance Fundamentals—A Programmed Text vs. A Conventional Text," *Personnel Psychology*, Vol. 9, No. 2 (1964) pp 165–171; McCormick and Tiffin, *Industrial Psychology*, p. 264.

10. William Tracey, *Designing Training and Development Systems*, p. 194.

11. William Tracey, *Designing Training and Development Systems*.

12. William Tracey, *Designing Training and Development Systems*, p. 30.

13. Robert J. House, *Management Development*, p. 74.

14. Robert J. House, *Management Development*, p. 75.

15. B. Taylor and G. L. Lippitt, *Management Development and Training Handbook* (London: McGraw-Hill, 1975) p. 223.

16. William Tracey, *Designing Training and Development Systems*, p. 205.

17. Norman R. F. Maier, Alan R. Solem, and Ayesha A. Maier, *The Role-Playing Technique* (LaJolla, Calif.: University Associates, 1975) pp. 21–35.

18. Kenneth N. Wexley and Wayne Nemeroff, "Effectiveness of Positive Reinforcement in Goal Setting as Methods of Management Development," *Journal of Applied Psychology*, Vol. 60, No. 4 (August 1975).

19. See Gary Dessler, *Organization and Management* (Englewood Cliffs, N.J.: Prentice-Hall, 1976) pp. 293–304.

20. "What is OD?" (NTL Institute: News and Reports from NTL Institute for Applied Behavioral Science) Vol. 2 June (1968) pp. 1–2. See also Gary Dessler, *Organization and Management*, p. 294; Wendell French, *The Personnel Management Process* (Boston: Houghton-Mifflin, 1974) p. 665.

21. Based on Warren G. Bennis, *Organizational Development: Its Nature, Origins, and Prospects* (Reading, Massachusetts: Addison-Wesley Publishing Co., 1969) p. 10.

22. John Kimberly and Warren Neilsen, "Organization Development and Change in Organizational Performance," *Administrative Science Quarterly* (June 1975) pp. 191–206.

23. Chris Argyris, "A Brief Description of Laboratory Education," *Training Directors Journal* (October 1963). Reprinted in Harold Lazarus, E. Kirby Warren, and Jerome Schnee, *The Progress of Management* (Englewood Cliffs, N.J.: Prentice-Hall, Inc., 1972) pp. 384–386.

24. J. P. Campbell, and M. Dunnette, "Effectiveness of T-group Experiences in Managerial Training and Development," *Psychological Bulletin*, Vol. 70 (1968) pp. 73–104; in W. Scott and L. Cummings, *Readings in Organizational Behavior and Human Performance* (Homewood: Irwin, 1973) pp. 568–595; Gary Dessler, *Organization and Management*, p. 300.

25. J. P. Campbell and M. Dunnette, "Effectiveness of T-group Experiences in Managerial Training and Development," *Psychological Bulletin*, Vol. 70 (1968) pp. 73–104.

26. John Kimberly and Warren Neilsen, "Organizational Development . . . ," p. 203; see also Peter B. Smith, "Controlled Studies of the Outcome of Sensitivity Training," *Psychological Bulletin*, Vol. 82, No. 4 (1976) pp. 597–622.

27. George Odiorne, "The Trouble with Sensitivity Training," *Training Directors Journal* (October 1963); George Odiorne, *Training By Objectives* (New York: Macmillan, 1970) Ch. 4; Robert J. House, *Management Development*, p. 71; Andre Delbecq, "Sensitivity Training," *Training and Development Journal* (January 1970) pp. 32–35, Reprinted in Fred Luthans, *Contemporary Readings in Organizational Behavior* (New York: McGraw-Hill, 1972) pp. 409–417.

28. Warren Bennis, *Organization Development: Its Nature, Origins, and Prospects*, p. 10.

29. Andre Delbecq, "Sensitivity Training," pp. 32–35.

30. Robert Blake and Jane Mouton, *Building a Dynamic Corporation Through Grid Organization Development* (Reading: Addison Wesley, 1969) pp. 76–109.

A Framework for Studying the Management Fundamentals

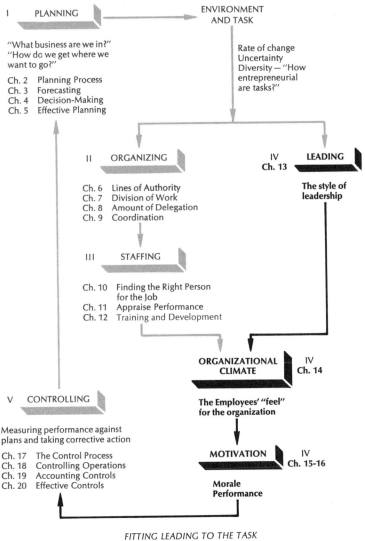

I   PLANNING

ENVIRONMENT AND TASK

"What business are we in?"
"How do we get where we want to go?"

Ch. 2   Planning Process
Ch. 3   Forecasting
Ch. 4   Decision-Making
Ch. 5   Effective Planning

Rate of change
Uncertainty
Diversity — "How entrepreneurial are tasks?"

II   ORGANIZING

Ch. 6   Lines of Authority
Ch. 7   Division of Work
Ch. 8   Amount of Delegation
Ch. 9   Coordination

III   STAFFING

Ch. 10   Finding the Right Person for the Job
Ch. 11   Appraise Performance
Ch. 12   Training and Development

IV   LEADING
Ch. 13

The style of leadership

ORGANIZATIONAL CLIMATE   IV   **Ch. 14**

The Employees' "feel" for the organization

V   CONTROLLING

Measuring performance against plans and taking corrective action

Ch. 17   The Control Process
Ch. 18   Controlling Operations
Ch. 19   Accounting Controls
Ch. 20   Effective Controls

MOTIVATION   IV   **Ch. 15-16**

Morale
Performance

FITTING LEADING TO THE TASK

Aspects of Leading	*Mechanistic*	*Organic*
Leadership Style	More autocratic	More democratic
Leadership Structure	Structured	Unstructured
Subordinate Motivation	Extrinsic (money, promotion)	Intrinsic (the job itself)
Psychological– Climate	Structured, performance-oriented	Supportive, development oriented

What we'll be discussing in this section:

Chap. 13
Leadership: Traits of effective leaders. Two basic styles of leadership. A situational approach to leadership. Summary: on an "ideal" leader.

Chap. 14
Organizational Climate and Employee Morale: Things that affect an employee's morale. Measuring organizational climate.

Chap. 15
Fundamentals of Motivation: What motivation is. An expectancy model of motivation. "What do people want?" All the management functions affect motivation.

Chap. 16
Motivation in Action: The role of incentives in motivation. Job enrichment. Management by objectives. Hints for motivating subordinates.

A Framework for Studying the Management Fundamentals

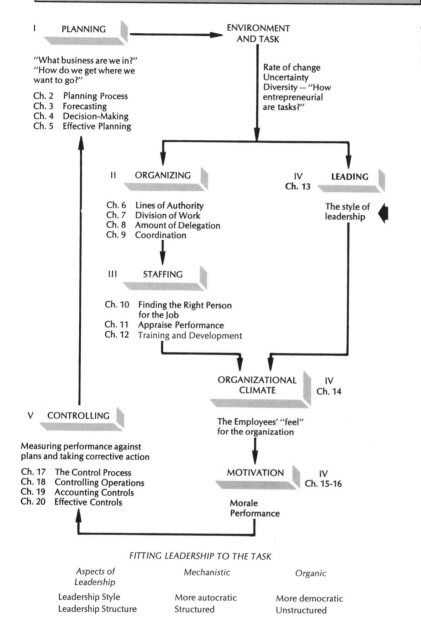

I   PLANNING

ENVIRONMENT AND TASK

"What business are we in?"
"How do we get where we want to go?"

Ch. 2   Planning Process
Ch. 3   Forecasting
Ch. 4   Decision-Making
Ch. 5   Effective Planning

Rate of change
Uncertainty
Diversity — "How entrepreneurial are tasks?"

Where we are now: Discussing the traits, styles, and "situational" aspects of effective leadership.

II   ORGANIZING

IV   LEADING
Ch. 13

Ch. 6   Lines of Authority
Ch. 7   Division of Work
Ch. 8   Amount of Delegation
Ch. 9   Coordination

The style of leadership

III   STAFFING

Ch. 10   Finding the Right Person for the Job
Ch. 11   Appraise Performance
Ch. 12   Training and Development

ORGANIZATIONAL CLIMATE
IV   Ch. 14

V   CONTROLLING

The Employees' "feel" for the organization

Measuring performance against plans and taking corrective action

Ch. 17   The Control Process
Ch. 18   Controlling Operations
Ch. 19   Accounting Controls
Ch. 20   Effective Controls

MOTIVATION
IV   Ch. 15-16

Morale
Performance

FITTING LEADERSHIP TO THE TASK

Aspects of Leadership	Mechanistic	Organic
Leadership Style	More autocratic	More democratic
Leadership Structure	Structured	Unstructured

When you have finished studying

13 Leadership

You should be able to:

1. *Explain leadership and its importance.*
2. *Discuss the four important components of leadership effectiveness.*
3. *Identify the traits possessed by successful leaders.*
4. *Distinguish between the two basic styles of leadership.*
5. *Describe the situational forces which you should consider before deciding on adoption of a leadership style.*
6. *Identify the leadership style which might be "best": 1) on an assembly line; 2) in a research laboratory; and 3) for a "staff" manager.*
7. *Discuss seven hints for being a more effective leader.*

INTRODUCTION

Leadership occurs whenever one person gets another to work toward some predetermined objective. Unlike many of your other management jobs, such as planning and organizing, leadership is a highly behavioral function that requires a substantial involvement in personal relationships.

The Four Components of Effective Leadership

Why do you think people like Winston Churchill, Dwight Eisenhower, and Joan of Arc were so effective as leaders? It may have been due to some traits *they had, such as physical attractiveness or self-assurance. Yet many leaders—Franklin Roosevelt, for example—were successful in spite of physical handicaps. Perhaps, then, they were successful because of their* style *of leadership; they may have been very considerate and democratic in their dealings with other people, for example. But some successful leaders, like Adolf Hitler, could hardly be described as considerate and democratic. Or perhaps these people were effective because they had the right combination of characteristics and style for the* job. *Maybe this is why Churchill, although a great wartime leader, lost reelection when the war ended. Finally, they may have been successful because of the* personalities and needs of the people being led. *Perhaps this is why a person who is effective as a foreman on an assembly line may not be effective in leading a group of scientists.*

Exhibit 13.1   Relationship of Leadership to Managing

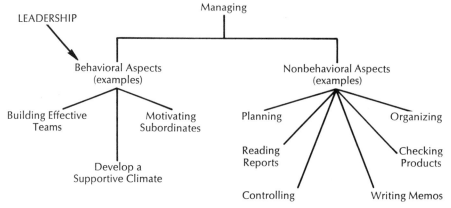

Note: Unlike many of the managers other functions, leading is highly behavioral in nature.

Source: Adapted from Massie and Douglas, *Managing: A Contemporary Introduction*, (Englewood Cliffs, N. J., Prentice-Hall, Inc., 1973) p. 296.

Actually these people were probably successful for all of these reasons. The chances are that (1) their traits, (2) their styles, (3) the nature of their jobs, and (4) the needs of their subordinates all combined to contribute to their success. Similarly, experts on leadership have found that there are four important factors which influence a leader's effectiveness. Let's discuss each in this chapter, and then finish with a picture of an "ideal" leader.

Exhibit 13.2   Four Important Aspects of Leadership Effectiveness

WHAT ARE THE TRAITS OF
EFFECTIVE LEADERS?

How would you describe the best leader you ever met? Did he have any particular characteristics which you think may have contributed to his success?

The idea that some leaders are characterized by certain traits was initially inspired by a "great-man" concept of leadership. Basically this concept held that people like Winston Churchill, Dwight Eisenhower, or Joan of Arc were great leaders because they were born with certain definable traits which made them so. Early researchers felt that if they studied the personality, intelligence, and attitudes of great leaders they would, sooner or later, stumble on the combination of traits which made these people outstanding leaders.

Some Important Traits

While most of the early studies were inconclusive, we now believe that effective leaders often do exhibit a certain pattern of traits. For example, a group of researchers found that successful managers were *brighter*, more *aggressive*, and more *self-reliant* than those who were not. They were also more *persuasive* and *better educated* than other managers.[1] You will also probably find that effective leaders *act* like leaders: they're somewhat withdrawn and not "one of the boys," for example.

The Ghiselli Study

In another study Edwin Ghiselli studied several hundred managers including foremen, middle managers, and top managers.[2] He usually found that effective leaders exhibited a number of traits including *intelligence, initiative, self-assurance,* and *"supervisory ability."* Ghiselli defined supervisory ability as the "effective utilization of whatever supervisory practices are indicated by the particular requirements of the situation." He felt that *intelligence,* and *supervisory ability* were the two factors which most distinguished between effective and ineffective leaders.

Some traits of effective leaders are summarized in Exhibit 13–3.

WHAT IS THE ''BEST'' STYLE
OF LEADERSHIP?

We also know that there are two basic functions leaders usually perform—*accomplishing the task,* and *satisfying the needs of subordinates.* These *task* and *people* functions of leadership are not necessarily opposites, although

Exhibit 13.3   Important Characteristics of Effective Leaders

they are sometimes viewed in this way. From a practical point of view, the two functions are probably best thought of as independent, with most leaders exhibiting aspects of both task and people leadership styles.

Exhibit 13.4   Several Different Ways of Describing "People" and "Task" Styles

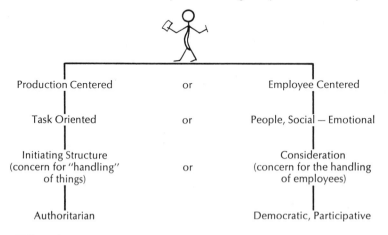

What do we mean by "leadership style"? By style, we mean what the leader does and how he behaves. As you can see in Exhibit 13–4, there are

actually several different ways of looking at the basic task-oriented style and people-oriented style. For example, writers typically distingiush between: 1) Structuring and Considerate leaders, as well as between 2) Job-centered and Employee-centered leaders; and 3) Autocratic and Participative leaders.

Which leadership style is most effective? While we don't have any positive answers, we do know that the people-oriented style is usually associated with higher employee morale. However, the task-oriented style is often associated with higher employee performance, and, on occasion, with high employee morale as well.[3]

Autocratic and Participative Leaders

For example, we now know quite a lot about the pros and cons of *autocratic* and *participative* leadership styles. As you can see in Exhibit 13–5, a major difference between these styles is that the autocratic leader wields much more power over his subordinates; he makes most of the decisions for the work group. The participative leader involves his group more in the decision-making; he lets them make more of their own decisions. Many behavioral scientists believe that participative leadership is more effective than autocratic leader-

Exhibit 13.5 Autocratic and Participative Leadership Compared

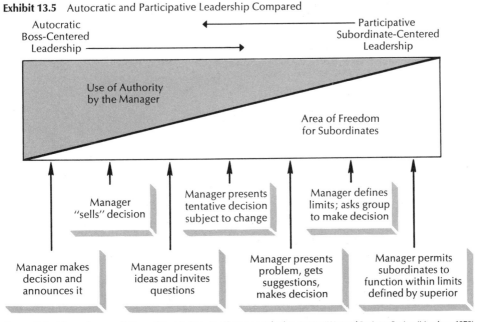

Source: Robert Tannenbaum and Warren Schmidt, "How to Choose a Leadership Pattern," *Harvard Business Review* (May-June 1973) pp. 162-180.

264 ship. This is based on the assumption that people derive a great deal of satisfaction from successfully planning and executing a task. Participative leaders supposedly encourage just that sort of job involvement.[4]

In practice, participative leadership does have its advantages. For example, several researchers have found that industrial work groups with participative leaders usually had higher morale as well as less turnover and fewer grievances. On the other hand, the performance of the groups which had *autocratic* leaders was considerably higher, although these employees quickly became dissatisfied.[5] In total, though, we will see the style of leader which is "best" really depends on many things, including the nature of the task and the subordinates.

Exhibit 13.6   You Have to Fit your Leadership Style to the Situation

Source: George Terry, *Supervisory Management* (Homewood: Richard D. Irwin, 1974) p. 20.

Can a Leader be Both "Things" and "People" Oriented?

In summary, there are two basic styles of leadership. The first is people-oriented. This leader is considerate, participative, and employee-centered. The second leader is task-oriented. He is autocratic, production-oriented, and structuring. One thing we have found is that the people-oriented leader usually has the most satisfied subordinates. On the other hand, it is often the task-oriented leader who has the most productive work group.

You might therefore reasonably ask: "Is it possible for me to have employees who are both highly productive and very satisfied?" The answer is yes. For one thing, most leaders have the potential for exhibiting *both* people-orientation and task-orientation.[6] In other words, there is no particular reason why you cannot push hard for production and at the same time be considerate, fair, and supportive of the needs of your subordinates. In fact, the

"Managerial Grid" program we discussed in Chapter 12 is aimed at developing leaders who can do just that.[7]

As you can see in Exhibit 13–7, Robert Blake and Jane Mouton contend that a leader can be both people- and task-oriented. Their *Managerial Grid* shows five basic types of leaders. Each reflects a different combination of people- and task-orientation.

Exhibit 13.7 The Managerial Grid

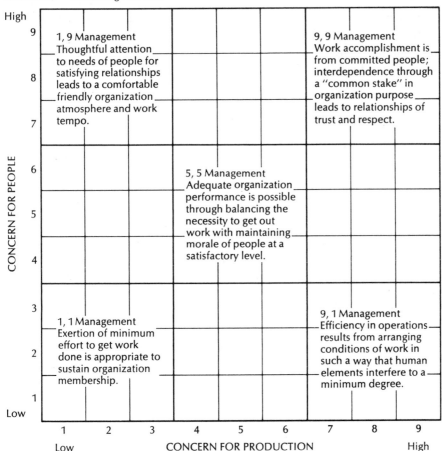

1, 9 Management Thoughtful attention to needs of people for satisfying relationships leads to a comfortable friendly organization atmosphere and work tempo.

9, 9 Management Work accomplishment is from committed people; interdependence through a "common stake" in organization purpose leads to relationships of trust and respect.

5, 5 Management Adequate organization performance is possible through balancing the necessity to get out work with maintaining morale of people at a satisfactory level.

1, 1 Management Exertion of minimum effort to get work done is appropriate to sustain organization membership.

9, 1 Management Efficiency in operations results from arranging conditions of work in such a way that human elements interfere to a minimum degree.

CONCERN FOR PEOPLE — High 9 8 7 6 5 4 3 2 1 Low

CONCERN FOR PRODUCTION — Low 1 2 3 4 5 6 7 8 9 High

Note: Notice that the "9-9" leader shows *both* high concern for people and high concern for production.

But remember that a style of leadership which might prove effective in one situation may prove less effective in another. Thus a person who is a great leader in a military battle might not necessarily be a very good host at a party for a group of strangers. Let's therefore look more closely at the "situational" factors that influence leader effectiveness, starting with the needs of the people being led.

FIT YOUR STYLE TO THE NEEDS OF YOUR SUBORDINATES

Their Values

One important way in which people differ is in their *values*. For example, we now know that the "Protestant Ethic" of hard work and doing a good job that drives some employees is lacking in others. Charles Hulin and Milton Blood have studied a large number of workers, and found that some workers have strong Protestant ethic values. These workers also seemed to prefer more job responsibility. Other workers did not have this strong work value. They tended to prefer less job responsibility, and more direction or "structure" from their leaders.

Their Personalities

Each of your subordinates will also have a unique *personality*. For instance, one of the things we have found is that some "authoritarian" people have to receive a lot more direction, clarification, and structure than some other people. In fact, we now know that such people do not react at all well to a participative leadership style. Several years ago Victor Vroom found that employees' reactions to participative leadership depended largely on how authoritarian they were. The nonauthoritarian employee's preference is for more discretion and flexibility, and the participative style seems to fill these needs very well. On the other hand, the more authoritarian employee prefers the kind of directive leadership that is associated with the autocratic style. We also know that the lower the level of your subordinate's competence, knowledge, or experience, the greater the chance he will tolerate more direction and "structure" from you.[8]

Their Motives

As we will see in Chapter 15, employees also vary widely in what *motivates them*. For example, we know that some people are highly "achievement" motivated; they are actively driven by a strong need to do a good job. Such people have to have clear and attainable objectives set for them, and also need a lot of feedback concerning their progress.[9]

FIT YOUR STYLE TO THE SITUATION   267

Tannenbaum and Schmidt's Three "Forces"

The idea that a leader has to be "right" for the job is now widely recongized. For example, Robert Tannenbaum and Warren Schmidt state that no set of leadership traits and no one style of leadership have been found to be universally applicable. Instead, "effective leadership depends on the leader, his followers, the situation, and the interrelationship between them." They contend that there are forces within the manager, forces within the subordinates, and forces within the situation which you should consider in deciding how people-oriented or task-oriented your leadership style should be.

The Managers: The *forces within the manager* include your values, the confidence you have in your subordinates, your inclinations toward one or the other style of leadership, and your feelings of security in an uncertain situation.

Your *value system* is important because it will influence the degree to which you feel your subordinates should share in decision-making. It also influences the amount of responsibility you feel you can *delegate* to them. Similarly your *confidence* in your subordinates will influence the amount of responsibility you think they can *assume*.

Your own *leadership inclinations* are also important, because some people are naturally more people-oriented (or task-oriented) leaders than others. And, your feeling of security in an uncertain situation is important since the outcome of a job usually becomes more uncertain whenever you delegate responsibility and decision-making to subordinates.

The Subordinate: There are also (to repeat) a number of *forces within the subordinate* which you need take into account when deciding on a leadership style. For example, many subordinates simply cannot tolerate a great deal of *ambiguity*, and prefer to be given clear-cut directions. In addition, your subordinate's readiness to assume *responsibilty* and the extent to which he understands and *identifies with the goals* of the organization are important. Furthermore, the extent to which he has the necessary *knowledge* and experience to deal with the problem will also enter into your decision concerning how much freedom he can be given.

The Situation: In addition to the forces within the manager and his subordinates, certain forces are operating within the *general situation* which help determine which leadership style is best. For one thing, organizations, like individuals have certain cherished values, *traditions*, and ways of doing things. Most new managers quickly discover that certain kinds of behavior are approved in their organizations, and others are not. For example, some

268 organizations are more structured than others; that is they have very rigid lines of communication, and clear-cut job descriptions. In such a situation, you might natually tend to be more structured and task-oriented in your style.

Summary: In summary, we now recognize that there are forces operating within the manager, the subordinates, and the situation which you should consider. The successful manager is the one who "maintains a high batting average in accurately assessing the forces that determine what his most appropriate behavior at any given time should be, and actually being able to behave accordingly." [10]

Fiedler's Contingency Theory

In contrast to Tannenbaum and Schmidt's intuitive approach, Fred Fiedler has conducted research aimed at finding out how "situational" factors actually influence a leader's effectiveness.[11] At the base of Fiedler's theory are three situational factors. He says that together they determine whether the people-oriented, or task-oriented leader style is called for:

1. *Position power.* This is "the degree to which the job itself enables the leader to get his group members to comply with and accept his direction and leadership."
2. *Task structure.* This refers to how routine and predictable the work groups' task is.
3. *Leader-member relations.* This refers to the extent to which the leader "gets along" with his men, as well as to the extent to which they have confidence in him and are loyal to him.

Basically, Fiedler has found that in situations where leader-member relations, task structure, and leader-position power are all either very high or very low, a more task-oriented leader is effective. This is summarized in Exhibit 13–8. On the other hand, in the mid-range where the situation facing the leader is not as clear-cut, a more people-oriented style is in order.

While Fiedler's work has been criticized, his findings have helped us to better understand the dynamics of leadership.[12] His evidence clearly shows that no single set of traits or style of leadership will be effective in all situations. Instead the leader has to be "right" for the job.

House's Path-Goal Approach to Leadership

Robert House has also proposed a "situational" theory of leadership. He calls it a "Path-Goal theory." He says that a leader's main functions are to set important *goals* for subordinates, and to clear their *paths* to these goals.

What does this mean in practice? For one thing, it means that if your subordinates are confused as to what to do next, it may be your duty to struc-

Exhibit 13.8   Effective Leadership Style Varies With the Situation

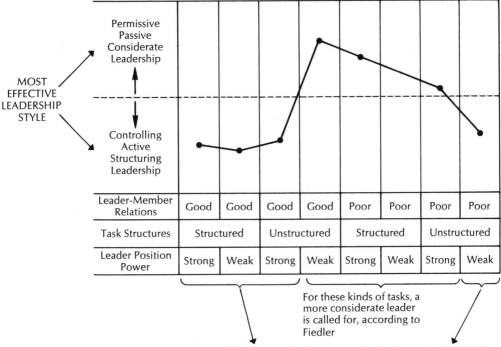

Source: Adapted from Fred Fiedler, *A Theory of Leadership Effectiveness* (New York: McGraw-Hill 1967) p. 176.

ture their jobs for them; that way, you give them a clear *path* to follow. It also means that if your subordinates' tasks are already very clear—they're working on an assembly line, for example—then you ought to "stay out of their hair." In this case, their "paths" are already clear enough. The path-goal theory also means that you have to set clear goals for your subordinates, and explain to them why these goals are important. Here, again, the research shows that you have to fit your leadership style to the situation.[13]

SUMMARY: HOW TO BE AN EFFECTIVE LEADER

Implications for the Management Fundamentals

The four components of leadership we discussed are all valuable. First, each has its own unique implications for the recruitment and development of leaders.[14] For example, we know that effective leaders are often characterized by *traits* such as intelligence and self-assurance. Thus, it is worthwhile for you to identify leadership traits which are associated with effective performance in your own organization; you can then test job candidates for these traits. In addition, training aimed at developing such traits becomes more important. For example, David McClelland says that leaders can be trained to be more achievement- and power-oriented,[15] and courses such as Dale Carnegie's are usually aimed at developing self-assurance and decisiveness.

Similarly, what we know about leadership *styles* tells us that management training which is aimed at both increasing leader consideration and getting leaders to be more flexible in using different styles can be useful. Finally, we also know that the leader has to be right for the *task*, and the *subordinates*. In fact, Fiedler says that it might often be easier to reorganize the job than to retrain the leader or hire a new one.

A Picture of an Ideal Leader

Beyond this, each component is of value because each contributes to our understanding of how to be an effective leader. First, from the trait components we see that an effective leader usually exhibits initiative, self-assurance, and decisiveness. He is also usually brighter, more competitive, but somewhat more withdrawn than others. Second, from the styles component, we know that the more successful leader is generally considerate and supportive of his subordinates. This does not mean that you shouldn't give orders and tell others what to do; instead it means that you have to recognize the individuality of your people and their need to feel important and useful. You then behave in such a way as to support these needs.

Finally the *situational component* tells us that in addition to these "universal" characteristics, the more effective leader has "supervisory ability." We can define this as the ability to provide the right amount of structure and direction for the task. For example, where the job calls for creativity and judgment, and your subordinates can assume the responsibility, you might give them more leeway to carry out their own jobs. To the extent that your subordinates are unable or unwilling to work unattended, you may insist on compliance with the company's rules and procedures.[16] In line with this, an effective leader is sensitive to the needs of the situation and of his subordinates. The "ideal" leader is able to adapt his style to fit those needs.

Seven Hints for Being an Effective Leader

There are no "sure-fire" guidelines for how to be an effective leader. But based on what we have discussed so far, we think the following hints can be useful.

1. *Know and Train Yourself:* From the traits aspect we now know
that more effective leaders tend to be persuasive intelligent, emotionally
stable, withdrawn, aggressive, self-assured, and to have initiative and
"supervisory ability." Prospective managers and leaders should therefore ask themselves how they rate on each of these traits. (Psychological
testing and counseling is available for getting more precise feedback
about yourself.) For both prospective and present leaders training in
areas such as decision-making, self-evaluation, and increasing self-
assurance is available.

2. *Know and Control Your Style:* Most leaders are probably inclined to be either task- or people-oriented. But the "best" style in
any particular case depends on many things, including the subordinate's need for structure and the ambiguity of the task. You should
therefore analyze and understand your own style; try to consciously
analyze your behavior, and maintain a flexibility which permits you
to fit your style to the situation.

3. *Know and Support Your People:* Each of your subordinates
has his own unique personality, values, and needs. Each expects to be
treated as an important, capable individual. One of your most important leadership jobs is to see to it that the atmosphere you create
is one that your subordinates feel is supportive of them as individuals.
Douglas McGregor, in his book *The Human Side of Enterprise*, says
that one way to do this is to *believe the best about your subordinates.*
Do not take what he calls a "theory X" perspective and assume that
people are lazy, dislike work, and do not want responsibility. Instead
assume that your people are intelligent and creative, and that they
are capable of doing a good job.

4. *Adapt to the Characteristics of the Work:* From people such
as Fred Fiedler we know that your leadership style has to fit the
task. For highly creative and entrepreneurial tasks, (such as starting up
a new company or inventing a new product), it is probably to your
advantage to set broad goals for your subordinates and then rely on
their judgment to get the job done. Where the job is more routine—
as it might be on an assembly line—the leader usually enforces a set
of prescribed rules for getting the job done.

5. *Act Like a Leader:* From the traits aspect of leadership we
know that more effective leaders *act* like leaders. Specifically, they tend
to be somewhat withdrawn and distant from their subordinates, and
while they may be friendly, they do not act like "one of the boys."
Thus in all respects you have to act like the kind of a person whom
the subordinates will want to look up to. In addition, from the styles
component we know that the more effective leader is also considerate,
fair, and nonarbitrary. Thus while your subordinates may occasionally
question the wisdom of some of your decisions, they should never have
to question your motives.

6. *Delegate—Don't Abdicate:* No one, no matter how competent,
can do all the work by himself. Part of the advantage of assuming the
best about your subordinates is that it allows you to delegate to them

as much as possible. This delegation not only frees you for more important things, but can motivate your competent subordinates. But you have to be careful not to delegate too much. Someone once said that the bad manager delegates nothing, and the mediocre manager delegates everything. The effective manager, on the other hand, *delegates selectively*. Specifically, you have to delegate as much as is practical to your subordinates, while retaining control over key result areas so that you can monitor the results.

7. ***Build an Effective Team:*** Rensis Likert says that an organization will function best when its personnel work not as individuals but as members of effective work groups. His research clearly shows that cohesive work groups—those in which all team members have a strong attraction and loyalty to the group—can result in increased productivity. Part of the reason is that such a group can impose its higher norms or standards on those employees who might normally be under-productive. Yet we also know that such a cohesive group can also *lower* productivity if it disagrees with the goals set by the leader. Therefore, one of your most important leadership jobs is to build such cohesive, effective, high-performing teams.

Some Important Things to Remember from This Chapter:

1. In order to be an effective manager, you will have to be an effective leader. Knowledge of the traits and skills of an effective leader can help you do just that.

2. But there are no simple answers to the question "What makes an effective leader?" Four factors—your leadership style, your personality traits, the nature of the task, and your subordinates themselves—will all interact in determining whether or not you will be an effective leader in any particular situation.

3. We know that effective leaders usually exhibit a number of characteristics. They are good decision-makers, self-assured, and persuasive. They are aggressive, and take the initiative. And they act like leaders—they are somewhat withdrawn or "above the crowd," and they treat their people with respect. They also have "supervisory ability" which we defined as fitting the amount of leader structure to the task.

4. From the work of people like Fiedler and House we know that it is very important for you to fit your leadership style to the task. Where creative, entrepreneurial activities are called for, and where your people have the discipline to manage themselves, the more unstructured and democratic approach is appropriate. But where routinization and efficiency are paramount, or an emergency situation exists, a more structured, autocratic approach is appropriate.

5. There are no sure-fire guidelines for *how* to be an effective leader; but we have seven useful hints for improving your own batting average: Know and train yourself; know and control your style; know and support your people; adapt to the characteristics of work; act like a leader; delegate—don't abdicate; and build an effective team.

STUDY ASSIGNMENTS

1. You have just read in the newspaper that an army colonel was passed over for promotion because he had "failed to exert leadership." What does it mean "to fail to exert leadership"?
2. Discuss the four important aspects of leadership effectiveness.
3. Discuss the traits possessed by successful leaders.
4. Compare and contrast the two basic styles of leadership.
5. Your boss has just asked you to give a short lecture to a group of new supervisors on "How to be an Effective Leader." What would you tell them?
6. Do you think it is more important for a leader to be respected, or to be popular? Why?
7. Explain the situational forces which a manager should consider before he decides on adopting a managerial style.
8. What leadership style would you exhibit under the following conditions:

   a) You have just been given a job as director of marketing services for an organization, and have been told by the president to "get those division managers to use some up-to-date marketing tools." He has also told you that you have no position power or authority over these division managers. How would you act as a leader?

   b) You have just been named the new manager of a large division. They have had four managers in three years, profits are declining, morale is at an all-time low, and the recent consultant's report states that "nobody knows what he is doing or what he is supposed to be doing." How would you act as a leader?

   c) The president of Central Steel wants to get his company into some new businesses, and has asked you to take charge of a recently organized new ventures department. The steel company has always been highly centralized, with top management making virtually all important decisions. Everyone has always "played it by the rules," and requests for deviations from standard practices traditionally have to be funnelled through the formal chain of command—a process which can take up to one year. How would you act as a leader?*

9. Write an essay entitled, "The most effective leader I have ever met." Make sure to discuss his leadership style and personality traits as well as any conditions which you feel contributed to his being effective.
10. Discuss seven hints for being a more effective leader.

---

* *Source:* This question is from Gary Dessler, *Organization and Management* (Englewood Cliffs, N.J.: Prentice-Hall, Inc., 1976) p. 177.

NOTES FOR THE CHAPTER

1. T. A. Mahoney, T. A. Jerdee, and A. N. Nash, "Predicting Managerial Effectiveness," *Personnel Psychology*, Vol. 13 (1960) pp. 147–163; Wendell French, *The Personnel Management Process* (Boston: Houghton Mifflin, 1974), pp. 318–321.

2. Edwin Ghiselli, "The Validity of Management Traits Related to Occupational Level," *Personnel Psychology*, Vol. 16 (1963) pp. 109–113; Abraham Korman, *Industrial and Organizational Psychology* (Englewood Cliffs, N.J.: Prentice-Hall, Inc., 1971) pp. 122–130.

3. R. M. Stogdill, *Managers, Employees, Organizations* (Columbus: Bureau of Business Research, Ohio State University, 1965) pp. 44–46; Abraham Korman, "Consideration; Initiating Structure; and Organizational Criteria—A Review," *Personnel Psychology*, Vol. 19, No. 4 (1966) pp. 349–361; Chester Schriesheim, Robert House, and Steven Kerr, *Leader Initiating Structure:* A reconciliation of discrepant research results and some empirical tests," *Organizational Behavior and Human Performance*, Vol. 15, pp. 297–321 (April 1976).

4. Stephen Sales, "Supervisory Style and Productivity: Review and Theory, *Personnel Psychology*, Vol. 19 (1966) pp. 275–286; L. L. Cummings and W. E. Scott, *Readings in Organizational Behavior and Human Performance* (Homewood: Irwin, 1969) pp. 596–652.

5. Nancy Morse and E. Reimer, "The Experimental Change of a Major Organizational Variable," *Journal of Abnormal and Social Psychology*, Vol. 51 (1956) pp. 120–129.

6. Walter Hill, "Leadership Style: Rigid or Flexible?" *Organizational Behavior and Human Performance*, Vol. 9 (1973) pp. 35–47.

7. Robert Blake and Jane Mouton, *Building a Dynamic Corporation Through Grid Organization Development* (Reading, Mass.: Addison-Wesley, 1969).

8. Steven Kerr, quoted in James Hunt and Lars Carson, *Contingency Approaches to Leadership* (Carbondale: SIU, 1974) p. 124.

9. Richard Steers, "Task Goal Attributes in Achievement, and Supervisory Performance," *Organizational Behavior and Human Performance*, Vol. 13, No. 3 (June 1975).

10. Based on Robert Tannenbaum and Warren Schmidt, "How to Choose a Leadership Pattern," *Harvard Business Review* (May-June 1973) pp. 162–180.

11. Fred Fiedler, *A Theory of Leadership Effectiveness* (New York: McGraw-Hill, 1967).

12. G. Graen, J. B. Orris, and K. M. Alvarez, "Contingency Model of Leadership Effectiveness: Some Experimental Results," *Journal of Applied Psychology*, Vol. 55 (1971) pp. 196–201; for a good review see Martin Chemers and Robert Rice, "A Theoretical and Empirical Examination of Fiedler's Contingency Model of Leadership Effectiveness" in Hunt and Larson, *Contingency Approaches to Leadership*, pp. 91–123.

13. See Robert House and Terence Mitchell, "Path-Goal Theory of Leadership," *Journal of Contemporary Business* (Autumn, 1974) pp. 81–99, for a good review of this theory.

14. This section is based on Gary Dessler, *Organization and Management* (Englewood Cliffs, N.J.: Prentice-Hall, Inc., 1976) p. 176.

15. David McClelland, "Achievement Motivation Can Be Developed," *Harvard Business Review* (November-December 1965).

16. See Stan Weed, Terence Mitchell, and Weldon Moffit, "Leadership Style, Subordinate Personality, and Task Type as Predictors of Performance and Satisfaction with Supervision," *Journal of Applied Psychology*, Vol. 61, No. 1 (February 1976).

A Framework for Studying the Management Fundamentals

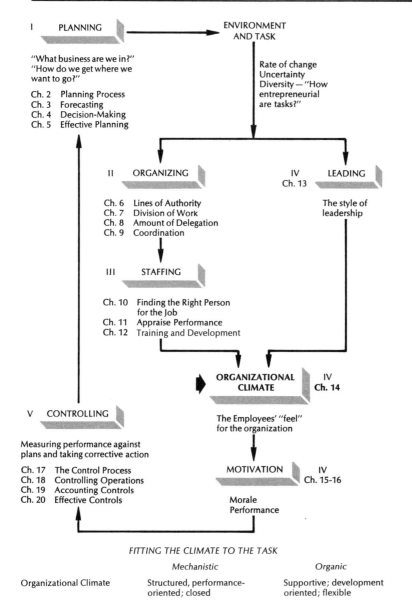

I   PLANNING → **ENVIRONMENT AND TASK**

"What business are we in?"
"How do we get where we want to go?"

Ch. 2   Planning Process
Ch. 3   Forecasting
Ch. 4   Decision-Making
Ch. 5   Effective Planning

Rate of change
Uncertainty
Diversity — "How entrepreneurial are tasks?"

II   ORGANIZING

Ch. 6   Lines of Authority
Ch. 7   Division of Work
Ch. 8   Amount of Delegation
Ch. 9   Coordination

IV   LEADING
Ch. 13

The style of leadership

III   STAFFING

Ch. 10   Finding the Right Person for the Job
Ch. 11   Appraise Performance
Ch. 12   Training and Development

ORGANIZATIONAL CLIMATE   IV   Ch. 14

The Employees' "feel" for the organization

V   CONTROLLING

Measuring performance against plans and taking corrective action

Ch. 17   The Control Process
Ch. 18   Controlling Operations
Ch. 19   Accounting Controls
Ch. 20   Effective Controls

MOTIVATION   IV   Ch. 15-16

Morale
Performance

FITTING THE CLIMATE TO THE TASK

Organizational Climate	*Mechanistic*	*Organic*
	Structured, performance-oriented; closed	Supportive; development oriented; flexible

Where we are now: Discussing organizational climate, which serves as a bridge between:
1. Objective aspects of the organization such as structure, and leader style, and
2. Employee morale and performance.

When you have finished studying

14 Organizational Climate and Employee Morale

You should be able to:

1. *Explain why a manager should aim at keeping his employees' morale high.*

2. *Discuss six important factors that affect employee morale.*

3. *Define organizational climate and explain how it acts as a "bridge."*

4. *Measure the organizational climate of your classroom or place of work.*

5. *Discuss the factors that we know affect an employee's perception of the world.*

6. *Cite four hints for developing a climate for high morale.*

INTRODUCTION

Do organizations really have "climates"? Do people develop a "feel" for the kind of organization in which they work? Does it matter whether your subordinates have high or low morale? Look at Exhibit 14–4 (page 284) for a moment. Can you use this questionnaire to describe the climate of your classroom or place of work? These are important questions for managers, and we will discuss them in this chapter.

DOES MORALE MATTER?

The Human Relations Approach

In Chapter 1 we discussed the Hawthorne studies whose findings became the basis of the Human Relations Movement. The essence of this movement was that managers could increase productivity by increasing the morale of their employees.[1]

There are at least three reasons why this assumption would be so appealing. For one thing, the idea that happy workers are better workers is *intuitively attractive.* Somehow it just seems more sensible to assume that

277

278   workers are more productive when they're satisfied than when they are dissatisfied.

Second, this assumption also fits the *value system* that prevailed when the Human Relations Movement was at its peak. Recall that after the Depression, people craved security and the desire to be happy at one's work took on added importance.

Finally, as we have discussed, some of the *evidence* from the Hawthorne plant seemed to show quite clearly that high morale and high productivity went hand in hand. Similarly in other experiments, restricted production was usually associated with low employee morale.[2]

But—Does Morale Matter?

In any event, the feeling that prevailed among writers during this period was that increased satisfaction undeniably led to increased productivity. But in the last few years writers have begun to question this assumption. In one famous review, for example, the authors concluded that "There is little evidence in the available literature that employee attitudes bear any simple—or, for that matter appreciable—relationship to performance on the job." [3]

Writers have therefore made something of an about face in the past few years. The prevailing assumption used to be, "Of course satisfaction leads to performance." But now the question is, "Does morale matter?" "Does it lead to high productivity?" "Does it lead to better attendance on the job?" "Does it lead to less employee turnover?"

It is obviously very important for you to have answers to these questions. Let's therefore look at some of the evidence.

Morale and Performance

How, if at all, are morale and *performance* related? The evidence is confusing, to say the least. There are three schools of thought on the matter, and the fact is they are probably all correct to some extent.[4]

First, there are some who assert that high satisfaction *leads to* high performance. The Hawthorne studies seem to support this position, as do the findings of a number of other studies.[5]

Second, there are those who take just the opposite position. For example, Lyman Porter and Edward Lawler say that satisfaction *results from* high performance. This is a familiar phenomenon. Most people have experienced the enormous feeling of satisfaction that comes from accomplishing some task, like making the Dean's list, building a radio, or clinching a sale. And, again, there is evidence to support this view.

Finally, there are those who claim that there is *no* consistent relationship between morale and performance. Victor Vroom reviewed 22 pertinent studies. He found significant relationships between morale and performance in only five of them.[6]

As you can see, there are no easy answers to the question "How are morale and performance related?" From a practical point of view it is mostly a matter of good judgment, and a big part of this is getting to know your employees. You will undoubtedly find some who do indeed work harder when they are more satisfied—with their pay, with the job itself, with working conditions, and so on. On the other hand, when *some* people's needs are satisfied—when they have *enough* security, or *enough* pay, or a good *enough* job, and the like—their performance starts to taper off because the "incentive" is gone. And undoubtedly there are some employees, on *some* jobs (such as a rigidly paced assembly line) for whom morale and performance are more or less unrelated.

Morale and Attendance

But the relationship between morale and *attendance* on the job *is* very clear and consistent. Employees with higher morale clearly have better attendance records and stay on their jobs longer than do employees with low morale.[7]

Therefore you, as a manager, certainly do not have to seek high morale for your employees "on faith." It is true that high morale and high performance do not necessarily go hand in hand. But it is also true that high morale does usually mean better employee attendance, and less employee turnover. And both attendance and turnover affect productivity and profits.

SOME THINGS THAT AFFECT MORALE

Why do some employees have higher morale than others? Is it because of their personalities, or backgrounds? Is it the nature of the organization? Is it the style of their supervisor? Actually, as we have summarized in Exhibit 14–1, all these affect morale. Let us look at some specifics.

The Employee's Age

Other things equal, who do you think are more satisfied—younger or older workers? Until quite recently most management writers would have answered "Both!" Many believed there was a "U"-shaped relationship between age and morale. They felt that morale was highest when people started on their job, but subsequently declined until people reached their late twenties.

Exhibit 14.1   Things that Affect an Employee's Morale

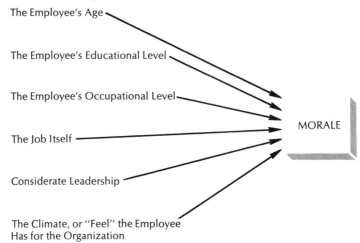

Then morale again began to rise.[8] But today we believe that age and morale are *directly* related: that, other things equal, older employees seem to have higher morale.[9]

What accounts for this? Frederick Herzberg says that employees who have *realistic expectations* about their jobs should be more satisfied than those with unrealistic expectations. And, probably, as an employee gets older he gradually lowers his aspirations and brings them into line with his abilities. Thus to the extent that older workers have more realistic expectations, they are more satisfied.

This does *not* mean that older employees don't need some extra care and coaching. Lester Bittel points out that older workers are usually somewhat slower and less resilient than younger ones. Sometimes it's harder for a worker to unlearn old habits and relearn new ones. So it's especially important here that you help him to see that he can do the job well, and help him build up his competence at it.[10]

The Employee's Educational Level

We also know that researchers usually find an inverse relationship between educational level and employee morale.[11] In other words, other things equal, the higher the educational level of an employee, the lower his job satisfaction (particularly with his pay). Why should this be the case? For one thing, people with higher educational levels also have higher "reference groups." These are groups both inside and outside of the company with which an employee compares his own attainments. Needless to say, the higher a person's reference point—the higher he thinks he *should* be—*the less* satisfied he may be at any particular point.

The Employee's Occupational Level

We also know that there is a direct relationship between occupational level and employee morale. Thus executives are on the whole more satisfied than managers; managers are more satisfied than their subordinates; and so forth.

The Job Itself

Charles Walker and Robert Guest studied workers in an automobile assembly plant. As you can see in Exhibit 14–2, they found that the more operations the workers performed, the more interesting they found their jobs.[12] From this and other studies we know that the job itself—how challenging it is; how interesting it is; and so forth—also influences morale.

Exhibit 14.2 Number of Operations Performed and How Interesting Workers Found their Jobs

Operations Performed	Very or Fairly Interesting	Not Very or Not At All Interesting
1	19	38
2-5	28	36
5 or more	41	18

Note: The more operations they performed, the more interesting the workers found their jobs.

Source: Charles R. Walker, and Robert H. Guest, *The Man on the Assembly Line* (Cambridge: Harvard University Press, 1952) p. 54; Joseph A. Litterer, *The Analysis of Organizations* (New York: Wiley and Sons, 1965) p. 189.

Considerate Leadership

In Chapter 13 we said that the more people-oriented, considerate leadership style is usually associated with higher employee morale. Being considerate and supportive of employees—treating them as valuable, capable individuals—is important for several reasons. First, "leader consideration" clearly raises employee morale. Furthermore, it is the more considerate leader who finds it easiest to "structure" his employees' jobs. For example, we know that when inconsiderate leaders try to give their employees orders, employee morale and performance usually drop. But when highly considerate leaders give orders, morale and performance usually stay high.[13]

Summary: Some Things That Affect Morale

There are many things that affect employee morale, and we could only touch on some of the most important ones here. These include:

1. *Age:* Other things equal—the higher the employee's age, the higher his morale.
2. *Educational Level:* Other things equal—the higher the employee's educational level, the lower his morale.
3. *Occupational Level:* Other things equal—the higher the employee's occupational level, the higher his morale.
4. *The Job Itself:* Other things equal—the more interesting the employee's job, the higher his morale (usually!).
5. *Considerate Leadership:* Other things equal—the more considerate and supportive the leader, the higher the morale of his subordinates.

In Exhibit 14–3 we have summarized these findings in terms of two extremes. Put a young employee with a high educational level into a boring low occupational level job, and saddle him with an inconsiderate leader, and you have the makings for a very dissatisfied employee. At the other extreme an older, less educated employee with an interesting, high occupational level job, and a considerate leader, will more likely have high morale.

Exhibit 14.3   Conditions for High and Low Morale

	Conditions Leading to High Morale:	*Conditions Leading to Lower Morale:*
Age	Younger (other things equal)	Older (other things equal)
Educational Level	Lower	Higher
Occupational Level	Higher	Lower
The Job Itself	More interesting	Less interesting
Considerate Leadership	More considerate	Less considerate

Organizational Climate

There is another very important determinant of employee morale, one that is much harder to "get a handle on" than are such things as employee age or occupational level. It is the organizational or psychological "climate" of the organization. Developing the right climate is such an important technique that we will devote the remainder of this chapter to it. First, though, let's see what we mean by "organizational climate."

ORGANIZATIONAL CLIMATE DEFINED   283

Do Organizations Really Have Climates?

Do organizations really have climates? While some writers would answer with a resounding "no," [14] most writers and managers would probably agree that they do.[15] Let's try a short experiment.

In Exhibit 14–4 you will find an "organization climate questionnaire." This can be used to give you a quick picture of the climate of some organization which you are familiar with. Notice that it focuses on things such as "warmth and support," "rewards," "conformity," and "leadership." As an example, think about the *best* class you ever had in college. Now for each of the seven climate dimensions in Exhibit 14–4, indicate with an "X" how you would rate this favorite class. Then do the same for your *worst* class, this time using checkmarks.

Could you discern any difference in climate between your *worst* and *best* classes? You may have found (as many students do) that the climate of your best class was much more open, warm, and supportive. Here students may have felt easier about expressing their opinions, criticism was held to a minimum, and challenging standards were set. A feeling of friendliness pervaded the class. You may have found that students not only learned better in this climate but were more creative as well.

On the other hand, many students find that their least favorite class had a very different climate. Here the climate could almost be described as oppressive. There was little or no friendly interchange between students and instructor. A rigid, unbending agenda and set of standards were adhered to, and criticism rather than rewards were used to "motivate" students.

Of course not all students feel that an open, warm, and supportive climate is necessarily "good"; or that a rigid, oppressive climate is necessarily "bad." In fact there are probably many classes where a lot more structure and "sticking to the rules" are quite appropriate. But the important point for us is that organizations do have climates. People do come away with some "feel" for the organization that transcends just the style of the leader, or the structure of the organization. And this climate can have an important influence on morale and behavior.

Organizational Climate Defined

George Litwin and Robert Stringer used the dimensions listed in Exhibit 14–5 to measure climate.[16] We know that dimensions like these are in

Exhibit 14.4 Organizational Climate Questionnaire

Introduction

For each of the seven organization climate dimensions described below place an (X) above the number that indicates your assessment of your favorite class's position on that dimension and a (✓) above the number that indicates your choice of your least favorite class on this dimension.

1. *Conformity*. The feeling that there are many externally imposed constraints in the organization; the degree to which members feel that there are many rules, procedures, policies, and practices to which they have to conform rather than being able to do their work as they see fit.

Conformity is not characteristic of this class (or other organization)	1 2 3 4 5 6 7 8 9 10	Conformity is very characteristic of this class (or other organization)

2. *Responsibility*. Members of the organization are given personal responsibility to achieve their part of the organization's goals; the degree to which members feel that they can make decisions and solve problems without checking with superiors each step of the way.

No responsibility is given in the organization	1 2 3 4 5 6 7 8 9 10	There is a great emphasis on personal responsibility in the organization

3. *Standards.* The emphasis the organization places on quality performance and outstanding production including the degree to which the member feels the organization is setting challenging goals for itself and communicating these goal commitments to members.

Standards are very low or nonexistent in the organization	1 2 3 4 5 6 7 8 9 10	High challenging standards are set in the organization

4. *Rewards.* The degree to which members feel that they are being recognized and rewarded for good work rather than being ignored, criticized, or punished when something goes wrong.

Members are ignored, punished, or criticized	1 2 3 4 5 6 7 8 9 10	Members are recognized and rewarded positively

5. *Organizational clarity.* The feeling among members that things are well organized and goals are clearly defined rather than being disorderly, confused, or chaotic.

The organization is disorderly, confused, and chaotic	1 2 3 4 5 6 7 8 9 10	The organization is well organized with clearly defined goals

6. *Warmth and support.* The feeling that friendliness is a valued norm in the organization; that members trust one another and offer support to one another. The feeling that good relationships prevail in the work environment.

There is no warmth and support in the organization	1 2 3 4 5 6 7 8 9 10	Warmth and support are very characteristic of the organization

7. *Leadership*. The willingness of organization members to accept leadership and direction from qualified others. As needs for leadership arise members feel free to take leadership roles and are rewarded for successfull leadership. Leadership is based on expertise. The organization is not dominated by, or dependent on, one or two individuals.

Leadership is not rewarded; members are dominated or dependent and resist leadership attempts	1 2 3 4 5 6 7 8 9 10	Members accept and reward leadership based on expertise

Source: David Kolb, Irwin Rubin, James McIntyre, *Organizational Psychology* (Englewood Cliffs, N. J., Prentice-Hall, 1971) pp. 75-6.

284

Exhibit 14.5 Sample Questions from Litwin and Stringer's Organizational Climate Questionnaire

1. *Structure*

The jobs in this Organization are clearly defined and logically structured.	Definitely Agree	Inclined to Agree	Inclined to Disagree	Definitely Disagree
In this Organization it is sometimes unclear who has the formal authority to make a decision.	Definitely Agree	Inclined to Agree	Inclined to Disagree	Definitely Disagree
Red tape is kept to a minimum in this Organization.	Definitely Agree	Inclined to Agree	Inclined to Disagree	Definitely Disagree
In some of the projects I've been on, I haven't been sure exactly who my boss was.	Definitely Agree	Inclined to Agree	Inclined to Disagree	Definitely Disagree

2. *Responsibility*

Our philosophy emphasizes that people should solve their problems by themselves.	Definitely Agree	Inclined to Agree	Inclined to Disagree	Definitely Disagree
There are an awful lot of excuses around here when somebody makes a mistake.	Definitely Agree	Inclined to Agree	Inclined to Disagree	Definitely Disagree
One of the problems in this Organization is that individuals won't take responsibility.	Definitely Agree	Inclined to Agree	Inclined to Disagree	Definitely Disagree

3. *Rewards*

We have a promotion system here that helps the best man rise to the top.	Definitely Agree	Inclined to Agree	Inclined to Disagree	Definitely Disagree
In this Organization the rewards & encouragements you get usually outweigh the threats and the criticism.	Definitely Agree	Inclined to Agree	Inclined to Disagree	Definitely Disagree
There is a great deal of criticism in this Organization.	Definitely Agree	Inclined to Agree	Inclined to Disagree	Definitely Disagree

4. *Risk*

Our business has been built up by taking calculated risks at the right time.	Definitely Agree	Inclined to Agree	Inclined to Disagree	Definitely Disagree
Decision making in this Organization is too cautious for maximum effectiveness.	Definitely Agree	Inclined to Agree	Inclined to Disagree	Definitely Disagree
Our management is willing to take a chance on a good idea.	Definitely Agree	Inclined to Agree	Inclined to Disagree	Definitely Disagree

5. *Warmth*

A friendly atmosphere prevails among the people in this Organization.	Definitely Agree	Inclined to Agree	Inclined to Disagree	Definitely Disagree
This Organization is characterized by a relaxed, easy-going climate.	Definitely Agree	Inclined to Agree	Inclined to Disagree	Definitely Disagree
People in this Organization tend to be cool and aloof toward each other.	Definitely Agree	Inclined to Agree	Inclined to Disagree	Definitely Disagree

6. *Support*

You don't get much sympathy from higher-ups in this Organization if you make a mistake.	Definitely Agree	Inclined to Agree	Inclined to Disagree	Definitely Disagree
People in this Organization don't really trust each other enough.	Definitely Agree	Inclined to Agree	Inclined to Disagree	Definitely Disagree
When I am on a difficult assignment I can usually rely on getting assistance from my boss and co-workers.	Definitely Agree	Inclined to Agree	Inclined to Disagree	Definitely Disagree

7. *Standards*

In this Organization we set very high standards for performance.	Definitely Agree	Inclined to Agree	Inclined to Disagree	Definitely Disagree
Our management believes that no job is so well done that it couldn't be done better.	Definitely Agree	Inclined to Agree	Inclined to Disagree	Definitely Disagree
In this Organization people don't seem to take much pride in their performance.	Definitely Agree	Inclined to Agree	Inclined to Disagree	Definitely Disagree

Exhibit 14.5   (continued)

8. *Conflict*

The best way to make a good impression around here is to steer clear of open arguments and disagreements.	Definitely Agree	Inclined to Agree	Inclined to Disagree	Definitely Disagree
The attitude of management is that conflict between competing units and individuals can be very healthy.	Definitely Agree	Inclined to Agree	Inclined to Disagree	Definitely Disagree
We are encouraged to speak our minds, even if it means disagreeing with our superiors.	Definitely Agree	Inclined to Agree	Inclined to Disagree	Definitely Disagree

9. *Identity*

People are proud of belonging to this Organization.	Definitely Agree	Inclined to Agree	Inclined to Disagree	Definitely Disagree
I feel that I am a member of a well functioning team.	Definitely Agree	Inclined to Agree	Inclined to Disagree	Definitely Disagree
As far as I can see, there isn't very much personal loyalty to the company.	Definitely Agree	Inclined to Agree	Inclined to Disagree	Definitely Disagree

Source: George Litwin and Robert Stringer Jr., *Motivation and Organizational Climate* (Boston: Division of Research, Graduate School of Business Administration, Harvard University, 1968).

fact representative of the climate of an organization.[17] Therefore we will define organizational climate as:

> The perceptions which the individual has of the kind of organization he is working in, and his "feel" for the organization, in terms of such dimensions as autonomy, structure, rewards, consideration, warmth and support, and openness.[18]

THE MECHANICS OF ORGANIZATIONAL CLIMATE

How Organizational Climate Works

As we have illustrated in Exhibit 14–6 (and in our framework) organizational climate acts as a bridge. On one side are the objective, tangible aspects of the organization such as structure, rules, and leadership styles. Climate is the perception or "feel" for these tangible aspects of the organization that the employees develop.

Exhibit 14.6   The Organizational Climate "Bridge"

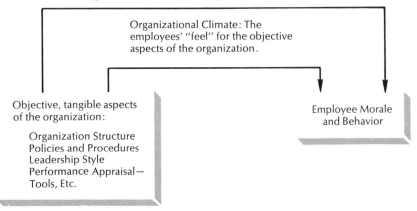

Organizational Climate: The employees' "feel" for the objective aspects of the organization.

Objective, tangible aspects of the organization:

Organization Structure
Policies and Procedures
Leadership Style
Performance Appraisal—
Tools, Etc.

Employee Morale and Behavior

Note: Organizational climate acts as a bridge between: (1) objective, tangible aspects of the organization such as structure, and leader style; and (2) the morale and behavior of employees.

On the other side of the climate "bridge" is the morale and behavior of the employees. Thus employee morale and behavior is not just a function of actual leadership style, or actual organizational structure. Instead (as we saw in Chapter 4) each person looks at the world through a window tinted by his own values, needs, and personality. And it is these *perceptions* of the world that influence his attitudes and behavior. Let's see how.

Perception

Everyone is familiar with how perception can distort a person's view of things. For example, a young supervisor once mentioned off-handedly to a subordinate that he would like to see him in his office later that afternoon. Actually he just wanted the subordinate's advice on some matter that had arisen. The subordinate didn't know that, though, and spent the rest of the day anguishing over what his boss might want. Needless to say, the supervisor was somewhat stunned when confronted later that day by his nervous and agitated subordinate. In this case, it clearly wasn't the actual reason for the meeting that had so upset the subordinate; it was his perception of it—his fear that he might be criticized or reprimanded.

Here are some of the things that we know affect perception: [19]

Self-Concept: This is the set of attitudes a person develops toward himself. For example, some people feel that they are competent, and capable of exercising a high degree of judgment on their jobs. Others do not feel so secure about their competence and prefer a strong hand guiding them.[20] As Saul Gellerman says:

The self-concept that the individual brings to his job is an amalgum of many things: the reception his parents gave him, the roles he has learned to play convincingly with his peers, his record of past successes and failures, and his notion of what rewards he deserves. His conduct at work will reflect this self-concept, and his morale will be heavily influenced by whether the job lets him be the kind of person he thinks he is.[21]

Group Pressure: Your subordinates' work group will also influence how he "sees" things. Thus in one famous study the researcher instructed five of six people in a group to give a wrong answer to a problem. Then the sixth person was brought in and confronted by the others giving the wrong answer. He also gave the wrong answer (although he knew it was wrong) just so that he could conform to the others!

Role: A person's position or role in the organization also affects how he perceives things. In one study researchers presented a group of business executives with a case which described a company with a number of general problems. The *sales* executives perceived them as sales problems, but the *production* executives perceived them as mechanical, "we need more structure" problems.[22] Your role as supervisor similarly influences how people perceive you. For example, as a supervisor, people will expect you to act like a leader and to not step out of that role very often.

Reference Groups: People often ask themselves, "I wonder what they will think of me if I do such and such?" This is an example of the use of reference groups. Such groups can have a very important influence on a person's perception. For example, you might tell a person that he can earn some extra money by speeding up his production. But very often his important reference group is his peers—the people he must work with day after day. If he thinks that working faster will make him look like a "company man" to his peers, he will probably forego the extra income rather than risk the criticism of his peers.

Summary.   In summary, here are four important things that affect perception—how your subordinate "sees" the world:

>   His self-concept;
>
>   Group pressure;
>
>   His role; and
>
>   His reference groups.

Organizational Structure and Climate

Organizational structure is one of the tangible aspects of the organization that affect its climate. For example, we know that school systems that operate with a formal chain of command, and that have large numbers of rules and regulations are more likely to be perceived as having closed, confining climates.[23]

Leadership and Climate

George Litwin and Robert Stringer carried out a study which showed how leadership style is another factor that affects climate.

As you can see in Exhibit 14–7, they set up three experimental companies. The leader of each was instructed to exhibit a different style. For example, in company A the leader was more "hard-nosed." He emphasized maintaining order and criticizing poor performance. At the other extreme,

Exhibit 14.7 Summary of Leadership Style Inputs

Climate Dimension	Organization A	Organization B	Organization C
1. Structure	maintain order, exercise authority and control	maintain informality	maintain informality
2. Standards, Responsibility			set high standards for individuals and organization encourage innovation
3. Reward and Punishment	criticize poor performance criticize deviation from rules	avoid individual punishment give general positive rewards (unconditional positive reward)	give individual and organizational rewards, praise, promotion reward excellent performance
4. Warmth and Support		create warm, friendly relationships create relaxed, easy-going atmosphere	give individual and organizational support
5. Cooperation and Conflict		stress cooperation avoid conflicts create warm, personal relationships with subordinates	stress cooperation in work tolerate personal and task-related conflict
6. Risk and Involvement	stress conservatism avoid deep involvement		stress moderate risks, create pride in organization, stress challenge, fun and excitement of work

Note: This summarizes the instructions Litwin and Stringer gave to each of their three "company presidents." They found that three different climates emerged.

Source: Litwin and Stringer, *Motivation and Organizational Climate.*

290   the leader of organization C emphasized maintaining an informal atmosphere and giving rewards and praise. Litwin and Stringer then administered their organizational climate questionnaire (Exhibit 14–5). They found that the employees of each company had clearly come away with very different impressions of their organizations' climate. Those in company A felt that their organization was "nonsupportive" and "highly structured." Those in company C felt that their organization was "closely structured" and "encouraged initiative." Thus as a leader *you're* going to have an important effect on your unit's climate.

Organizational Climate and Employee Morale and Performance

Structure and leadership affect climate.[24] In turn we know that organizational climate has been found to have an important effect on the *morale* of many different types of employees.[25] And as you have probably found in some of your college classes, climate can also influence *performance*. For example, in a study of 260 middle managers it was found that more open, supportive climates resulted in higher performance than did more oppressive climates.[26]

Summary: The Mechanics of Organizational Climate

In summary, organizational climate acts as a bridge between 1) the tangible aspects of the organization (such as structure and leadership); and 2) the morale and behavior of employees. Climate itself represents the perceptions or "feel" that employees have for an organization. This perception is influenced by several things, including group pressure, the employee's self-concept, his organizational position (or "role"), and his reference group.

FOUR HINTS FOR DEVELOPING A CLIMATE FOR HIGH MORALE

How do you go about developing the right climate? This is no easy matter. It doesn't just involve using the right leadership style, or establishing the right organization structure. Climate, remember, is the perception or feel for these tangible things that employees have. And we know that each employee is going to develop his own picture of the world, one that is tinted by his own unique values, needs, and self-concepts.[27] So, keeping this in mind, here are some hints for developing the right climate.

Hint 1. Find Out What Your Organization's Climate Is Now

Your first step in developing the "right" climate is to find out what the climate is *now*. You could use the organizational climate dimensions from Exhibits 14–4 and 14–5 to guide you. Ask questions such as: "Do your subordinates feel they have sufficient autonomy?" "Do they feel too constrained to do their jobs well?" "Do they feel that there is adequate structure?" "Do they feel they are rewarded for a job well done?" "Do they feel that they are treated with consideration and support?"

Hint 2. Remember: It's Not Just What You Do—It's How You Do It

The climate that emerges will be a product of a consistent, honest, and continuous effort on your part. A multitude of things will contribute to that climate—not just your leadership style and what you say. Your facial expressions, whether you carry through on promises, whether you implement subordinates' suggestions, and whether in all your dealings with them you are honest, unbiased, and open, will all contribute to the climate that emerges.

Hint 3. Develop a Supportive Climate

Dale Carnegie has said that the *"big secret of dealing with people"* is to give them what they want most in the world. He says that almost every normal adult wants certain things, including:

a) Health and the preservation of life.
b) Food.
c) Sleep.
d) Money and the things money will buy.
e) The well-being of our children.
f) A feeling of importance.[28]

And he goes on to say that almost all these wants are gratified—except one:

> But there is one longing almost as deep, almost as imperious, as the desire for food or sleep which is seldom gratified. It is what Freud calls "the desire to be great." It is what Dewey calls "the desire to be important." [29]

We will come across this idea again in the next chapter. It is very similar to what psychologists like Frederick Herzberg and Abraham Maslow say motivates people. Herzberg says that improving physical aspects of people's jobs—

such as pay and working conditions—won't really motivate them. Instead, he says, you have to build "motivators" into the job; and one of the most important motivators is *recognition* for a job well done.

Similarly, we will see that Abraham Maslow says that there is a hierarchy of needs that motivate people. He says that the highest level needs—and those which are usually never completely fulfilled—are those for "esteem and self-actualization." Self-actualization is the need people have to become the persons they are capable of becoming. It is the need to achieve all that they feel they are capable of achieving. It is the need to be and feel important, in one's own eyes as well as in the eyes of others.

So "What is the big secret of dealing with people?" There is obviously no sure-fire formula. But from experts like Carnegie, Herzberg, and Maslow, we know that satisfying the need to feel important is one ingredient. Therefore Hint 3 is: Develop a supportive climate—one that allows your subordinates to feel that they are treated as important, capable individuals.

Hint 4. Make Sure the Climate Fits the Task

In previous chapters we said that things like organization structure, rules, and leadership style have to be appropriate for the task. But John Morse has found that *it is not enough* to have the appropriate structure, rules, and leadership style.[30] In addition, the *organizational climate must be appropriate.* In a research lab, for example, an open and flexible climate where each scientist perceives himself as having a great deal of autonomy may be appropriate. At the other extreme, a more structured, directive (but still supportive) climate may be appropriate for routine, assembly-line type tasks.

In summary, then, make sure the climate is right for the task. Ask such questions as: "Does the task call for greater autonomy on the part of employees?" "Would the employees themselves prefer a more structured climate?" And "Do you need the sort of open climate that encourages creativity?" Here's what Morse concluded:

	in the Mechanistic Organization	in the Organic Organization
Organization Structure	Highly structured	Low degree of structure
Use of rules	Many, specific	Minimal, flexible
Organization Climate	Closed, rigid	Open, adaptable

Some Important Things to Remember from This Chapter:

1. The evidence concerning how morale and performance are related is conflicting. Some say that high satisfaction leads to high performance; some say that high performance leads to high satisfaction; and some say the two are not really related at all. The answer is probably that we just can't generalize. You will have to use your judgment in light of what you know about your employees and their jobs.

2. We know that the relationship between morale and attendance on the job *is* very consistent. Employees with higher morale clearly have better attendance records.

3. You need only look around you to see that some employees have higher morale than others. An employee's morale (how satisfied he is) is, we know, a function of many factors. Among these are his age; his educational level; his occuptional level; the job itself; how considerate his leader is; and the organizational climate.

4. Organizational climate is the perception the individual has of the kind of organization in which he is working, and his "feel" for the organization in terms of such dimensions as autonomy, structure, rewards, consideration, warmth and support, and openness.

5. Employee morale and behavior are not just a function of actual leadership style or actual organizational structure. Instead each person looks at the world through a window tinted by his own values, needs, and personality. It is these perceptions of the world that influence his attitudes and behavior. Thus organizational climate (the employee's perceptions of the kind of organization he is working in) acts as a bridge between 1) objective, tangible aspects of the organization; and 2) his morale and behavior.

6. We discussed four hints for developing a climate for high morale. They were:

   a) Find out what your organization's climate is now.
   b) Remember, it is not just what you do, it's how you do it.
   c) Develop a supportive climate.
   d) Make sure the climate fits the task.

STUDY ASSIGNMENTS

1. Measure the climate of your classroom or place of work, using the questionnaire in Exhibit 14–4.
2. Explain why a manager should aim at keeping his employees' morale high.
3. Discuss six important factors that affect employee morale.
4. In your own words, explain how organizational climate can influence employee morale and motivation.
5. Define organizational climate.
6. Discuss the factors that we know affect an employee's perception of the world. Why are they important to you as a manager.

7. Discuss four hints for developing a climate for high morale.

8. "It is not enough to have an organization structure that fits the task; the climate has to be appropriate too." Explain whether you agree or disagree with this statement, and why.

9. What was the essense of the "human relations" approach? What made the human relations approach so appealing to so many managers?

10. Consider the classroom or work situation which you think has the worst organization climate you have ever experienced. If you were called in as a consultant, what would you do to improve that climate?

NOTES FOR THE CHAPTER

1. Victor H. Vroom, *Work and Motivation* (New York: John Wiley and Sons, 1964); L. L. Cummings and W. E. Scott, *Readings in Organizational Behavior and Human Performance* (Homewood, Ill.: Irwin, 1969) Ch. 3.

2. Edward Lawler and Lyman Porter, "The Effect of Performance on Job Satisfaction," Industrial Relations, Vol. 7, No. 1 (October 1967) pp. 20–28; reprinted in Cummings and Scott, *Readings in Organizational Behavior and Human Performance.*

3. Arthur Brayfield and Walter Crockett, "Employee Attitudes and Employee Performance," *Psychological Bulletin,* Vol. 52 (September 1955) pp. 396–424; Donald Schwab and Larry Cummings. "Theories of Performance and Satisfaction: A Review," *Industrial Relations,* Vol. 9, No. 4 (October 1970) pp. 408–430; reprinted in W. E. Scott, Jr. and L. L. Cummings, *Readings in Organizational Behavior and Human Performance* (Homewood, Ill.: Irwin, 1973) pp. 130–139.

4. Victor H. Vroom, *Work and Motivation* (New York: John Wiley and Sons, 1964); also see, for example, Constance Nathanson and Marshall Becker, "Job Satisfaction and Job Performance: An Empirical Test of Some Theoretical Propositions," *Organizational Behavior and Human Performance,* Vol. 9 (1973) pp. 267–279; John Wanous, "A Causal-Correlational Analysis of the Job Satisfaction and Performance Relationship," *Journal of Applied Psychology,* Vol. 59, No. 2 (1974) pp. 139–144.

5. F. Herzberg, B. Mausner, and D. B. Snyderman, *The Motivation to Work* (New York: John Wiley & Sons, 1959).

6. Victor Vroom, Work and Motivation.

7. H. Mann and H. Baumgartel, "Absence and Employee Attitudes in an Electric Power Company" (Survey Research Center, University of Michigan, December 1952); Ernest J. McCormick and Joseph Tiffin, *Industrial Psychology* (Englewood Cliffs, N.J.: Prentice-Hall, 1974) pp. 325–330.

8. John Hunt and Peter Saul, "The Relationship of Age, Tenure and Job Satisfaction in Males and Females," *Academy of Management Journal,* Vol. 18, No. 4 (December 1975) pp. 690–702.

9. Abraham Korman, *Industrial and Organizational Psychology* (Englewood Cliffs, N.J.: Prentice-Hall, 1971) pp. 163–177; John Hunt and Peter Saul, "The Relationship of Age, Tenure and Job Satisfaction in Males and Females."

10. Lester R. Bittel, *What Every Supervisor Should Know* (New York: McGraw-Hill, 1974) pp. 334–341.

11. Abraham Korman, *Industrial and Organizational Psychology,* p. 163; S. Klein, and J. Maher, "Educational Level and Satisfaction with Pay," *Personnel Psychology,* Vol. 19 (1966) pp. 195–208.

12. Charles Walker and Robert Guest, *The Man on the Assembly Line* (Cambridge: Harvard University Press, 1952) p. 54; in Joseph Litterer, *The Analysis of Organizations* (New York: John Wiley & Sons, 1965) p. 189.

13. E. A. Fleishman and E. Harris, "Patterns of Leadership Behavior Related to Employee Grievances and Turnover," *Personnel Psychology,* Vol. 15 (1962) pp. 42–56; Charles N. Greene, "The Reciprocal Nature of Influence Between Leader and Subordinate," *Journal of Applied Psychology,* Vol. 60, No. 2 (April 1975).

14. Robert Guion, "A Note on Organizational Climate," *Organizational Behavior and Human Performance*, Vol. 9 (1973) pp. 120–125.　　　　　　　　　　　　295

15. See, for example, William LaFollette and Henry Sims, Jr., "Is Satisfaction Redundant with Organizational Climate?" *Organizational Behavior and Human Performance*, Vol. 13 (1975) pp. 257–278.

16. George Litwin and Robert Stringer, *Motivation and Organizational Climate* (Boston: Division of Research, Graduate School of Business Administration, Harvard University, 1968).

17. Henry Sims, Jr. and William LaFollette, "An Assessment of the Litwin and Stringer Organization Climate Questionnaire," *Personnel Psychology*, Vol. 28 (1975) pp. 19–38.

18. Gary Dessler, *Organization and Management: A Contingency Approach* (Englewood Cliffs, N.J.: Prentice-Hall, 1976) p. 187; J. P. Campbell, M. Dunnette, E. E. Lawler, and K. E. Weick, Jr., *Managerial Behavior, Performance, and Effectiveness* (New York: McGraw-Hill Book Company, 1970).

19. These are based on Joseph A. Litterer, *The Analysis of Organizations*, pp. 51–65.

20. See Saul Gellerman, *Motivation and Productivity* (New York: American Management Association) p. 185.

21. Saul Gellerman, *Motivation and Productivity*, p. 187.

22. D. Dearborn and H. Simon, "Selective Perception: A Note on the Departmental Identifications of Executives," *Sociometry*, Vol. 21 (1958) p. 142.

23. J. George and L. Bishop, "Relationship of Organizational Structure and Teacher Personality Characteristics Toward Organizational Climate," *Administrative Science Quarterly*, Vol. 16 (1971) pp. 467–476; Don Hellriegel and John Slocum, Jr., "Organizational Climate: Measures, Research, and Contingencies," *Academy of Management Journal* (June 1974), pp. 255–280 .

24. Hermon Lyon and John Ivancevich, "An Exploratory Investigation of Organizational Climate and Job Satisfaction in Hospitals," *Academy of Management Journal*, Vol. 17, No. 4 (December 1974).

25. T. Cawsey, "The Interaction of Motivation and Environment in the Prediction of Performance Potential on Satisfaction in a Life Insurance Industry in Canada," paper presented at the 16th annual Midwest Academy of Management meeting, Chicago, Illinois, April 1973; for some contradictory evidence, see Benjamin Schneider and Robert Snyder, "Some Relationships Between Job Satisfaction and Organizational Climate," *Journal of Applied Psychology*, Vol. 60, No. 3 (June 1975) p. 318.

26. N. Frederickson, "Some Effects of Organizational Climates on Administrative Performance," Research Memorandum, RM-66-21, Educational Testing Service, 1966.

27. H. Russell Johnston, "A New Conceptualization of Source of Organizational Climate," *Administrative Science Quarterly*, Vol. 21, No. 1 (March 1976) pp. 95–103.

28. Dale Carnegie, *How to Win Friends and Influence People* (New York: Pocketbooks, 1968) p. 31.

29. Dale Carnegie, *How to Win Friends and Influence People*, p. 31.

30. John Morse, "Organizational Characteristics and Individual Motivation," in *Studies in Organizational Design*, ed. Jay Lorsch and Paul Lawrence (Homewood, Ill.: Irwin, 1970) pp. 84–100.

A Framework for Studying the Management Fundamentals

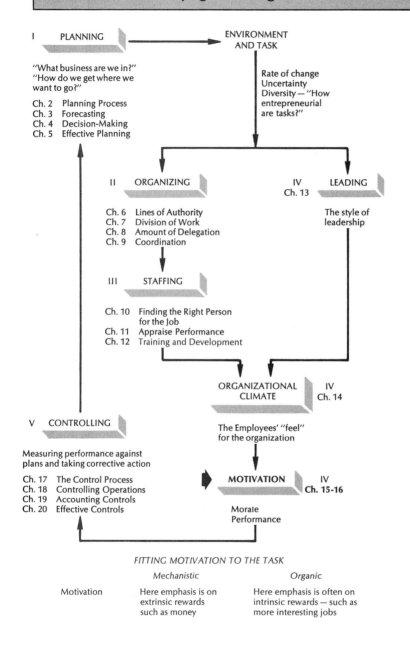

I   PLANNING   ENVIRONMENT
                                                 AND TASK

"What business are we in?"   Rate of change
"How do we get where we   Uncertainty
want to go?"   Diversity — "How
                                                 entrepreneurial
Ch. 2   Planning Process   are tasks?"
Ch. 3   Forecasting
Ch. 4   Decision-Making
Ch. 5   Effective Planning

II   ORGANIZING   IV   LEADING
                                    Ch. 13

Ch. 6   Lines of Authority   The style of
Ch. 7   Division of Work   leadership
Ch. 8   Amount of Delegation
Ch. 9   Coordination

III   STAFFING

Ch. 10   Finding the Right Person
          for the Job
Ch. 11   Appraise Performance
Ch. 12   Training and Development

ORGANIZATIONAL   IV
CLIMATE   Ch. 14

V   CONTROLLING   The Employees' "feel"
                                     for the organization

Measuring performance against
plans and taking corrective action

Ch. 17   The Control Process   MOTIVATION   IV
Ch. 18   Controlling Operations   Ch. 15-16
Ch. 19   Accounting Controls
Ch. 20   Effective Controls   Morale
                                     Performance

FITTING MOTIVATION TO THE TASK

                        Mechanistic   Organic

        Motivation   Here emphasis is on   Here emphasis is often on
                        extrinsic rewards   intrinsic rewards — such as
                        such as money   more interesting jobs

Where we are now: Discussing motivation, which emerges out of the climate you set.

When you have finished studying

15 Fundamentals of Motivation

You should be able to:

1. *Explain what motivation is.*

2. *Develop an "expectancy model" diagram of motivation.*

3. *Discuss the Maslow Needs Hierarchy.*

4. *Compare and contrast the Maslow and the Herzberg motivation theories.*

5. *Summarize what we know about "What do people want?"*

6. *Explain how all the management functions influence motivation.*

INTRODUCTION

How would you respond to the following questions?

	Yes	No
1. When you start a task, do you stick with it?		
2. Do you try to find out how you are doing, and do you try to get as much feedback as possible?		
3. Do you respond to difficult, challenging situations? Do you work better when there is a deadline or some other challenge involved?		
4. Are you eager to accept responsibility? Do you set (and meet) measurable standards of high performance?		
5. Do you seem to enjoy a good argument?		
6. Do you seek positions of authority where you can give orders rather than take them? Do you try to take over?		
7. Are status symbols especially important to you, and do you use them to gain influence over others?		
8. Are you especially eager to be your own boss, even when you need assistance, or when joint effort is required?		

SECTION IV: LEADING

<table>
<tr><td></td><td>Yes</td><td>No</td></tr>
</table>

9. *Do you seem to be uncomfortable when you are forced to work alone?*

10. *Do you interact with other workers, and go out of your way to make friends with new workers?*

11. *Are you always getting involved in group projects, and are you sensitive to other people (especially when they are "mad" at you)?*

12. *Are you an "apple polisher," and do you try hard to get personally involved with your superiors?*

According to George Litwin and Robert Stringer, "yes" answers to questions 1 through 4 mean that you have a high need to achieve.[1] You *prefer situations which have moderate risks, in which you can identify your own contribution, and in which you receive concrete feedback concerning your performance.*

"Yes" answers to questions 5 through 8 mean that you have a high need for power. You *prefer situations in which you can get and maintain control of the means for influencing others.*

Finally, "yes" answers to questions 9 through 12 mean that you have a high need for affiliation. *You have a strong desire to maintain close friendships and positive emotional relationships with others.*

Of course a quick test like this can only give you the roughest of guidelines about what your needs are. But it does point up the fact that people's specific needs are highly individualized, and that the things that will motivate them must also be highly individualized.

What are these "needs" that are so important in motivating people? How do you go about motivating someone? These are two of the most important questions you'll face as a manager, and they are the questions we will try to answer in this chapter.

WHAT IS MOTIVATION?

Motivating—Simple Yet Complex.

Motivating is one of the simplest yet most complex of your management jobs. It is simple because *people are basically motivated or driven to behave in a way that they feel leads to rewards.*[2] So motivating someone should be easy; just find out what he wants, and hold it out as a possible reward (or "incentive").

But this is where the complexity of motivating comes in. For one thing, what one person considers an important reward, another person might consider useless. For example, a glass of water would probably be a lot more "motivating" to a person who has just spent three hours on a hot beach, than it would be to someone who had just downed three cold beers. And even holding out a reward that *is* important to someone is certainly no guarantee that it will motivate him. The reason is that the reward itself (the glass of water, a date with some movie star, a promotion, and so on) won't motivate him *unless he feels that effort on his part will probably lead to his obtaining that reward.* People differ greatly in how they size up their chances for success on different jobs. So you can see that a task which one person might feel *would* lead to rewards, might be viewed by another as impossible.

But, the complexities of motivation notwithstanding, there's no doubt that motivation is the "bottom line" of management. Managers get things done through people, and if you can't somehow motivate your people, you'll probably not make it in management. Therefore, let's accept the complexity of motivation as a fact of life, and instead take a close look at what we *do* know about motivating employees.

Some Basic Terminology

Before proceeding, let's briefly review some basic terminology.

Most writers agree that some sort of "internal tensions" are at the root of motivation, and that *motivated behavior* is aimed at reducing these tensions.[3] For example, everyone has a *need* to eat. But right after you finish a big meal, this need to eat would probably be *satisfied*. Thus someone couldn't "motivate" you by offering you a big steak dinner. But if you *hadn't* eaten for a few days, the need to eat would undoubtedly become activated. An internal *tension* would develop: On the one hand, you have a basic need to eat; but on the other hand, you haven't eaten for days. Now if someone were to offer you a steak dinner (an *incentive* or *reward*) you might jump for it—be motivated to get it.

Now let's suppose that someone throws a barrier (say, a fence) between you and that steak dinner. You would find your *path* to the *goal* (the steak dinner) blocked by the fence, and would probably become *frustrated*. Frustrated or not, of course, if the goal was important enough you might find some ingenious way of getting around the fence. But what we find more often in industry is that when the paths of workers are blocked, they often just "give up." *Morale* (satisfaction) drops; they sit around with their friends and gripe, and, in some cases, retaliate by throwing a wrench (sometimes literally) into the machinery. This is summarized in Exhibit 15–1.

Exhibit 15.1 How Motivation, Incentives, and Frustration are Related

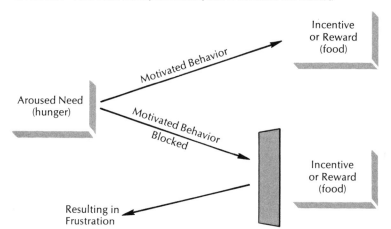

Note: Motivation takes place when you see an incentive or reward that can satisfy an *AROUSED* need. Frustration occurs when a barrier is placed between you and that incentive or reward.

An Expectancy Model of Motivation

We said that to motivate someone, it's not enough to just offer him something to satisfy his important needs. The reason for this (to repeat) is that in order for him to be motivated, he will also have to be reasonably convinced he has the ability to obtain the reward. For example, telling a person you will appoint him sales manager if he increases sales in his district will probably not motivate him if he knows the task is virtually impossible.

Victor Vroom has developed a theory of motivation which takes into account the person's *expectations* for success.[4] Basically, as depicted in Exhibit 15–2, he says that motivation will take place if two things occur:

If the "valence" or value of the particular outcome (such as becoming a sales manager) is very high for the person; and

If the person feels he has a reasonably good chance of accomplishing the task and obtaining the outcome.

Exhibit 15.2 Outline of Vroom's Theory of Motivation

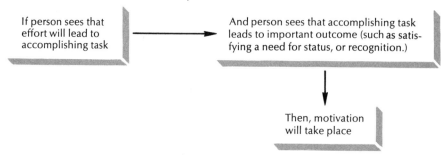

Vroom's theory makes a lot of common sense. And while not all the research findings support it,[5] much of it does.[6] Therefore we are going to use Vroom's model in this chapter as a framework for explaining how motivation takes place.

In summary, Vroom's expectancy model says that people are motivated or driven to behave in a way that they feel leads to rewards. But motivating someone is easier said than done, since no two persons' needs are quite the same. Therefore the next thing we should do is delve into the question of what people want—what motivates them.

WHAT DO PEOPLE WANT?

Let's look at what five psychologists have to say about "what do people want?" Then at the end of this section we'll tie together their ideas in a summary.

Abraham Maslow and the Needs Hierarchy

Abraham Maslow says that man has five basic categories of needs—physiological, safety, social, ego, and self-actualization needs.[7] He says that these needs form a hierarchy or ladder (as in Exhibit 15–3) and that each need becomes active only when the next lower-level need is satisfied.

Exhibit 15.3 Maslow's Needs Hierarchy

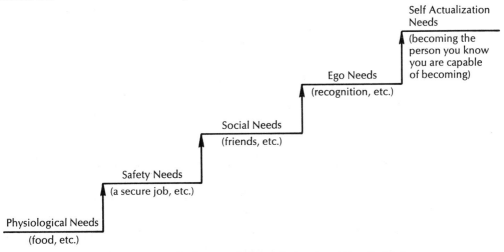

Note: Each higher order needs become active only when succeeding lower level needs are fairly well satisfied.

The Physiological Needs: The lowest level in Maslow's hierarchy are the physiological needs. These are the most basic needs we all have; for example, the needs for food, drink, shelter, and rest.

The Safety Needs: When the physiological needs are reasonably satisfied—when you are no longer thirsty, have had enough to eat, have a roof over your head, and so forth—then the safety needs become activated. They become the needs which the person tries to satisfy; the needs that motivate him. These are the needs for protection against danger or deprivation; the need for security.

The Social Needs: Once a man's physiological and safety needs are satisfied then, according to Maslow, they no longer motivate behavior. Now the social needs become the active motivators of behavior; needs such as for affiliation, for giving and receiving affection, and for friendship.

The Ego Needs: Next in the hierarchy are the ego needs, which Douglas McGregor has interpreted as:

1. Those needs that relate to one's self-esteem—needs for self-confidence, for independence, for achievement, for confidence, for knowledge; and
2. Those needs that relate to one's reputation—needs for status, for recognition, for appreciation, for the deserved respect of one's fellows.

One of the big differences between ego needs and the physiological, safety, and social needs is that *the former needs are rarely satisfied.* Thus, according to Maslow, people have a constant craving for more achievement, more knowledge, and more recognition. But, as with the other needs, ego needs only motivate behavior once the lower-level needs are reasonably satisfied.

Self-Actualization Needs. Finally there is an ultimate need; a need that only begins to dominate a person's behavior once all lower-level needs are satisfied. This is the need for self-actualization or fulfillment, the need we all have to become the person we feel we have the potential for becoming. This is the need that drives an artist to express himself on canvas; the need that motivates a student to work all day and then take a college degree in night school. This need, as with the ego needs, is rarely if ever satisfied.

Frederick Herzberg and the Motivator-Hygiene Theory

Frederick Herzberg says that man has two different sets of needs.[8] One, "lower-level" set derives from man's desire to avoid pain and satisfy his basic needs. These include the needs for such things as food, clothing, and shelter, as well as the need for money to pay for these things.

Man also has a "higher-level" set of needs. This other set of needs
"relates to that unique human characteristic: the ability to achieve, and to
experience psychological growth." Included here are the needs to achieve a
difficult task, to obtain prestige, and to receive recognition.

Herzberg has carried out studies in order to more precisely determine
what people want, and what motivates them. In one study he asked several
hundred engineers and accountants to explain things about their jobs that they
found "exceptionally good" (and therefore motivating) or "exceptionally
bad."

His findings are summarized in Exhibit 15–4.[9] According to Herzberg,
these findings mean that *the work factors which lead to job satisfaction and
motivation (the "motivators") are different from those (the "hygienes") which*

Exhibit 15.4   Summary of Herzberg's Motivator-Hygiene Findings

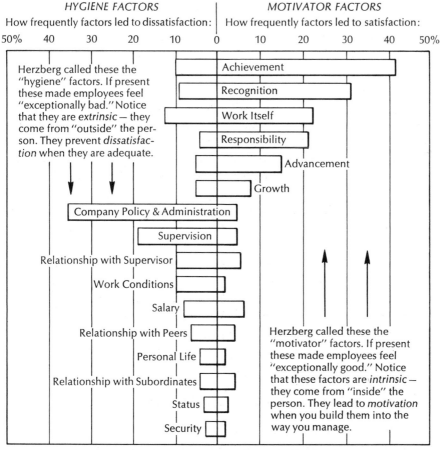

Source: Adapted from Frederick Herzberg, "One More Time: How Do You Motivate Employees," *Harvard Business Review*
(January-February 1968).

304   *lead to job dissatisfaction.* Specifically, if these "hygiene" factors (such as better working conditions, salary, supervision) that appear on the left of Exhibit
15–4 are absent, the employee becomes dissatisfied. But—and this is extremely
important—adding more and more of these hygiene factors (like salary) to the
job will not motivate him once the factor (like salary) is adequate: these
"hygienes" can only keep him from becoming dissatisfied.

On the other hand, the "job content" or "motivator" factors on the
right of Exhibit 15–4 (achievement, recognition, etc.) can motivate employees. Thus, according to Herzberg, if you continue to build more opportunities for achievement and recognition into the job then your employees
should become more motivated. (This is the basis for the "Job Enrichment"
approach that we will discuss in Chapter 16.)

Atkinson and McClelland—The Need to Achieve, the Need for Power, and the Need for Affiliation

Several writers, most notably John Atkinson and David McClelland,
say that all people have a need for *achievement, power,* and *affiliation.*
(These were the three needs that you "tested" yourself for at the beginning
of this chapter.)

We know that people with a high need to achieve prefer situations
which have moderate risks and in which they can see their own contributions.
They also prefer to receive quick, concrete feedback concerning their performance. They are motivated by the need to accomplish challenging tasks.

People with a high need for *power* prefer situations in which they can
get and maintain control of the means for influencing others. They like being
in the position of making suggestions, giving their opinions, and talking
others into things. This satisfies their need for "power." Others have a high
need for *affiliation.* They have a strong desire to maintain close friendships and
to receive affection from others. They are constantly seeking to establish
friendly relationships.

McClelland has found that everyone has each of these needs to some
degree.[10] However, no two people have them in exactly the same proportions.
For example, one person may be very high in his need for achievement but
low in his need for affiliation. Another person might be high in his need for
affiliation but low in his need for power.

Saul Gellerman on the Meaning of Motivation

Saul Gellerman agrees that we all have needs for things such as
money, status, achievement, and recognition. And he agrees that if one of
these needs is not satisfied, then a person will be motivated to satisfy it. But

he also says that we don't only seek money, or status, or achievement for its own sake. Instead these are only vehicles which the person uses in his constant quest to be himself, or to be the kind of person he thinks he should be:

> The ultimate motivation is to make the self-concept real: to live in a manner that is appropriate to one's preferred role, to be treated in a manner that corresponds to one's preferred rank, and to be rewarded in a manner that reflects one's estimate of his own abilities. Thus we are all in perpetual pursuit of whatever we regard as our deserved role, trying to make our subjective ideas about ourselves into objective truths.[11]

Gellerman has put his finger on a very important aspect of motivation. Above all, most people have a need to be treated as valuable individuals. Each has his or her own concepts of who he is, and what he deserves, and each wants to be treated in a manner that supports this self-concept. Each person is strongly motivated to behave in a way that satisfies that need.

This is also, in large part, what Maslow and the other psychologists we discussed are saying. Whether we call it the need for self-actualization, or for achievement, or for recognition, each is saying that we all have this need to be ourselves, and to be treated as valuable individuals. And a key to your success as a manager will be your ability to motivate your subordinates by appealing to and supporting this "higher level" need.

So: What Do We Know about "What Do People Want?"

Do needs really form a "hierarchy?" Can a satisfied need still be a motivator? [12] Let us try to answer some of these questions now.

1. *People have many different needs.* These include, for example:

   a. A number of "existence" or physiological needs, including hunger, sex, thirst, and oxygen.
   b. A security need.
   c. A social need.
   d. A need for esteem and recognition.
   e. A need for self-control and independence.
   f. A need for confidence, achievement, and self-actualization.

No two people have exactly the same proportion of any of these needs.

2. *A satisfied need is not a motivator.* From research findings we know that when a need is satisfied it becomes much less important as a "motivator." [13]

3. *Needs are arranged in a two-level hierarchy.* At the lower level are physiological and security needs. At the higher level are social, esteem, autonomy, and self-actualization needs. These are the needs to feel im-

306 portant, and to be treated as a capable individual. We know that needs don't fall into a neat five-step hierarchy the way Maslow proposes.[14] It is more useful to assume a two-level hierarchy, in which the higher level needs become active only when the lower level needs are satisfied.

Thus a person won't start craving achievement, recognition, or a more interesting job, until his lower-level needs for existence and security are fairly well fulfilled.

Don't forget, though, that this is a little more complicated than it may at first appear. One reason for this is that these lower-level needs are somewhat relative. The person who is accustomed to owning three homes, a Rolls Royce, and a yacht, might view a salary of $150,000 a year as "subsistence"; to another, it might be a windfall. That's why it's not surprising to meet high-salaried executives who seem motivated by nothing but "lower-level" needs, such as money.

4. *The needs differ in what will satisfy them.* Notice that the first five needs on the above list ("a" through "e"—security, recognition, and so on can really be satisfied only by outcomes which are concrete and *external* to the person. These external (or "extrinsic") outcomes include things such as food, money, and praise. On the other hand, "the need for self-actualization and competence seems to be satisfied only by outcomes given *intrinsically* by persons to themselves." [15] Thus the person himself has to derive a sense of accomplishment from performing a difficult task, painting a picture, or some other.

5. *More than one need is active at a time.* A person can be motivated by more than one need at a given point in time. He will continue to be motivated by these needs until they are satisfied, or until satisfaction of lower-order needs is threatened.

6. *Money fulfills several different needs.* At first glance, money would seem to be one of the "lower-level" needs, a need that is quickly satisfied and

Exhibit 15.5   Money Fulfills Several Different Needs

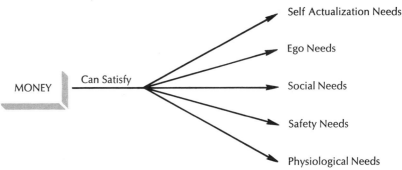

quenched. But in reality this is usually not the case. The reason, of course, is that money is more than just a medium of exchange. It is more often a vehicle through which you can satisfy other, higher-order needs. So the person who goes out to buy a fancy new car is doing more than just spending his money; he is buying—at least in his own eyes—prestige, recognition, and a visible symbol of his achievements. Thus he has used his money to satisfy some of his higher-order needs.[16]

Summary

In summary, here are some important things we know about what people want:

1. People have many different needs.
2. A satisfied need is not a motivator.
3. Needs are arranged in a two-level hierarchy.
4. The needs differ in what will satisfy them.
5. More than one need is active at a time.
6. Money fulfills several different needs.

A MODEL OF MOTIVATION

We have summarized much of what we have talked about to this point in Exhibit 15–6.[17] Read the exhibit carefully. As you can see, this model answers the question "Will motivation take place?" The answer is yes, *if* the incentive is important to the person, and *if* he feels that effort will result in obtaining the incentive.

HOW ALL THE MANAGEMENT FUNCTIONS AFFECT MOTIVATION

People are motivated to accomplish those tasks which they feel will lead to rewards. What implication does this have for leadership? For organizing? For the climate you establish? Let's try to answer these questions.

Throughout this book we've said that the organization has to "fit" the task. And we've seen that when the organization and its management *are* appropriate, the firm is usually more effective. (Remember what Burns and Stalker, Chandler, and Lawrence and Lorsch found, for example.)

Exhibit 15.6 A Model of Motivation

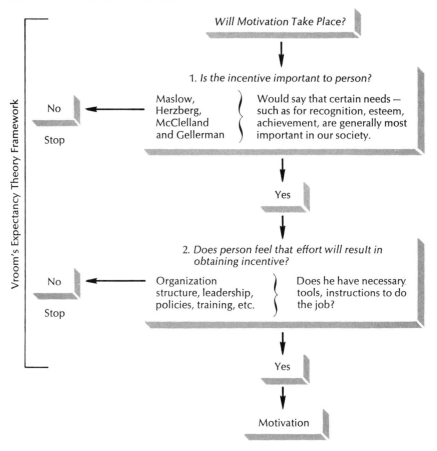

John Morse says that organizations that "fit" their tasks are more effective *because they raise the chances that an employee can successfully complete his task.* In other words, employees are more motivated (and the firm is more effective) because they are convinced that they can accomplish their tasks—that effort on their part *will* lead to rewards. As Morse says:

> . . . an organizational fit situation motivates individuals precisely because it leads to a sense of competence from mastering a particular task environment.[18]

(His ideas are summarized in Exhibit 15–7. This means that fitting the management function to the task can increase your subordinates' sense of achievement or "competence" motivation by helping him do a better job. In other words, it helps him see that effort on his part *will* lead to his accomplishing his task.

Here are some examples of how:

	In Mechanistic Situations (Emphasis on *Efficiency*)	*In Organic Situations* (Emphasis on *Creativity*)
Planning	Using more precise plans, rules, and procedures facilitates planning what the most efficient courses of action are.	Using less precise plans and fewer rules lets people adapt their behavior to rapidly changing conditions.
Organizing	Providing clear job descriptions gives each employee a clear idea of what's expected of him, and keeps "wasted motions" to a minimum.	Flexible, enlarged jobs, and less adherence to the chain of command let employees redefine their jobs and make quick, on-the-spot decisions in response to changing conditions.
Staffing	You have to "fit the people to the task" too. Here, for example, there might be more emphasis on recruiting people whose personalities allow them to work better in a more structured environment.	Here people who work better in ambiguous, unpredictable environments are recruited.
Leading	It is *always* important to treat employees fairly and with respect:	
	But here the leader's style is usually more directive. The leader stands by to provide directions, assure adherence to rules, etc., all of which keep efficiency high. There's also more emphasis on satisfying "lower-level" needs, such as for pay and security.	Here people work best where the leader just provides rough guidelines. He then lets *them* do the task as they see fit. And there's more emphasis on participation, and other techniques aimed at satisfying "higher-level" needs, such as for recognition and achievement.
Controlling	Here clear, precise standards, frequent checks on performance, and more *imposed* control helps insure that tasks are accomplished efficiently, and as planned.	Here broad milestones, less frequent checks on performance, and more *self-control* allows employees to adapt *how* they do their jobs to changing conditions.

Exhibit 15.7 Summary of Morse's Findings

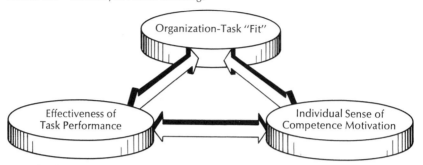

Note: When the organization *fits the task,* your subordinates can do their jobs better, and derive a sense of competence or *achievement motivation* from this. They are thus motivated, and *performance* is higher.

Source: John Morse, and Jay Lorsch, "Beyond Theory Y," *Harvard Business Review,* May-June 1970.

Some Important Things to Remember from This Chapter:

1. Basically, people are motivated or driven to behave in a way which they feel leads to rewards. Thus there are two basic requirements for motivating someone: 1) the incentive or reward must be important to the person; and 2) he must feel that effort on his part will probably lead to his obtaining the reward. This is the essence of Vroom's expectancy theory of motivation.

2. Abraham Maslow says that people's needs can be envisioned in a hierarchy. Each succeedingly higher level need does not become aroused until the next lower-level need is fairly well satisfied. Working up the hierarchy the five Maslow needs are: physiological; safety; social; ego; and self-actualization.

3. Herzberg says that the work factors involved in producing job satisfaction and motivation are separate and distinct from those which lead to job dissatisfaction. Those leading to job dissatisfaction (if they are absent) are the hygiene factors. These include "extrinsic" factors such as supervision, working conditions, and salary. The factors leading to satisfaction and motivation (if they are present) include intrinsic job factors such as achievement and recognition.

4. All the researchers we have discussed seem to agree on at least one important thing: that the ultimate need for which we all strive is "to be ourselves"; to be the kind of people we think we have the potential for becoming. Thus we are all constantly pursuing what we regard as our deserved role; striving to feel important, useful, and recognized.

5. Motivating someone hinges on knowing what he wants. Here are some important things to keep in mind about what people want—what their needs are:

1. People have many different needs.
2. A satisfied need is not a motivator.
3. Needs are arranged in a two-level hierarchy.
4. The needs differ in what will satisfy them.
5. More than one need is active at a time.
6. Money fulfills several different needs.

6. Don't expect to rely on just your knowledge of motivation theory and
techniques when it comes to motivating your subordinates. Motivation really involves all the management functions—from developing the appropriate plans and hiring the right people for the right jobs, to insuring that your organization structure fits the task. All the management functions contribute directly or indirectly to the motivation of your subordinates.

STUDY ASSIGNMENTS

1. If you have not already done so, fill in the questionnaire in the introduction to this chapter. What would you say this tells you about your important needs? About the tasks for which you would be best suited?
2. Explain what motivation is.
3. Develop an "expectancy model" diagram of motivation.
4. Discuss the Maslow needs hierarchy.
5. Compare and contrast the Maslow and Herzberg motivation theories.
6. Compare and contrast the Vroom and Herzberg theories of motivation. Are they compatible?
7. Summarize what we know about "What do people want?" How would you make use of this knowledge as a manager.
8. Explain how *all* the management functions influence motivation.
9. How can developing the "right" climate increase motivation?
10. "I don't need to know about any fancy motivation theories," your boss tells you, "what they all come down to is that you should practice the Golden Rule—do unto others as you would have others do unto you." Explain why you agree or disagree with this statement, and why.

NOTES FOR THE CHAPTER

1. George Litwin and Robert Stringer, Jr., *Motivation and Organizational Climate* (Boston: Division of Research Graduate School of Business Administration, Harvard University, 1968) pp. 173–174; by permission, Harvard University Press.
2. Edward Lawler III and John Grant Rhode, *Information and Control in Organizations* (Pacific Palisades: Goodyear, 1976).
3. See, for example, Joel Leidecker and James Hall, "Motivation: Good Theory—Poor Application," *Training Development Journal* (June 1974) pp. 3–7.
4. Victor H. Vroom, *Work and Motivation* (New York: John Wiley & Son, 1964).
5. See, for example, Frederick Starke and Orlando Behling, "A Test of Two Postulants Underlying the Expectancy Theory," *Academy of Management Journal*, Vol. 18, No. 4 (December 1975); and Leon Reinharth and Mahmoud Wahba, "Expectancy Theory as a Predictor of Work Motivation, Effort Expenditure, and Job Performance," *Academy of Management Journal*, Vol. 18, No. 3 (September 1975).
6. See, for example, Robert Pritchard, Philip DeLeo, and Clarence VonBergen, Jr., "The Field Experimental Test of Expectancy—Valence Incentive Motivation Techniques," *Organizational Behavior and Human Performance*, Vol. 15, No. 2 (April 1976).
7. This section is based on Douglas McGregor, "The Human Side of Enterprise," *The Management Review* (November 1957) pp. 22–28, 88–92; reprinted in Max Richards

312   and William Nielander, *Readings in Management* (Cincinnati: Southwestern, 1974) pp. 433–441.

8. This section is based on Frederick Herzberg, "One More Time: How Do You Motivate Employees?" *Harvard Business Review* (January-February 1968).

9. F. Herzberg, D. Mausner, D. B. Snyderman, *The Motivation to Work* (New York: John Wiley & Sons, 1959). You should keep in mind that a number of writers have attacked Herzberg's "Interview" approach and theory, so the findings are not as clear-cut as they might at first appear. For a discussion, see Steven Kerr, Anne Harlan, and Ralph Stogdill, "Preference for Motivator and Hygiene Factors in a Hypothetical Interview Situation," *Personnel Psychology*, Vol. 27 (1974) pp. 109–124.

10. David Kolb, Irwin Rubin, James McIntyre, *Organizational Psychology* (Englewood Cliffs, N.J.: Prentice-Hall, 1971) p. 67.

11. Saul Gellerman, *Motivation and Productivity* (New York: American Management Association, 1963) p. 290.

12. This section is largely based on Edward E. Lawler III and John Grant Rhode, *Information and Control in Organizations*, pp. 11–30.

13. Lawler and Rhode, *Information and Control in Organizations*, p. 15.

14. See, for example, Mahmoud A. Wahba and Lawrence G. Bridwell, "Maslow Reconsidered: a Review of Research on the Need Hierarchy Theory," *Organizational Behavior and Human Performance*, Vol. 15, No. 2 (April 1976): Vance Mitchell and Pravin Moudgill, "Measurement of Maslow's Need Hierarchy," *Organizational Behavior and Human Performance*, Vol. 16, No. 2 (August 1976) pp. 334–349.

15. Lawler and Rhode, *Information and Control in Organizations*, p. 14.

16. Lawler and Rhode, *Information and Control in Organizations*, p. 17; Robert Opsahl and Marvin Dunnette, "The Role of Financial Compensation in Industrial Motivation," *Psychological Bulletin*, Vol. 66, No. 2 (1966), pp. 94–118; in W. E. Scott, Jr. and L. L. Cummings, *Readings in Organizational Behavior and Human Performance* (Homewood, Ill.: Irwin, 1973) pp. 350–371.

17. Gary Dessler, *Organization and Management: A Contingency Approach* (Englewood Cliffs, N.J.: Prentice-Hall, 1976) p. 205.

18. John Morse, "Organizational Characteristics and Individual Motivation," in Jay Lorsch and Paul Lawrence (Eds.), *Studies in Organization Design* (Homewood, Ill.: Irwin Dorsey, 1970) pp. 84–100.

A Framework for Studying the Management Fundamentals

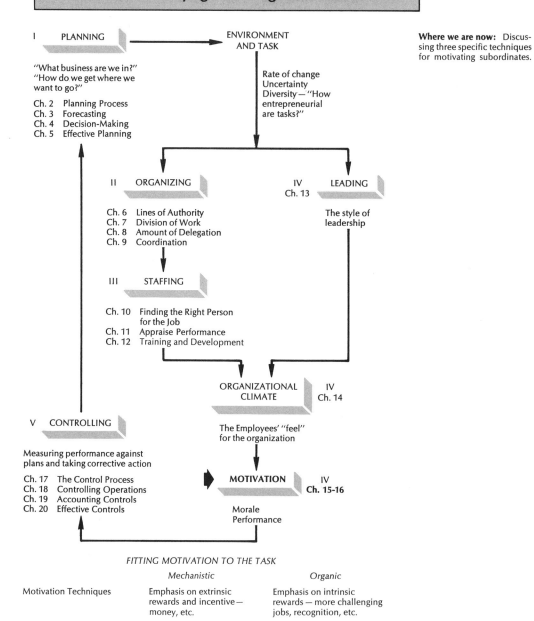

I   PLANNING

ENVIRONMENT
AND TASK

"What business are we in?"
"How do we get where we
want to go?"

Rate of change
Uncertainty
Diversity — "How
entrepreneurial
are tasks?"

Ch. 2   Planning Process
Ch. 3   Forecasting
Ch. 4   Decision-Making
Ch. 5   Effective Planning

Where we are now: Discussing three specific techniques for motivating subordinates.

II   ORGANIZING

IV   LEADING
Ch. 13

Ch. 6   Lines of Authority
Ch. 7   Division of Work
Ch. 8   Amount of Delegation
Ch. 9   Coordination

The style of
leadership

III   STAFFING

Ch. 10   Finding the Right Person
         for the Job
Ch. 11   Appraise Performance
Ch. 12   Training and Development

ORGANIZATIONAL
CLIMATE

IV
Ch. 14

V   CONTROLLING

The Employees' "feel"
for the organization

Measuring performance against
plans and taking corrective action

Ch. 17   The Control Process
Ch. 18   Controlling Operations
Ch. 19   Accounting Controls
Ch. 20   Effective Controls

MOTIVATION

IV
Ch. 15-16

Morale
Performance

FITTING MOTIVATION TO THE TASK

	Mechanistic	*Organic*
Motivation Techniques	Emphasis on extrinsic rewards and incentive — money, etc.	Emphasis on intrinsic rewards — more challenging jobs, recognition, etc.

When you have finished studying

16 Motivation in Action

You should be able to:

1. *Explain the pros and cons of using positive or negative incentives to motivate subordinates.*

2. *Give several concrete examples of how you would "enrich" a subordinate's job.*

3. *Cite the conditions under which job enrichment will more likely result in increased motivation.*

4. *List the steps you would use in implementing a management by objectives program.*

5. *Discuss the three foundations of management by objectives.*

6. *List the barriers you would expect to encounter in implementing a management by objectives program.*

7. *Discuss ten hints for motivating subordinates.*

INTRODUCTION

Motivation theories like those of Maslow and Herzberg are very useful. They help explain what motivates people, and they help us to see what sorts of needs managers can focus on satisfying.

But when it comes to managing, what you also need are some specific techniques for applying these theories—techniques for motivating employees. You will find that whenever managers talk about motivating employees the discussion inevitably turns to three such techniques: "KITA" (positive and negative incentives); job enrichment; and management by objectives. Therefore, let's briefly discuss the nature and pros and cons of each technique.

USING KITA (POSITIVE AND NEGATIVE INCENTIVES) TO MOTIVATE SUBORDINATES

The first prize in any contest for the "most widely recommended motivation technique" would undoubtedly go to incentives—either positive ones (like money) or negative ones (like threats).[1] Frederick Herzberg says

316   that they are popular because "the surest and least circumlocuted way of getting someone to do something is to kick him in the pants—give him what might be called the KITA." [2]

A "'kick in the pants'" (either positive or negative) can be useful. Most people work to earn a living, and paying a salary is therefore a prerequisite for keeping them on the job. And beyond that, incentives (such as more pay, fringe benefits, or threats) do "motivate" people—at least in the short run. The problem, though, is that once the incentive is removed—or the need for money, security, and so on, is satisfied—the "motivation" often disappears. Thus KITA only results in short-term movement. As often as not, when you turn your back you will find that your subordinate is no longer "motivated." As Herzberg says:

> Why is KITA not motivation? If I kick my dog (from the back or the front) he will move. And when I want him to move again, what must I do? I must kick him again. Similarly I can charge a man's battery, and then recharge it, and recharge it again. But it is only when he has his own generator that we can talk about motivation. He then needs no outside stimulation. He *wants* to do it.[3]

So, in summary, KITA is an effective motivation tool—especially for "motivating" short run bursts of activity. But in the long run it's probably more useful (but not always possible!) to get your subordinate to genuinely *want* to do the job.

USING JOB ENRICHMENT TO MOTIVATE SUBORDINATES

What Is Job Enrichment?

Herzberg says that the way to motivate someone (to make him *want* to do it) is to build "motivators" like opportunities for growth into the job. (Recall his motivator-hygiene theory from Chapter 15.) One way to do this is through *job enrichment*, in which you reorganize your subordinate's job so as to make it more interesting and challenging. The job is designed to be less specialized and more "enriched." Usually this is accomplished by giving the worker more autonomy, and by allowing him to do much of the planning and inspection formerly done by his supervisor.

An example from what Herzberg calls a "highly successful job enrichment experiment" is illustrated in Exhibit 16–1. (In this case the jobs were those of people responsible for corresponding with a large corporation's stock-

Exhibit 16.1 An Outline of a Successful Job Enrichment Project

Specific changes aimed at enriching jobs	"Motivators" these changes are aimed at increasing
A. Removing some controls while retaining accountability	Responsibility and personal achievement
B. Increasing the accountability of individuals for own work	Responsibility and recognition
C. Giving a person a complete natural unit of work (module, division, area, and so on)	Responsibility, achievement, and recognition
D. Granting additional authority to an employee in his activity; job freedom	Responsibility, achievement, and recognition
E. Making periodic reports directly available to the worker himself rather than to the supervisor	Internal recognition
F. Introducing new and more difficult tasks not previously handled	Growth and learning
G. Assigning individuals specific or specialized tasks, enabling them to become expert	Responsibility, growth, and advancement

Source: Frederick Herzberg, "One More Time: How Do You Motivate Employees?"

holders—answering their questions, and so on.) On the left of the Exhibit are listed some of the changes which were aimed at enriching the job, such as "removing some controls while retaining accountability." On the right of the exhibit are listed the "motivators"—such as for recognition—these job changes are aimed at satisfying.

Why is Job Enrichment Supposed to Work?

There are two reasons why job enrichment is supposed to result in increased morale and performance. First, by building into the job more challenge and opportunities for achievement, you are supposedly appealing to your employee's higher order needs—such as for achievement. Thus he should now get so much satisfaction out of doing the job well that he is motivated to do it whether you watch him closely or not. Second, many believe that very specialized jobs are inherently demoralizing. The assumption here is that (as illustrated in Exhibit 16–2) specialized, repetitive jobs lead to monotony, boredom, and dissatisfaction. This finally leads to absenteeism and reduced performance. Job enrichment is supposed to "short circuit" this by resulting in jobs which are less specialized.

Exhibit 16.2   Why Should Unenriched, Repetitive Jobs be Demoralizing?

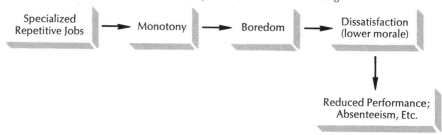

Source: Based on Charles Hulin and Milton Blood, "Job Enlargement, Individual Differences, and Worker Responses", *Psychological Bulletin*, Vol. 69, No. 1 (1968), pp. 41-55.

We know that these two assumptions are more applicable to some situations than to others. We know, for example, that people who are more "*authoritarian,*" or whose major satisfactions come not from work but from nonwork interests such as hobbies, don't find specialized jobs so demoralizing. We also know that many people do not exhibit *strong higher-order* needs, such as for achievement: The design of the job (enriched vs. nonenriched) often has no effect at all on these people.[4] The *job itself* is also important. Jobs that have "traction"—a smooth, uninterrupted machine-like process—are usually not as demoralizing as those where the worker is constantly interrupted by problems and outsiders.[5]

Does Job Enrichment "Work"?

Does job enrichment "work"? While there's no simple answer to this question, the prevailing evidence seems to say yes—*if* you are careful how and when you implement it. For example, we know that in some companies and in some jobs, (particularly those higher in the organization), job enrichment has been successful. Morale rose, quality went up, and production costs went down.[6] Yet in other situations, such as when job enrichment did not involve a commensurate pay raise, workers showed no marked preference for the more enriched jobs. We also know that job enrichment is not recommended where there are severe difficulties—such as low morale due to low pay levels.[7] And usually (as illustrated in Exhibit 16–3) job enrichment is more successful in improving the *quality* of the work than its quantity.

Some Hints—When to Use Job Enrichment

How can you help ensure that you use job enrichment most effectively? Here, based upon the research findings are some hints. You should consider using job enrichment as a motivation technique when:

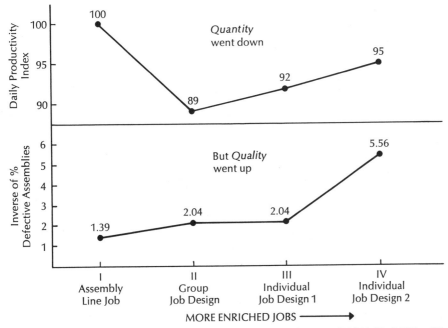

Source: Adapted from Louis Davis, "Job Design and Productivity: A New Approach, *Personnel*, Vol. 31, (March 1957) p. 425; Filley and House. Managerial Process and Organizational Behavior (Glenview; Scott, Foresman, 1969) ch. 9.

1. Quality of work is a primary consideration.
2. The job requires a good deal of originality and judgment.[8] Here the motivation has to come more from *inside* your subordinate.
3. The workers themselves clearly prefer less structured, less routine jobs.
4. The organization itself is organic and is preoccupied with making creative, entrepreneurial decisions.
5. You know that the employees clearly have strong "higher-order" needs, such as for achievement.
6. The jobs are those of professionals and other higher-level employees.
7. You're not trying to deal with an acute morale problem caused by some "non job factor" such as low pay, job security, or poor supervision.

USING MANAGEMENT BY OBJECTIVES TO MOTIVATE SUBORDINATES

What Is Management By Objectives?

As a manager, you will hear a lot about the advantages of management by objectives (or "MBO"). Although MBO has something of an aura of mystery about it, it really is a fairly simple procedure. It consists of five basic steps as follows: [9]

1. Set organization's goals. Establishment of an organizationwide strategy, and goals.

2. Joint goal setting. Establishment of short-term performance targets between you and your subordinate.

3. Performance reviews. Frequent performance review meetings between you and your subordinate.

4. Set checkpoints. Establishment of major checkpoints to measure progress.

5. Feedback. Discussion between you and your subordinate at the end of a defined period (say six months or a year) to assess the results of your subordinate's efforts.

You can use many aspects of MBO (such as joint goal setting, and performance reviews) on a day-to-day basis. In this regard MBO does have potential as a technique for motivating lower-level employees, particularly those with less routine "unprogrammed" tasks. But keep in mind that, as of today, major company-wide MBO programs are mostly aimed at managers and technical-professional personnel.[10]

The Three Foundations of MBO

MBO developed out of the practical experiences of managers, but it is also based on three sound psychological foundations: 1) goal setting; 2) feedback; and 3) participation.

Exhibit 16.4   Why Management by Objectives is Supposed to be Effective:

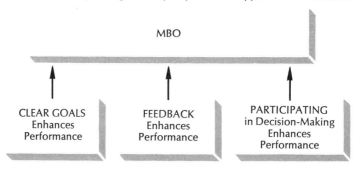

For example, MBO involves mutual *goal setting* and we know that employees who have clear goals usually perform better than those who don't.[11] Clear, attainable goals help channel energies in specific directions, and let your subordinate know the basis on which he will be rewarded. We also know that employees who receive frequent *feedback* concerning their performance are usually more highly motivated than those who don't. Feedback that is specific, relevant, and timely helps satisfy the need most people have for knowing where they stand.

We know, too, that allowing subordinates to genuinely *participate* in establishing their own goals can increase their commitment to these goals and thereby their performance. It can make them feel more involved, and can thus appeal to their "higher-level" needs. Thus while participation is not effective under all conditions—it's not as effective with more "authoritarian" people who prefer more direction, for example—we know that it *can* lead to increased performance.

Finally, goal-setting helps clarify your subordinate's *goals*. And participation in goal-setting helps to insure that the goal is attainable, and that the path to this goal is clear. So MBO also fits in with our *expectancy model of motivation*.

Some Benefits You Can Expect From MBO

We know that many MBO programs are quite successful.[12] Here, based on the research findings are some of the benefits you can expect from such programs.

MBO Helps Motivate Managers.   We have seen that goal-setting, feedback, and participation lead to increased acceptance of goals and increased motivation and performance. Thus, because they are shooting for targets that are clear and attainable, MBO should result in improved motivation.[13]

MBO Directs Work Activity Toward Organizational Goals.   MBO results in a "means/ends" chain. Managers at succeedingly lower levels in the organization establish targets which are integrated with those at the next higher level. Thus MBO can help insure that everyone's activity is ultimately aimed toward the organization's goals.

MBO Forces and Aids in Planning.   MBO forces top management to establish a strategy, and goals for the entire organization. It also requires other managers to set their own targets and plan how they will reach them. Thus MBO forces and aids in planning.

MBO Provides Clear Standards for Control.   The goals or targets that emerge from the MBO process provide (or should provide) clear standards for control.

MBO Reduces Role Conflict and Ambiguity.   We say that *role conflict* exists when a person is faced with conflicting demands from two or more supervisors. *Role ambiguity* exists when a person is uncertain as to how he will be evaluated, or what he has to accomplish. We know that both role conflict and role ambiguity can result in lower morale, higher tension, and decreased performance. Since MBO is aimed at providing each manager with clear targets and their order of priority, MBO should reduce role conflict and ambiguity.

322   *MBO Provides More Objective Appraisal Criteria.* The targets that emerge from the MBO process should provide a sound set of criteria for evaluating the manager's performance.

MBO Identifies Problems Better. Frequent performance review sessions are an integral part of MBO. This increased interaction between you and your subordinate should help identify problems early, before they get too big.

MBO Aids in the Development of Personnel. MBO has a variety of uses. It can help *motivate* managers, and help make *planning* and *control* more effective. And in many books you will find MBO included in the "training and development" chapter, since MBO is also an effective *training and development* technique. It helps identify performance deficiencies, and enables you and your subordinate to set individualized self-improvement goals.

Barriers to Avoid (or Minimize) When Using MBO

While MBO can be effective, we also know that many programs also fail. Much of the reason for these failures stems from certain barriers and problems that can often be avoided. The following are the most important ones.[14]

Commitment of Time. MBO programs can require a great deal of time, energy, and form-completing on the part of managers (and subordinates). For example, you may have to fill out a form such as that in Exhibit 16–5, in order to specify goals for your subordinate. Then you have to meet with him, review his accomplishments, and discuss plans for the ensuing time period. All this can add up to a tremendous commitment of time.

Lack of Performance Measurement. In some areas, such as cutting costs or increasing sales, measuring performance is a straightforward and more or less objective matter. But in many other areas, such as subordinate development, appraising performance can be an acute problem.

Lack of Awareness. Often there is a lack of awareness on the part of managers of the rationale and value of MBO. This can make the time they have to spend on it seem even more exasperating.

Inadequate Time. Subordinates often feel that not enough time is spent on the goal-setting or feedback stages.

Unclear Goals. Everybody involved in the process sometimes lacks an understanding of how to set clear goals or targets.

Tug of War. There is sometimes a "tug of war" in which the subordinate tries to set the lowest targets possible, and the supervisor the highest.

In summary, MBO can be an effective technique for motivating subordinates. But keep in mind *why* it's supposed to work (goal-setting, feedback, participation), and also plan to deal with the potential barriers.

Exhibit 16.5   A Form Used in an Actual MBO Program   323

Black & Decker   OVERALL PERFORMANCE WORK SHEET

Fiscal Year 19 _____

Grade _____

Age _____

Years With Company _____

Years in Present Job _____

GENERAL INSTRUCTIONS

OBJECTIVES

The four objectives of this Program are to:

1. Help the individual to improve his knowledge and skill.

2. Assure continuing two-way communications between the individual and his immediate supervisor.

3. Convert Black & Decker's goals into targets for the individual.

4. Realistically appraise the individual's performance.

TARGET SETTING PROCEDURES

1. The manager of each division, department or section should meet with his subordinates in a briefing session to discuss the overall targets of the group. Also, the manager should discuss how the group's targets can be converted to targets for each individual.

2. After the briefing session, each individual should review the group's targets and determine what his own targets should be to help the group achieve its overall targets. Then the individual should prepare the first three elements of the Work Sheet, Parts A through C. Each manager should do the same for each individual reporting to him.

3. Finally, the individual should again meet with his manager and mutually agree on his personal and job targets and principal job responsibilities for the next year.

NOTE: Both the manager and the individual will have a copy of the Work Sheet. The individual's copy is his working copy to be used throughout the year. The manager's copy is his working copy and becomes the permanent file copy at the end of the year.

REVIEW AND APPRAISAL

During the year the manager should hold periodic meetings with the individual to review target progress, discuss any help or assistance needed to achieve a target and make any target changes necessary.

At year-end the manager completes Parts A through E, evaluating how well the individual performed. Then he should meet with the individual to discuss the overall performance appraisal.

WHAT IS THE PURPOSE OF THIS JOB IN TERMS OF THE CONTRIBUTION IT SHOULD MAKE TO THE BUSINESS?

_____

_____

_____

A   Instructions

1. Describe, as specifically as possible, the type of work this individual desires in the near future (2-3 years) and in the long range.

2. List the individual's personal and professional strengths on which he can build to achieve his future aspirations.

3. Indicate those personal and professional areas where he needs further development.

4. Discuss personal development with the individual and together develop a plan to attempt to attain his objectives. Then select a few personal targets which will increase his present knowledge, skills and potential to help him achieve his career aspirations.

NOTE: These targets should largely be determined by the factors that affected the individual's performance last year. . . . see Part D.

A.   PERSONAL DEVELOPMENT

1.   Career Aspirations: _____

_____

_____

2.   Areas of Greatest Strengths: _____

_____

_____

_____

_____

3.   Areas Requiring Further Development: _____

_____

_____

4. Personal Targets for the Year	How Well Were Targets Accomplished?

Exhibit 16.5 (continued)

B Instructions

Suggestions:

Review the individual's job responsibilities to develop a current list of all his functions and responsibilities. These are job functions for which the individual is held accountable.

Next, select and list only the major job responsibilities which are the PRIMARY functions of the individual's job.

At the year-end review the manager should analyze the individual's overall performance on the primary responsibilities, write his appraisal in the space provided and then discuss it with the individual.

B. PRINCIPAL JOB RESPONSIBILITIES

C Instructions

Select the specific job targets (Projects, programs, assignments) the individual is expected to accomplish. The targets should be specific, mutually understood and agreed upon. Also, to the extent possible, indicate priorities, completion times, and results expected. If a target is complex or requires a prolonged period for completion, break it into separate phases showing when certain elements or parts will be completed.

During the year, the manager should meet at least quarterly with the individual to:

1. Review his progress towards target completion.

2. Discuss any help or assistance he needs to achieve the targets.

3. Make any changes necessary to current targets; add new targets if workload permits.

Also, the manager should indicate in the space provided, what action was taken on each target.

At year-end, the manager should evaluate the results accomplished in the column provided, noting the quality and quantity of the work done. This should then be discussed with the individual.

C. SPECIFIC JOB TARGETS | 1st Quarter Review

D Instructions

This part is to be completed at the year-end review. This section is not to be completed in advance.

The manager should:

1. Analyze the other critical factors which in your judgment have interfered with the individual's performance through the year, e.g., knowledge the man brings to the job, technical and managerial skills, and personal characteristics.

2. Select those factors which have MOST adversely affected his performance last year, describe and give examples in the space provided.

3. These factors should be considered when the individual's personal targets (Part A, #3 and #4) are established next year.

D. OTHER FACTORS AFFECTING JOB PERFORMANCE

HOW WELL DID HE PERFORM?

2nd Quarter Review	3rd Quarter Review	4th Quarter Review	Results

DESCRIBE AND GIVE EXAMPLES

Exhibit 16.5 (continued)

E **Instructions**

To be completed by the manager:

1. **Check the statement which best describes the individual's overall job performance.**
2. **Then support this performance rating by giving a word picture of the individual's performance.**
3. **Review the individual's career aspirations on page one. Then, based on present performance and overall growth potential, recommend a career path or future jobs you feel the individual is capable of achieving. It will be helpful to consult with other managers in other divisions for their opinions about the individual's performance and potential.**

NOTE:
All factors in this overall performance appraisal should be considered when preparing next year's targets for the individual.

If the individual or the rater's superior would like to comment on this appraisal, attach his statement to the completed Work Sheet.

E. OVERALL PERFORMANCE SUMMARY

1. HOW WELL DID HE MEET STANDARDS OF JOB PERFORMANCE?

____FAR EXCEEDS: Outstanding Performance in Present Assignment in practically every respect.

____EXCEEDS: Above Average Perfomance in Present Assignment in most respects.

baseline performance level

____MEETS NORMAL REQUIREMENTS: Average or Satisfactory Performance in PRIMARY FUNCTIONS, JOB TASKS and MANNER.

baseline performance level

MEETS MINIMUM REQUIREMENTS: Acceptable but does not meet average performance in the majority of primary functions, job tasks and manner.

2. EXPLAIN IN DETAIL:

3. CAREER PATH RECOMMENDATIONS:

SIGNATURES:

Individual Rated ____________________ Date ____________

Rater ____________________ Date ____________

Rater's Superior ____________________ Date ____________

☐ SEE ATTACHED STATEMENT

Form No. 2283

Source: Courtesy of Black and Decker. Reproduced in Stephen Carroll Jr., and Henry Tosi, Jr., *Management by Objectives* (New York: Macmillan, 1973) pp. 195-98.

IN CONCLUSION: TEN HINTS FOR MOTIVATING SUBORDINATES

1. Let your people know that you consider them valuable, capable individuals. In these last four chapters the need to treat people with respect and honesty has emerged as a very important element in motivation. The fact is that in our country today most employee's basic needs—for food, health, money, and so on—are fairly well satisfied. But there is one need which is seldom gratified. Maslow refers to this as the need for esteem and for self-actualization. Herzberg calls it recognition. McClelland calls it the need to achieve. Gellerman calls it the need to be yourself. But in one form or another it is a fundamental need we all have to express ourselves, to feel important, and to be treated as valuable and respected individuals; ones who are capable of getting the job done.

2. Make sure your subordinate has the tools to get the job done. No matter how important the reward your subordinate is not going to be motivated unless he thinks he can accomplish the task, and get that reward. If he needs training, see that he gets it. Beyond this, see that he has the organization structure, the manpower, and so forth to accomplish the task. Remember that *all* the management functions—not just "leading" affect motivation.

3. Fit the person to the job. For example, if he is achievement oriented, put him in a job where he can set his own standards, get concrete feedback, and deal with moderate risks.

4. Avoid building "dissatisfiers" into the job. Make sure that factors like salary and working conditions are at least adequate. Build "motivators" such as advancement and recognition into the job on this sound foundation.

5. Get to know your people. Find out what things are important to him. Is he an achiever? Does he need a higher salary? Does he want a chance to express himself creatively?

6. Set fair, achievable goals and communicate them. People work better when they know what their goals are and that the standards by which they will be evaluated are consistent and fair. Understanding what he is shooting for also helps your subordinate to equate accomplishing his task with his own personal needs.

7. Never belittle or criticize your subordinates in front of others. Everyone wants to be made to feel important and useful. Reprimanding an employee—particularly in public—could very well demolish him.

8. Always give your subordinates your undivided attention at least occasionally. Each of your subordinates wants to believe that he has something important to contribute. And each wants to be recognized as being

328   someone special—an individual. You can help satisfy this need by giving your subordinates your undivided attention, at least occasionally.

9. Let your people know how they are doing.   Feedback improves performance and morale, especially for achievement-oriented people.

10. Use KITA, MBO, and job enrichment.   We know that these techniques can be effective. But before applying them, also remember their limitations. For example, job enrichment may not be appropriate if morale is low due to low pay levels.[15]

Some Important Things to Remember from This Chapter:

1. KITA (positive and negative incentives) can be useful. They do "motivate" people—at least in the short run. The problem is that once the incentive is removed, or the need for money, security, and so on, is satiated, the "motivation" disappears. So KITA is especially effective for motivating short-run bursts of activity, or for tasks where you can closely watch the work.

2. In job enrichment, the worker's job is made interesting and challenging. You would usually accomplish this by giving the worker more autonomy, and by allowing him to do much of the planning and inspection you have formerly done yourself.

3. Job enrichment is especially effective when: quality of work is a primary consideration; the job requires a good deal of originality and judgment; and the workers themselves clearly prefer less structured jobs. On the other hand, it is not as effective where there are severe difficulties—such as low morale due to pay levels.

4. In simplest terms, management by objectives involves 1) establishing short-term performance targets between you and your subordinate, and 2) periodically discussing his progress toward these targets with him.

5. We know that MBO should be effective because goal-setting, feedback, and participation all enhance performance. We also know that often MBO programs are quite successful. They result in more highly motivated managers, help direct work activity toward organizational goals, and provide clear standards for control. Excessive paper work, a lack of awareness concerning the value of MBO, and unclear targets *are* some important problems to watch out for.

6. Our ten hints for motivating subordinates are as follows:

    1. Let your people know that you consider them valuable individuals.
    2. Make sure your subordinate has the tools to get the job done.
    3. Fit the person to the job.
    4. Avoid building "dissatisfiers" into the job.
    5. Get to know your people.
    6. Set fair, achievable standards and communicate them.
    7. Never belittle or criticize a subordinate in front of others.
    8. Always give your subordinate your undivided attention at least occasionally.
    9. Let your people know how they are doing.
    10. Use KITA, MBO, and job enrichment.

STUDY ASSIGNMENTS

1. Explain how would you apply what we know about "What do people want?" to the three motivation techniques discussed in this chapter—KITA, job enrichment, and MBO.
2. Explain why motivation techniques like those discussed in this chapter are not, by themselves, sufficient to motivate employees.
3. Explain the pros and cons of using positive or negative incentives to motivate subordinates.
4. Give several concrete examples of how you would "enrich" a subordinate's job.
5. Would you recommend job enrichment for the workers of the sanitary company we discussed in the introduction to Chapter 12? Why?
6. Discuss the conditions under which job enrichment will more likely result in increased motivation.
7. Discuss how you would go about implementing a management by objectives program.
8. Discuss the barriers you might expect to encounter in implementing a management by objectives program.
9. "To believe in job enrichment, you have to believe that people don't like routine jobs." Explain why you agree or disagree with this statement.
10. Would you consider a professor's job enriched or not enriched? What would you do to make it more enriched? What would you do to make it less enriched?

NOTES FOR THE CHAPTER

1. Morale is another cherished "motivator"; we discussed this in Chapter 14.
2. This section is largely based on Frederick Herzberg, "One More Time: How Do You Motivate Employees?" *Harvard Business Review* (January-February 1968). Also see W. E. Scott and L. L. Cummings, *Readings in Organizational Behavior and Human Performance* (Homewood: Irwin, 1973) pp. 350–378.
3. Herzberg, "One More Time: How Do You Motivate Employees?"
4. Edward Lawler III and John Grant Rhode, *Information and Control in Organizations* (Pacific Palisades: Goodyear, 1976) p. 66; Richard Hackman and Greg Oldham, "Motivation Through the Design of Work: Test of a Theory," *Organizational Behavior and Human Performance*, Vol. 16 (August 1976) pp. 250–279.
5. For a good review of many of these findings, see Alan Filley, Robert House, and Steve Kerr, *Managerial Process and Organizational Behavior* (Glenview: Scott, Foresman, 1976).
6. See, for example, Frederick Herzberg, "One More Time: How Do You Motivate Employees?"; M. D. Kilbridge, "Reduced Costs Through Job Enlargement: A Case," *Journal of Business* (October 1960) pp. 357–362; Filley, House, and Kerr, "Managerial Process and Organizational Behavior"; Dennis Umstot, Cecil Bell, Jr., and Terrence Mitchell, "Effects of Job Enrichment and Task Goals on Satisfaction and Production: Implications for Job Design," *Journal of Applied Psychology*, Vol. 61, No. 4 (1976) pp. 379–394.
7. Rollin H. Simmons, and John N. Oriff, "Worker Behavior vs. Enrichment Theory," *Administrative Science Quarterly*, Vol. 20, No. 4 (1975) p. 606; David Whitsett, "Where Are Your Unenriched Jobs?" *Harvard Business Review*, Vol. 53, No. 1 (January-February 1976); Greg Oldham, J. R. Hackman, and J. Pearce, "Conditions Under Which

330   Employees Respond Positively to Enriched Work," *Journal of Applied Psychology*, Vol. 61, No. 4 (August 1976) pp. 395–403.

8. See, for example, Saul Gellerman, *Motivation & Productivity* (New York: AMA, 1963) p. 218.

9. Steven Carroll and Henry Tosi, *Management by Objectives* (New York: Macmillan, 1973) p. 3; Harry Levinson, "Management by Whose Objectives?" *Harvard Business Review* (July-August 1970).

10. Carroll and Tosi, *Management by Objectives*, p. 140.

11. Carroll and Tosi, *Management by Objectives*, pp. 3–8.

12. Henry Tosi, John Hunter, Rob Chesser, Jim Tartar, and Steven Carroll, "How Real are Changes Induced by Management by Objectives?" *Administrative Science Quarterly*, Vol. 21, No. 2 (June 1976).

13. These benefits based on Carroll and Tosi, *Management by Objectives*, pp. 130–138.

14. Carroll and Tosi, *Management by Objectives*, pp. 14–15, 60–61; Levinson, *Management by Whose Objectives*; Bruce Kirchoff, "A Diagnostic Tool For Management by Objectives," *Personnel Psychology*, Vol. 28 (Autumn, 1975).

15. Several of these hints are based on Mortimer Feinberg, *Effective Psychology for Managers* (Englewood Cliffs, N.J.: Prentice-Hall, 1965), pp. 133–141.

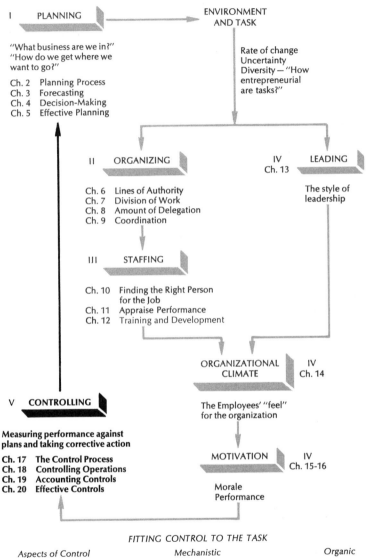

I   PLANNING

ENVIRONMENT
AND TASK

"What business are we in?"
"How do we get where we
want to go?"

Rate of change
Uncertainty
Diversity — "How
entrepreneurial
are tasks?"

Ch. 2   Planning Process
Ch. 3   Forecasting
Ch. 4   Decision-Making
Ch. 5   Effective Planning

What we'll be discussing in this section:
Chap. 17
The Control Process: What
control is, why it's necessary,
and how to set standards.
Chap. 18
Controlling Operations:
Some nuts and bolts tech-
niques for controlling operations — such as production
control, and quality control.
Chap. 19
*Understanding Management
Accounting Controls:* How
to use budgets, standard costs,
and financial ratios.
Chap. 20
Making Control Effective:
How and why control sys-
tems backfire. Fitting control
to the task. Hints for developing effective control
systems.

II   ORGANIZING

IV   LEADING
Ch. 13

Ch. 6   Lines of Authority
Ch. 7   Division of Work
Ch. 8   Amount of Delegation
Ch. 9   Coordination

The style of
leadership

III   STAFFING

Ch. 10   Finding the Right Person
         for the Job
Ch. 11   Appraise Performance
Ch. 12   Training and Development

ORGANIZATIONAL
CLIMATE

IV
Ch. 14

V   **CONTROLLING**

The Employees' "feel"
for the organization

**Measuring performance against
plans and taking corrective action**

Ch. 17   The Control Process
Ch. 18   Controlling Operations
Ch. 19   Accounting Controls
Ch. 20   Effective Controls

MOTIVATION

IV
Ch. 15-16

Morale
Performance

FITTING CONTROL TO THE TASK

Aspects of Control	Mechanistic	Organic
Standards	Very specific; emphasis on efficiency	Broad; emphasis on "milestones" and "getting the job done"
Self vs. imposed control	Control Imposed — through formal budgets, close supervision, etc.	Emphasis on self-control
How frequently you check on performance	Check frequently	Infrequent checks
Control emphasis	Emphasis on process — on *how* job gets done	Emphasis on outcome on "getting the job done"; let employee work out *how*

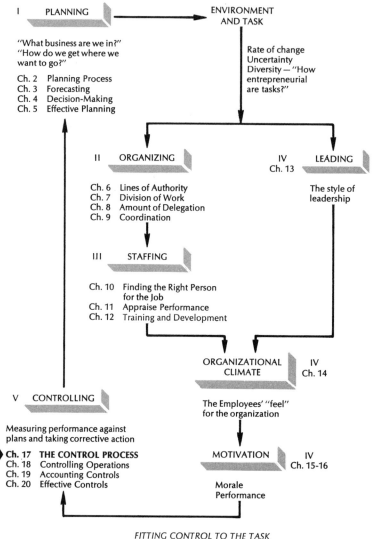

A Framework for Studying the Management Fundamentals

I   PLANNING → ENVIRONMENT AND TASK

Where we are now: Discussing the basic control process, and how to set effective standards.

"What business are we in?"
"How do we get where we want to go?"

Ch. 2 Planning Process
Ch. 3 Forecasting
Ch. 4 Decision-Making
Ch. 5 Effective Planning

Rate of change
Uncertainty
Diversity — "How entrepreneurial are tasks?"

II   ORGANIZING

IV LEADING
Ch. 13

Ch. 6 Lines of Authority
Ch. 7 Division of Work
Ch. 8 Amount of Delegation
Ch. 9 Coordination

The style of leadership

III   STAFFING

Ch. 10 Finding the Right Person for the Job
Ch. 11 Appraise Performance
Ch. 12 Training and Development

ORGANIZATIONAL CLIMATE

IV
Ch. 14

V   CONTROLLING

The Employees' "feel" for the organization

Measuring performance against plans and taking corrective action

Ch. 17 THE CONTROL PROCESS
Ch. 18 Controlling Operations
Ch. 19 Accounting Controls
Ch. 20 Effective Controls

MOTIVATION

IV
Ch. 15-16

Morale
Performance

FITTING CONTROL TO THE TASK

	Mechanistic	*Organic*
Standards	Specific; emphasis on efficiency	General; emphasis on "milestones"
Self vs. imposed control	Control imposed — through formal budgets, etc.	Emphasis on self-control
How frequently you check on performance	Check frequently	Infrequent checks
Control Emphasis	Emphasis on process — on *how* he gets job done	Emphasis on "getting the job done" let employees work out *how*

When you have finished studying

17 The Control Process

You should be able to:

1. *Explain why control is necessary.*

2. *Describe the three steps in the control process.*

3. *Discuss the way in which four dimensions of control should "fit" the task.*

4. *Explain at least seven hints for setting effective standards.*

5. *Set effective standards for your subordinates.*

INTRODUCTION

Control is the last of the management functions, but it's also a very important topic. You might excel at planning, organizing, staffing, and leading, but the real test of your management ability is the results you achieve. And it's through control that you monitor performance and get actual achievements back in line with those planned. One problem with "losing" control is illustrated in Exhibit 17–1.

WHAT IS CONTROL?

Control is the task of insuring that activities are providing the desired results. All control systems collect, store, and transmit information on profits, sales, or some other factor. And all control systems are aimed at influencing behavior. (This is one reason why "controlling someone" often has negative overtones.) Control also requires that targets, standards, or goals be set. This is why the word "planning" is always used along with the word "control."

Why Control, Both Formal and Informal, Is Necessary

If you could be sure that every task you assigned would be perfectly executed you really wouldn't need to "control." But things rarely go this smoothly. Most plans are executed by people, and people vary widely in their

334   abilities, motivation, and honesty. Furthermore, plans themselves become outdated and require revision. For these
reasons, and more, control is clearly a
very important management job.

People sometimes equate formal companywide accounting systems
with the word control. But control certainly doesn't only refer to such large-
scale companywide control systems;
instead it applies to "controlling" *every*
task—large and small—that you delegate. In some cases the task you delegate may be so unimportant, or your
subordinate so competent, that you
don't need to bother with controls. But
most managers quickly learn that abdi-
cation of this sort can be a dangerous
way to manage. As we discussed in
Chapter 13:

A poor manager delegates nothing,
and a mediocre manager delegates
everything. An effective manager
delegates all that he can to his subordinates, while at the same time establishing sufficient checkpoints so
that he knows how the work has been
performed.

Exhibit 17.1

FBI Chief Denies He Plans to Quit

WASHINGTON — (UPI) — FBI
Director Clarence Kelley, in a newspaper interview Sunday, denied
rumors that he considered resigning
in the wake of damaging new dis-
closures about FBI burglaries in the
1970s. . . .

Kelley said a year ago that the
FBI stopped using "black-bag jobs"
in domestic security investigations
in 1966. But it recently was dis-
closed that the Justice Department
is looking into domestic break-ins
committed by FBI agents in New
York and possibly elsewhere during
the past five years.

KELLEY CONFIRMED last week
that "a limited number of surrepti-
tious entries" were carried out in
1972 and 1973. He said he did not
know about them previously. . . .

"I can see where people might
think that Kelley doesn't know
what's going on in his own organization," the FBI director said in the
interview. . . .

Therefore, for every task you delegate you'll need to set up some
formal, or informal control mechanism.

Dimensions of Control

We will see that control systems come in a variety of shapes and formats. They may consist of quality control charts, PERT networks, or budget
systems. Or they may simply involve assigning some project to a subordinate,
and then monitoring that project's progress. But while these control systems
are all different, they all have certain important dimensions in common. These
include: [1]

1. *Degree of Imposed vs. Self-Control:* The extent to which control is
   imposed—through rules, close supervision, etc.—rather than left to
   the *self-control* of the person or department doing the job.

2. A *Performance Criteria:* All control systems have some standard of
   performance—dollar sales, number of defects, etc.
3. *How Frequent Are Checks?* How often is performance monitored
   and checked?
4. *Degree of Control of Goal vs. Control of Process:* Do you keep close
   tabs on the detailed process or method being used to carry out the
   task, or do you only check on the actual outcome?

We know that you have to try to "fit" these dimensions to the task.
For mechanistic tasks such as running bookkeeping departments, control is
usually *imposed* through a system of rules and procedures. Very *specific efficiency* criteria—such as "cut costs by 10 percent"—are emphasized. Progress
is monitored and checked *frequently.* You not only monitor and control the
outcomes, (such as number of products manufactured per month), you also
closely control the *process* or "means" through which your subordinates do
their jobs.

But we know that control systems for organic, entrepreneurial tasks
(such as running a research laboratory) are quite different. Here you depend
more on self-discipline or *self-control.* The emphasis is on broad results, such
as developing a new product, rather than on specific efficiency criteria. You
check performance *infrequently* and instead focus on "milestones." And here
the focus is on the *outcome*—getting the job done—rather than on the exact
means through which the job gets done.[2] This is illustrated in Exhibit 17–2.

Exhibit 17.2   Develop Controls to "Fit" the Situation

	Mechanistic	*Organic*
Typical Application	Mass production Unskilled labor Bookkeeping Department	Hand (one at a time) production Highly skilled labor Research Development Department
Imposed vs. Self Control	Imposed "Close" supervision "Rigid" rules	Self control "General" supervision Autonomy
Performance Criteria	Specific: Unit sales Unit output Unit defects	General: Total sales Total output Total defects
Frequency of Checks	Frequent checks	Infrequent checks
Process Control vs. Goal Control	"Process Control" Emphasis on *how* work carried out	"Goal Control" Emphasis on quality of final product

THE CONTROL PROCESS

Whether the "controller" is the foreman on an assembly line or the
president of General Motors, the control process remains essentially the same.
As in Exhibit 17–3 it involves three steps:

Exhibit 17.3   The Control Process

Set Performance Standard →	*Measure Actual Performance* →	*Take Corrective Action*
(*targets, goal, quota*)	(*yardstick, measure*)	(*change, alter*)
Examples:	Examples:	Examples:
Sales quota	Planned sales versus Actual Sales	Increase sales calls; Sales training
Production quota	Planned Output versus Actual Output	Change methods; Change materials; Change design

Source: Courtesy of Professor Robert Miller.

1. Establish some type of standards or targets.
2. Measure actual performance against these standards.
3. Identify deviations and take corrective action.

Step 1. Establish Some Sort of Standard

Control begins by setting standards of some sort. Often these standards are expressed in *monetary* terms. Thus a salesman might be told that his quota is $8,000 worth of products per month; or a production foreman may be told to cut costs by $2,000 per week. Standards of performance are also expressed in terms of *time*—such as having to meet a certain sales quota in a week, a month, or a year.

Other standards of performance are *quantitative*. Thus production foremen are usually responsible for producing a specified number of units of product per week. The number of labor hours used per unit of output is another example of a quantity standard. Still other standards are expressed in terms of *quality*. These are often expressed in terms of reject rates in quality control, or in grades of products sold—such as "grade A."

Other types of standards are related to the completion of *projects*. If you tell a subordinate to develop a sales forecast for your department, then the standard of performance is the forecast itself. Similarly, if you ask your secretary to make plane reservations for your business trip then obtaining the right reservations is the standard of performance.

Step 2. Measure Actual Performance Against Standards

The second control step involves measuring actual performance against the standard. The simplest and most prevalent way of doing this is by personal observation. For example, a new employee might be given on-the-job training, with his performance personally observed by his supervisor. Sales managers typically make sales calls with their salesmen once or twice a year in order to observe their performance. Or a production foreman personally observes each of his subordinate's performance on an assembly line.

You'll find that this kind of simple, direct observation becomes more difficult as you take on more and more responsibilities. In a two- or three-man organization you could exercise control by simply observing the work being done. But as the responsibilities increase—for example, as the members of salesmen or assemblers increase—it becomes more difficult to directly observe each subordinate's performance. This is summarized in Exhibit 17–4.

Exhibit 17.4   The Problem with Relying on Personal Observation for Control

Monitoring performance through personal observation becomes more difficult as the number of subordinates becomes larger.

With just a few subordinates you could control each by closely watching each one.

But as your subordinates increase in number, you have to start relying more on formal, written control reports.

When the job gets "too big" for one man to handle, two things usually happen. First, a division of work takes place. For example, a sales manager might hire two assistant managers to supervise salesmen in different areas; or a production foreman might hire two assistant foremen to manage each of the plant's assembly lines. But even with this extra help the original manager still needs some way of controlling performance. The fact is that having two assistant sales managers or assistant foremen is no guarantee that the salesmen or assemblers will perform adequately. It's at this point that formal written control reports become more important. These reports, as we'll see, may be in the form of budgets, statistical reports, charts, or narratives.

338

Step 3. Identify Deviations (from Standard) and Take Corrective Action.

Once you've compared actual with planned performance, you'll have to clearly identify any important deviations, and take corrective action. For this you'll want to apply many of the concepts and techniques we discussed in . previous chapters.

From our discussion of decision-making, for example, you know it's important to clearly identify the central problem. Inadequate performance is usually just a symptom, and so you'll therefore want to find out *why* performance is not up to par. For example, ask "Are the plans themselves in need of revision?"; "Is the organization structure inadequate?"; "Are my people not up to the task?"; "Is training and development called for?"; "Is the deviation due to low morale?"; and so forth. And of course in actually taking remedial action you'll want to keep in mind some of the hints we've discussed—on how to counsel, and motivate subordinates, for example.

HOW TO SET EFFECTIVE STANDARDS: SOME HINTS

In the next two chapters we'll be discussing the "measure performance" step in control. We just saw that much of what we've discussed up to now deals with how to "take corrective action." Since it's also important for you to be able to "set effective standards" we'll focus on this step in the remainder of this chapter.

Why Setting Effective Standards Is Important

People are motivated to perform in a way that they feel leads to rewards.[3] If you set targets too high, your subordinates will assume the targets are unreachable—that effort on their part *won't* lead to rewards. If targets are unclear, they won't have any way of gauging the likelihood of success. In any case, setting effective standards—and communicating them—is an essential task.

What "Fairness" Has to Do With the Standards You Set

Setting standards which are perceived as fair and attainable is probably the single most important ingredient in developing effective control systems. Several years ago, Herbert Simon carried out a study and his conclusions are as appropriate now as they were then:

Interview results show that a particular figure does not operate as a norm, . . . simply because the controller's department calls it a standard. It operates as a norm only to the extent that the executives and supervisors, whose activity it measures, accept it as a fair and attainable yardstick of their performance. Generally, operating executives were inclined to accept a standard to the extent that they were satisfied that the data were *accurately reported,* that the standard level was *reasonably attainable,* and that the variables it measured were controllable by them.[4]

Set High Standards for Your Subordinates

We know that when individuals are given low, medium, and high standards it is the employees with the high standards who are consistently the most productive.[5] Set standards so that there is little less than a fifty-fifty chance of success.[6] Make sure they're high, but *reasonable.*[7]

Set Specific Standards—Don't Just Tell Your Subordinates to "Do Their Best"

Studies have been carried out in which some employees were given specific standards (low and high) and others were simply told to "do their best." The employees who were assigned low standards did the worst. Those who were told to do their best had performance in the medium range. Employees who were assigned the highest standards did the best.[8] So assigning high standards is more effective than telling someone to do his best.

Raise Your Subordinates' Standards When They Meet Your Previous Standards

You should raise your subordinates' standards—but not too much. In one study the researcher set new standards at 20, 40, 60, 80 and 100 percent above what the subjects had previously achieved. Performance increased with each higher standard, up to the point where standards were 80 percent higher than previously. For example, productivity increased 25 percent when standards were set 20 percent higher than previously. But when standards were set at 80 percent above previous performance, productivity went up only by 12 percent. And when standards were doubled—100 percent of the previous performance—productivity declined. On the whole, the best results were obtained where standards were set at about 20 percent above previous performance.[9]

Let Your People Know How They Are Doing

Employees who are given feedback on their achievements usually have higher morale and perform better.[10] We also know that providing feedback is especially important where you have assigned high standards to your subordinates. In other words, providing feedback is more important when you set high standards than when standards are just average, or when you simply tell a subordinate to "do his best." [11] As a general rule, feedback should be fast and frequent. This is especially so for lower-level jobs which are often routine and quickly completed.[12]

Set High Standards for Quality and Quantity:
Standards Should Be Complete

Employees concentrate their efforts where results are measured.[13] Therefore you can use standards to help focus your employee's attention on critical areas. If quality is paramount (as it might be where heart pacemakers are manufactured) then set higher standards for quality. If quantity (or some other factor) is paramount, then set high quantity standards; but remember that your employees will take their cues from you. If you set standards only on quantity, they will emphasize quantity. If you set them only on quality, they will emphasize quality.[14] If both quality and quantity are important to you, then you'd best set clear standards for both.

Setting High Standards Is Also a Good Idea for Employees
Who Are Not Highly Motivated

We know that setting high standards for low-motivated groups usually results in sharper increases in performance than does setting high standards for highly motivated groups. And not only does the former's performance increase sharply, their interest in the task sharply increases as well.[15]

Remember to Use MBO

Setting goals, evaluating performance, and providing feedback is the essence of the MBO procedure. In one respect MBO is a method for motivating employees because the process of setting goals, exercising self-discipline, and getting feedback on results can be highly motivating. But, MBO can also be viewed as a control system as it involves setting standards, evaluating performance, and rewarding or correcting deviations from standards.

One principle of classical management writers was called "Management by Exception." This principle held that only significant deviations (exceptions) from standards should be brought to the manager's attention. For example, suppose you establish a quality control standard which says that three defects per 100 units produced is permissible. Under the Management by Exception principle, only significant deviations from this standard—four or more defects per 100 units in this case—should be brought to your attention.

Summary

In summary, the "perfect standard" (if there was such a thing) would be:

1. Viewed as *fair* by your subordinates.
2. High, but reasonable—there would be about a 50/50 chance of success at reaching it.
3. Specific.
4. Set about 20% above previous performance.
5. Communicated to your subordinate, provide feedback.
6. Complete—for example, don't just focus on *quantity*, and disregard *quality*, unless that's your intention.
7. Used within the context of MBO and management by exception.

Some Important Things to Remember from This Chapter:

1. Control is the task of insuring that activities are providing the desired results. Unless the task you delegate is unimportant, or your subordinate completely competent, you ought to have a way of controlling every task you delegate.

2. Establishing standards or targets is the first step in the control process. These targets may be expressed in monetary terms; in terms of time; in quantitative terms; in terms of quality; and in terms of the completion of a project.

3. Measuring performance against these standards is the second step in control. In small two- or three-man units, you might be able to accomplish this step simply by personally observing the work being done. But as your subordinates increase you will find yourself depending more on the kind of formal written control devices we will discuss in the next two chapters.

4. Identifying and correcting deviations from standards is the third and final step in control. This step will involve all the problem-identifying, decision-making, organizing, and leadership skills discussed in the book up to this point.

5. Control devices always contain four basic dimensions:

   1. The degree of imposed vs. self-control.
   2. Performance criteria or standards.
   3. How frequently performance is checked.
   4. The extent to which the goal vs. the process is controlled.

342 For mechanistic tasks, such as running bookkeeping departments, control is imposed; standards are very specific; performance is frequently checked; and both the goals and the process are controlled. At the other extreme control systems for organic, entrepreneurial tasks such as running a research laboratory, emphasize self-control; broad performance standards; infrequent checks; and a focus on the outcome rather than the process.

6. Much of what we discussed in Chapters 1 through 16 was involved with the "how" and "why" of taking corrective action. In the next two chapters we'll focus on control devices for measuring actual performance against standards. So in the last part of this chapter we have focused on the first step in the control process: setting standards. We concluded that the "perfect standard" would be: fair; high, but reasonable; specific; about 20% above previous performance; communicated; complete; and used within the context of MBO and management by exception.

STUDY ASSIGNMENTS

1. Explain why control is necessary.
2. Describe the three steps in the control process.
3. Discuss the relationship between delegation, control, and management effectiveness.
4. Briefly describe how you would control each of the following activities: You ask your secretary to analyze last month's sales figures and send a short report to each of your salesmen; you ask your spouse to make sure to mail out all the bills that are due; you ask a subordinate to analyze the feasibility of a new plant site you are considering.
5. Discuss the way in which four dimensions of control must "fit the task."
6. Explain at least seven hints for setting effective standards.
7. Write an essay discussing the effectiveness of the standards which your instructor in this course has set for you. Explain whether you think they are effective and why.
8. "Your leadership style really reflects your attitude toward control." Is there any relationship between leadership style and our four dimensions of control? Explain your answer.
9. Why is setting effective standards so important?
10. Explain some of the different types of standards you can set.

NOTES FOR THE CHAPTER

1. Gary Dessler, *Organization and Management: A Contingency Approach* (Englewood Cliffs, N.J.: Prentice-Hall, 1976) p. 361.

2. See for example, William H. Newman, "Strategy and Management Structure," *Journal of Business Policy*, Vol. 2, No. 1 (Winter, 1971–1972) pp. 56–66.

3. Edward Lawler and John Rhode, *Information and Control in Organizations* (Pacific Palisades: Goodyear, 1976).

4. Herbert Simon et al., *Centralization vs. Decentralization in Organizing the*

Controller's Department (New York: Controllership Foundation, Inc., 1954) p. 29; quoted
in Charles T. Horngren, *Accounting for Management Control* (Englewood Cliffs, N.J.: Prentice-Hall, 1970), p. 363.

5. Edwin Locke, "Toward a Theory of Task Motivation and Incentive," *Organizational Behavior and Human Performance*, Vol. 3 (1968) pp. 168–171; Lawler and Rhode, *Information and Control in Organizations*, pp. 69–72. Donald Campbell and Daniel Ilgen, "Additive Effects of Task Difficulty and Goal-Setting on Subsequent Task Performance," *Journal of Applied Psychology*, Vol. 61 (June 1976).

6. Lawler and Rhode, *Information and Control in Organizations*, pp. 69–72.

7. Much of the remainder of this section is based on Arlyn Melcher, *Structure and Process of Organizations* (Englewood Cliffs, N.J.: Prentice-Hall, 1976) pp. 227–253. He presents an excellent discussion of standards.

8. Edwin Locke, "The Relationship of Intentions to Level of Performance," *Journal of Applied Psychology*, Vol. 50 (1966) pp. 60–66; see also Gary O. Latham and J. James Baldes, "The Practical Significance of Locke's Theory of Goal Setting," *Journal of Applied Psychology*, Vol. 60, No. 1 (February 1975).

9. Mukul K. Day and Gurmindd Kaur, "Facilitation of Performance by Experimentally Induced Ego Motivation," *Journal of General Psychology*, Vol. 73 (1965) pp. 237–247.

10. Arlen Melcher, *Structure and Process of Organizations*, p. 229.

11. Edwin Locke, "Motivational Effect of Knowledge and Results: Knowledge or Goal Setting?" *Journal of Applied Psychology*, Vol. 51 (1967) pp. 324–329.

12. Lawler and Rhode, *Information and Control in Organizations*, pp. 54–55.

13. Lawler and Rhode, *Information and Control in Organizations*, p. 47.

14. Arlen Melcher, *Structure and Process of Organizations*, p. 252; V. F. Ridgway, "Dysfunctional Consequences of Performance Measurements," *Administrative Science Quarterly*, Vol. 1, No. 2, pp. 240–247, 1956, in John Turner, Alan Filley, Robert House, *Studies in Managerial Process and Organizational Behavior* (Glenview: Scott Foresman, 1972) p. 190.

15. Judith Bryan and Edwin Locke, "Goal Setting As a Means of Increasing Motivation," *Journal of Applied Psychology*, Vol. 51 (1967) pp. 274–277.

A Framework for Studying the Management Fundamentals

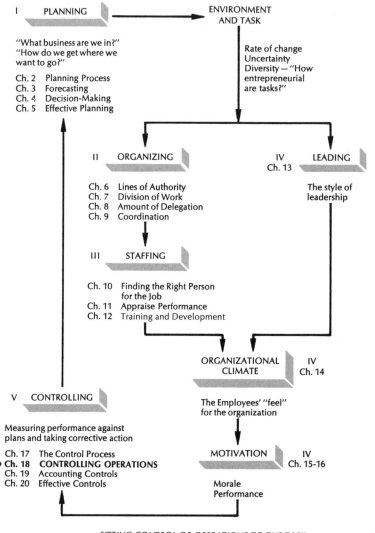

I PLANNING → ENVIRONMENT AND TASK

Where we are now: Discussing techniques for controlling operations — production, inventory, and quality.

"What business are we in?"
"How do we get where we want to go?"

Ch. 2 Planning Process
Ch. 3 Forecasting
Ch. 4 Decision-Making
Ch. 5 Effective Planning

Rate of change
Uncertainty
Diversity — "How entrepreneurial are tasks?"

II ORGANIZING

Ch. 6 Lines of Authority
Ch. 7 Division of Work
Ch. 8 Amount of Delegation
Ch. 9 Coordination

IV LEADING
Ch. 13

The style of leadership

III STAFFING

Ch. 10 Finding the Right Person for the Job
Ch. 11 Appraise Performance
Ch. 12 Training and Development

ORGANIZATIONAL CLIMATE   IV Ch. 14

V CONTROLLING

The Employees' "feel" for the organization

Measuring performance against plans and taking corrective action

Ch. 17 The Control Process
Ch. 18 CONTROLLING OPERATIONS
Ch. 19 Accounting Controls
Ch. 20 Effective Controls

MOTIVATION   IV Ch. 15-16

Morale
Performance

FITTING CONTROL OF OPERATIONS TO THE TASK

Dimensions of Control to Remember When Controlling Operations	*Mechanistic*	*Organic*
Standards	Specific; emphasis on efficiency	General; emphasis on "milestones"
Self vs. imposed control	Control imposed — through formal budgets, etc.	Emphasis on self-control
How frequently you check on performance	Check frequently	Infrequent checks
Control Emphasis	Emphasis on process — on *how* he gets job done	Emphasis on "getting the job done" let employees work out *how*

18   Controlling Operations

1. *Cite the steps in "order control."*

2. *Develop the following production control forms:*
A sales order
A bill of materials
A job cost sheet
A route sheet
A GANTT chart
A PERT chart
A shop order

3. *Explain the purpose of inventory control.*

4. *Set up two types of inventory control systems.*

5. *Develop a working quality control system.*

INTRODUCTION

When Bob Ellis started his electronics firm two years ago he carefully constructed each calculator himself and kept no inventories. Therefore, controlling operations was not much of a problem for him. But today he has 10 assembly line workers assembling his products, a constant flow of new orders, and an inventory that's worth $200,000. He comes to you with the following questions:

1. What type of production planning and control system should I install?
2. What type of inventory control system should I install?
3. What type of quality control system can I install to monitor production?

By the time you have finished this chapter you should be able to answer these questions and help Bob install the necessary production, inventory, and quality control systems.

346 *PRODUCTION PLANNING AND CONTROL*

Whether you are producing cars or Broadway shows you have to have some system for planning and controlling production. Let's therefore begin our discussion of controlling operations with this topic. *Production planning* is aimed at determining what products you will produce, and where, when, and how you will produce them. *Production control* is aimed at assuring that the production plans or schedules you establish are being met.

The most common type of production planning and control is called *order control.*[1] It is used in "job shops" where custom products, such as cabinets or iron gates are made. It involves six basic steps:

1. *Receive the orders* from customers.
2. Develop *lists of required materials.*
3. Develop a *route* sheet.
4. Develop *production schedules.*
5. *Dispatch* notices to operators to begin work.
6. *Follow-up/expedite* to see that schedule is being met.

Let's look at each of these steps in turn.

Step 1. Receive Orders

You start with the receipt of an order from a customer. The sales order (such as that in Exhibit 18–1) usually contains information on things such as product and model to be produced, requested delivery date, and required quantities.[2] Sometimes products are manufactured for stock or inventory rather than for immediate sale. In that case an order form, such as shown in Exhibit 18–2, is issued by the person in charge of maintaining inventories.

Step 2. Develop the Bill (or list) of Materials

Next you compile a list of the raw materials and parts required to fill the order. Many companies maintain forms, such as that in Exhibit 18–3. These list the required parts and materials for each product they manufacture. Without such a list, it may be necessary to have a specialist analyze the customer's order and develop a special list of required materials.

In any case this step usually culminates in a job cost sheet (such as that in Exhibit 18–4). This lists the materials, labor, and overhead costs involved in filling the customer's order. Among other things, you can use this for estimating how profitable (or unprofitable) it will be for your company to fill this particular order.

Exhibit 18.1   A Sales Order

SALES ORDER

Nov. 10	1052
ENTRY DATE	ORDER NO.
3	147
QUANTITY	MODEL NO.

SOLD TO

ABC Appliance Company
535 Terrace Street
Newark 3, New Jersey

RADIO CONSOLE
PRODUCT DESCRIPTION

Jan. 8	
DATE WANTED	SCHEDULE PERIOD

IMPORTANT: Enter On One Order Only Items of
Identical Specifications and Delivery Date

SPECIFICATIONS

Moderne	Blonde Maple		115	60	H.D.	25	H.F.
STYLE	FINISH		VOLTS	CYCLES	TYPE	WATTS	TYPE
CABINET			POWER UNIT			AMPLIFIER	

25	Hi Fi	Frequency Modulation		High Fidelity	
WATTS	TYPE	TUNING UNIT		PHONOGRAPH UNIT	
SOUND REPRODUCER					

USE SPACE BELOW FOR SPECIAL INSTRUCTIONS, ACCESSORIES, AND OPTIONAL DEVICES

External Frequency Modulation Dipole Antenna

Source: Reproduced in Mayer, *Production and Operations Management,* p. 267.

Exhibit 18.2 Interdepartment Production Shipping Request

Ship to Department ☐ 1   Number _____

☐ 2   Date _____

☐ 3

☐ 4

☐ 5

Item Code	# Units	Description

Step 3. Develop the Route Sheet

Routing determines the sequence of operations to be performed and the path (or route) to be taken by the order. The route sheet itself is a form such as that in Exhibit 18–5. This lists the types of machines required to get each part of the job done, and the time required for each step in the operation.[3]

Exhibit 18.3 Standard Bill of Material

Assembly No. __4xy__   Description: __Card Table__

Part Number	Quantity	Description
A 403	4	Steel legs
A 501	1	Table top
P 42	16 sq. ft.	Plastic cover
P 48	6 oz.	Adhesive
B 5	1	Bolt kit

Note: The Standard Bill (or list) of Material shows all the material needs for, in this case, the card table.

Source: Charles Horngren, *Accounting for Management Control,* Englewood Cliffs, N. J., Prentice-Hall Inc., 1970) p. 266.

		Cost Summary					DATE	
FORM 541								A
PREPARED BY:		APPROVED BY:						
PART NUMBER		QUANTITY		UNIT OF MEASURE		JOB NO.		
DESCRIPTION				CUSTOMER		CUSTOMER NO.		

DATES: RECEIVED		PROMISED		FINISHED		QUOTED		INVOICED	

DATE	LABOR					MATERIAL						TOTALS	
	OPERATION	CLASS	HRS.	RATE	AMOUNT	DESCRIPTION	QUAN.	UNIT	UNIT COST	AMOUNT	DESCRIPTION	AMOUNT
											LABOR	
											FACTORY OVERHEAD	
											MATERIAL	
											MATERIAL BURDEN	
											SALES OVERHEAD	
											ADMINISTRATIVE	
											ACTUAL COST	
	TOTAL LABOR					TOTAL MATERIAL					NET RESULT	

COST SUMMARY

Don't guess at your costs. This Cost Summary sheet insures that you consider and include all the cost elements. Then your quoted prices will be sure to lead to profits.

Source: Courtesy Van DeMark, Inc., (Form 541).

Step 4. Develop the Production Plan or Schedule

The production schedule is usually in the form of a chart which shows in detail what manufacturing operations are to be carried out, and when. Usually this information exists in other records, such as route sheets. The value of putting the information on a chart "lies in its ability to consolidate this scattered mass of information and present it in a form that is easy to read and understand." [4]

A GANTT chart, such as that in Exhibit 18–6, is one widely used scheduling chart. It shows, for each order, when each required operation should be completed.

A PERT chart, such as that in Exhibit 18–7, is also used for scheduling projects. (PERT stands for "Program Evaluation Review Technique.) The two major components of a PERT network are *events* and *activities*. Events are depicted by circles, and represent specific accomplishments. Activities are represented by arrows, and are the time-consuming aspects of the project. By carefully studying the PERT chart the scheduler can determine the "critical path." This is the sequence of events which, in total, requires the most time to complete.

In practice, most production schedulers work from the required delivery date backwards. They determine how long each assembly will take, how

350   **Exhibit 18.5** Example of a Route Sheet

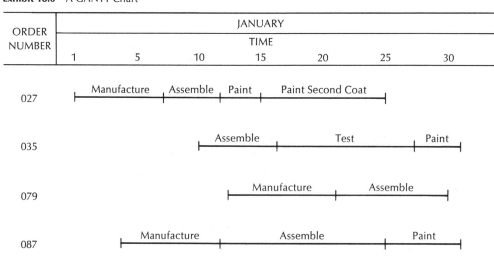

ROUTE SHEET

Assembles in orderly fashion all material needs, operation sequence, equipment and tooling required, and time standards. Use for all manufactured parts, sub-assemblies and finished goods.

Source: Courtesy of Van DeMark, Inc., (Forms 532: 531).

Exhibit 18.6 A GANTT Chart

ORDER NUMBER	JANUARY						
	TIME						
	1	5	10	15	20	25	30
027	Manufacture	Assemble	Paint	Paint Second Coat			
035			Assemble		Test		Paint
079				Manufacture		Assemble	
087		Manufacture		Assemble		Paint	

Note: The GANTT chart shows, for each order, when each operation (manufacture, assemble, etc.) is to start and stop.

Exhibit 18.7 A PERT Chart

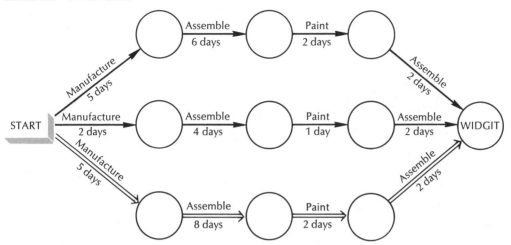

Note: This PERT Chart shows the schedule, and "critical path" for manufacturing and assembly of the three components for a widget.
\# days for component #1: 5 + 6 + 2 + 2 = 15
\# days for component #2: 2 + 4 + 1 + 2 = 9
\# days for component #3: 5 + 8 + 2 + 2 = 17

So component 3 construction is the "critical path" and is shown with double lines. Now you could put the people here on overtime, or hire additional help to speed up work on this component.

long it will take to obtain raw materials, and so forth. Based on this, they can determine whether the required delivery date can be met, and what bottlenecks they should be prepared to unravel.

Step 5. Dispatching

Dispatching means issuing the orders for performing the work. The orders themselves are contained on written forms. These are often called shop orders, job tickets, or manufacturing orders, and are illustrated in Exhibit 18–8. They not only specify the work to be performed, but also authorize release of the necessary materials, labor, and tools. The shop order provides a space where operators and inspectors can sign after each operation has been completed; then it goes with the work to the next operation. *Requisitions* for materials, parts, and tools, such as illustrated in Exhibit 18–9, are used to authorize the shop to obtain necessary materials.

Step 6. Follow-up/Expedite

In production management jargon production control is often called follow-up, or expediting: it is the "control" aspect of production planning and control. Its aim is to insure that the production schedule is being adhered to. The control standards might be the scheduled completion dates, the required quantities, and, perhaps, the required product quality levels.

352   **Exhibit 18.8**   A Shop Order and a Job Ticket

Used to Order the Shop to Carry Out Appropriate Activities.

MANUFACTURING ORDER ROUTE SHEET										

MANUFACTURING ORDER NO. 24347 · **PART NO.** 3143211 **MODEL NO.** 8461 **SHEET** 1 **OF** 1

ORDER QUANTITY 656 **PART DESCRIPTION** ACTUATOR SCREW **BY** LB

DATE START 1016 **DATE COMPLETE** 1124 **DATE ISSUE** 1002 **RAW MATERIAL NO.** 60431 **RAW MATERIAL DESCRIPTION** 241 SP. 1/2" RD.

TOTAL QUANTITY RAW MATERIAL 81.25 FT. **RAW MATERIAL PER UNIT** .125 FT. **DELIVER TO DEPT.** 14

SCHEDULE DATE COMPLETE	WORK CENTER	OPER. NO.	OPERATION DESCRIPTION	TOOLS AND FIXTURES	SPEED	FEED	JOB CODE	SET-UP HOURS	STANDARD HOURS PER HUNDRED	PIECES PER HOUR
1018	142	10	TURN .475 DIA., TURN .350 DIA. TURN FOR 1/4 – 16 THREAD, GROOVE, DEBURR, CUT OFF				197	1.50	3.300	30
1022	282	20	DRILL (1) .135/.140 DIA. HOLE REAM (1) .135/.140 DIA. HOLE							
1025	543	30	MILL TEETH							
1030	549	40	STRADDLE MILL .312 DIAM.							
1102	549	50	RADIUS CORNERS PER END VIEW							
1105	920	60	DEBURR AND RADIUS							
1107	950	70	CLEAN FOR HEAT TREAT							
1109	901	80	HEAT TREAT							
1126	314	85	GRIND 1/4 – 16 THREADS							
1128	951	90	DEGREASE							

WORK CENTER OPERATION TICKET							

MANUFACTURING ORDER NO. 24347 **PART NO.** 3143211 **MODEL NO.** 8461

ORDER QUANTITY 656 **PART DESCRIPTION** ACTUATOR SCREW

DATE START 1016 **DATE COMPLETE** 1124 **DATE ISSUE** 1002 **RAW MATERIAL NO.** 60431 **RAW MATERIAL DESCRIPTION** 241 SP. 1/2" RD.

TOTAL QUANTITY RAW MATERIAL 81.25 FT. **RAW MATERIAL PER UNIT** .125 FT.

SCHEDULE DATE COMPLETE	WORK CENTER	OPER. NO.	OPERATION DESCRIPTION	JOB CODE	SET-UP HOURS	STANDARD HOURS PER HUNDRED	PIECES PER HOUR
1018	142	10	TURN .475 DIA., TURN .350 DIA. TURN FOR 1/4 – 16 THREAD, GROOVE, DEBURR, CUT OFF	197	1.50	3.300	30
DATE							
BAL. PCS.							

Source: Job Ticket (Courtesy of Royal McBee Corporation). Reproduced in Mayer, *Production and Operations Management*, p. 279.

There are many different techniques for controlling production.[5] One is for the foreman to prepare, at the end of each day, *a report* listing orders received, orders processed, and orders remaining. In some companies this reporting process has been computerized: IBM-type computer cards are punched at the job site, with information on each job. This information is then fed into computer terminals, again at the job site. Then it is summarized in daily computerized production *control reports*, such as that illustrated in Exhibit 18–10.

Another production control technique makes use of the *shop orders*. As each operation is completed, the operator initials the shop order. Actual and planned completion dates as listed on the shop orders are then reviewed each day by the foreman.

Exhibit 18.9   Material Requisition

MATERIAL REQUISITION
(NOT A PURCHASE ORDER)

No.

To					Date	19	
Deliver To					Charge To Job		
QUANTITY		STOREKEEPER: PLEASE SUPPLY			PRICE	AMOUNT	
1							
2							
3							
4							
5							
6							
7							
8							
9							

PRICED BY	EXTENDED BY	CHECKED BY	ENTERED BY	
				Signed

Source: Courtesy of Professor Robert Miller.

Some companies use *move orders* to authorize a transfer of partially finished goods from one operation to another. Copies of these move orders are sent to the production control department after each "move." These can be another effective production control technique.

Another technique makes use of *inspection reports*. Most companies require periodic inspection after each completed operation, and often these inspections are summarized on inspection forms. Copies of these inspection forms, sent to the production control department, are another effective control technique.

Exhibit 18.10   A Production Control Report

WORK-IN-PROCESS STATUS

SHOP DATE 615

RAMAC ADDR.	SHOP ORDER		STOCK DATE	QUANTITY ORDERED	TOTAL STD. HRS.	TOT. ACT. HRS. TO DATE	STD. HRS. TO COMPL.	NO. OPS.	LAST OP.		DAYS		REASON CODE
	PART NO.	LOT NO.							DAY	NO.	EARLY	LATE	
20400	358006	020-0	632	68	1597	269	1414	13	612	50		3	1
20800	358006	030-0	649	69	1615	80	1582	13	613	20	2		
21800	358117	040-0	617	100	976	815	161	16	614	180		1	4

Source: Courtesy of International Business Machines Corporation. Reproduced in Mayer, *Production and Operations Management*, p. 286.

354   Still other companies make use of their *GANTT* scheduling charts for controlling production. As you can see in Exhibit 18–11, you can develop a chart which shows both scheduled and actual progress for each order. These charts show quickly and concisely whether the production department is meeting its planned schedules.

Exhibit 18.11   A GANTT Chart Showing Scheduled and Actual Progress

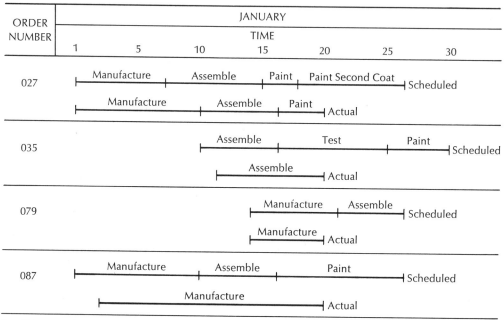

Note: This GANTT Chart shows, for each order, when each operation (manufacture, assemble, etc.) was to start and stop, *and* where each order *actually* stands as of January 20. Note that orders 027, 035, and 087 are behind, and order 079 is ahead of schedule.

After comparing actual and planned progress, you may find that some orders are well behind schedule. This might not only affect the required shipping date, but might have a "domino" effect by disturbing established schedules for other scheduled orders. Because of this, many companies retain special "expediters." Their speciality is solving production problems and breaking up production bottlenecks. Corrective action might entail hiring extra labor, working overtime, or subcontracting some of the work, for example.

Summary: Production Planning and Control

The production planning and control process is a good example of what might be called the planning-action-control cycle. Based on the order, the bill of materials, and the route sheet, a production schedule is *planned*. This sets standards for what is to be produced, and how, when, and where it is to be produced. Then orders are dispatched to the production shop so that actual production activities (*action*) can take place. Next, production *control* is carried out. Foremen's reports, shop orders, "move" orders, inspection reports, and GANTT charts are some of the devices used to compare actual with planned progress. Should a significant unfavorable discrepancy exist, corrective action—such as hiring additional help—is initiated.

INVENTORY CONTROL

Inventory control is a second important technique for controlling operations.

The Purpose of Inventory Control

Inventory control is aimed at maintaining supplies of inventory at levels appropriate to meet production and sales requirements. The supplies stocked in inventory might be raw materials, or components used in the manufacture of your company's products. Or it might be the finished products from which customer's orders are filled.

There are three basic problems you want to avoid by using inventory control. The first is *overinvestment* in inventories. This ties up money, crowds available space, and hikes losses due to deterioration and obsolescence. At the other extreme, *underinvestment* makes your company unable to fill production orders, and discourages customers. The third problem is *unbalanced inventory*. Here some items are understocked and others are overstocked. Let's look at two inventory control tools.

ABC Inventory Control

This is a simple, effective inventory control system.[6] It helps you to focus your control efforts where they're most needed: on those items with the highest dollar volume.

Here's the basic idea. Most companies find that 25 or 30 percent of the items in their inventory account for 70 or 80 percent of their annual dollar volume. (You find an item's annual dollar volume by multiplying its cost per item times the number of items used in a year.) With the ABC system you divide your inventory into three-dollar volume categories, A, B, and C, with the A items the most active. You then concentrate most of your control efforts on the "A" items. For example, you order these most often, and see to it they don't sit around your bins too long.

Let's look at an example.[7] Suppose a company has 2,000 items in inventory, with a total annual dollar volume of $100,000. As you can see in Exhibit 18–12, the person controlling inventories discovers that 500 of these items (25 percent) actually account for $65,000 (65 percent) of the annual dollar volume. He decides to put these in class "A." (This is a somewhat arbitrary decision. He could have put the items accounting for 60 percent or 80 percent of volume, or some other, into class "A.") Next, he puts those items which account for, say, 20 percent of the annual volume into class B. This leaves the 1,000 items which account for the remaining 15 percent of volume to be placed in class C. Now instead of dividing his attention evenly among all 2,000 items, he can focus his time on the 500 items that account for his biggest investment—those in class A.

Exhibit 18.12   The ABC Inventory Control System

# of Items	% of Items	Annual Dollar Volume	% of Annual Dollar Volume	Inventory Class
500	25	$65,000	65	A
500	25	$20,000	20	B
1,000	50	$15,000	15	C

Note: That 25 percent of the items account for 65 percent of the dollar volume of inventory. These 500 items are the ones you want to focus on; you want to order them the most often so your day to day supply of them is never to large. And you want to see that they don't lie around your bins too long.

The Economic Order Quantity Inventory Control Model

Another widely used inventory control technique is the Economic Order Quantity (EOQ) model. You can use it to determine what quantity to order in order to minimize total inventory costs. Exhibit 18–13 illustrates the relationships involved. As you can see, the two major costs, *carrying* (warehouse storage costs, and so on) and *ordering* (filling in purchase requisitions, and the like) tend to offset each other. One reason for this is that ordering in large quantities usually allows you to obtain volume discounts, but at the same time it also involves higher storage costs.

Inventory Control in Action—An Optional Example

Example: Let's look at an example to see how carrying and ordering costs offset each other, and how to use the EOQ model in practice.[8] Suppose you want to determine the Economic Order Quantity—the best quantity to buy—for an item with the following attributes:

Cost: $15.00 per unit.

Annual Usage Rate: 300 units used per year.

Restocking Cost (Cost of *ordering*—Purchase Orders, etc.): $10.00 per order.

Annual *Carrying Cost* (Warehouse costs, etc.): 20 percent of value of inventory.

Exhibit 18.13 The Economic Order Quantity Model:

A. *The Relationships Involved:*

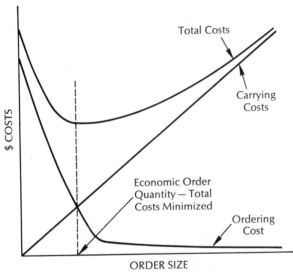

B. *Plugging in the Data Given in the Text and Calculating the E.O.Q.*

EOQ Formula:

$$Q = \sqrt{\frac{2\ U.S.}{CI}}$$

So, for Our Example,

$$Q = \sqrt{\frac{2(300)\ (10)}{(15)\ (.20)}} = 44.72$$

Where

Q = Economic Order Quantity

U = Annual Usage

S = Restocking (or ordering) Cost

C = Cost Per Unit

I = Annual Carrying Cost

Note: As the order size goes up, costs per order go down — due to discounts, etc. But as order size goes up, you order less often and carry more inventory — so carrying costs go *UP*.

Carrying Costs: To begin with, suppose you bought the entire year's supply of 300 units at once. Then your inventory level will vary from 300 units at the beginning of the year to none at the end of the year. Thus you'll have an average of 150 units (300 ÷ 2) in inventory during the year. But if during the year you placed 10 orders for 30 units each, your inventory would range from 30 to 0 units during each of the 10 periods and so your average inventory would be only 15 units. As you can see, *the more often you order, the lower is your average inventory, and therefore your carrying costs.*

Ordering Costs: The problem, though, is that *the more often you order, the higher your ordering costs go.* For one thing, you usually forego some volume discounts. For another, it usually costs you and your company about the same thing (for clerical time, purchase requisitions, and so forth) to order 30 units as it does to order 300. In our example, the ordering

358   cost is $10 whether you order 300 units or 30 units. Therefore the paperwork cost involved with ordering 300 units at once is $10. But if you order 30 units ten times during the year, then your total ordering cost woud be 10 × $10 or $100.

So as you can see in Exhibit 18–13, the smaller the order size the higher the annual *ordering* cost. But the smaller the order size the lower the average inventory and therefore *carrying costs*: ordering and carrying costs offset each other.

Using the Model. In Exhibit 18–13 we have "plugged" the appropriate costs and quantities into our EOQ model. As you can see, the EOQ—the economic or best order quantity—is 45 units. In this case, you will minimize your total inventory costs if you submit orders for 45 units at a time. You would therefore have to order six or seven times per year.

QUALITY CONTROL

Let's look at a third important aspect of controlling operations: quality control.

The Quality Control Process

The quality control process consists of establishing quality standards, inspecting goods, and taking corrective action as necessary.

Establishing quality *standards* doesn't necessarily mean that quality must be high, since "quality" means different things to different people. To some, for example, the word brings to mind diamonds and Rolls Royce cars. But to a manufacturer, quality means whatever he says it means and his standards certainly don't have to be high. In fact many companies are quite successful aiming their sights on producing low quality (and low cost) merchandise.

Inspection is the task of comparing actual quality to these established standards. Most companies have some type of formal inspection procedure in which inspectors test and measure the merchandise against the established standards. Inspection might also be informal and carried out by workers using their physical senses to get a feel for the quality of the product. In some manufacturing processes, such as the production of heart pacemakers, 100 percent inspection is typical. Here each product is inspected in relation to the established standards. But more often *sampling inspection* is used. Here some proportion—perhaps only 2 or 5 percent—of the merchandise is inspected. Inspection often results in reports such as illustrated in Exhibit 18–14.

Exhibit 18.14 Inspection Report for Quality Control

INSPECTION REPORT	CAN REWORK ☐ CAN SALVAGE ☐ MUST SCRAP ☐	DATE INSPECTED	INSPECTED BY	FOR VENDOR, USE THIS NO. ON THE CARDS **IR 14750**

PART OR MATERIAL DESCRIPTION | PART NO. | MATERIAL

REASON FOR REJECTION SPECIFICATION SHOULD BE | SPECIFICATION | JOB NO. | P.O. NO.

LAST SPECIFICATION NO. | RECEIVING REPORT NO.

VENDOR

WHO IS RESPONSIBLE | CLOCK NO. | MACHINE NO.

QUANTITY INSPECTED

TOTAL	GOOD	REJECTED

NATURE OF REJECTS

VENDOR	OUR SCRAP	VENDOR'S SCRAP

REVIEW

DATE | INSPECTION | ENGINEERING | PRODUCTION | B.O. | VENDOR

DISPOSITION

1—RETURN TO VENDOR:
☐ FOR CREDIT ONLY
☐ FREIGHT COST
☐ FOR CREDIT AND REPLACEMENT
☐ FREIGHTING

2—REWORK IN OUR PLANT
☐ VENDOR'S EXPENSE
☐ OUR EXPENSE

3—SCRAP
☐ CHARGE TO VENDOR
☐ OUR EXPENSE

OPER. NO.	MACH. NO.	REWORK INSTRUCTIONS	TOOLING	EST.TIME

INSPECTION DATE | 1—DISPATCH | PURCHASING O.H.

Source: Dean S. Ammer, *Materials Management* (Richard D. Irwin, Inc., 1974).

360   If inspection identifies a variation or discrepancy, *corrective action* is initiated. This involves identifying the cause of the deviation (which might be a worn-out machine part, lack of employee attention, and so on), and rectifying it.

    The Four Stages of Quality Control: You can't expect quality control standards to emerge spontaneously in the production shop. Elwood Buffa says there are four stages of quality control and that these begin at the highest levels in the enterprise. These are summarized in Exhibit 18–15.[9] According to Professor Buffa, quality control policies should begin with top management.

Exhibit 18.15   The Four Stages of Quality Control

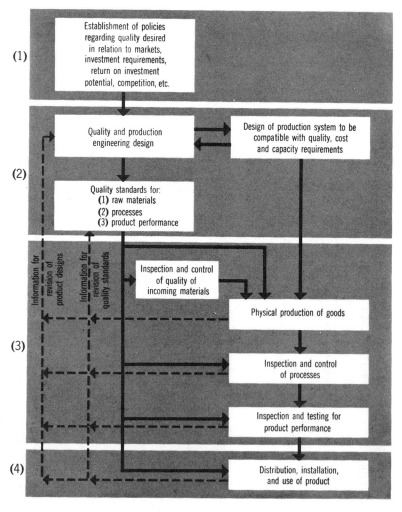

Note: This outlines the role of quality control throughout the planning, production, and distribution of a product.

Source: Ellwood Buffa, *Modern Production Management*, p. 644 (New York: John Wiley & Sons, 1973).

They establish policies regarding desired quality in relation to markets, competition, and so forth. These quality standards then permeate the product design stage, the manufacturing stage, and finally the installation stage of the product.

Quality Control Charts

Many companies use charts such as that in Exhibit 18–16 to control the quality of their products.[10] There are many different types of charts, but the basic idea is always the same. As in this Exhibit, upper and lower limits are drawn on the chart. Then some measurable aspect of the merchandise, such as length or weight, is inspected and measured. If it (the length, weight, etc.) begins to trend toward the upper or lower control limits, then quality may be "going out of control," and the reason for the trend has to be checked.

Exhibit 18.16   Example of Quality Control Chart

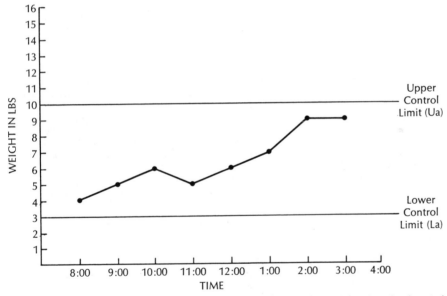

Note: You draw upper and lower "control limits." Then, each hour (or day, etc.) you check the weight (or length, etc.) of your product. That way you can keep track of the trends, to see that things don't get "out of control."

Quality Control in Action—An Optional Example

The most widely used quality control charts are called $\overline{X}$ and R charts. $\overline{X}$ stands for arithmetic mean (average length, average weight, and the like). R stands for range (the highest and lowest length, weight, and so on) for a sample of merchandise. The two charts are used together to control quality.

The best way to learn how to develop $\overline{X}$ and R charts is by working through an example.[11] Let's assume that we want to develop control charts to

362 monitor the weight in ounces of the contents of containers we're filling on an assembly line. The containers should hold at least 60 ounces. In order to guarantee the weight, the machinery must be set to deliver slightly more than 60 ounces. We don't want to inspect all the hundreds of bottles produced every hour. So we take *samples* of five containers every three minutes for an hour (20 samples in all). (In practice, it's really up to you how many samples you choose, and when.) The weights of each container we sample are presented in Exhibit 18–17. For each of the 20 samples we also show the average weight ($\overline{X}$) and the range (R). Notice for example, that the average weight for sample number one was calculated by adding up the weights of the five containers in this sample and then dividing by five:

$$
\begin{array}{c}
61.3 \\
60.5 \\
62.4 \\
62.4 \\
62.0 \\
\hline
308.6 \\
\end{array}
$$

$$\frac{308.6}{5} = 61.7 \text{ ounces}$$

Exhibit 18.17   Basic Data for Example Discussed in Text

The Weight of the Containers in Ounces

| | Sample Number | Sample Values | | | | | For Each Sample: | |
		(1)	(2)	(3)	(4)	(5)	Mean $\overline{X}$	Range R
For each	1	61.3	60.5	62.4	62.4	62.0	61.7	1.9
sample (1-20),	2	59.6	61.7	63.0	61.4	62.8	61.7	3.4
we tested 5	3	61.4	62.4	61.7	61.4	62.4	61.9	1.0
containers,	4	62.0	61.9	63.2	61.9	62.2	62.2	1.3
then took the	5	62.4	61.9	61.7	61.6	60.5	61.6	1.9
mean ($\overline{X}$)	6	63.8	62.5	63.9	61.9	61.4	62.7	2.5
and range (R)	7	63.3	61.6	63.2	60.7	61.4	62.0	2.6
samples	8	61.1	61.3	63.2	62.8	62.0	62.1	2.1
	9	62.5	61.9	63.8	61.6	63.0	62.6	2.2
	10	62.1	61.7	62.0	61.7	62.9	62.1	1.2
	11	61.7	62.6	62.3	61.2	60.8	61.7	1.8
	12	63.8	62.3	63.4	64.1	61.3	62.8	2.8
	13	60.6	61.8	63.1	62.8	61.7	62.0	2.5
	14	62.0	61.2	62.1	61.7	62.1	61.8	0.9
	15	61.5	63.1	63.9	61.9	60.7	62.2	3.2
	16	63.4	62.6	62.4	61.9	61.8	62.4	1.6
	17	62.1	63.1	64.1	61.4	62.3	62.6	2.7
	18	61.5	63.2	62.4	62.6	62.2	62.4	1.7
	19	61.8	62.2	61.5	61.2	60.8	61.5	1.4
	20	61.5	61.4	63.1	61.6	60.8	61.7	2.3
								41.0

Source: Agee, Taylor, and Torgerson, *Quantitative Analysis for Management Decisions*, p. 166.

Thus the average weight ($\overline{X}$) for sample one is 61.7 ounces.
The range (R) of sample one is simply the difference between the heaviest and lightest container in this sample:

62.4 — 60.5 = 1.9 ounces

Constructing the R Chart. Let's construct the range (R) chart first. We start by calculating the average range for all 20 samples. We do this by adding up the ranges for all samples (1.9, 3.4, 1.0, and so on) and then dividing by the total number of samples, which is 20. Thus the average range is

$$R = 1.9 + 3.4 + 1.0 + \ldots + 2.3 = \frac{41}{20} = 2.05$$

Next we calculate the upper and lower control limits for our R chart. For this we use the special table developed for this purpose. It is presented in Exhibit 18–18. It can be used to help you develop almost any $\overline{X}$ and R chart.

Exhibit 18.18 Special Chart for Use in Constructing any $\overline{X}$ and R Chart

First: Just choose your sample size	Sample Size, n	R Chart: Multiplier for Upper Limit	Multiplier for Lower Limit	$\overline{X}$ Chart Multipliers
	2	3.27	0	1.88
(We used a sample size of 5 in our example)	3	2.58	0	1.02
	4	2.28	0	0.73
	5	2.12	0	0.58
	6	2.00	0	0.48
	7	1.92	0.08	0.42
	8	1.86	0.14	0.37
	9	1.82	0.18	0.34
	10	1.78	0.22	0.31

Second: These are your "special multipliers" for the upper and lower *ranges*.

Third: These are your "special multipliers" for the $\overline{X}$ chart.

Source: Adapted from Agee, Taylor, Torgerson, *Quantitative Analysis for Management Decisions*, p. 165.

Notice from this table that with our sample size of 5 containers, the *special multipliers* for the upper and lower range limits are 2.12, and 0, respectively. We calculate the upper control limit range for our R chart by multiplying 2.12 times the average range for all our samples, which is 2.05:

Upper range control limit = 2.12 × 2.05 = 4.35.

364   Similarly, we calculate our lower contol limit range by multiplying the special multiplier (0) for the lower range times the average range for all 20 samples, which is 2.05. Thus:

Lower range control limit $= 0 \times 2.05 = 0.$

In Exhibit 18–19 we have constructed our range chart. The line we draw for the upper range control limit is at 4.35 ounces. The lower range control limit is at 0 ounces. We have also plotted the range for each of our 20 samples. In a moment we'll see how to use this chart.

Exhibit 18.19   An *R* Chart for the Data of Exhibit 18.17

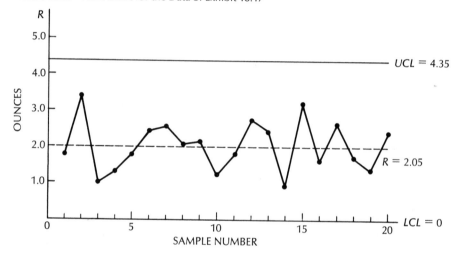

Source: Agee, Taylor, Torgerson, *Quantitative Analysis for Management Decisions*, **p. 167**; copyright © 1976, Prentice-Hall, Inc., Englewood Cliffs, N.J. Reprinted by permission.

Constructing the $\overline{X}$ Chart: First, though, let's construct our $\overline{X}$ chart. First, we calculate the average of all the average weights of our 20 samples as follows:

$$\frac{\text{Overall}}{\text{Average}} = \frac{61.7 + 61.7 + 61.9 + \ldots + 61.7}{20} = 62.09$$

From our special table in Exhibit 18–18, we see that the control limit multiplier for the $\overline{X}$ chart is .58: you use it for both the upper and lower limits. The formula for calculating the upper $\overline{X}$ control limit is:

Upper control limit = overall average + (special multiplier $\times$ average *range*)

In our case, the *upper* control limit $= 62.09 + (.58 \times 2.05) = 63.28$

We construct the *lower* control limit by using the following formula:

Lower control limit = overall average — (special multiplier $\times$ average *range*)

Therefore the lower control limit in this case equals:

$$62.09 - (5.8 \times 2.05) = 60.90$$

In Exhibit 18–20 we have constructed our $\bar{X}$ chart. The upper control limit line is drawn at 63.28 ounces. The lower control limit line is drawn at 60.90 ounces. We've plotted the average weight of each of our samples on the chart.

Exhibit 18.20   An $\bar{X}$ Chart for the Data of Exhibit 18.17

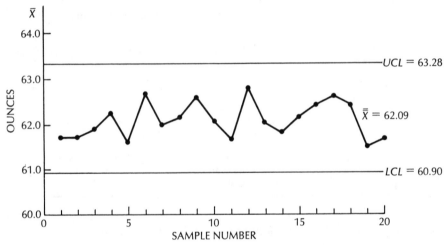

Source: Agee, Taylor, Torgerson, *Quantitative Analysis for Management Decisions*, p. 168.

Using the Charts.   Our $\bar{X}$ and R charts are now ready to be used to control production quality. Samples of five containers would be taken—perhaps every 30 minutes, or perhaps only once or twice a day. The mean or average weights of this sample of five units would be plotted on the $\bar{X}$ chart. The range would be plotted on the R chart. So long as both values fall within their respective control limits, we would assume that the process is "in control." As soon as an $\bar{X}$ value—one of the *average sample weights*—starts pushing the control limits on our $\bar{X}$ chart, we would assume that the average weight of our process has shifted. And if the *range* for a sample starts pushing the upper or lower limits on our R chart, we would assume that the range of our process has increased. In either case, we would now have to seek the cause of the variation and take the appropriate corrective action. The steps in constructing $\bar{X}$, and R charts are summarized in Exhibit 18–21.

Exhibit 18.21 Steps in Developing $\bar{X}$ and R Charts for Quality Control

1. Take *samples* of several (five or six) items every few minutes until you have 20 or 25 samples (each with five or six items).

2. List, for each sample the weight (or length, etc.) of each item in the sample.

3. Compute the Average weight ($\bar{X}$) (or length etc.) for each sample.

4. Compute the range (R) for each sample by subtracting the heaviest (or longest, etc.) item in that sample from the lightest (or shortest, etc.).

5. Compute the overall average range: add up all the 20 (or 25) ranges and divide by 20 (or 25).

6. Using Exhibit 18-18, compute the upper range control limit, and the lower range control limit.

7. Draw your range (R) chart: draw in the upper and lower control limits, and plot the range for each of your 20 or 25 samples.

8. Compute the overall average weight (or length): add up all the 20 (or 25) average weights and divide by 20 (or 25).

9. Using Exhibit 18-18, compute the upper average control limit and the lower average control limit.

10. Draw your average ($\bar{X}$) chart: draw in the upper and lower control limits, and plot the average weight (or length, etc.) for each of your 20 or 25 samples.

11. Take a sample of several (five or six—the same as originally) occasionally. Plot the range (R) and average ($\bar{X}$) on the appropriate chart. If a plot starts pushing a control limit, check to see if the process is going out of control.

Some Important Things to Remember from This Chapter:

1. The most common type of production planning and control is called Order Control. It has six basic steps: 1) receive the orders; 2) develop lists of required materials; 3) develop a route sheet; 4) develop production schedules; 5) dispatch notices to operators to begin work; and 6) follow-up/expedite.

2. Exhibits 18–1 to 18–11 have presented some very important production control charts and forms. These actually form the heart of your production planning and control system; therefore, at this point, you might want to review them so that you can develop your own when the need arises.

3. There are three basic problems you want to avoid by using inventory control: overinvestment; underinvestment; and unbalanced inventory.

4. ABC inventory control is a simple, effective inventory control system. It helps you to focus your control efforts where they are most needed; on those items with the highest dollar volume. Many companies use the economic order quantity (EOQ) model. You can use it for determining what quantity should be ordered in order to minimize total inventory costs.

5. The quality control process consists of establishing quality standards, inspecting goods, and taking corrective action as necessary. Inspection is often

informal, and carried out by workers using their physical senses to get a feel for
the quality of the product. But often you also need a more formal, methodical
quality control system. Inventory control charts (such as the $\overline{X}$ and R charts discussed in this chapter) are simple, effective quality control systems. The steps
in developing $\overline{X}$ and R charts are summarized in Exhibit 18–21; you should review
them again at this point.

STUDY ASSIGNMENTS

1. Answer the questions Bob Ellis posed in the introduction to this
   chapter. For each question indicate what additional information, if
   any, you would need before answering.
2. Discuss the steps in "order control."
3. Briefly explain the basic information you would expect to find in: the
   sales order; a bill of material; a job cost sheet; a route sheet; and a
   shop order.
4. Explain some of the techniques you could use in actually controlling
   production.
5. Draw a PERT chart for some project with which you are familiar (i.e.,
   getting admitted to college; finding a job; tuning an automobile).
6. Compare and contrast a PERT chart and a GANTT chart.
7. Explain the purpose of inventory control.
8. Explain how you would set up an ABC inventory control system.
9. Compute the economic order quantity for the following item: cost,
   $20 per unit; annual usage rate, 250 units per year; cost of ordering,
   $12 per order; annual carrying costs, 15 percent of inventory.
10. Explain how you would go about developing $\overline{X}$ and R charts for qual-
    ity control.

NOTES FOR THE CHAPTER

1. Richard Hopeman, *Production: Concepts, Analysis, Control* (Columbus: Charles
Merrill, 1976) p. 307.
2. Norman Mayer, *Production and Operations Management* (New York: McGraw-
Hill, 1975) p. 266.
3. Richard Hopeman, *Production: Concepts, Analysis, Control*, p. 310.
4. *Prentice-Hall Encyclopedic Dictionary of Systems and Procedures*, (Englewood
Cliffs, N.J.: Prentice-Hall, 1966) p. 502.
5. See Raymond Mayer, *Production and Operations Management*, pp. 282–286.
6. *Prentice-Hall Encyclopedic Dictionary of Systems and Procedures*, pp. 1–2.
7. *Prentice-Hall Encyclopedic Dictionary of Systems and Procedures*, pp. 1–2.
8. *Prentice-Hall Encyclopedic Dictionary*   pp. 203–205.
9. Elwood S. Buffa, *Modern Production Management* (New York: John Wiley,
1973) pp. 643–647.
10. This section and the next adapted from Marvin Agee, Robert Taylor, and
Paul Torgerson, *Quantitative Analysis for Management Decisions* (Englewood Cliffs, N.J.:
Prentice-Hall, 1976) pp. 164–169.
11. This section and the example are from Marvin Agee, Robert Taylor, and
Paul Torgerson, *Quantitative Analysis For Management Decisions*, pp. 164–169.

A Framework for Studying the Management Fundamentals

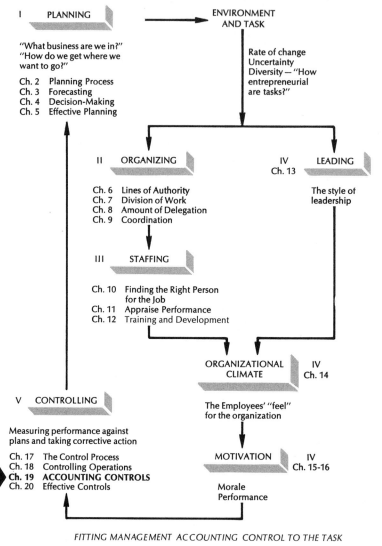

I   PLANNING

"What business are we in?"
"How do we get where we
want to go?"

Ch. 2   Planning Process
Ch. 3   Forecasting
Ch. 4   Decision-Making
Ch. 5   Effective Planning

ENVIRONMENT
AND TASK

Rate of change
Uncertainty
Diversity — "How
entrepreneurial
are tasks?"

Where we are now: Discussing basic management accounting control devices like budgets and performance reports.

II   ORGANIZING

Ch. 6   Lines of Authority
Ch. 7   Division of Work
Ch. 8   Amount of Delegation
Ch. 9   Coordination

IV   LEADING
Ch. 13

The style of
leadership

III   STAFFING

Ch. 10   Finding the Right Person
         for the Job
Ch. 11   Appraise Performance
Ch. 12   Training and Development

ORGANIZATIONAL
CLIMATE

IV
Ch. 14

The Employees' "feel"
for the organization

V   CONTROLLING

Measuring performance against
plans and taking corrective action

Ch. 17   The Control Process
Ch. 18   Controlling Operations
Ch. 19   ACCOUNTING CONTROLS
Ch. 20   Effective Controls

MOTIVATION

IV
Ch. 15-16

Morale
Performance

FITTING MANAGEMENT ACCOUNTING CONTROL TO THE TASK

Dimensions of Control to Remember When Using Management Accounting Controls	*Mechanistic*	*Organic*
Standards	Specific; emphasis on efficiency	General; emphasis on "milestones"
Self vs. imposed control	Control imposed — through formal budgets, etc.	Emphasis on self-control
How frequently you check on performance	Check frequently	Infrequent checks
Control Emphasis	Emphasis on process — on *how* he gets job done	Emphasis on "getting the job done" let employees work out *how*

When you have finished studying

19 Understanding Management
Accounting Controls

You should be able to:

1. *Discuss the importance of the sales budget in the budgeting process.*

2. *Develop a budget.*

3. *Develop a standard cost sheet for a product.*

4. *Explain how you would compute price and quantity variances.*

5. *Compare and contrast "flexible" and "static" budgets.*

6. *Develop a flexible budget.*

7. *Compute at least eight important financial ratios.*

INTRODUCTION

Many people don't like dealing with accounting data, but there's no avoiding the fact that accounting is the language of business. As a manager of any sort —production foreman, sales manager, hospital director, or company president —your ability to understand accounting data will be a very large factor in your success.

You'll have to know how to read financial performance reports, and how to compute the cost of a product. You'll have to know how to budget. And you'll have to know how to analyze a financial statement and draw conclusions about profitability and resource usage.

These are, therefore, some of the crucial management accounting fundamentals we'll deal with in this chapter. We'll focus on four management accounting tools: budgeting; standard costs; flexible budgets; and ratio analysis.

369

BUDGETARY PLANNING AND CONTROL

Budgets and Performance Reports: An Overview

Budgets are formal, financial expressions of a manager's plans. They show targets for things such as sales, cost of materials, production levels, and profits, usually expressed in dollars. These planned targets are the standards against which actual performance is compared and controlled. Budgets are the most widely used control device. Each manager, from first-line foreman to company president, usually has his own budget to use as a standard of comparison.[1] However budgets (as shown in Exhibit 19–1) only represent the standard-setting step in the control process. Actual performance still needs to be measured and compared to these budgeted standards. Then, any necessary corrective action needs to be taken.

Exhibit 19.1   An Example of a Budget

Budget for Machinery Department, June 1978	
Budgeted Expenses:	Budget
Direct Labor	$2,107
Supplies	$3,826
Repairs	$ 402
Overhead (Electricity, etc.)	$ 500
TOTAL EXPENSES:	$6,835

Your company's accountants are responsible for collecting data on actual performance. They then compile this financial data and feed it back to the appropriate manager. The most common form of feedback is a *performance report* like that in Exhibit 19–2. Typically you would receive a report like this for your unit at the end of some time period (say, each

Exhibit 19.2   An Example of a Performance Report

Performance Report for Machinery Department, June, 1978			
	Budget	Actual	Variance	Explanation
Direct Labor	$2,107	$2,480	$373 over	had to put men on overtime.
Supplies	$3,826	$4,200	$374 over	wasted 2 crates of material.
Repairs	$ 402	$ 150	$252 under	—
Overhead (Electricity, etc.)	$ 500	$ 500	0	—
TOTAL	$6,835	$7,330	$495 over	

month). As in Exhibit 19–2, the performance report shows budgeted or *planned* targets. Next to these, it shows your department's *actual* performance. The report also lists the differences between budgeted and actual amounts (these are usually called "variances"). There is also sometimes a space on the report for you to explain any such variances. After reviewing the performance report, you and your boss can then take any corrective action that seems warranted.

Steps in the Budgeting Process

The Sales Forecast. The first step in budgeting is to develop a sales forecast and sales budget such as that in Exhibit 19–3. As you can see, the sales budget shows the number of units to be shipped in each period (usually per month) and the sales revenue expected from these sales.

Exhibit 19.3 A Sales Budget for the XYZ Company

		First Quarter	Second Quarter	Third Quarter	Fourth Quarter
Eastern Division	Number of Units	400	501	600	480
	$*	$800	$1,002	$1,200	$960
Western Division	Number of Units	350	380	400	301
	$*	$700	$760	$800	$602
	Total Units	750	881	1,000	781

*At average of $200 per unit.

The Production and Materials Budgets. Next, as you can see in Exhibit 19–4 you can develop your other budgets. These show what you expect to spend for materials, labor, administration, and so forth, in order to fulfill the requirements of the sales budget. For example, the production budget (Exhibit 19–5) shows the number of units you have to manufacture in order to fill monthly sales requirements.

From its bills of materials and route sheets (discussed in Chapter 18) your production department knows the raw materials, components, and labor required for each product. Therefore costs of materials budgets and cost of labor budgets, such as those in Exhibit 19–6, can be developed next.

There's No Ironclad Procedure. In practice each department in your company usually has its own budget. The marketing department might have a budget such as in Exhibit 19–7. This shows how much they expect to spend on salesmen and other expenses in order to fulfill the sales target. Other budgets will be developed for the personnel department, research depart-

Exhibit 19.4   The Sales Budget is the Foundation for All your Other Budgets

The Central Importance of the Sales Budget

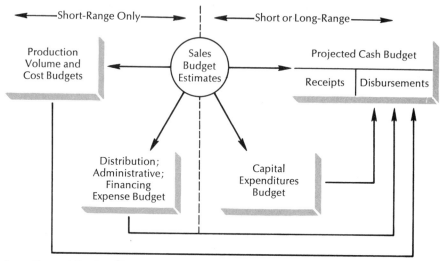

Source: Figure and Note From Winston Korn and Thomas Boyd, *Managerial Accounting* (New York: Wiley 1975) p. 269.

Note: The sales budget is the most important individual budget; all other budgets depend upon its forecast of sales volume. For example, production can be determined in advance only when expected sales volume is known, and only when production has been set can material, labor, and overhead cost standards be established. Similarly the volume of cash that will be available for the forthcoming period cannot be determined without a sales volume estimate. The dependence of the various budgets on the sales budget is shown in the figure.

ment (and even the accounting department). These budgets specify targets in dollar terms for things such as sales revenue, labor costs, insurance costs, taxes, and so forth.

In practice, managers do not stick to a rigid sequence of steps when developing budgets. Instead,

> . . . . Tentative budgets are proposed, discussed, and revised again and again as they move upward toward final approval. The process is one of progressive dialogue; an executive seldom receives a budget proposal from a subordinate without having discussed vital aspects of it ahead

Exhibit 19.5   Production Budget for XYZ Company

	First Quarter	Second Quarter	Third Quarter	Fourth Quarter
Est. Sales in Units	750	881	1,000	781
Less: Inventory at Start of Period	200			
TOTAL Units to be Produced	550	881	1,000	781

Exhibit 19.6   Cost of Materials and Labor Budget of XYZ Company

	First Quarter	Second Quarter	Third Quarter	Fourth Quarter
Total Units to be Produced	550	881	1,000	781
Cost of Materials	$225	$440	$500	$391
Cost of Labor	$112	$220	$225	$195

of time. Through vertical and horizontal communication within the management group, these plans are adjusted and readjusted until they become a set of integrated and realizable objectives consistent with overall company policies.[2]

An Example of the Budgeting Process

Let's look at an example to see how budgeting works in practice

The Organization. The organization chart of the Clean-Em Soap Company is presented in Exhibit 19–8. The firm manufactures hand soaps for both industrial and consumer markets. There is an industrial sales division whose salesmen sell to factories and office buildings. There is a consumer sales division whose salesmen sell to retail outlets such as supermarkets and drugstores. Although the packages are a bit different, the "industrial" and "consumer" soaps are about the same and both are produced by Clean-Em's production division.

Whether industrial or consumer, Clean-Em sees itself as the "no frills" soap company. Their soaps are inexpensive ("Cheap," says the president) but effective ("Works great," he says). They accomplish the latter by using good raw materials. They keep the cost down by using inexpensive packaging, minimizing advertising, and leaving "frills" such as perfumes out of their products.

Exhibit 19.7   Marketing Department Budget – XYZ Company

	First Quarter	Second Quarter	Third Quarter	Fourth Quarter
Est. Sales in Units	750	881	1,000	781
Salesmen's Expenses	$300	$300	$300	$300
Advertising Expenses	$150	$200	$250	$250
General Administrative Expenses	$100	$100	$100	$100
TOTAL BUDGET EXPENSES	$550	$600	$650	$650

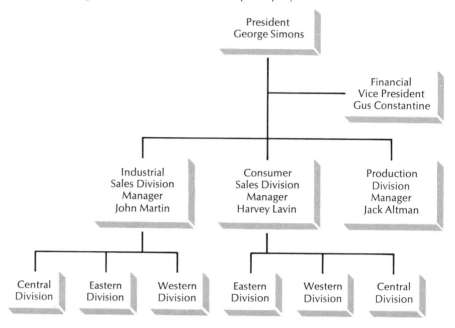

The Marketing Plan. Clean-Em's fiscal or budget year begins on July 1, each year. Early in March 1978, the president, George Simons asks each of his sales-division managers to submit a tentative marketing plan (or budget). He asks them to show their estimated sales in units, the estimated size of their sales forces, the promotion and advertising they intend to use, and also their anticipated revenues and expenses.

Harvey Lavin, the manager of the consumer products division, starts by asking all his regional salesmen for a forecast of expected sales in each of their districts. He also asks each of them to spell out in detail a marketing program for the coming year, and to estimate its costs and its result on sales volume. The marketing plans are to include recommendations on advertising expenditures, product displays, additional sales help, and so forth. John Martin, industrial sales division manager, follows a similar procedure.

Both sales managers then review the projected sales and the underlying marketing plans with their salespeople. Mr. Lavin, for example, compares the ratio of expenses to sales for each of his salesmen with the 1977 ratio and with the ratios for other regions. He recommends that his central division salesman add new sales agents to service the rapidly growing discount drugstores. He turns down a proposal from the eastern division salesman for an increase in television advertising. He says it is too costly and also incompatible with the "no frills" image Clean-Em tries to project.

After additional discussion the two sales managers present the tentative sales and expense budgets shown in Exhibit 19–9 to Gus Constantine,
the financial vice-president.

Exhibit 19.9 Budgeted Sales, and Marketing Expenses, by Division for the Clean-Em Company

	First Quarter	Second Quarter	Third Quarter	Fourth Quarter
Industrial Division				
Sales in Units	150	175	180	200
Sales in Dollars	$30,000	$35,000	$36,000	$40,000
Salesmen's Expenses	$ 1,000	$ 1,000	$ 1,000	$ 1,000
Advertising Expenses	$ 1,000	$ 1,200	$ 1,000	$ 1,500
Administrative Expenses	$ 1,500	$ 1,500	$ 1,500	$ 1,500
Consumer Division				
Sales in Units	200	300	450	600
Sales in Dollars	$40,000	$60,000	$90,000	$120,000
Salesmen's Expenses	$ 1,500	$ 2,000	$ 3,000	$ 3,500
Advertising Expenses	$ 800	$ 900	$ 1,000	$ 1,000
Administrative Expenses	$ 1,800	$ 1,800	$ 1,800	$ 1,800
Totals:				
Sales in Units	350	475	630	800
Expenses	$7,600	$8,400	$9,300	$10,300

Mr. Constantine questions John Martin, the industrial sales manager,
about the slow growth of sales in his division and also about the high ratio
of marketing expenses to sales. When confronted with the expense/sales
ratios for the company as a whole, Mr. Martin decides to revise his plans. He
particularly wants to concentrate on cutting advertising expenses.

The Production Plan. At this point Mr. Constantine asks the two
sales managers to meet in his office with Jack Altman, the production manager. The sales managers give Mr. Altman their proposed sales budgets and
forecasts. Mr. Altman complains that he can't meet these sales forecasts with
his current level of manpower. He says he either has to hire additional operators, or have more of his people work overtime; in any case, production
expenses will have to rise. He proposes the production division budget presented in Exhibit 19–10. At this point Mr. Simons, the president, walks in.
He has been kept up to date on all the discussions, and concurs with the
recommended marketing and production budgets.

The Profit Plan. After the meeting, Mr. Constantine assembles the
available data into a tentative profit plan for the coming year. This tentative
profit plan is usually called a "budgeted *income statement*," or "pro forma
income statement." As you can see in Exhibit 19–11 it shows expected sales,
expected expenses, and expected income or profits for the year.

Exhibit 19.10   Production Budget for Clean-Em Company — Including Plant Expenses

	First Quarter	Second Quarter	Third Quarter	Fourth Quarter
Estimated Sales in Units	350	475	630	800
Cost of Materials	$1,750	$2,380	$3,150	$4,000
Cost of Labor	$ 700	$ 950	$ 760	$1,000
Plant Overhead	$ 400	$ 400	$ 400	$ 400
TOTAL COSTS	$2,850	$3,750	$4,310	$5,400

The Cash Budget.   Mr. Constantine knows that cash usually doesn't flow into Clean-Em in such a way as to coincide precisely with cash disbursements. For example, some customers may take 35 days to pay their bills, but employees expect to be paid every week. Therefore, he develops the cash budget presented in Exhibit 19–12. This shows, for each month, the amount of cash the company can expect to receive and the amount it can expect to disburse. There should be a cash shortage in June. Mr. Constantine expects to rectify this by having the company take out a short term loan from its bank.

The Balance Sheet.   Finally, Mr. Constantine draws up a budgeted *balance sheet* for the company. This is a (projected) statement of the financial position of Clean-Em. It shows assets (such as cash and equipment), liabilities (such as long term debt), and net worth, (the excess of assets over other liabilities). It is presented in Exhibit 19–13. It shows managers, owners, and creditors what the company's projected financial picture will be in terms of assets, liabilities, and net worth at the end of the year. The company now has a complete set of budgets for use in planning and control for the coming year.[3]

Exhibit 19.11   Budgeted Income Statement for Clean-Em Company for 197_

Sales Revenues	$451,000	
Less: Cost of materials		$11,280
Cost of Labor		$ 3,410
Plant Overhead		$ 1,600
Marketing Expenses		$35,600
TOTAL EXPENSES		$51,890
Net Income Expected		$399,110
Sales in Units = 2,255		

Exhibit 19.12   Cash Budget for Clean-Em Company

Necessary Because Cash Revenues Do Not Always Coincide Exactly With Cash Disbursements.

	First Quarter	Second Quarter	Third Quarter	Fourth Quarter
Cash Receipts From Customers	$20,000	$22,000	$85,000	$214,000
Cash Disbursements				
Materials	$ 1,750	$ 2,380	$ 3,150	$ 4,000
Salaries	$ 3,200	$ 3,950	$ 4,760	$ 5,500
Other	$15,400	$18,050	$16,150	$ 18,800
TOTAL	$22,850	$24,280	$24,050	$ 28,300
Cash Excess (or deficiency)	($2,850)	($2,280)	$60,950	$185,700
Borrow	$2,850	$2,280		
Repay			$ 2,850	$ 2,280

USING STANDARD COSTS FOR CONTROL

Standard costing is a second widely used management accounting control tool.

Standard Product Costs

In our example the production manager of the Clean-Em Company was asked to estimate his production expenses based on the sales forecast he was given. He can do this because his company's accountants have developed a file of "standard costs" for each product the firm manufactures.

A standard cost sheet for one of Clean-Em's soap products is shown in Exhibit 19–14. From the *bill of materials* the accountants knew the materials to be used in this product. From the *route sheet* they knew the jobs to be performed in the manufacture of the product, the kinds of labor to be used, and the amount of labor time that should be necessary to perform each operation. *And from past experience they know the standard costs of each of these bits of material and labor involved in the manufacture of the product.*

On a standard cost sheet like that in Exhibit 19–14 they list all the materials and all the operations involved in manufacturing the product. Also listed is the standard (or, if not available, estimated) cost for each. Then all these costs are added up in order to get the standard cost for the product— a bar of soap. The company's accountants have a standard cost sheet for each of Clean-Em's products.

Exhibit 19.13   Budgeted Balance Sheet for Clean-Em Company, 197_

ASSETS	
Current Assets	
Cash	$ 83,420
Accounts Receivables	$100,000
Inventory	$ 10,000
Marketable Securities	$100,000
Equipment and Plant	$200,500
TOTAL ASSETS	**$493,920**

LIABILITIES AND OWNERS' EQUITY*	
Current Liabilities	
Accounts Payable	$280,000
Owners' Equity	$213,920
TOTAL LIABILITIES AND OWNERS' EQUITY	**$493,920**

*These may be viewed as *claims against assets*; this is why total assets will always equal total liabilities.

Exhibit 19.14   A Standard Cost Sheet for Clean-Em Soap Product "A"

Standard Cost Sheet

Product: **"A"**   Quantity :   10,000

Description: hand soap

Standard Cost: $1000   Standard Cost Per Unit: $0.10

Operation or Item	Materials			Labor		
	Quantity	Price	Total	Hours	Rate	Total
Raw materials	4,000 LBS	.20 per lb	$800			
Mix material in vats				100	$2.00 per hr.	$200
TOTAL			$800			$200

Standard Costs in Action—An Optional Example   379

Suppose that during the year the production manager of Clean-Em receives the performance report presented in Exhibit 19–15.[4] For the month of May the factory produced, as planned, 10,000 bars of hand soap. According to the standard cost sheet for this product (Exhibit 19–14) these should have cost the company $1000 to produce—$800 for material, and $200 for labor.

Exhibit 19.15   Performance Report for Clean-Em Company Production Department, May

PERFORMANCE REPORT FOR CLEAN-EM COMPANY
PRODUCTION DEPARTMENT, MAY

10,000 Bars of Soap

	Budgeted*	Actual	Variance
Material	$800	$1,100	$300 over
Labor	$200	$ 200	0

*Based on standard costs.

These standard costs for material and labor are shown on the performance report in Exhibit 19–15. They are the targets the production manager was shooting for but, as you can see, the *actual* material cost was $1,100. So the factory overspent here. Actual labor costs, though, were right on target.

The production manager knows that there are two reasons why his material expenses may be higher than planned. Perhaps his factory used *more material* than was budgeted. Or they may have used the right quantity of materials, but had to pay a *higher price* for this material than planned. Based on the information contained in the standard cost sheet for this bar of soap (Exhibit 19–14) the manager makes some quick calculations. These are summarized in Exhibit 19–16. First he wants to see if the overspending is the result of using too much material—a *quantity variance*. For 10,000 bars of soap the factory should have used 4,000 pounds of materials; but actually they purchased (and used) 5,000 pounds. The quantity variance is:

(5,000 pounds — 4,000 pounds) times the standard cost per pound of materials (20¢). Thus the quantity variance is
$$1,000 \times .20, \text{ or } \$200.$$

380   Next the production manager computes the *price variance*. This is the difference between the standard price and the actual price paid, multiplied by the actual quantity purchased:

(actual price paid — standard price) × actual quantity purchased.

In this case the standard price per pound was 20¢; but actually the factory paid 22¢ per pound. Since the factory purchased (and used) 5,000 pounds of material, the price variance was:

5,000 × (.22¢ — .20¢), or $100

Exhibit 19.16   The Production Manager's Calculations

Why the Plant Spent Too Much on Materials

For 10,000 bars of soap:

Should have used 4,000 lbs of material at .20 ¢/lb

Instead, Plant actually used: 5,000 lbs of material at .22¢/lb

Quantity Variance	5,000 lbs
	−4,000 lbs
	1,000 lbs, X $.20 =	$200

Price Variance	5,000 lbs (actually used)
	X$.02 (actual minus standard price per lb)
	$100

$200 + $100 = $300 = total materials variance

Standard Costs in Action—Taking Corrective Action

Let's see how we could use standard cost information for taking corrective action. In our example, the production manager knew that his department had spent $300 more on material than planned. He finds (after doing his standard cost computations) that of this $300, $200 was spent using 1,000 pounds more material than planned. The extra $100 resulted from spending 2¢ more per pound than was anticipated.

The fact that too much material was used is a problem he discusses with his production foreman. When confronted, the foreman explains that about 1,000 pounds of material was wasted when a new employee inadvertently opened the wrong valve on a machine. The production manager recommends that the foreman meet with the plant personnel manager in order to tighten up hiring and training procedures so that accidents such as this don't happen again.

Next, the production manager meets with his plant purchasing manager. The latter is the person most responsible for controlling the prices paid for raw materials. The purchasing manager explains that they had to pay an extra 2¢ per pound because they have been ordering in smaller quantities than usual, thus losing their volume discounts. The purchasing manager recommends that they meet with the plant's inventory control manager. The former says that although they have been cutting down on storage costs they have done so at the expense of large order-volume discounts. He suggests reevaluating these inventory policies. The production manager concurs and sets up a meeting between the three of them for later that day. With the help of budgets, performance reports, and standard costs, he has compared actual to planned performance, identified problems, and initiated corrective action.

FLEXIBLE BUDGETS FOR CONTROL

Eariler in this chapter we discussed budgeting. Now let's turn to another management accounting tool: flexible budgets.

What Is a Flexible Budget?

Unlike the budgets we discussed earlier, flexible budgets are prepared for a *range* of activity. Thus a flexible budget might show target sales expenses, materials expenses, profits, and so on, for 3,000, 4,000, 5,000, and 6,000 units of production. This provides a *dynamic* basis for comparison. The flexible budget approach says, "You tell me what your output was during the month. I'll provide a budget that specifies what costs should have been *for that specific output*." Flexible budgets are also sometimes called variable budgets.[5]

Why Use Flexible Budgets for Controlling?

Look at the budget and performance report in Exhibit 19–17. This manager's department was budgeted to produce 5,000 units of merchandise. And *at this level of output* they were budgeted to spend $2,100 for labor, $500 for supplies, and $500 for repairs. Notice, though, that their actual production was only 4,700 units—they produced 300 units less than expected. Since they produced less merchandise than planned, their costs were also lower than planned. For example, they spent $100 less on labor than planned, and $10 less on supplies.

Suppose you were this manager's boss. What would this performance report tell you about his performance? For one thing, you would see that his department has not been *effective* in carrying out its goals—it produced 300

Exhibit 19.17   "Static" Performance Report for Department for Month of June, 197X

	Actual	Budget	Variance
Units Produced	4,700	5,000	300 under
Labor Cost	$2,000	$2,100	$100 under
Supplies Cost	$ 490	$ 500	$ 10 under
Repairs Cost	$ 500	$ 500	0
TOTAL COSTS	$2,990	$3,100	

Note: Did they spend less than planned because they were efficient, or because they produced 4,700 units instead of 5,000 units?

fewer units than planned. But the performance report wouldn't tell you anything about his department's *efficiency*. Certainly, according to the performance report, he used less labor and fewer supplies than planned. But was this because of efficiency? Or was it simply because they produced 300 fewer units than planned? You can't answer this from the performance report, since the target costs assume a production level of 5,000 units rather than the 4,700 units actually produced.

Flexible Budgeting in Action

Let's see how using flexible budgeting for control could clarify the situation. In Exhibit 19–18, you'll find a flexible budget for this same department for the month of June. Based on the standard costs per unit for labor, supplies, and repairs, this flexible budget shows the expected costs for *several* levels of activity from 4,600 units to 5,200 units. For example, if 4,600 units are produced, the expected labor costs are $1,932. The expected labor costs if 5,200 units are produced would be $2,184.

Exhibit 19.18   A "Flexible" budget for the Same Department as in Exhibits 19.17

	Various Levels of Activity			
Units Produced	4,600	4,700	5,000	5,200
Labor (.42/unit)	$1,932	$1,974	$2,100	$2,184
Supplies (.10/unit)	$ 460	$ 470	$ 500	$ 520
Repairs (.10/unit)	$ 460	$ 470	$ 500	$ 520
TOTAL EXPENSES	$2,852	$2,914	$3,100	$3,224

Now look at the performance report in Exhibit 19–19. This report (as did Exhibit 19–17) shows the actual costs incurred in producing 4,700 untis. *But this time the budgeted targets are also based on 4,700 units.* Now by comparing the budgeted costs for 4,700 units of production with the actual costs, you can see just how efficient this manager was. He actually spent more on labor, supplies, and repairs than was budgeted for this level of production (4,700 units). His explanations are noted on the performance report. Now you would be in a good position for initiating some type of corrective action.

Exhibit 19.19 Performance Report Based on "Flexible" Budget for Same Department Described in Exhibit 19.17

	Actual	Budget*	Variance	Explanations
Labor	$2,000	$1,974	$26 over	none offered
Supplies	$ 490	$ 470	$20 over	one assembly wasted when machine left running
Repairs	$ 500	$ 470	$30 over	machine inadvertently left running
TOTALS	$2,990	$2,914	$76 over	

Units Originally Scheduled: 5,000
Units Actually Produced: 4,700

*For 4,700 units actually produced

Note: With this flexible budget, you can see that this manager actually *overspent* a bit; in Exhibit 19.17 it seemed he had *underspent*, since in Exhibit 19.17 you had to compare his actual expenditures at 4,700 units with his budgeted expenditures at 5,000 units.

CONTROL THROUGH RATIO ANALYSIS, AND RETURN ON INVESTMENT (ROI)

The last management accounting control tool we'll discuss focuses on ratio analysis. A ratio is a measure of the relationship between two figures. It can be expressed as a percentage ($\frac{1}{4} \times 100 = 25\%$); a proportion (1:4); or a fraction ($\frac{1}{4}$). A *financial* ratio compares one financial measure (such as profits) to another (such as sales).

When you analyze a financial statement (such as a balance sheet) a single figure like "profits" or "sales" really doesn't tell you much. Usually you're more interested in things such as profits relative to last year, or sales relative to those of competitors, or profits relative to sales. It is this kind of *relative* comparison that financial ratio analysis provides for you.

Some of the most common financial ratios are presented in Exhibit 19–20. There are four basic categories: 1) liquidity ratios; 2) leverage ratios; 3) activities ratios; and 4) profitability ratios. Let's look at each.

384   **Exhibit 19.20**   Some Common Financial Ratios

Name of Ratio	*Formula*

1. *Liquidity Ratios* (measuring the ability of the firm to meet its maturing obligations)

Current ratio	$\dfrac{\text{Current assets}}{\text{Current liabilities}}$
Acid-test ratio	$\dfrac{\text{Cash and equivalent}}{\text{Current liabilities}}$
Cash velocity	$\dfrac{\text{Sales}}{\text{Cash and equivalent}}$
Inventory to net working capital	$\dfrac{\text{Inventory}}{\text{Current assets—Current liabilities}}$

2. *Leverage Ratios* (measuring the contributions of financing by owners compared with financing provided by creditors)

Debt to equity	$\dfrac{\text{Total debt}}{\text{Net worth}}$
Coverage of fixed charges	$\dfrac{\text{Net profit before fixed charges}}{\text{Fixed charges}}$
Current liability to net worth	$\dfrac{\text{Current liability}}{\text{Net worth}}$
Fixed assets to net worth	$\dfrac{\text{Fixed assets}}{\text{Net worth}}$

3. *Activities Ratios* (measuring the effectiveness of the employment of resources)

Inventory turnover	$\dfrac{\text{Sales}}{\text{Inventory}}$
Net working capital turnover	$\dfrac{\text{Sales}}{\text{Net working capital}}$
Fixed-assets turnover	$\dfrac{\text{Sales}}{\text{Fixed assets}}$
Average collection period	$\dfrac{\text{Receivables}}{\text{Average sales per day}}$
Equity capital turnover	$\dfrac{\text{Sales}}{\text{Net worth}}$
Total capital turnover	$\dfrac{\text{Sales}}{\text{Total assets}}$

(Continued)

Name of Ratio	Formula
4. *Profitability Ratios* (indicating degree of success in achieving desired profit levels)	
Gross operating margin	$\dfrac{\text{Gross operating profit}}{\text{Sales}}$
Net operating margin	$\dfrac{\text{Net operating profit}}{\text{Sales}}$
Sales margin	$\dfrac{\text{Net profit after taxes}}{\text{Sales}}$
Productivity of assets	$\dfrac{\text{Gross income less taxes}}{\text{Total assets}}$
Return on capital	$\dfrac{\text{Net profit after taxes}}{\text{Net worth}}$
Net profit on working capital	$\dfrac{\text{Net operating profit}}{\text{Net working capital}}$

Source: W. Warren Haynes, Joseph L. Massie, and Marc J. Wallace, Jr., *Management: Analysis, Concepts, and Cases*, 3rd Ed. (Englewood Cliffs, N. J.: Prentice-Hall, Inc., 1975 pp. 264-66.

Liquidity Ratios

Liquidity ratios measure the ability of your firm to meet its "current" financial obligations—those that come due during the coming year. They help answer questions such as "Do we have enough cash on hand to repay the loans that come due this year?" One measure of liquidity is the *current ratio,* which is the ratio of current assets to current liabilities:

$$\frac{\text{Current Assets}}{\text{Current Liabilities}}$$

From the financial statements in Exhibit 19–21 we see that the current assets for the Ajax Company amount to $3,400. Current liabilities amount to $2,800. Therefore, their current ratio =

$$\frac{\text{Current assets}}{\text{Current liabilities}} = \frac{\$3,400}{\$2,800} = 1.21.$$

In other words, this company has 1.21 times more current assets than current liabilities.

Another test of liquidity is the *asset-test* or *"quick"* ratio. This is the ratio of:

$$\frac{\text{Cash and current assets equivalent to cash}}{\text{Current liabilities}}$$

Exhibit 19.21 Balance Sheet, and Income Statement for the Ajax Company

Balance Sheet	
Assets	
Current Assets	$3,400
Cash	1,000
Inventory	2,400
TOTAL	$3,400
Equipment	$8,000
TOTAL ASSETS	$11,400
Liabilities	
Current liabilities	
Accounts payable	2,800
Long Term Debt (Bonds) Payable	$4,000
Owner's Equity	2,600
TOTAL LIABILITIES	$11,400

Income Statement	
Sales Revenues	$35,000
Expenses	
Interest on Bonds	2,000
Labor	13,000
Materials	11,820
Other	3,500
TOTAL	$30,320
NET INCOME	$4,680

This test shows the ratio of those current assets that can be *quickly converted* into cash, divided by current liabilities. (Current assets such as inventories usually cannot be quickly converted into cash.) The asset-test ratio therefore helps show the company's ability for repaying current liabilities *quickly*.

For the Ajax Company the asset-test ratio equals

$$\frac{\$1,000}{\$2,800} = .36$$

Leverage Ratios

Leverage ratios measure your firm's ability to pay its total (current *and* long-term) debts—its "solvency." They also measure the ratio of the funds contributed to the company by owners, compared to the funds contributed by creditors (banks, bond holders, and so on). One such measure is the "*debt to equity ratio.*" This measures:

$$\frac{\text{Total debt}}{\text{Net worth}} \, ^6$$

For the Ajax Company the debt to equity ratio is

$$\frac{\$6,800}{\$2,600} = 3.07$$

Another leverage ratio is called "*coverage of fixed charges.*" This shows the firm's ability to pay its fixed charges for interest payments, bank loans, and so forth. For the Ajax Company the coverage of fixed charges is:

$$\frac{\text{Net Profit Before Fixed Charges}}{\text{Fixed Charges (i.e.: for Interest)}} = \frac{\$6,680}{\$2,000} = 3.34$$

Activities Ratios

Activities ratios measure how effectively your company is using its resources. The higher the activity ratio, the more effective your company is at using its resources. For example, "*inventory turnover*" is the ratio of:

$$\frac{\text{Sales}}{\text{Inventory}}$$

For the Ajax Company the inventory turnover is:

$$\frac{\$35,000}{\$2,400} = 14.58 \text{ times}$$

Another activities ratio is "*total capital turnover.*" This is equal to:

$$\frac{\text{Sales}}{\text{Total Assets}}$$

For the Ajax Company total capital turnover equals:

$$\frac{\$35,000}{\$11,400} = 3.07 \text{ times}$$

Profitability Ratios

Profitability ratios relate profits to things such as sales or total assets. Most owners are not interested in just how much profits ($100,000; $150,000; and so on) the company makes in a year. Instead they also want to know how profitable the company was *relative to the amount of money invested in the company*. One measure of this is the "*rate of return on investment*." This is equal to:

$$\frac{\text{Net profit}}{\text{Total assets}}$$

For the Ajax Company the rate of return on investment is:

$$\frac{\$4,680}{\$11,400} = 41\%$$

Another widely used profitability ratio is the "sales margin" or "profit margin." This measures the ratio of:

$$\frac{\text{Net profit}}{\text{Sales}}$$

It tells you how efficient and productive the company has been in generating "profits" from its sales revenue. For the Ajax Company the sales or profit margin equals:

$$\frac{\$4,680}{\$35,000} = 13\%$$

Using Financial Ratio Analysis for Control

Let's look at an example to see how to use ratio analysis for control.

Ajax's managers have set standards or targets for various ratios: they are presented in Exhibit 19–22. Such target ratios may be based on the company's experience for the past few years. But you can also obtain published industry norms from financial services. An example of the industry averages (or norms) for various industries' ratios are presented in Exhibit 19–23.

By comparing Ajax's actual ratios with their own target ratios the managers are able to identify unfavorable discrepancies. They can then take corrective action as necessary. For example, in comparing their actual ratios with their target ratios (Exhibit 19–22) Ajax managers find that their current ratio is well below target. This could mean that unless the company quickly replenishes its cash balances it may have problems paying for its current commitments.

Exhibit 19.22   Target and Actual Financial Ratios for Ajax Company

Ratios	Target	Actual	Implication
Current ratio	2.50	1.21	Too low; take out long term loan from bank
Quick ratio	.40	.36	—
Coverage of Fixed charges	2.50	3.34	Could increase long-term debt payments
Inventory turnover	15.00	14.58	—
Total capital turnover	3.00	3.07	—
Return on investment	.35	.41	—
Profit margin	.20	.13	Too low; find out why expenses too high, and take corrective action.

Notice also that the sales or profit margin is also well under target. This is an indication that Ajax needs to get better control over its expenses and thereby raise its profits.

Controlling Performance Through Return on Investment (ROI)

Many managers control performance through a network of *interlocking financial ratios*. One such system is diagrammed in Exhibit 19–24.

Notice that the overall (and most important) measure of profitability is the return on investment (ROI). Also notice from the diagram that the ROI itself can be broken down into two component financial ratios: *profit margin*, and *turnover*. In other words

Profit margin $\times$ turnover $=$ ROI, or:

$$\frac{\text{Profit}}{\text{sales}} \times \frac{\text{sales}}{\text{investment}} = \frac{\text{Profit}}{\text{investment}} = \text{ROI}$$

Similarly, the profit margin and the turnover rate can each be broken down into their components.

The ROI approach can help keep performance in perspective. For example, you can see that the ROI as a measure of overall profitability can be influenced by factors such as excessive investment and high selling expenses. Thus by doing a little detective work you could use this ROI approach to help encouver the causes of poor performance. For example, it could turn out that Ajax's low profit margin is related to unusually high selling expenses. Then management could begin tracking down the central problem: Do the salesmen need better training? Is the sales manager not up to the job? Is the company spending too much on advertising? Once the problem was isolated, corrective action could be taken.

Exhibit 19.23 Some Financial Ratios for Several Industries

Line of Business	Year	Current Assets to Current Debt (Times)	Net Profit on Net Sales (Percent)	Net Profit to Tangible Net Worth (Percent)	Net Sales to Tangible Net Worth (Times)	Collection Period (Days)	Net Sales to Inventory (Times)	Fixed Asset to Tangible Net Worth (Percent)	Total Debt to Tangible Net Worth (Percent)	Inventory to Net Working Capital (Percent)
Agricultural Chemicals	65	1.80	1.34	4.36	3.37	45	7.5	57.8	132.9	83.1
	67	1.88	2.17	6.90	3.08	56	6.9	53.2	115.9	74.4
	69	1.86	1.45	5.30	2.78	57	6.6	43.8	123.3	76.5
	71	2.06	2.08	7.11	2.84	57	8.5	41.7	139.4	59.8
	73	1.98	3.65	16.15	3.39	50	9.9	36.2	100.4	55.1
Airplane Parts & Accessories	65	2.15	3.78	10.03	2.90	48	6.8	46.8	74.5	84.7
	67	1.78	4.44	16.67	3.23	39	5.9	55.1	93.5	103.7
	69	2.16	3.04	9.06	2.92	59	5.2	53.6	72.4	86.6
	71	2.47	1.63	3.60	2.24	58	4.9	57.5	107.2	82.0
	73	2.24	3.94	12.70	2.81	52	4.7	50.1	120.6	88.2
Bakery Products	65	1.89	1.52	8.40	4.49	17	27.2	80.2	67.7	54.3
	67	1.84	2.37	10.21	4.15	18	30.4	78.8	57.3	61.7
	69	1.88	2.54	8.70	4.08	22	28.9	80.8	49.6	57.9
	71	2.07	1.77	6.58	4.18	21	27.5	79.5	55.8	51.5
	73	1.90	1.37	6.45	4.25	26	22.7	74.9	77.7	62.5
Blast Furnaces, Steel Works & Rolling Mills	65	*	*	*	*	*	*	*	*	*
	67	2.58	4.07	8.01	1.90	35	4.9	61.4	50.8	92.4
	69	2.56	3.66	8.66	1.98	43	5.4	58.5	55.9	81.1
	71	2.90	2.70	6.37	2.15	39	4.8	80.5	69.9	95.7
	73	2.13	4.31	10.11	2.72	41	6.7	69.9	74.5	91.4
Book Publishing & Printing	65	2.97	7.36	14.74	2.12	71	3.8	31.3	66.0	67.3
	67	2.63	5.20	10.44	2.32	58	4.1	28.8	77.2	71.4
	69	2.52	4.70	8.04	2.13	61	4.4	34.8	52.3	72.0
	71	2.59	4.71	8.15	1.94	68	4.1	36.0	57.8	65.6
	73	2.49	4.76	10.14	1.98	64	4.2	35.2	83.1	62.5

Note: Median values taken from Dun's Reviews. *Data not available or not applicable.

Source: Reprinted with special permission of *Dun's Review*, November, 1965, 1967, 1969, 1971, and 1973, Dun and Bradstreet Publications Corporation. Presented in Robert C. Schirley, Michael H. Peters, and Adel I. El-Ansary, *Strategy and Policy Formation: A Multinational Orientation*, (Santa Barbara: John Wiley and Sons, 1976) . 183.

Exhibit 19.24 Relationship of Factors Affecting Return on Investment

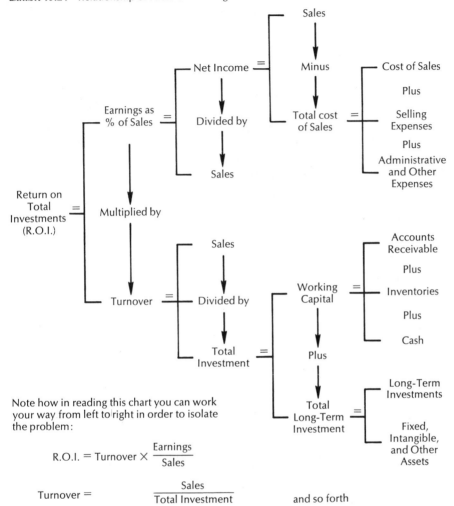

Note how in reading this chart you can work your way from left to right in order to isolate the problem:

$$R.O.I. = Turnover \times \frac{Earnings}{Sales}$$

$$Turnover = \frac{Sales}{Total\ Investment}$$ and so forth

Some Important Things to Remember from This Chapter:

1. Budgets are formal, financial expressions of managers' plans. They show you targets for things such as sales, costs of material, production levels, and profits, usually expressed in dollars.

2. A performance report like that in Exhibit 19–2 complements the budget; it provides you with data on both actual and budgeted figures, and summarizes the discrepancies or variances. It also usually provides a space for explanations.

3. The budgeting process for your company always begins with the development of a sales budget. Then once you know the quantity of goods to be sold in each period, you can develop production budgets, purchasing budgets, cost of goods sold budgets, and so forth.

4. A standard cost sheet, as shown in Exhibit 19–14, is the heart of your standard costing control system. You can use it to estimate the cost of a sales order. And you can compare the standard labor and standard materials costs for the product with the costs you have actually incurred. This can help you to determine the cause of the discrepancy. Was the price paid for material too high? Was too much material used? And so forth.

5. A flexible budget is prepared for a range of activity. The performance report based on the flexible budget shows the actual expenses and the budgeted or target expenses at the *actual* level of production. You can therefore use it to compare actual costs at, say, 4,000 units of production with the costs that were budgeted at 4,000 units of production. In contrast, with a static budget and performance report you might end up comparing actual costs at 4,000 units of production with budgeted costs for 6,000 units of production.

6. A financial ratio compares one financial measure (such as profits) to another (such as sales). We discussed four basic categories of ratios: 1) liquidity ratios; 2) leverage ratios; 3) activities ratios; and 4) profitability ratios. These are presented in Exhibit 19–20, and you might want to review them again at this point.

7. You can use a network of interlocking financial ratios, such as shown in Exhibit 19–24, for controlling return on investment (ROI) and for identifying problems. It is built on the assumption that each ratio (such as return on investment) can itself be broken down into component ratios. In the case of ROI, for example, its two components are the profit margin and turnover. By starting with some discrepancy—such as an ROI that is too low—you can move from left to right of Exhibit 19–24, methodically zeroing in on the problem: Is investment excessive? Are selling expenses too high? And so forth.

STUDY ASSIGNMENTS

1. Discuss the importance of the sales budget in the budgeting process.
2. Explain the difference between the budget and the performance report.
3. What is the basic information you would expect to find in a standard cost sheet for a product? Explain how you would go about developing a standard cost sheet.
4. Discuss how you would use standard costs for taking corrective action.
5. Explain how you would compute price and quantity variances.
6. Compare and contrast "flexible" and "static" budgets.
7. Explain how you would go about developing a flexible budget.
8. Explain and give examples of liquidity ratios; leverage ratios; activities ratios; and profitability ratios.
9. Pick out a company in which you may wish to invest. From its annual report or from a financial service such as Standard and Poors (which you will probably find in your school library) compute the following ratios: current ratio; debt to equity ratio; coverage of fixed charges; inventory turnover; total capital turnover; rate of return on investment; profit margin. Do you think this would be a good company to

invest in? Why? To what other sources of information would you want
to refer?

10. Explain and diagram how you would go about controlling overall performance through return on investment (ROI).

NOTES FOR THE CHAPTER

1. Charles Horngren, *Accounting for Management Control* (Englewood Cliffs, N.J.: Prentice-Hall, 1970) p. 188.

2. Myron Gordon, and Gordon Shillinglaw, *Accounting: A Management Approach* (Homewood, Ill.: Richard D. Irwin, 1974) p. 505.

3. This section was partly based on an idea in Myron Gordon and Gordon Shillinglaw, *Accounting: A Management Approach*, pp. 507–511.

4. See Horngren, *Accounting for Management Control*, pp. 260–269; Gordon and Shillinglaw, *Accounting: A Management Approach*, pp. 646–650.

5. The following discussions are partly based on Charles T. Horngren, *Accounting for Management Control* (Englewood Cliffs, N.J.: Prentice-Hall, 1970) pp. 269–273.

6. Net worth or "owner's equity" is equal to the excess of assets over all other liabilities.

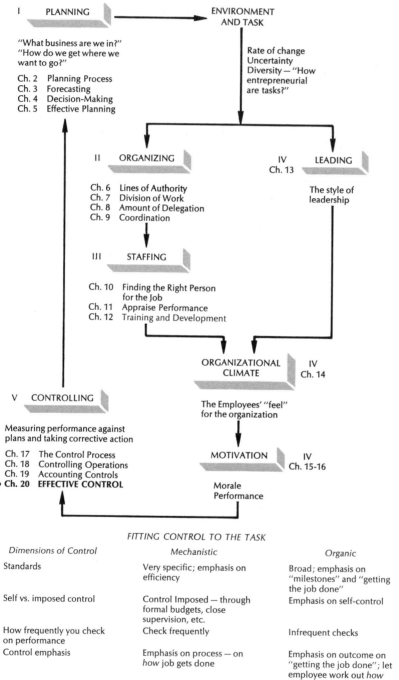

A Framework for Studying the Management Fundamentals

I   PLANNING → **ENVIRONMENT AND TASK**

"What business are we in?"
"How do we get where we want to go?"

Ch. 2   Planning Process
Ch. 3   Forecasting
Ch. 4   Decision-Making
Ch. 5   Effective Planning

Rate of change
Uncertainty
Diversity — "How entrepreneurial are tasks?"

Where we are now: Discussing why control systems backfire and what you can do to make your controls more effective.

II   ORGANIZING

Ch. 6   Lines of Authority
Ch. 7   Division of Work
Ch. 8   Amount of Delegation
Ch. 9   Coordination

IV   LEADING
Ch. 13

The style of leadership

III   STAFFING

Ch. 10   Finding the Right Person for the Job
Ch. 11   Appraise Performance
Ch. 12   Training and Development

ORGANIZATIONAL CLIMATE   **IV**   Ch. 14

The Employees' "feel" for the organization

V   CONTROLLING

Measuring performance against plans and taking corrective action

Ch. 17   The Control Process
Ch. 18   Controlling Operations
Ch. 19   Accounting Controls
Ch. 20   EFFECTIVE CONTROL

MOTIVATION   **IV**   Ch. 15-16

Morale
Performance

FITTING CONTROL TO THE TASK

Dimensions of Control	Mechanistic	Organic
Standards	Very specific; emphasis on efficiency	Broad; emphasis on "milestones" and "getting the job done"
Self vs. imposed control	Control Imposed — through formal budgets, close supervision, etc.	Emphasis on self-control
How frequently you check on performance	Check frequently	Infrequent checks
Control emphasis	Emphasis on process — on *how* job gets done	Emphasis on outcome on "getting the job done"; let employee work out *how*

When you have finished studying

20 Making Control Effective

You should be able to:

1. Compare and contrast "imposed control" with "self control."

2. Explain why control systems backfire.

3. Discuss three techniques that employees use to beat the control system.

4. Explain how you would "fit control to the task" in practice.

5. Cite six hints for developing more effective control systems.

INTRODUCTION

"During the spring of 1972, the Air Force recalled General John D. Lavelle from his command in Vietnam and demoted him for conducting 28 raids on North Vietnam that were in violation of White House rules. (Time, 1972). How did General Lavelle manage to conduct 28 raids before he was caught? The General and his subordinates had developed a double accounting system. The Air Force required reports on all missions and checked them to be sure they violated no rules. According to Sergeant Lonnie Franks, however, he and 200 other men often made out two sets of reports—one true and one false. The false report was forwarded to the Pentagon, which became aware that it was receiving false information only some time later. Thus, the Pentagon lost control over the activities of General Lavelle at the same time that Henry Kissinger and the U.S. Government were trying to negotiate the Vietnam peace treaty. Consequently, when delicate coordination was most needed between the military and civilian segments of government, it was not present because a vital information system was not functioning effectively." *

Why do employees try to "beat the system"? What can you do to make your control system more effective? These are two of the critical issues we'll discuss in this chapter.

---

* Quoted from Edward E. Lawler III and John Grant Rhode, *Information and Control in Organizations* (Pacific Palisades: Goodyear, 1976) p. 1.

CONTROLS AND THEIR EFFECTS ON PEOPLE

Control—A Central Issue in Managing

The question of how to maintain control lies at the very core of your job as a manager. Every day you will be faced with questions such as, "How do I get someone to do what I want?" "How do I see to it that he does his job?" To a large extent, the answer to both questions is, "By imposing controls."

But if tightly controlling employees was the only (or best) way to insure effective performance, we could disregard half of this book. For example, we would not need to know very much about what motivates people, what leadership style is best, or how to develop a supportive climate.

But the fact is that you can't rely exclusively on controls for keeping your subordinates' performance high. For one thing, employees sometimes retaliate against controls—through absenteeism, turnover, poor quality output, and so forth. And in practice you just can't develop a system of rules and controls so complete that you can keep track of everything your employees do on the job.

How Control Systems Backfire

One of the problems with overrelying on formal controls is that they often result in undesirable reactions from employees. Elmer Burack has summarized how this can occur; [1] his ideas are presented in Exhibit 20–1. He says that managers often attempt to impose tighter controls in order to improve the efficiency of their units. Symptoms of this include more routine jobs and higher performance standards.

But although these tighter controls may result in improved performance in the short run, they often result in low morale and higher absenteeism. Performance, in other words, begins deteriorating. Then as performance declines management often reacts with new, tighter controls.[2] This, in turn, leads to increased alienation on the part of employees, a further deterioration of performance, and attempts to "beat" the system. Edward Lawler and John Rhode say that there are several techniques employees use to resist and "beat" control systems. Here's what to watch out for: [3]

"Rigid Bureaucratic Behavior." This refers to the tendency of people to try to look good in terms of the control system. They concentrate their efforts where results are measured, often disregarding the organization's more important goals. The problem stems mostly from incomplete standards. For example, in one state employment agency, employees found that they were measured on the number of job seekers they *interviewed* rather than on the number they placed in jobs. The number of interviews soared but little

Exhibit 20.1 How Control Systems Backfire

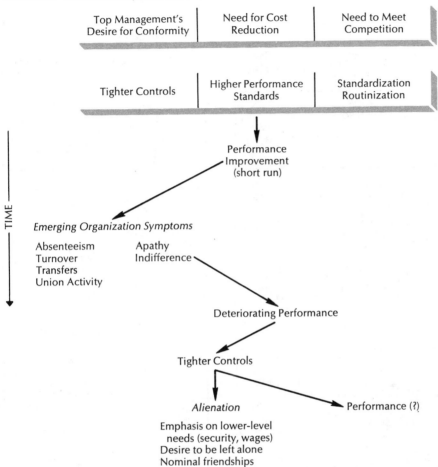

Source: Elmer H. Burack, *Organizational Analysis: Theory and Applications* (New York: The Dryden Press, Holt, Rinehart and Winston, 1975). Copyright © 1975. Reprinted by permission.

attention was focused on adequately counseling applicants. When it became apparent what was happening several new standards (such as the ratio of placements to interviews) were devised. These were aimed at providing a more complete—and acceptable—set of standards for the counselors.[4]

"Strategic Behavior." Anyone who has ever worked for a government agency is probably familiar with "strategic behavior." This refers to the tendency of people to provide information in such a way that they look good for a certain time period. As an example, many government agencies assign budgets to departments with the stipulation that any funds not spent by the end of the year be returned. What often happens (as in Exhibit 20–2) is that

398   **Exhibit 20.2**   Strategic Behavior: One Popular Way for Getting Around Controls

at the end of the year, employees rush to spend all their available funds—often for unnecessary "frills." They look good (they've spent their yearly allocation) but their expenditures are often frivolous. However, you don't have to be in a government agency to incur this problem. It can happen whenever a project you assign must be completed within a certain time period.

"*Invalid Data Reporting.*" Sometimes employees beat the system by simply reporting back invalid, erroneous information. For example, this is apparently how Air Force General Lavelle's men were able to make 28 unauthorized bombing raids before they were caught. Three important techniques employees use to resist control systems are summarized in Exhibit 20–3.

Exhibit 20.3   Summary Barriers to Effective Control

Courtesy of Professor Robert Miller.

FITTING CONTROL TO THE TASK

One way to make sure your control system doesn't backfire is to make sure it's appropriate for the job you're controlling. Let's therefore discuss what we know about how to fit control to the task.

The Lawrence and Lorsch Findings

Paul Lawrence and Jay Lorsch studied control in companies in the plastics, foods, and container industries. They defined a person's level of control in terms of how much influence he exerted over others in the company. Their findings are summarized in Exhibit 20–4.

Notice how in the plastics and food firms the amount of organizational control (or influence) was fairly evenly distributed. In other words, managers at all levels—first-line foremen, department managers, plant managers—all exhibited a good deal of self-control. But in the container firms only top-level managers exerted much influence. Lower-level people had very little control or influence in the organization.

Exhibit 20.4 Lawrence & Lorsch Findings: How Control was Distributed in Three Organizations

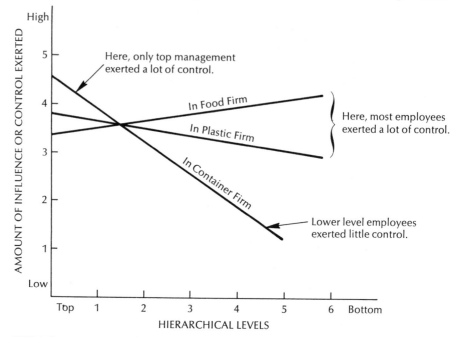

NOTE: In the more entrepreneurial, uncertain food and plastics firms, total control was high and people at *all* levels exerted high control. In the more mechanistic container firm, employees at lower levels had little autonomy; people at higher levels exerted most of the control, and those at lower levels simply followed orders.

Source: Paul Lawrence and Jay Lorsch, *Organization and Environment* (Boston, Harvard University, 1967) p. 143.

Lawrence and Lorsch say that control has to fit the situation. In the plastics and food firms, innovation and creativity were paramount. Quick decisions had to be made. Here it was important for *all* managers to have a good deal of influence, so they could make quick, on-the-spot decisions.

In the container firms, efficiency (rather than innovation) was paramount. Here quick, creative decisions were not as necessary. It was more important for everyone to "stick to the rules" and be highly efficient. So here only top managers exercised a great deal of control or influence. Lower-level managers followed orders and monitored production.

Bell's Findings

Gerald Bell carried out another important study of control patterns.[5]

First he studied employees who had very unpredictable jobs. These jobs were often interrupted by unexpected events, and were not at all routine or repetitive. He found that these employees' supervisors exerted very little control over how they did their jobs. For example, their supervisors did not keep close tabs on how they were doing, and only occasionally checked on performance. Next he studied employees who had routine, predictable tasks. They were much more tightly controlled. Their supervisors closely observed the work they were doing, and frequently checked on their performance.

How to Fit Control to the Task

David Katz and Robert Kahn help us to put these other findings into perspective. They say that there are four basic ways for you to get a subordinate to perform satisfactorily.[6] These are summarized in Exhibit 20–5. At one extreme is "legal compliance." Here you depend on close supervision, and on formal control tools like budgets and standard cost systems. Employees obey these because they are enforced by legal sanctions. This is *imposed control.*

Exhibit 20.5   Katz and Kahn's Control Continuum

They Say That There Are Basically Four Ways to "Control" Someone

Imposed (legal compliance)	Instrumental Satisfaction (rewards)	Job Identification (job satisfaction)	Internalization of Organization Goals (adoption of organizational goals)

(imposed control) ←————————————————————————→ (self-control)

Note that they range from *enforcement* to *self control.*

But they say that there are three other ways for you to get someone to perform satisfactorily. These ways emphasize *self-control*:

1. *"Instrumental satisfaction."* Here your subordinate does his job well because he knows he will be *rewarded* for performing satisfactorily.
2. *"Job identification."* Here he does a good job because he derives satisfaction from *the job itself.*
3. *"Internalization of organizational goals."* This occurs when your subordinate *adopts the organization's goals* as his own.

Many of the concepts and tools we've discussed in this book are aimed at developing "instrumental satisfaction," "job identification," and "internalization of organizational goals." These include management by objectives; effective leadership; job enrichment; counseling; orientation; and training. They are aimed at instilling in employees the desire to do their jobs well, and at developing in the employee the willingness to exercise self-control in the performance of his duties.

Formal, imposed control systems, such as those discussed in the last three chapters, are necessary management tools; they provide management with vital information about actual company performance. But remember that they are not, by themselves, sufficient to insure effective performance. At some point you will have to rely on the self-control and self-discipline of your subordinates. And this self-control is largely developed through application of concepts and tools like MBO, effective leadership, and job enrichment.

Summary. In summary, we know from studies like those of Lawrence and Lorsch, and Bell that for mechanistic tasks such as running a bookkeeping department, tight control is usually *imposed*. Performance is closely supervised, and there is an elaborate system of rules and procedures. Very *specific efficiency* criteria—such as "cut costs by 10 percent"—are empasized. Progress is monitored and *very frequently checked*.

And we know that controls for organic, creative, entrepreneurial tasks such as running a research laboratory are quite different. Here you depend more on *self-control*. The emphasis is on *broad results* (such as developing a new product) rather than on specific efficiency criteria. You check performance *infrequently*, and instead focus on *"milestones."* This is summarized in Exhibit 20–6.

GUIDELINES FOR DEVELOPING EFFECTIVE CONTROLS

Let's briefly discuss six guidelines for developing effective controls.

Practice "Preventive" Control

The best time to impose controls is not when things start going wrong, but earlier, before problems start. To do this, remember (as summarized in our framework) that you can't separate control from the other management functions. "Preventive" control begins with effective planning—with making accurate forecasts, deciding on a sound strategy, and setting effective standards. And it requires an effective organization structure—the necessary organization charts, a structure that fits the task, and so forth. It requires effective staffing—hiring competent, effective people to begin with, and providing them with the necessary training.[7] And of course it requires effective leadership—choosing the right leadership style, developing a supportive climate, and motivating your subordinates. In summary, practice preventive control: avoid problems *before* they start.

Exhibit 20.6 How to Fit Control to the Task

Dimensions of Control	Mechanistic (Ex: Assembly Line) HERE CONTROL *IMPOSED*	Organic (Ex: New Product Development Department) HERE *SELF CONTROL* STRESSED
Type of *Standards* That You Set	Complete and specific; Stress on efficiency. Ex: very specific, quantified production, inventory, quality and budgetary control standards.	Broad; emphasis on milestones. Ex: more use of overall ROI than on monitoring inventory levels, or production costs; more use of flexible budgets.
Degree of *Self-Control* vs *Imposed Control*	Control imposed. Ex: workers not actively involved in setting production, sales, or cost standards; performance controlled through very complete, detailed production, inventory, quality, and budgetary control reporting system.	Emphasis on self-control. Ex: workers participate in setting standards. Less emphasis on using rules, close supervision, daily production and quality control reports. More emphasis on letting employees control themselves.
How *Frequently* You Check on Performance	Very frequent. Ex: daily reports on production, inventory levels, quality. Daily feedback on budgeted standards.	Infrequently. Ex: progress toward completing project just checked weekly or monthly.
Stress "Goal" (Getting Job Done) or "Process" (*How* Job is Done)	Emphasis on process; on closely supervising work in process. Ex: employees given production and budget standards which specify how work is to be carried out; management receives complete, detailed, (and frequent) production and budget reports on how work is progressing.	Emphasis on "getting the job done"—let employees work out details of "how" themselves. Ex: more use of "project" standards and on "getting the job done." Less emphasis on specifying and measuring (via close supervision, detailed production and budget control reports, etc.) *how* job should be (or is) being carried out.

Source: Based on Gary Dessler, *Organization and Management,* p. 361-62.

Set Effective Standards

Remember that our "perfect" standard would be:

1. Viewed as fair by your subordinates.
2. High—but reasonable—there would be about a 50/50 chance of success at reaching it.
3. Specific.
4. Set about 20% above previous performance.

5. Communicated to your subordinate; use feedback.
6. Complete—for example, don't just focus on *quantity*, and disregard *quality*, unless that's your intention.
7. Used within the context of MBO and management by exception.

Familiarize Yourself with Available Control Techniques

We discussed some of the most popular techniques—budgets, standard costing, EOQ models, GANTT charts, and so forth. Familiarize yourself with these and others, know when and how to apply them, and avoid "just winging it" when you could be using a proven control device.

Take Effective Corrective Action

Recall that for this you'll want to apply many of the concepts and techniques we discussed throughout this book. From our discussion of decision making, for example, you know (to repeat) that it's important to clearly identify the central problem. Inadequate performance is usually just a symptom, and so you'll therefore want to find out *why* performance is not up to par. For example, ask "Are the plans themselves in need of revision?"; "Is the Organization Structure inadequate?"; "Are my people not up to the task?"; "Is training and development called for?"; "Is the deviation due to low morale?"; and so forth. And of course in actually taking remedial action you'll want to keep in mind some of the hints we've discussed—on how to counsel and motivate subordinates, for example.

Fit Your Controls to the Task

Remember that for mechanistic, assembly-line type tasks tight control is usually *imposed*. Performance is closely supervised, specific efficiency criteria are stressed, and progress is checked frequently. For organic, entrepreneurial tasks you depend more on self-control. The emphasis here is on broad results, you check performance infrequently, and focus more on "milestones."

Don't Overrely on Formal Controls

Finally, remember not to overrely on formal controls like budgets, or return on investment. These are very valuable management tools, but they're also far from perfect. Don't make the mistake that many managers do of becoming so hypnotized by the data from your controls that you start to lose track of what's really happening "down in the shop": You're going to find that sometimes one visit to that shop is worth a thousand pages of budget figures.

Some Important Things to Remember from This Chapter:

1. You can't rely exclusively on controls for keeping your subordinates' performance high. For one thing, employees sometimes retaliate against controls—through absenteeism, poor quality output, and so forth. And in practice you just can't develop a system of rules and controls so elaborate and so complete that you can keep track of everything your employees do on the job.

2. At some point you will have to rely on the self-control and self-discipline of your subordinates. This can be encouraged through "instrumental satisfaction" (providing rewards); "job identification" (where the job itself provides satisfaction); or "internalization of organizational goals" (where your subordinate adopts the organization's goals as his own). This kind of self-control is largely developed through the application of concepts and tools like MBO, effective leadership, and job enrichment.

3. Trying to tighten up on controls can sometimes lead you into a vicious cycle. When you tighten controls, morale drops, absenteeism rises, and before you know it you have to tighten controls even further. Be on your guard against such "escalating" controls.

4. Employees use at least three basic techniques to resist and "beat" control systems: Rigid bureaucratic behavior (just concentrating effort where results are measured); "strategic behavior" (making themselves "look good" in the short run); and "invalid data reporting" (reporting back invalid, erroneous information).

5. One way to make sure your control system doesn't backfire is to make sure it's appropriate for the job you are controlling. Thus for mechanistic tasks, such as running bookkeeping departments, tight control is usually imposed; specific efficiency criteria are emphasized; and progress is frequently checked. But for organic, entrepreneurial tasks such as running a research laboratory, you depend more on self-control. The emphasis here is on broad results and on "milestones."

6. Our six guidelines for developing effective controls included:

1. Practice "preventive" control.
2. Set effective standards.
3. Familiarize yourself with available control techniques.
4. Take *effective* corrective action.
5. Fit your controls to the task.
6. Don't overrely on formal controls.

STUDY ASSIGNMENTS

1. If you were the Secretary of Defense, how would you go about avoiding the kind of problem that is described in the introduction to this chapter?
2. Compare and contrast imposed controls with self-control.
3. What are some of the techniques, discussed in this book, which are aimed at developing *self-control.*
4. Why is it always necessary to depend to some extent on your subordinates' self-control?
5. Explain why control systems backfire.

6. Discuss three techniques employees use to beat the control system.
7. Explain how you would "fit control to the task" in practice. For example, what sort of control system would you establish if you were: A supervisor of an assembly line in a production plant; the manager of a bookkeeping department; the chairman of the management department in a business school; a sales manager; or the manager of a new product development department?
8. Discuss our six guidelines for developing more effective control systems.
9. Explain the relationship between planning and control.
10. "If you do a good job of planning, organizing, staffing, and leading, you will just about eliminate the need for any type of controls." Explain why you agree or disagree with this statement.

NOTES FOR THE CHAPTER

1. Elmer H. Burack, *Organization Analysis: Theory and Applications* (Hinsdale, Ill.: The Dryden Press, 1975) pp. 158–160.
2. For a discussion of this see Alvin Gouldner, *Patterns of Industrial Bureaucracy* (New York: Glencoe, 1954) pp. 157–180; Excerpted in Joseph Litterer, *Organizations: Structure and Process* (New York: John Wiley & Sons, 1969) pp. 378–387.
3. These are based on Edward Lawler III and John Grant Rhode, *Information and Control in Organizations*, Ch. 6. In their book they present a scholarly, comprehensive, yet practical analysis of control in organizations.
4. P. M. Blau, *The Dynamics of Bureaucracy* (Chicago: University of Chicago Press, 1955), in Lawler and Rhode, *Information and Control in Organizations*, pp. 83–84; V. F. Ridgway, "Dysfunctional Consequences of Performance Measurements," *Administrative Science Quarterly*, Sept., 1956, Vol. 1, No. 2, pp. 240–247, reprinted in John Turner, Alan Filley, and Robert House, *Studies in Managerial Process and Organizational Behavior* (Glenview: Scott-Foresman, 1972) pp. 190–191.
5. Gerald Bell, "Predictability of Work Demands and Professionalization as Determinants of Worker Discretion," *Journal of the Academy of Management*, Vol. 9, No. 1, March 1966, pp. 20–28, reprinted in Joseph Litterer, *Organizations: Structure and Behavior* (New York: John Wiley & Sons, 1969) pp. 446–452.
6. David Katz and Robert Kahn, *The Social Psychology of Organizations* (New York: John Wiley & Sons, 1966); based on John Baum and Stewart Youngblood, "Impact of an Organizational Control Policy on Absenteeism, Performance, and Satisfaction," *Journal of Applied Psychology*, Vol. 60, No. 5 (1975) pp. 688–694.
7. See for example Warren B. Brown, "The Organization and Socio-Technical Control," *MSU Business Topics*, Winter 1968, pp. 39–46, in John Turner, Alan Filley, and Robert House, *Studies in Managerial Process and Organizational Behavior*.

A Framework for Studying the Management Fundamentals

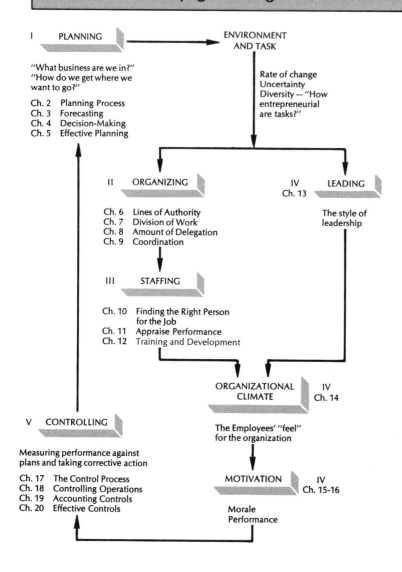

I   PLANNING → ENVIRONMENT AND TASK

"What business are we in?"
"How do we get where we
want to go?"

Ch. 2 Planning Process
Ch. 3 Forecasting
Ch. 4 Decision-Making
Ch. 5 Effective Planning

Rate of change
Uncertainty
Diversity — "How
entrepreneurial
are tasks?"

II   ORGANIZING

Ch. 6 Lines of Authority
Ch. 7 Division of Work
Ch. 8 Amount of Delegation
Ch. 9 Coordination

III   STAFFING

Ch. 10 Finding the Right Person
         for the Job
Ch. 11 Appraise Performance
Ch. 12 Training and Development

IV LEADING
Ch. 13

The style of
leadership

ORGANIZATIONAL CLIMATE   IV Ch. 14

The Employees' "feel"
for the organization

V   CONTROLLING

Measuring performance against
plans and taking corrective action

Ch. 17 The Control Process
Ch. 18 Controlling Operations
Ch. 19 Accounting Controls
Ch. 20 Effective Controls

MOTIVATION   IV Ch. 15-16

Morale
Performance

Where we are now: Tying together our discussion of the management fundamentals, and discussing the ethics and social responsibility management.

When you have finished studying

Management Fundamentals: An Integrated View

You should be able to:

1. *Discuss how you might avoid your own management "Watergate."*

2. *Compare and contrast the "maximize profit" and "social responsibility" approaches to the manager's job.*

3. *Summarize our discussions of the management fundamentals.*

4. *Explain why you need to take an "integrated" view of the management fundamentals.*

5. *Develop a table which shows how the management functions have to fit the task.*

6. *Discuss why you think you would (or would not) be an effective manager.*

INTRODUCTION

Spindel Rayon Mill had moved to the small Southern community in which Frank Jones lived in 1958. Frank accepted a job on the construction crew and was later employed to install and maintain lights, air conditioning, generator, steam plant, and miscellaneous equipment.

By 1965, floor space had tripled and the work force had increased by several hundred. Frank found that his responsibilities had grown commensurately. He was often required to work overtime and occasionally returned to the plant during the night to make necessary repairs. He performed his work in a conscientious manner and was considered to be a devoted and loyal employee. It was necessary to add men to his crew, and in late 1973 he found himself with a salary, a title as Director of Physical Plant, and responsible for the efforts of 16 men.

It was noted, however, that he still preferred to personally repair the machines rather than direct his subordinates to do so. The plant manager

410 *told him one man could no longer perform all the work required of his department. He encouraged him to do less of the repair work himself, but instead to select, train, and direct capable subordinates.*

Frank made an attempt to do so. He even dressed like the other supervisors and organized his crew in such a way that he could spend most of his time in the office. It was not long, however, before department heads were complaining that machinery needed repairs and work schedules were disrupted due to idle machines. It was reported that when physical-plant repairmen were summoned, more likely than not they were incapable of of completing the repairs without calling Frank. One department head complained to the plant manager that Frank was possessive about the machinery: He was deliberately not selecting and training qualified repairmen because he seemed to feel secure only if others regarded him as indispensible.

The plant manager took under advisement the action to be taken. He knew that Frank was not performing the supervisory function, yet he remembered the years and loyalty Frank had devoted to the company.*

1. *What was the problem here?*
2. *What would you do if you were the plant manager? Make sure to list several alternatives, and your recommendation.*
3. *How would you apply ideas we discussed in this book (planning, organizing, staffing, leading, and controlling) to this case?*

MANAGEMENT FUNDAMENTALS AND MANAGEMENT VALUES

Managers apply the management fundamentals within the framework of their own values and beliefs. Decisions such as which plan to accept, or which person to hire, usually don't just reflect what is "best" in a given situation. Instead they also reflect the personal values of the manager. Probably never before have the personal values of managers undergone so much scrutiny (or so much change) as during the past few years. Questions of management ethics and the social responsibility of business abound. There is no doubt that these will be critical issues in the next decade.

So it is fitting that we start this final chapter with a brief review of management values, and in particular the questions of ethics and social responsibility. For these values are the ultimate framework within which you'll apply the management fundamentals.

---

* *Source*: John Champion and John James, *Critical Incidents in Management* (Homewood, Ill.: Richard D. Irwin, 1975) pp. 230–233.

The Question of Ethics

It sometimes seems as if we live in an age of management scandals. Whether it is Watergate or illegal campaign contributions we are reminded almost daily that many managers seem to be operating without their ethical compasses. Their decisions often seem to be based more on expediency than on any concept of what is right.

Are the managers themselves to blame? Or are such things simply part and parcel of being a manager? The answer, probably, is a little of both. As a manager you are going to bring to your job your own concept of what is right and what is wrong. As with other facets of your personality, your ethics represent the sum total of your experiences, education, and upbringing. Every decision you make and every action you take will reflect, for better or for worse, the application of these standards to the questions at hand.

But—and this is extremely important—even managers with a well honed concept of what is right and what is wrong run the risk of doing the "wrong" thing. This happens when they are confronted with the pressures and realities of organizational life. There is the pressure for productivity. There is the pressure to conform to the values and norms of your boss. And there is the ever-present temptation that comes with the autonomy most managers have. So in decisions both large and small, even managers who know better sometimes make expedient rather than wise decisions.

What can you do to avoid this? Some managers find that they are able to make the "right" choice by simply taking the time to ask what the right decision is. Before making some decision they ask themselves whether they believe that they're doing the right thing. They make every decision as if they have an independent auditor looking over their shoulders. They ask: *"Would I make the same decision if I had to make a full and public disclosure of my actions?"*

What is the Purpose of a Business? The Question of Social Responsibility

But what is the "right" thing to do when it comes to "social responsibility"? This is one of the most critical issues managers will face in the next decade. Is it a manager's job simply to maximize profits? Or should he also be vitally concerned with using his organization to carry out other social responsibilities? These might include creating jobs for minorities, controlling pollution, or supporting education, for example. Let's look at two sides of the argument.

The "Maximize Profit" Argument.   Many people believe that everyone is better off when business managers concentrate on maximizing profits. This

412   idea can be traced back at least two hundred years to Adam Smith. He said that the "invisible hand" of the market would insure that everyone did his best, and that all society would gain the most when businessmen focused on maximizing profits. One of the most effective contemporary proponents of this view is Milton Friedman, who says:

> The view has been gaining widespread acceptance that corporate officials and labor leaders have a "social responsibility" that goes beyond serving the interest of their stockholders or their members. This view shows a fundamental misconception of the character and nature of the free economy. In such an economy, there is one and only one social responsibility of business—to use its resources and engage in activities designed to increase its profits so long as it stays within the rules of the game, which is to say, engages in open and free competition, without deception or fraud . . . few trends could so thoroughly undermine the very foundation of our free society as the acceptance by corporate officials of a social responsibility other than to make as much money for their stockholders as possible.[1]

The "Social Responsibility" Argument.   But there is another view of what is meant by the "social responsibility" of business. Many people say that the social responsibility of business goes well beyond maximizing profits.[2]

Every day business managers are being asked to assume broader responsibilities to society than ever before. These include providing advancement opportunities for minorities, assisting in overcoming urban blight, supporting education and the arts, and others.

Such a view of business and commerce actually is not new.[3] But never before have managers been buffeted from so many different directions with demands for increased social responsibility. "Self-appointed guardians of the public interest," such as Ralph Nader, and a multitude of minority group spokesmen all insist on greater corporate social responsibility.[4]

Apparently these pressures have been successful. In Exhibit 21–1 you will find the results of a Harris Poll. It shows what a sample of Americans stated were their expectations of companies at three different points in time—1966, 1971, and 1972. There has been a steady increase in the number who feel that companies should "give leadership" in such areas as controlling pollution, and wiping out poverty.

Business managers themselves are increasingly accepting this view and attempting to cope with the need to make their organizations more socially responsible.[5] Even investment companies (which buy shares of stock and thereby become partial owners of corporations) today focus more attention on social responsibility. For example, the Dreyfus Third Century Fund stated in its prospectus of March 1972 that:

. . . . The Fund intends to consider performance by companies in the areas of (1) the protection and improvement of the environment and the proper use of our natural resources, (2) occupational health and safety, (3) consumer protection and product purity, and (4) equal employment opportunity.[6]

Exhibit 21.1   The Changing Expectations Americans Have of Business Enterprises

"Do You Think (READ LIST) is a Problem That Businessmen and Companies Should Give Some Special Leadership to, or Not?"

	Should Give Leadership		
	1972	1971	1966
Controlling air and water pollution	92%	89%	69%
Eliminating economic depressions	88	83	76
Rebuilding our cities	85	84	74
Enabling people to use their creative talents fully	85	85	73
Eliminating racial discrimination	84	81	69
Wiping out poverty	83	81	69
Raising living standards around the world	80	74	43
Finding cures for disease	76	70	63
Giving a college education to all qualified	75	70	71
Controlling crime	73	64	42
Cutting down highway accidents	72	67	50
Raising moral standards	70	64	48
Reducing threat of war	68	61	55
Eliminating religious prejudice	63	52	37
Cutting out government red tape	57	50	34
Controlling too rapid population growth	44	43	17

Source: Corson and Steiner, "Social Responsibility: A New Dimension of Corporate Accountability," reprinted in Koontz and O'Donnell, p. 55.

Today, therefore, every manager, from first-line foreman to president, must cope with a variety of new problems. These range from pollution control, to minority recruiting, to occupational safety.

Reporting to the Government.   You may find that this emphasis on social responsibility is most apparent in the variety of reports you'll have to fill out for the federal government. The Food and Drug Administration and the Federal Trade Commission have elaborate reporting requirements for describing the characteristics of products. The Environmental Protection Agency requires information on air pollution. The Securities and Exchange Commission has new disclosure rules that require managers to present detailed information on their operations.

The Equal Employment Opportunity Commission requires the submission of data on employment of minority group members. Managers need to develop detailed reports on their affirmative action programs, based on checklists such as shown in Exhibit 21–2. The Department of Labor requires every establishment covered by the Occupational Safety and Health Act to maintain

Exhibit 21.2 Employment Self Evaluation Checklist

EMPLOYMENT SELF EVALUATION CHECKLIST

Title IX of the Education Amendments of 1972 requires all institutions (and others) receiving federal education funds to undertake a self evaluation of policies and practices concerning both students and employees. Institutions which have received federal contracts (and are thereby covered by Executive Order 11246) have undoubtedly already conducted such analyses concerning employees in order to develop their affirmative action plans. The process of self analysis provides the institution with an opportunity to analyze its policies and practices in a systematic manner and to determine which policies and practices it wants to change or retain.

The short checklist which follows is aimed primarily at those institutions which have not been covered by the affirmative action requirements of the Executive Order and have not been previously involved in any self evaluation process concerning employees. The list is by no means complete, and is intended only to highlight some of the areas that need to be examined. Institutions will no doubt want to add other items.

Institutions may find it helpful to follow the general strategy listed below:

- Identify the person(s) who will be responsible for implementation
- Develop a timetable for implementation
- Identify problems by organizational unit and/or job category
- Analyse problems, collecting data when necessary
- Develop and adopt solutions; modify policy and procedures when necessary
- Develop a timeframe for re-evaluation and monitoring progress

I. Administrative Component
   A. Evaluate and assign responsibility for administration and implementation
      1. Identify the organizational structure of the institution
      2. Determine who has supervisory responsibility within each organizational unit
      3. Identify who has hiring responsibility within each organization unit
      4. Appoint an affirmative action officer and spell out her/his duties, responsibilities, and authority
      5. Select an affirmative action committee and spell out its duties, responsibilities, and authority
      6. Develop a monitoring and reporting system specifying:
         a. who will conduct the monitoring and how?
         b. what kind of reports will be necessary?
         c. how often reports will be submitted?
      7. Develop a grievance procedure
      8. Set a timetable for implementation
   B. Identify how the policy will be disseminated to the following groups:
      1. Employees and prospective employees
      2. Minority and female interest groups on campus
      3. External groups and organizations
      4. Contractors, subcontractors, vendors and suppliers

II. Policy Component
   A. Develop and publish an equal employment/affirmative action statement
   B. Evaluate the following areas for sex discrimination and develop nondiscriminatory policies as necessary:
      1. Childbearing and childrearing leave
      2. Nepotism policies
      3. Standards and procedures for promotion, tenure and seniority
      4. Part-time employment
      5. Mandatory and optional retirement
      6. Other policy areas as appropriate
      7. Recruiting, hiring and promoting faculty, administrators, and non-academic personnel

III. Analysis Component: Evaluate Policies and Collect Data
   A. Evaluate the hiring process for possible sex bias
      1. Job descriptions
      2. Advertisement and recruitment
      3. Search committees screening processes
      4. Referral sources, including internal referrals
      5. Applicant flow, including hiring and rejection ratios by sex by race
      6. Testing and evaluation
      7. New hires
         a. full time
         b. part time
         c. temporary
   B. Evaluate fringe benefits for sex bias:
      1. Health insurance and benefits
      2. Life insurance
      3. Pensions
      4. Disability insurance
      5. Sick leave
      6. Tuition benefits for self and family
      7. Training opportunities
   C. Evaluate job mobility for sex bias
      1. Transfers
      2. Promotions
      3. Terminations and layoffs

(continued)

    D. Evaluate rank and salary for sex bias: Analyze salaries by race by sex for each job level within each organizational unit, as well as in the institutions as a whole
        1. Starting salaries
        2. Average salaries
        3. Present salaries
        4. Rate of progression
        5. Salary increments
        6. "Hard" money vs. "soft" money
    E. Evaluate other benefits and employment responsibilities for sex bias
        1. Tenure and seniority
        2. Committee assignments and responsibilities
        3. Opportunities to apply for research grants
        4. Opportunity for sabbatical leave and leave without pay
        5. Access to facilities, such as faculty/staff clubs and recreational facilities
        6. Use of credit unions, etc.
        7. Availability of child care
    F. Evaluate contractual and other agreements for sex bias
        1. Union contracts
        2. Civil service (if applicable)
    G. Evaluate student employment for sex bias
        1. Graduate students
        2. Undergraduate students
    H. Evaluate agreements with contractors and vendors for sex bias
        1. Areas of activity
        2. Number of minority and/or female contractors and vendors

IV.   Utilization Analysis: Compare the Percent of Available Qualified Women and Minorities with the Actual Number and Percent of Women and Minorities in Each Organizational Unit
    A. Academic
    B. Non-academic

* * * * *

 association of american colleges 1818 R STREET, N.W. · WASHINGTON, D.C. 20009

Source: Project on the Status and Education of Women, Association of American Colleges, 1818 R Street N.W., Washington, D. C.

a log such as that in Exhibit 21–3. Every occupational illness or injury suffered by an employee must be logged. This record must be available when the Department of Labor inspector visits your establishment.

Summary. What is the purpose of a business? Is it simply to maximize profits? Or does business also have a wider social responsibility—one measured in terms of things such as pollution control and consumer protection? As of today the latter seems to be the prevailing view. And although the question continues to be debated, as a manager today you will have to be attentive to a variety of goals beyond profit maximization.

IS MANAGING FOR YOU?

What do managers do? What does it take to be an effective manager? Is managing for you? These were the sort of questions we said you'd be better able to answer after studying this book, and they are crucial questions indeed.

Exhibit 21.3 Log of Occupational Injuries and Illnesses

OSHA NO. 100

LOG OF OCCUPATIONAL INJURIES AND ILLNESSES

Form Approved
OMB NUMBER 44R 145:

					DESCRIPTION OF INJURY OR ILLNESS		EXTENT OF AND OUTCOME OF INJURY OR ILLNESS				
							Fatalities	Lost Workday Cases		Nonfatal Cases Without Lost Workdays	
Case or file no.	Date of injury or initial diagnosis of illness. If diagnosis of illness was made after first day of absence enter first day of absence. (mo./day/yr.)	Employee's Name (First name, middle initial, last name)	Occupation of injured employee at time of injury or illness	Department to which employee was assigned at time of injury or illness	Nature of injury or illness and part(s) of body affected (Typical entries for this column might be: Amputation of 1st joint right forefinger Strain of lower back Contact dermatitis on both hands Electrocution—body)	Injury or illness code *See codes at bottom of page.*	Enter date of death (mo./day/yr.)	Enter workdays lost due to injury or illness (*see instructions on back.*)	If, *after* lost workdays, the employee was permanently transferred to another job or was terminated, enter a check in the column below	If no entry was made in columns 8 or 9, but the injury or illness did result in: Transfer to another job or termination, or; medical treatment, other than first aid, or; diagnosis of occupational illness, or; loss of consciousness, or; restriction of work or motion; Enter a check in the column below	If a check in column 11 represented a transfer or termination, enter another check in column 12
1	2	3	4	5	6	7	8	9	10	11	12

Company Name --

Establishment Name --

Establishment Location ------------------------------------

Injury Code
10 All occupational injuries

Illness Codes
21 Occupational skin diseases or disorders
22 Dust diseases of the lungs (pneumoconioses)
23 Respiratory conditions due to toxic agents
24 Poisoning (Systemic effects of toxic materials)
25 Disorders due to physical agents (other than toxic materials)
26 Disorders due to repeated trauma
29 All other occupational illnesses

Note: Examples of one of the forms businessmen must fill out to comply with the Federal Occupational Safety and Health Act.

Source: Reprinted in Andrew F. Sikula, *Personnel Administration and Human Resources Management,* (Santa Barbara: Wiley/Hamilton, 1976) pp. 356-358.

Real success in a wide range of occupations—from accountant to lawyer to Indian chief (especially Indian chief!)—will hinge on how good a manager you are. So if you have any doubts about your management potential you'd better clear them up soon. Do so before locking yourself into what, for you, could turn out to be a dead-end occupation.

What Do Managers Do? A Summary

Throughout this book we used our framework to tie together the management fundamentals we discussed. Now let's use it to summarize our discussion to this point.

Planning. First (see Exhibit 21–4), we said that effective managing requires planning—planning what your people do day to day, what your monthly quotas are, and what the central guiding concept of your enterprise is. It requires forecasting and developing planning premises. And it requires effective decision-making—the ability to zero in on the "central problem," analyze alternatives, and make a good decision. As a manager, your most important decision may be your choice of "central guiding concept." This answers the question "what business are we in?" It therefore determines the sort of environment and tasks your enterprise has to deal with. For instance, are quick, entrepreneurial decisions called for? Is efficiency paramount or flexibility? And so forth. This central concept is the ultimate target for your organization. It is the overall standard against which every decision you make is evaluated.

Organizing. Next (Exhibit 21–5) we saw that effective managing requires organizing. This involves giving each subordinate a separate, distinct task and insuring that these tasks are coordinated so that your organization accomplishes its goals. We saw that your organization structure has to fit the task. Remember that routine, mechanistic tasks call for a different type of structure than do entrepreneurial, organic ones.

Staffing. And (Exhibit 21–6) effective managing requires staffing your organization. You have to analyze the jobs you've organized, draw up job descriptions, decide what sorts of people to hire, and then recruit, select, and orient them. You'll also have to appraise their performance relative to your planned standards, counsel them, and train them.

Leading. Managers get things done through people, so to be an effective manager, you'll also have to be an effective leader (Exhibit 21–7). You'll have to be able to fit your style to the task, and *act* like a leader. You'll have to develop the right climate, and try to motivate your people to *want* to do a good job without you standing over them all day.

Controlling. But while you might excel at planning, organizing, staffing, and leading, the real test of your ability lies in the results you achieve. And

Exhibit 21.4 Planning

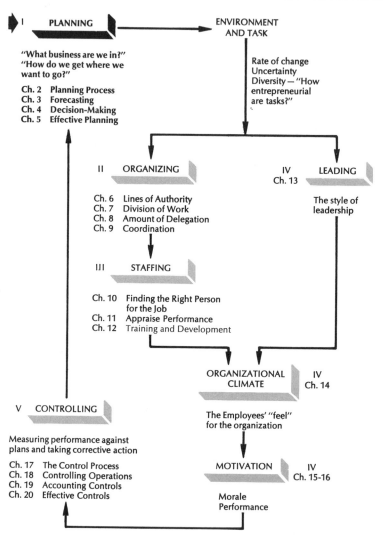

A Framework for Studying the Management Fundamentals

I PLANNING

ENVIRONMENT
AND TASK

"What business are we in?"
"How do we get where we
want to go?"

Rate of change
Uncertainty
Diversity — "How
entrepreneurial
are tasks?"

Ch. 2 Planning Process
Ch. 3 Forecasting
Ch. 4 Decision-Making
Ch. 5 Effective Planning

II ORGANIZING

IV LEADING
Ch. 13

Ch. 6 Lines of Authority
Ch. 7 Division of Work
Ch. 8 Amount of Delegation
Ch. 9 Coordination

The style of
leadership

III STAFFING

Ch. 10 Finding the Right Person
for the Job
Ch. 11 Appraise Performance
Ch. 12 Training and Development

ORGANIZATIONAL
CLIMATE

IV
Ch. 14

V CONTROLLING

The Employees' "feel"
for the organization

Measuring performance against
plans and taking corrective action

Ch. 17 The Control Process
Ch. 18 Controlling Operations
Ch. 19 Accounting Controls
Ch. 20 Effective Controls

MOTIVATION

IV
Ch. 15-16

Morale
Performance

it's through control (Exhibit 21–8) that you monitor results and bring them back in line with those planned. You'll have to be able to set fair, acceptable standards, make use of a wide variety of control devices, and take effective corrective action. And the latter will require all the decision-making, staffing, and leading skills you can bring to bear.

An Integrated View. To be an effective manager you're also going to have to take a "systems," "everything is related" view of your job. Your

Exhibit 21.5 Organizing   419

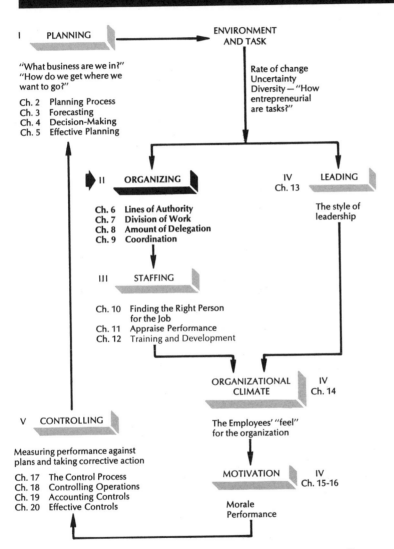

A Framework for Studying the Management Fundamentals

I   PLANNING   ENVIRONMENT
                                                 AND TASK

"What business are we in?"   Rate of change
"How do we get where we   Uncertainty
want to go?"   Diversity — "How
                                                 entrepreneurial
Ch. 2   Planning Process   are tasks?"
Ch. 3   Forecasting
Ch. 4   Decision-Making
Ch. 5   Effective Planning

        II   ORGANIZING   IV   LEADING
                                          Ch. 13

        Ch. 6   Lines of Authority   The style of
        Ch. 7   Division of Work   leadership
        Ch. 8   Amount of Delegation
        Ch. 9   Coordination

        III   STAFFING

        Ch. 10 Finding the Right Person
                for the Job
        Ch. 11 Appraise Performance
        Ch. 12 Training and Development

                              ORGANIZATIONAL   IV
                              CLIMATE   Ch. 14

V   CONTROLLING   The Employees' "feel"
                                       for the organization

Measuring performance against
plans and taking corrective action

Ch. 17 The Control Process   MOTIVATION   IV
Ch. 18 Controlling Operations   Ch. 15-16
Ch. 19 Accounting Controls
Ch. 20 Effective Controls   Morale
                                       Performance

subordinates' morale and performance emerges from the climate you set. Climate, in turn, is their perception of the organization's structure and your leader behavior. In turn, these last factors have to fit your organization's environment and task: And your firm's central concept determines the sort of environment and tasks it has to cope with.

Changing any aspect of the organization—how much is delegated, the firm's central concept, and so forth—has implications for everything else in

420   **Exhibit 21.6**   Staffing

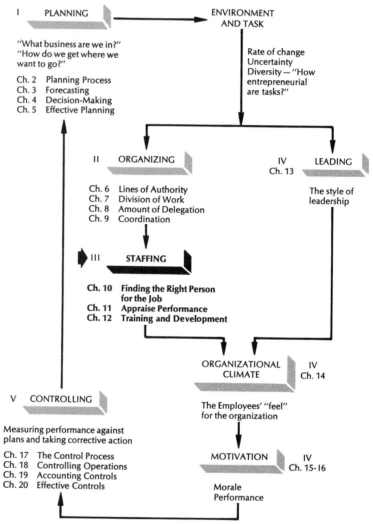

A Framework for Studying the Management Fundamentals

I   PLANNING

"What business are we in?"
"How do we get where we
want to go?"

Ch. 2   Planning Process
Ch. 3   Forecasting
Ch. 4   Decision-Making
Ch. 5   Effective Planning

ENVIRONMENT
AND TASK

Rate of change
Uncertainty
Diversity — "How
entrepreneurial
are tasks?"

II   ORGANIZING

Ch. 6   Lines of Authority
Ch. 7   Division of Work
Ch. 8   Amount of Delegation
Ch. 9   Coordination

IV   LEADING
Ch. 13

The style of
leadership

III   STAFFING

Ch. 10   **Finding the Right Person
for the Job**
Ch. 11   **Appraise Performance**
Ch. 12   **Training and Development**

ORGANIZATIONAL
CLIMATE

IV
Ch. 14

V   CONTROLLING

Measuring performance against
plans and taking corrective action

Ch. 17   The Control Process
Ch. 18   Controlling Operations
Ch. 19   Accounting Controls
Ch. 20   Effective Controls

The Employees' "feel"
for the organization

MOTIVATION

IV
Ch. 15-16

Morale
Performance

the organization. Thus your subordinates' motivation is not just a function of how you *lead*. It's also a function of how you structure their jobs, appraise their performance, and set their standards. Or, suppose you change the central concept of your enterprise from one emphasizing quality to one emphasizing high volume. This will affect the type of departmentation that's appropriate, the kind of people you hire, the leadership style you'll need, and the climate that emerges.

Exhibit 21.7 Leading

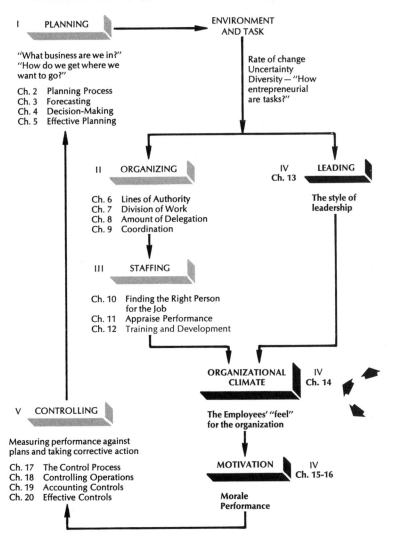

A Framework for Studying the Management Fundamentals

I PLANNING → ENVIRONMENT AND TASK

"What business are we in?"
"How do we get where we want to go?"

Ch. 2 Planning Process
Ch. 3 Forecasting
Ch. 4 Decision-Making
Ch. 5 Effective Planning

Rate of change
Uncertainty
Diversity — "How entrepreneurial are tasks?"

II ORGANIZING

Ch. 6 Lines of Authority
Ch. 7 Division of Work
Ch. 8 Amount of Delegation
Ch. 9 Coordination

IV LEADING
Ch. 13

The style of leadership

III STAFFING

Ch. 10 Finding the Right Person for the Job
Ch. 11 Appraise Performance
Ch. 12 Training and Development

ORGANIZATIONAL CLIMATE
IV Ch. 14

The Employees' "feel" for the organization

V CONTROLLING

Measuring performance against plans and taking corrective action

Ch. 17 The Control Process
Ch. 18 Controlling Operations
Ch. 19 Accounting Controls
Ch. 20 Effective Controls

MOTIVATION
IV Ch. 15-16

Morale
Performance

Related to this, remember that different organizations are appropriate for different tasks. At one extreme are organizations for performing routine tasks like assembling autos. Here efficiency is emphasized, and successful organizations tend to be "bureaucratic," or "'mechanistic." [7] They have specialized divisions of work, directive leadership, and stress adherence to rules and to the chain of command. At the opposite extreme, organizations such as product development departments have unpredictable tasks. Here entrepre-

Exhibit 21.8 Controlling

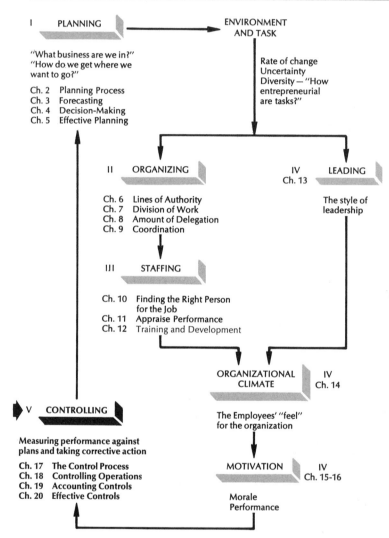

A Framework for Studying the Management Fundamentals

I PLANNING

ENVIRONMENT
AND TASK

"What business are we in?"
"How do we get where we
want to go?"

Rate of change
Uncertainty
Diversity — "How
entrepreneurial
are tasks?"

Ch. 2 Planning Process
Ch. 3 Forecasting
Ch. 4 Decision-Making
Ch. 5 Effective Planning

II ORGANIZING

IV LEADING
Ch. 13

Ch. 6 Lines of Authority
Ch. 7 Division of Work
Ch. 8 Amount of Delegation
Ch. 9 Coordination

The style of
leadership

III STAFFING

Ch. 10 Finding the Right Person
for the Job
Ch. 11 Appraise Performance
Ch. 12 Training and Development

ORGANIZATIONAL
CLIMATE

IV
Ch. 14

V CONTROLLING

The Employees' "feel"
for the organization

Measuring performance against
plans and taking corrective action

Ch. 17 The Control Process
Ch. 18 Controlling Operations
Ch. 19 Accounting Controls
Ch. 20 Effective Controls

MOTIVATION

IV
Ch. 15-16

Morale
Performance

neurial, creative activities are emphasized. To encourage such activities, these organizations are "behavioral" or "organic." They don't urge employees to "play it by the rules" or to closely abide to the chain of command. Here leadership tends to be more participative, and jobs tend to be less specialized. Some important differences between mechanistic and organic organizations are summarized in Exhibit 21–9.

Exhibit 21.9 How the Management Functions Have to Fit the Task

		MECHANISTIC *Closed* *(Classical Orientation)*	*ORGANIC* *Open* *(Behavioral Orientation)*
P L A N	Goals	Specific; output-oriented	General; development-oriented
	Standards	Rigid	Flexible
	Rules and Procedures	Many; specific	Few; broad
	Plan (Means/End)	Detailed, inflexible	Broad, flexible
	Forecasts	Historical trend	Qualitative; future projection
	Decision-making	Management Science Techniques	Creativity; intuition
O R G A N I Z E	Lines of Authority	Clear—no deviations	Broad—permit deviation
	Line and Staff	Clear distinction	Little distinction
	Departmentation	By Function or Process	By Purpose
	Specialization	Highly developed	Low—generalization
	Delegation	Little	Much
	Span of Control	Narrow	Wide
	Coordinate	Use "chain"	Committees
S T A F F	Job Descriptions	Clear—limited scope	Clear—"open-ended"
	Job Specification	Background, skills	Background, potential
	Selection Methods	Specific Performance Tests—Reference checks	General Aptitude and Interest Tests—Interview
	Performance Criteria	Specific; output oriented	General; development oriented
	Performance Evaluation	Graphic Rating Scale	Critical Incidents
	Training & Development	On the job training	Organizational development
L E A D	Leadership Style	More Autocratic	More Democratic
	Leadership Structure	Structured	Unstructured
	Subordinate Motivation	Extrinsic (money, promotion)	Intrinsic (the job itself)
	Established Climate	Structured, performance-oriented	Supportive, development-oriented
C O N T R O L	Standards	Set specific, efficiency	General, "milestones"
	Control Measures	Imposed	Self-set
	Performance Checks	Frequent	Infrequent
	Control emphasis	Process oriented	Goal-oriented

So: Is Managing for You?

That gives you a brief summary of the management fundamentals and of what managers do. Remember, though that the view of an effective manager as a "human computer" carefully planning, organizing, staffing, leading, and controlling is a bit utopian. In Chapter 1 we saw that you'll also be constantly working against deadlines, putting out fires, and interacting with people. And you'll have a multitude of roles, such as "liaison," "disturbance handler," and "spokesman." You'll always have to be on guard to do the "right" thing, and to weigh the often conflicting demands of owners and social responsibility advocates. Needless to say, this often won't leave you much time for planning, or capital budgeting, or MBO, or those other fundamentals we discussed—unless you can make the time.

Is managing for you? Can you effectively Plan, Organize, Staff, Lead, and Control? Can you do this while constantly "under the gun" to produce? Can you be an effective leader? Are you willing to assume the responsibilities of being a manager in order to reap its tremendous rewards? We can't answer these questions for you. But you now have much of the information about managing that you need in order to answer them for yourself.

Some Important Things to Remember from This Chapter:

1. As a manager, you will bring to your job your own concept of what is right and what is wrong. And every decision you make, every action you take will reflect, for better or worse, the application of these standards to the questions at hand. But even managers with well-honed concepts of what is right and what is wrong, run the risk of doing the "wrong" thing. This happens when they are confronted with the pressures and realities of organizational life. Some managers find that it helps to make every decision as if they had an independent auditor looking over their shoulders. They ask "would I do what I'm doing if I had to make a full and public disclosure of my actions?"

2. There is controversy and ongoing debate concerning whether managers should simply attempt to maximize profits, or instead pursue a wider social responsibility. Those favoring the latter approach believe that business has a responsibility to society in areas such as pollution control, and minority recruiting. The profit maximizers believe that a manager must focus on maximizing profits, and on his own self-interests. Then, and only then, will every manager and every business work as hard as possible and produce the best goods at the lowest costs. This is an area in which you will have to develop your own philosophy, as you will your own overall philosophy of management.

3. It is important to see how we use our framework to tie together the management fundamentals. Morale and performance are related to organizational climate. Climate, in turn emerges from your organization's structure and leader

behavior. These in turn have to fit your organization's environment and task. The firm's central concept determines the sort of environment and task with which your firm will have to cope.

4. Examples of this interrelatedness between the management functions abound. For example, you may often find it nearly impossible to "motivate" subordinates even after trying every motivation technique discussed in Chapters 13 through 16. This is because motivation really begins with your staffing decisions—with finding the right person for the right job. And it is further influenced by all the other management functions—the way you organize the job, the types of controls you impose, and your policies and procedures.

5. Different types of organizations are appropriate for different tasks. At one extreme are organizations for performing routine tasks such as assembling automobiles. Here efficiency is emphasized, and successful organizations tend to be "bureaucratic" or "mechanistic." At the opposite extreme, organizations such as product development departments have unpredictable tasks. Here entrepreneurial creative activities are emphasized. To encourage such activities, organizations are "behavioral" or "organic." Some of the differences between these two types of organizations are summarized in Exhibit 21–9. You might review them again at this point.

STUDY ASSIGNMENTS

1. Answer the questions from the introduction to this chapter.
2. Explain why you need to take an "integrated" view of the management fundamentals. Be sure to give some specific examples.
3. Develop a table which shows how the management functions have to fit the task.
4. FBI Director Clarence Kelley was recently the center of some debate. He had allegedly accepted several gifts from subordinates, and allegedly permitted the FBI carpentry shop to build and install some drapery valances in his private apartment. His boss, the Attorney General, recommended that he not be fired for these incidents. Would you have accepted that recommendation? Why?
5. One of the reasons American businesses have been so successful is the profit motive. By aiming to maximize profits and minimize costs they are able to produce their goods as cheaply as possible. If you want to see what happens when the government starts tampering with this profit motive, just take a look at the inefficiency and confusion of some of our government agencies such as HEW, which don't have this profit motive to guide them? Is this a legitimate comparison? Do you agree that without the profit motive inefficiency and confusion will result? Why?
6. Discuss how management scandals like Watergate might be avoided.
7. Pick out an organization with which you are familiar—this university, a local business, and the like. Then make a list of the local, state, and federal forms and reports which that organization's managers typically have to file. How much of their time do these managers say they have to devote to government reporting?

426   8. Explain in your own words how the central concept of an enterprise has an impact on each of the five management functions.

9. Explain in your own words the difference between mechanistic and organic organizations.

10. Write an essay explaining why you think you would (or would not) make an effective manager. Use specific examples from your experiences to substantiate your case.

NOTES FOR THE CHAPTER

1. Milton Friedman, *Capitalism and Freedom* (Chicago: The University of Chicago Press, 1962) p. 133.

2. Don Corson and George Steiner, "Social Responsibility: A New Dimension of Corporate Accountability," from *Measuring Business and Social Performance: The Corporate Social Audit* (New York: Committee for Economic Development, 1974) pp. 1–20. Reprinted in Harold Koontz and Cyril O'Donnell, *Management: A Book of Readings* (New York: McGraw-Hill, 1976) pp. 48–58.

3. Fred Luthans and Richard Hodgetts, *Social Issues in Business* (New York: Macmillan, 1976) Chapter 1.

4. Corson and Steiner, "Social Responsibility: A New Dimension of Corporate Accountability."

5. See for example, Corson and Steiner's article, "Social Responsibility, etc."

6. Quoted by Corson and Steiner in "Social Responsibility, etc."

7. Based on Gary Dessler, *Organization and Management: A Contingency Approach* (Englewood Cliffs: Prentice-Hall, 1976) pp. 11–13.

INDEX